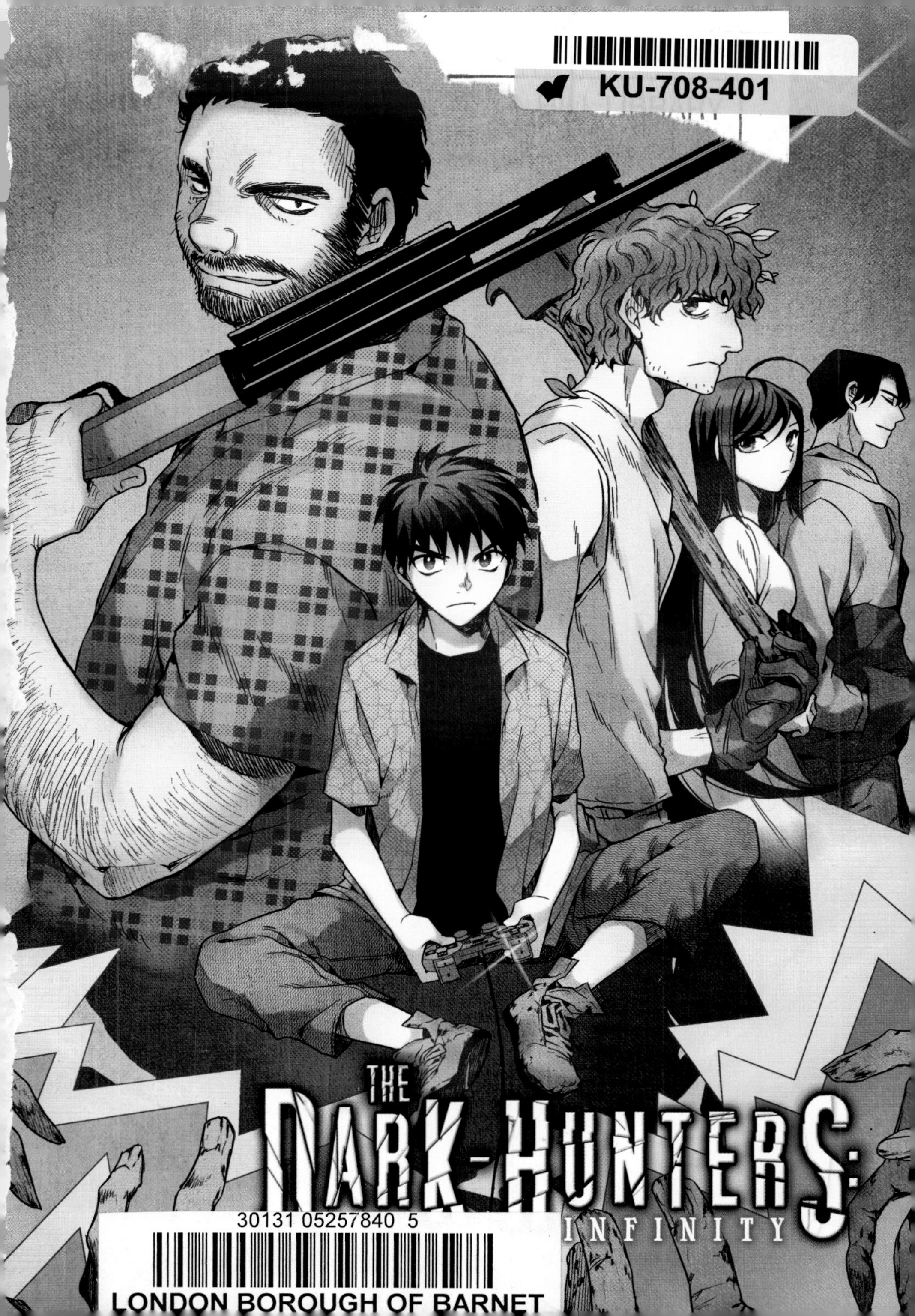
THE
DARK-HUNTERS:
INFINITY

THE DARK-HUNTERS: INFINITY

SHERRILYN KENYON
ART BY JIYOUNG AHN

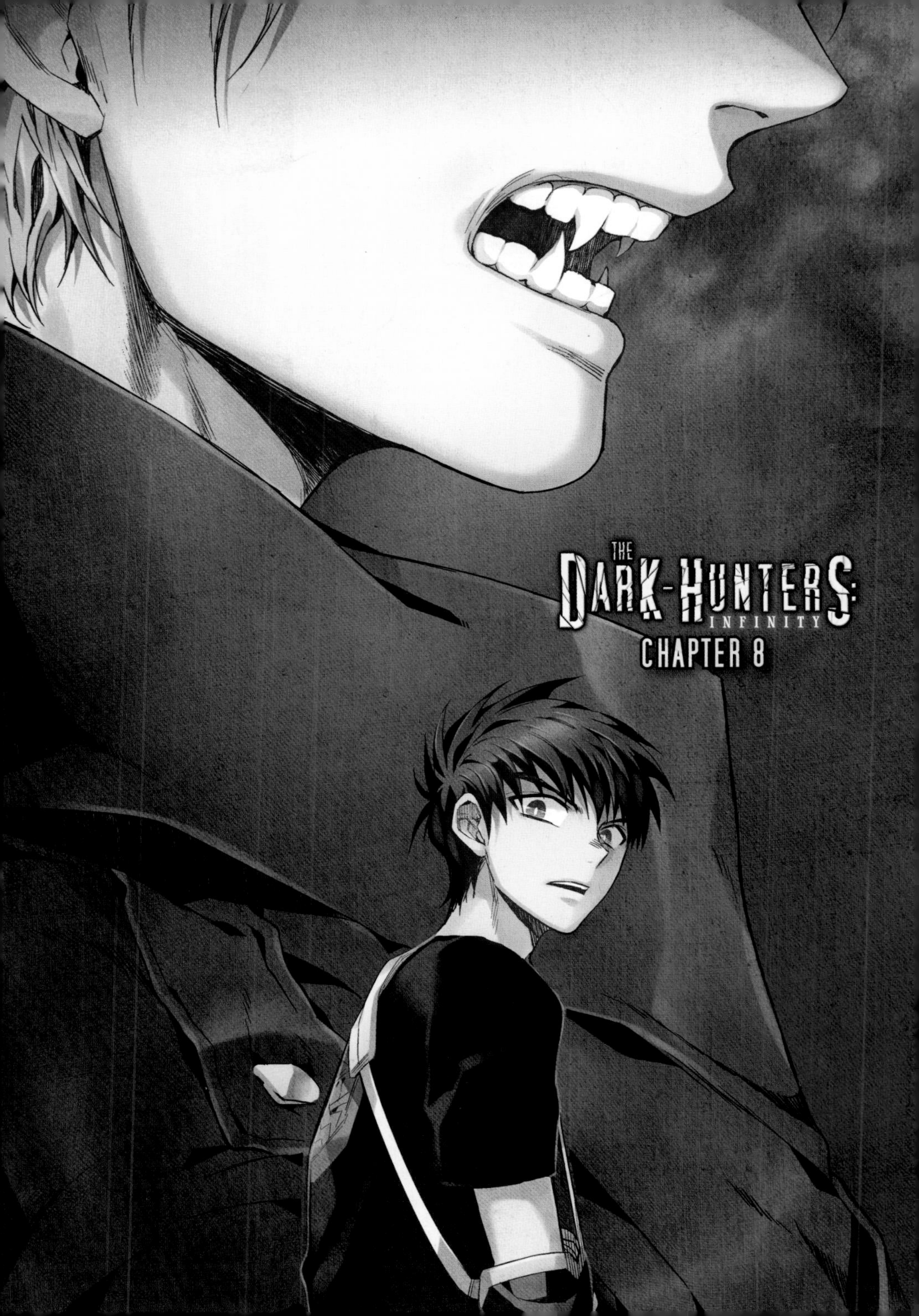
THE DARK-HUNTERS: INFINITY
CHAPTER 8

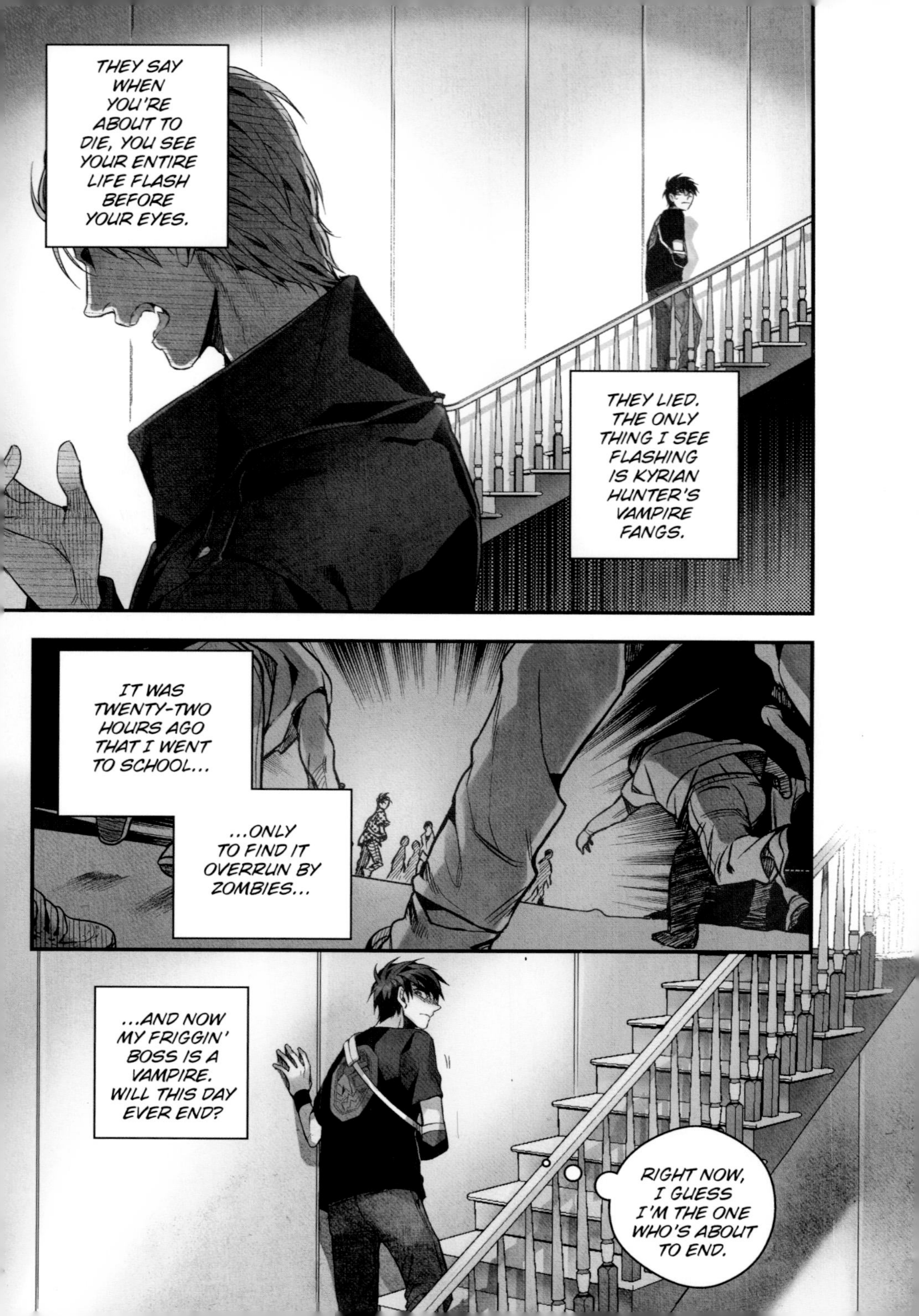
THEY SAY WHEN YOU'RE ABOUT TO DIE, YOU SEE YOUR ENTIRE LIFE FLASH BEFORE YOUR EYES.
THEY LIED. THE ONLY THING I SEE FLASHING IS KYRIAN HUNTER'S VAMPIRE FANGS.
IT WAS TWENTY-TWO HOURS AGO THAT I WENT TO SCHOOL...
...ONLY TO FIND IT OVERRUN BY ZOMBIES...
...AND NOW MY FRIGGIN' BOSS IS A VAMPIRE. WILL THIS DAY EVER END?
RIGHT NOW, I GUESS I'M THE ONE WHO'S ABOUT TO END.

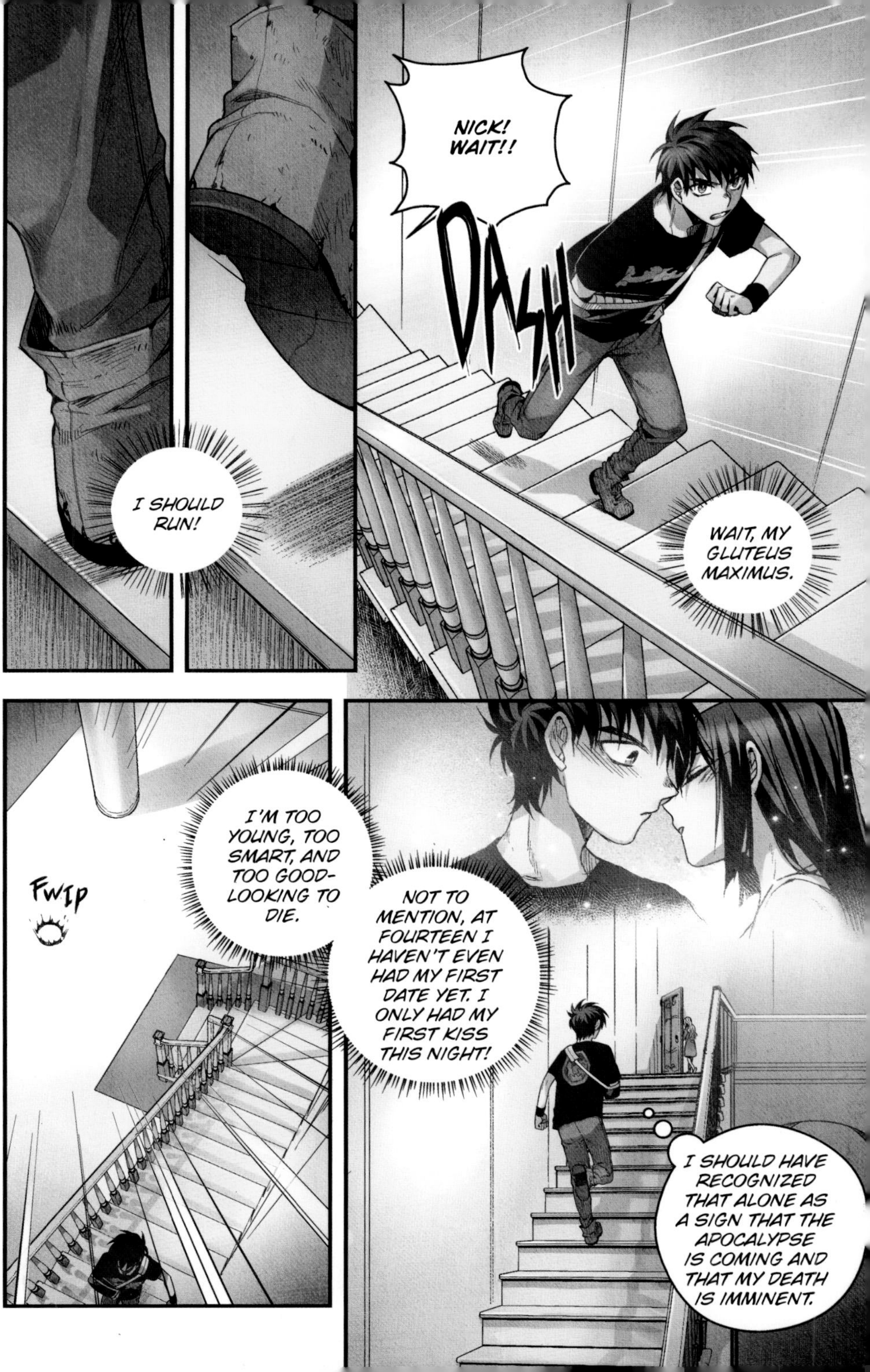
NICK! WAIT!!
DASH
I SHOULD RUN!
WAIT, MY GLUTEUS MAXIMUS.
I'M TOO YOUNG, TOO SMART, AND TOO GOOD-LOOKING TO DIE.
FWIP
NOT TO MENTION, AT FOURTEEN I HAVEN'T EVEN HAD MY FIRST DATE YET. I ONLY HAD MY FIRST KISS THIS NIGHT!
I SHOULD HAVE RECOGNIZED THAT ALONE AS A SIGN THAT THE APOCALYPSE IS COMING AND THAT MY DEATH IS IMMINENT.

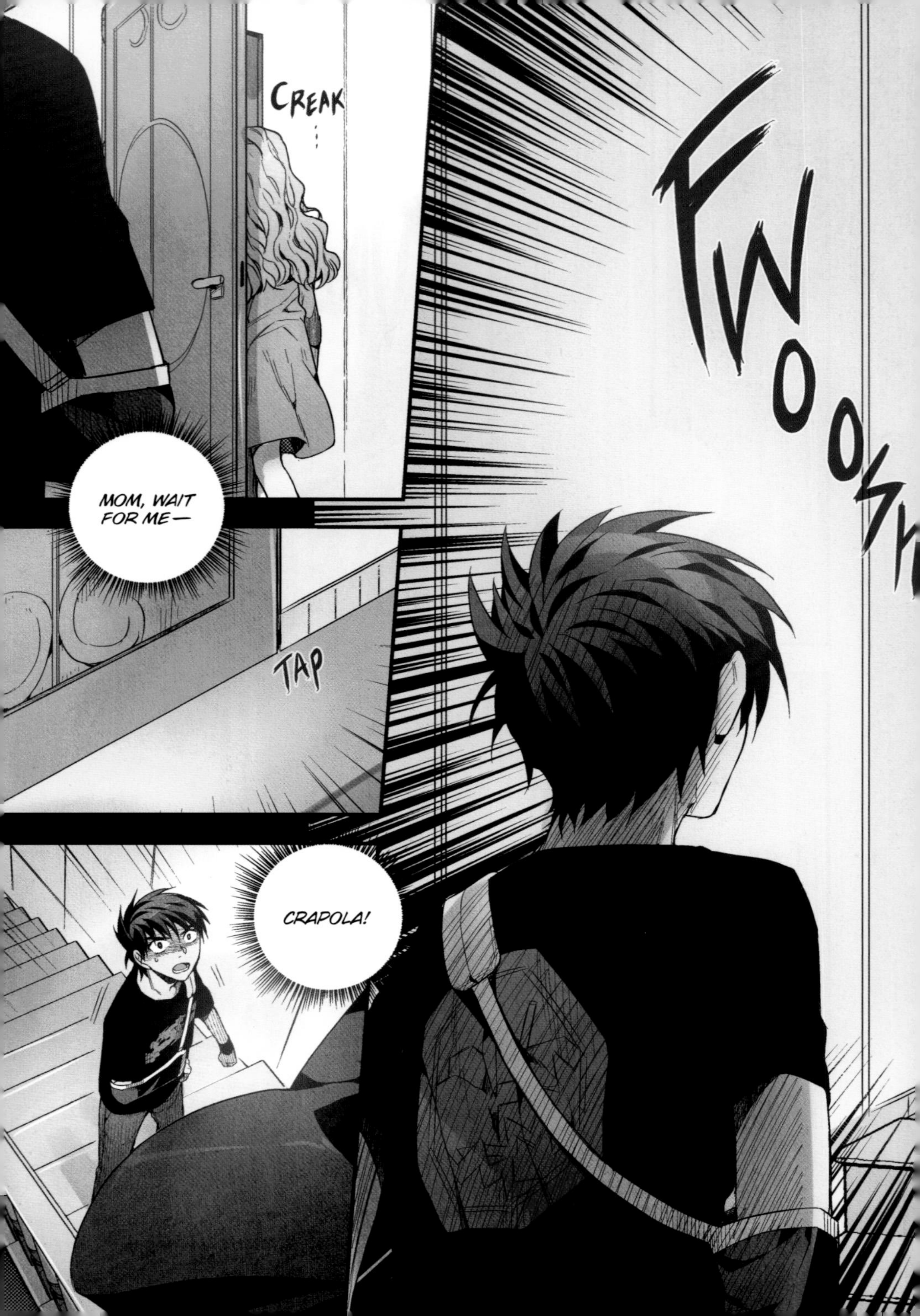

CREAK
FWOOSH
MOM, WAIT FOR ME—
TAP
CRAPOLA!

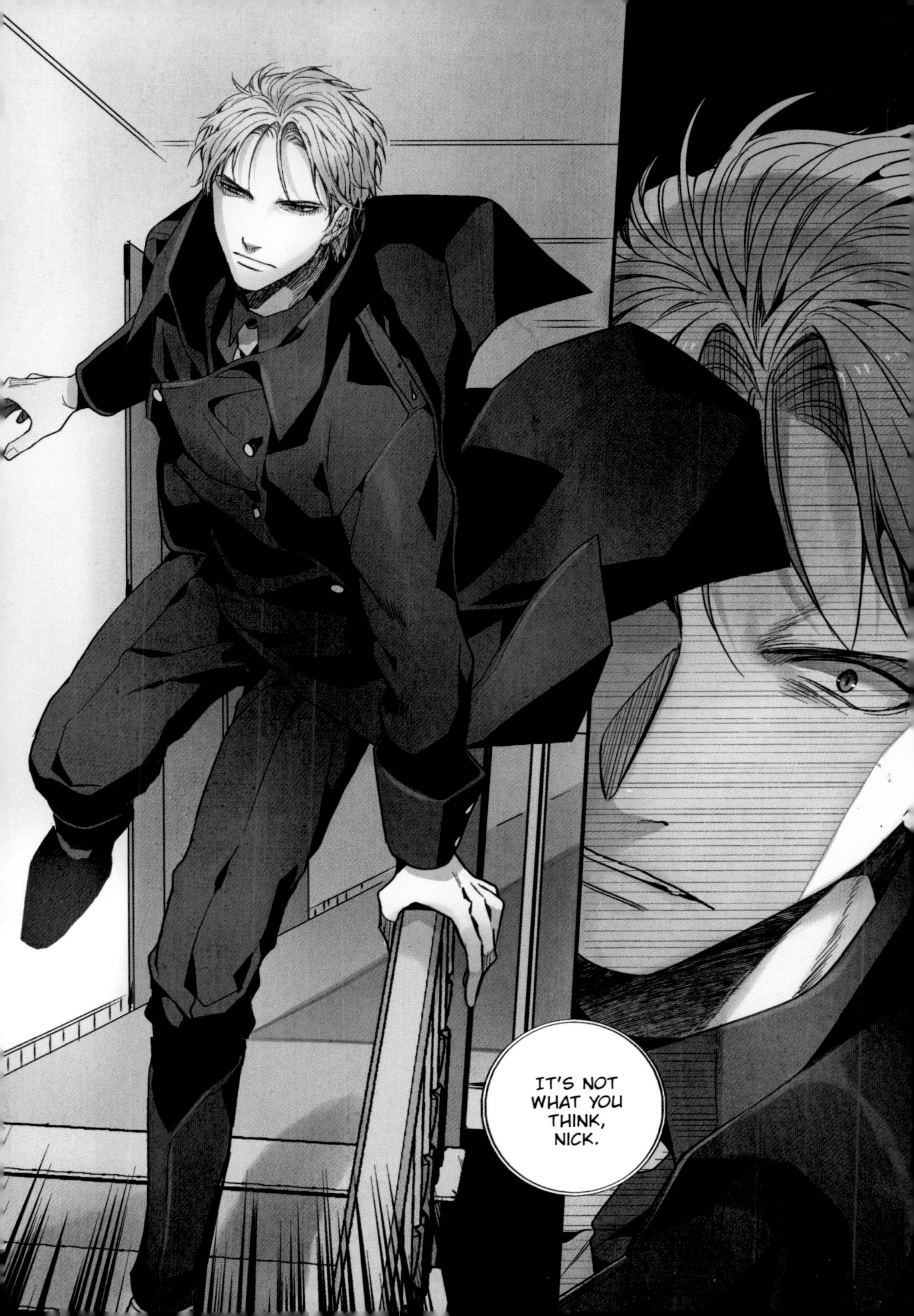
IT'S NOT WHAT YOU THINK, NICK.

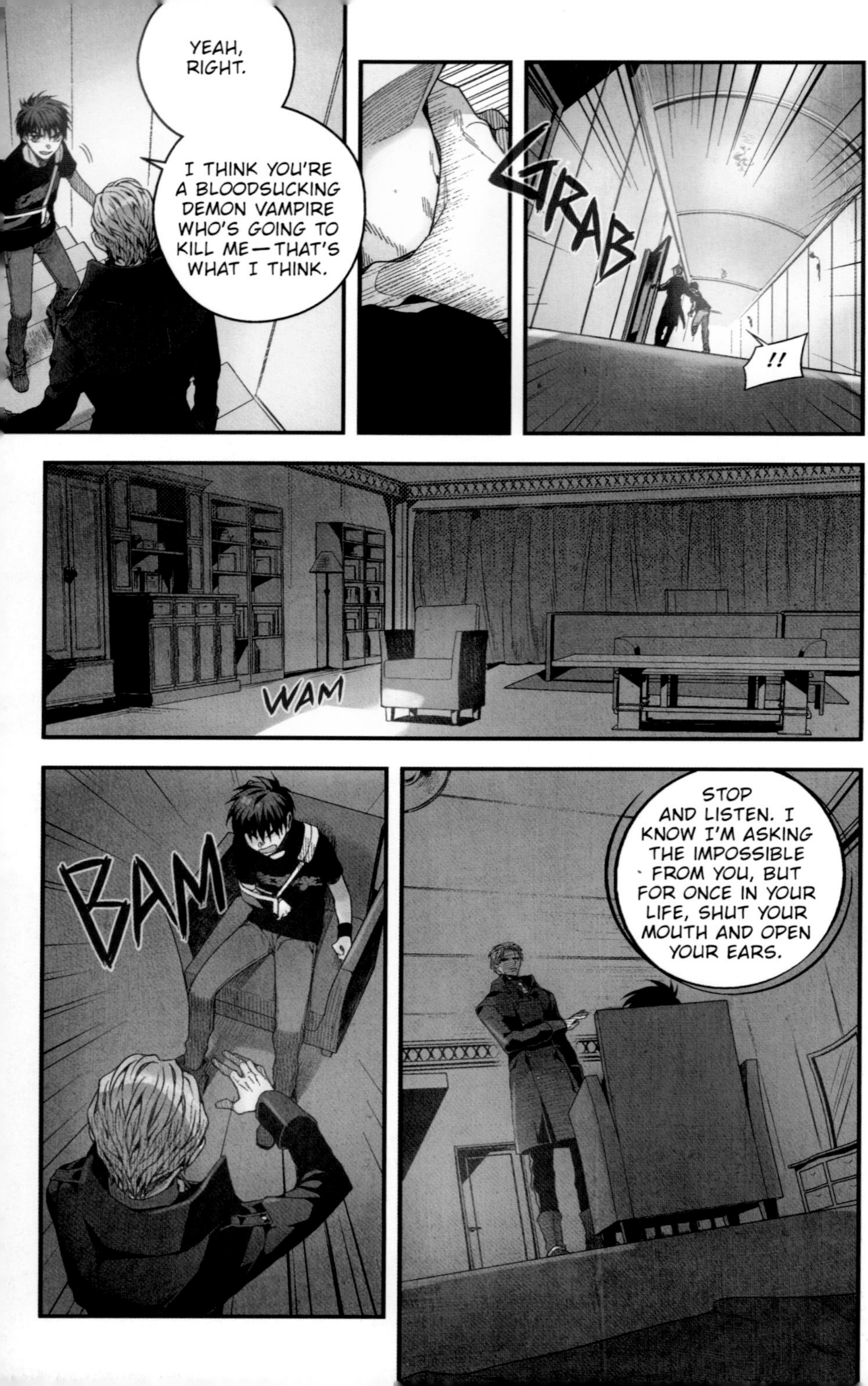
YEAH, RIGHT.
I THINK YOU'RE A BLOODSUCKING DEMON VAMPIRE WHO'S GOING TO KILL ME—THAT'S WHAT I THINK.
GRAB
!!
WAM
BAM
STOP AND LISTEN. I KNOW I'M ASKING THE IMPOSSIBLE FROM YOU, BUT FOR ONCE IN YOUR LIFE, SHUT YOUR MOUTH AND OPEN YOUR EARS.

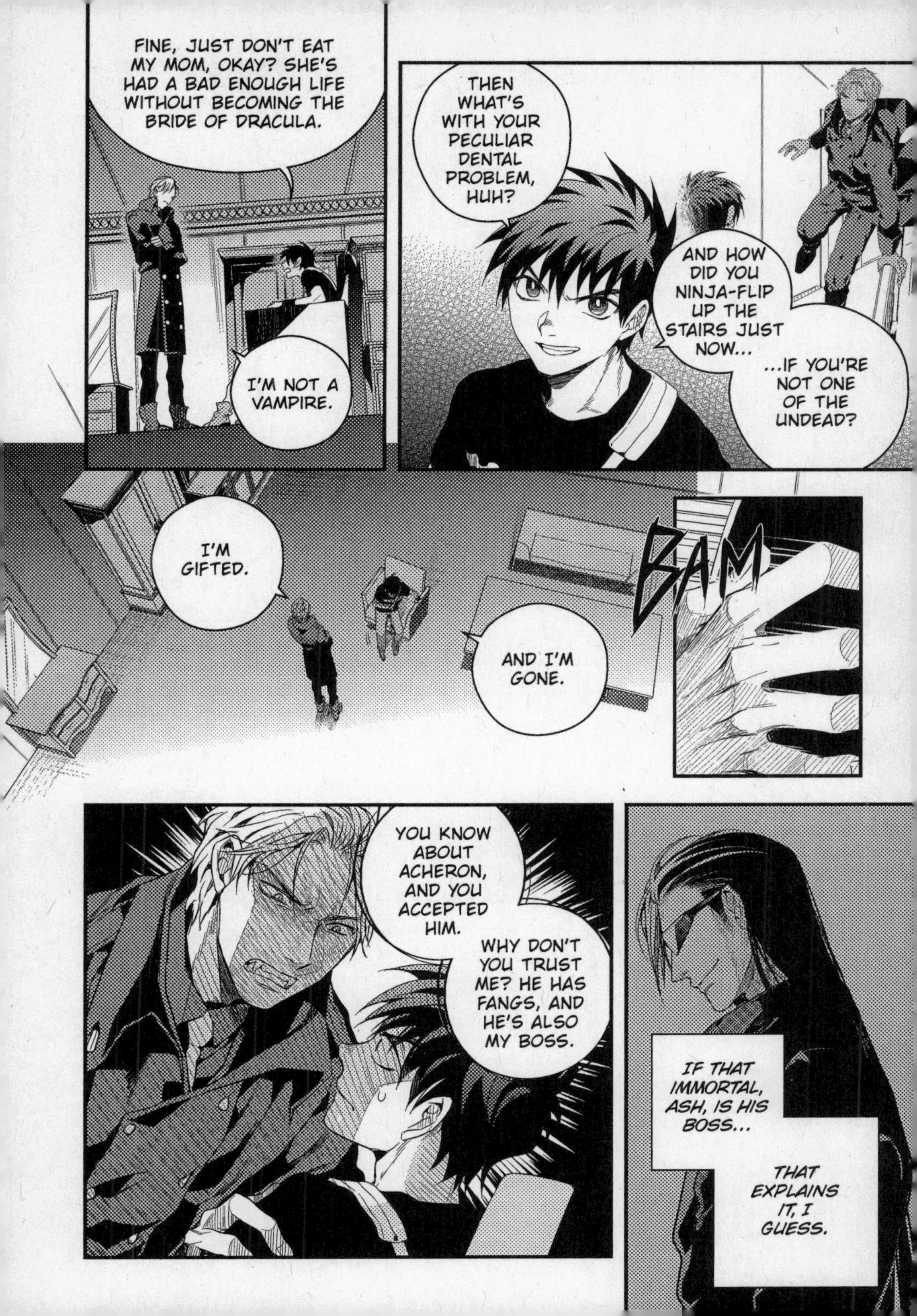
FINE, JUST DON'T EAT MY MOM, OKAY? SHE'S HAD A BAD ENOUGH LIFE WITHOUT BECOMING THE BRIDE OF DRACULA.
I'M NOT A VAMPIRE.
THEN WHAT'S WITH YOUR PECULIAR DENTAL PROBLEM, HUH?
AND HOW DID YOU NINJA-FLIP UP THE STAIRS JUST NOW...
...IF YOU'RE NOT ONE OF THE UNDEAD?
I'M GIFTED.
AND I'M GONE.
BAM
YOU KNOW ABOUT ACHERON, AND YOU ACCEPTED HIM.
WHY DON'T YOU TRUST ME? HE HAS FANGS, AND HE'S ALSO MY BOSS.
IF THAT IMMORTAL, ASH, IS HIS BOSS...
THAT EXPLAINS IT, I GUESS.

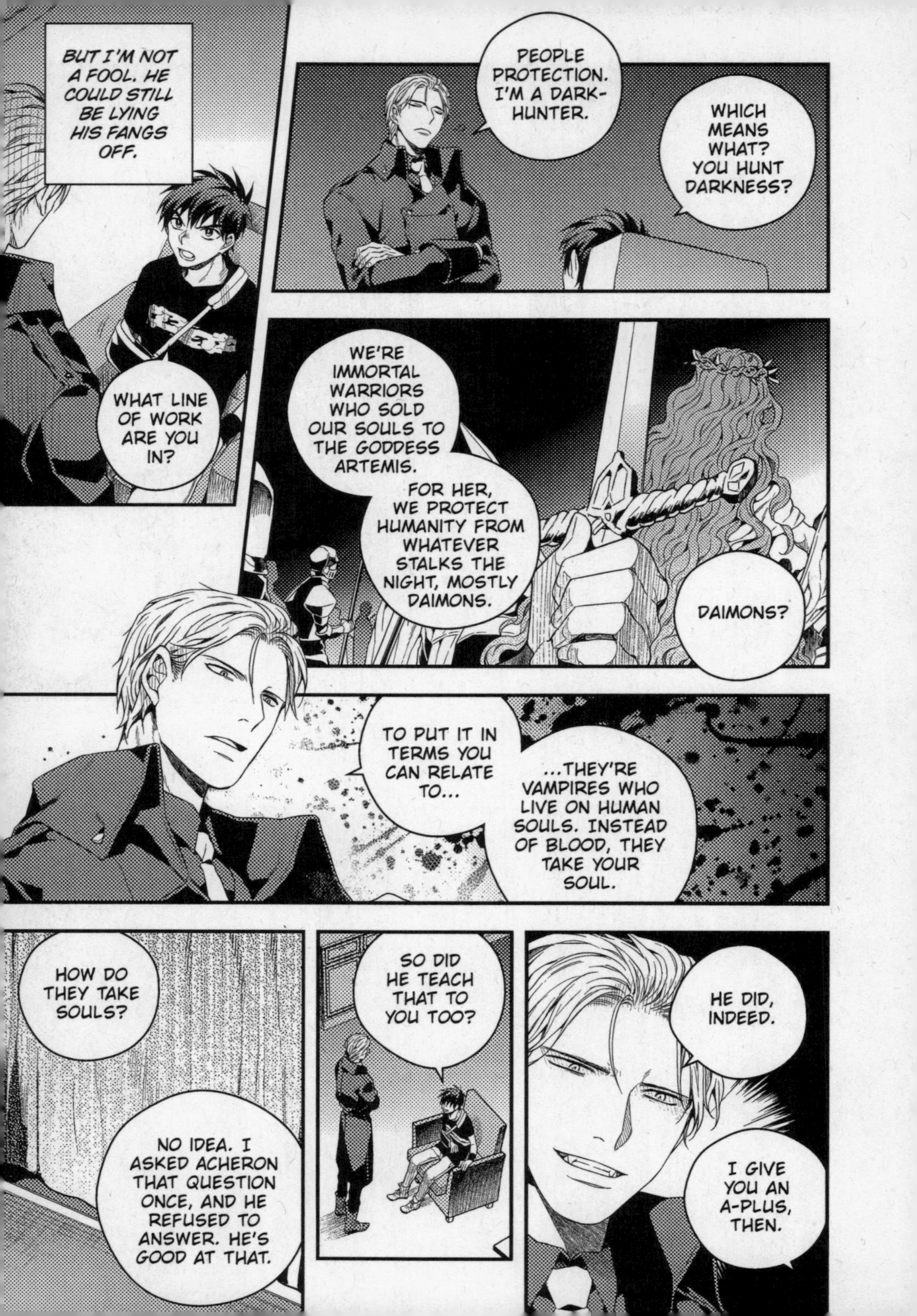
BUT I'M NOT A FOOL. HE COULD STILL BE LYING HIS FANGS OFF.
WHAT LINE OF WORK ARE YOU IN?
PEOPLE PROTECTION. I'M A DARK-HUNTER.
WHICH MEANS WHAT? YOU HUNT DARKNESS?
WE'RE IMMORTAL WARRIORS WHO SOLD OUR SOULS TO THE GODDESS ARTEMIS.
FOR HER, WE PROTECT HUMANITY FROM WHATEVER STALKS THE NIGHT, MOSTLY DAIMONS.
DAIMONS?
TO PUT IT IN TERMS YOU CAN RELATE TO...
...THEY'RE VAMPIRES WHO LIVE ON HUMAN SOULS. INSTEAD OF BLOOD, THEY TAKE YOUR SOUL.
HOW DO THEY TAKE SOULS?
NO IDEA. I ASKED ACHERON THAT QUESTION ONCE, AND HE REFUSED TO ANSWER. HE'S GOOD AT THAT.
SO DID HE TEACH THAT TO YOU TOO?
HE DID, INDEED.
I GIVE YOU AN A-PLUS, THEN.

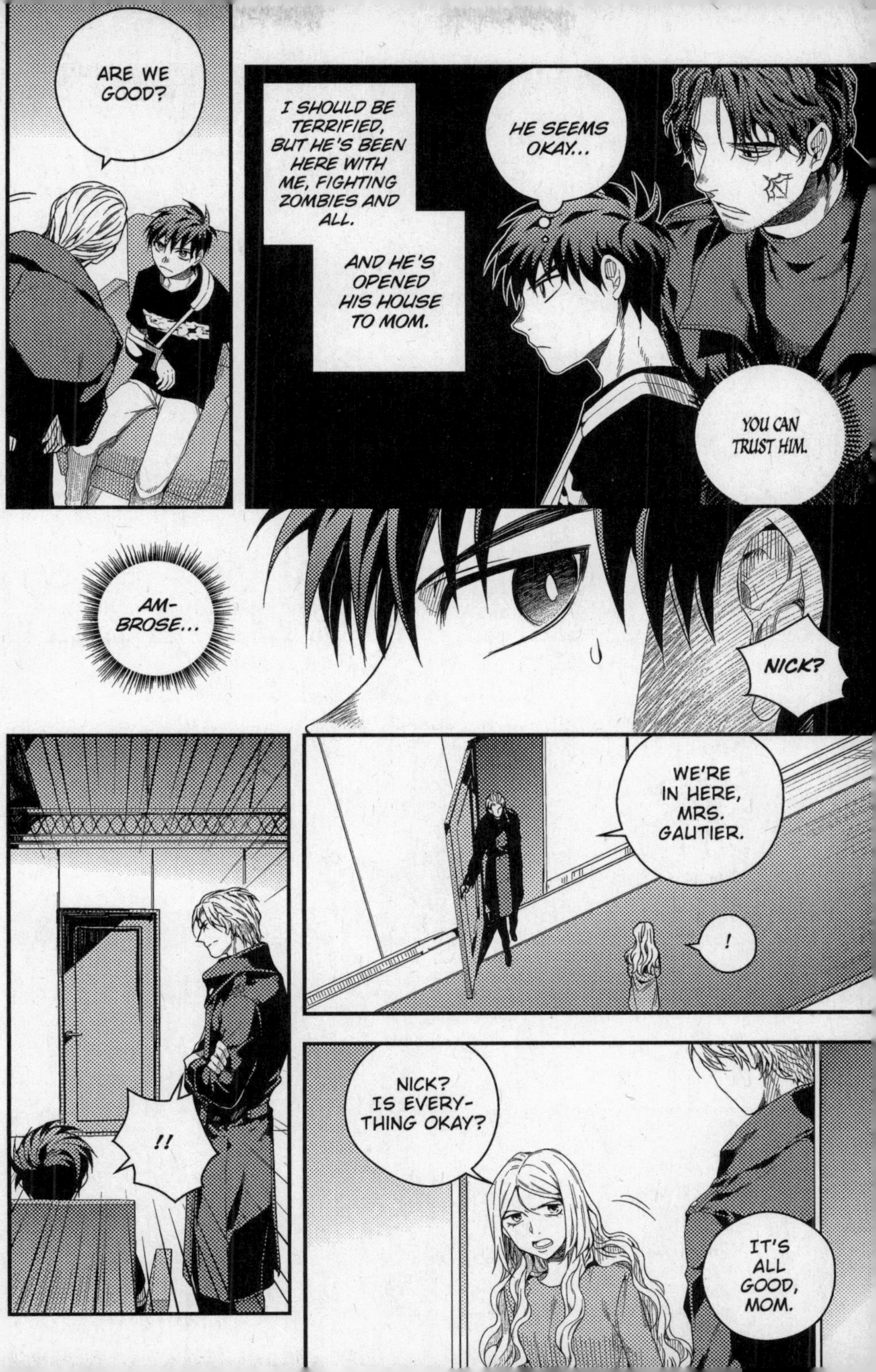
ARE WE GOOD?
I SHOULD BE TERRIFIED, BUT HE'S BEEN HERE WITH ME, FIGHTING ZOMBIES AND ALL.
AND HE'S OPENED HIS HOUSE TO MOM.
HE SEEMS OKAY...
YOU CAN TRUST HIM.
AM-BROSE...
NICK?
WE'RE IN HERE, MRS. GAUTIER.
!
!!
NICK? IS EVERY-THING OKAY?
IT'S ALL GOOD, MOM.

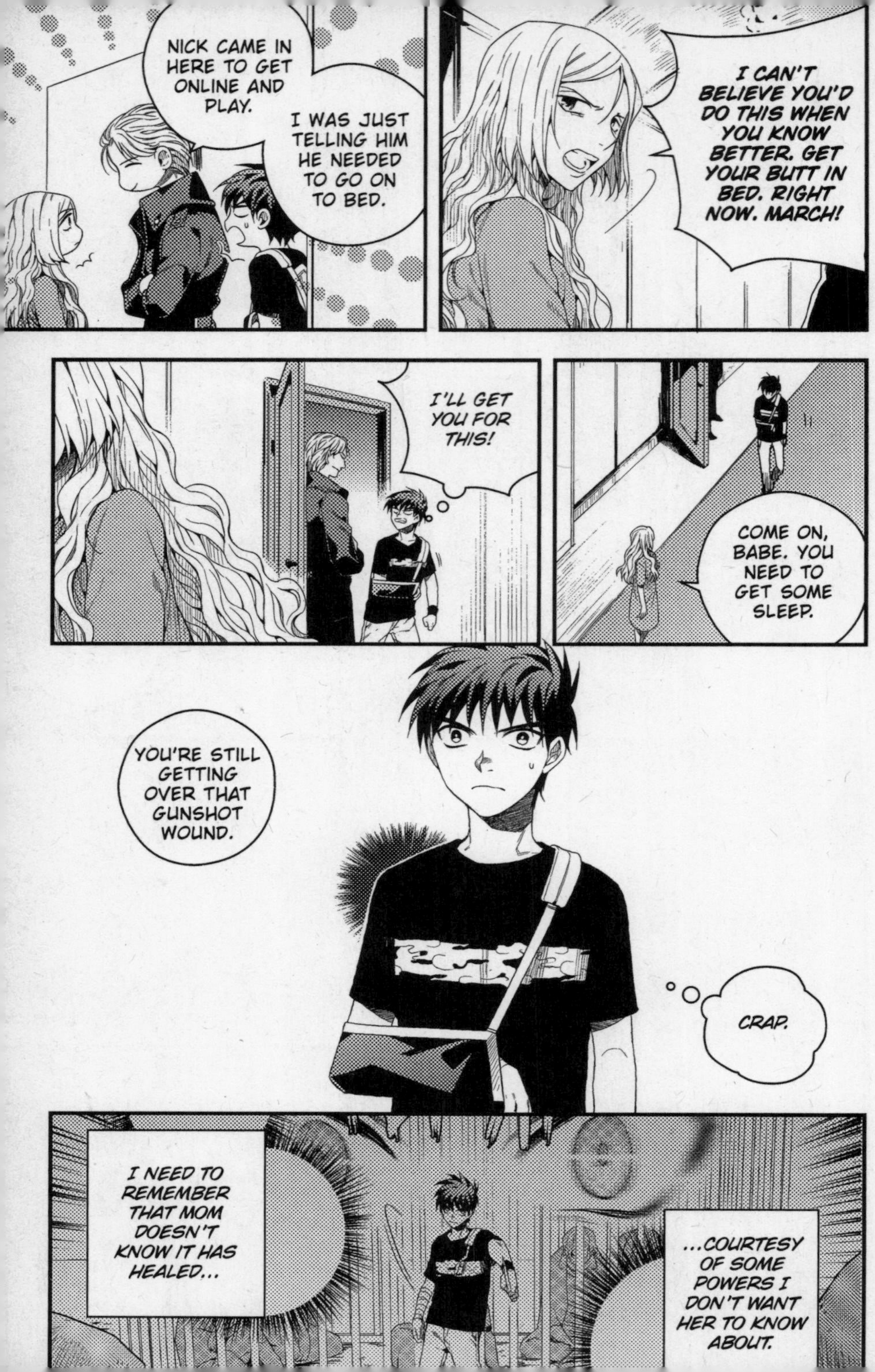
NICK CAME IN HERE TO GET ONLINE AND PLAY.
I WAS JUST TELLING HIM HE NEEDED TO GO ON TO BED.
I CAN'T BELIEVE YOU'D DO THIS WHEN YOU KNOW BETTER. GET YOUR BUTT IN BED. RIGHT NOW. MARCH!
I'LL GET YOU FOR THIS!
COME ON, BABE. YOU NEED TO GET SOME SLEEP.
YOU'RE STILL GETTING OVER THAT GUNSHOT WOUND.
CRAP.
I NEED TO REMEMBER THAT MOM DOESN'T KNOW IT HAS HEALED...
...COURTESY OF SOME POWERS I DON'T WANT HER TO KNOW ABOUT.

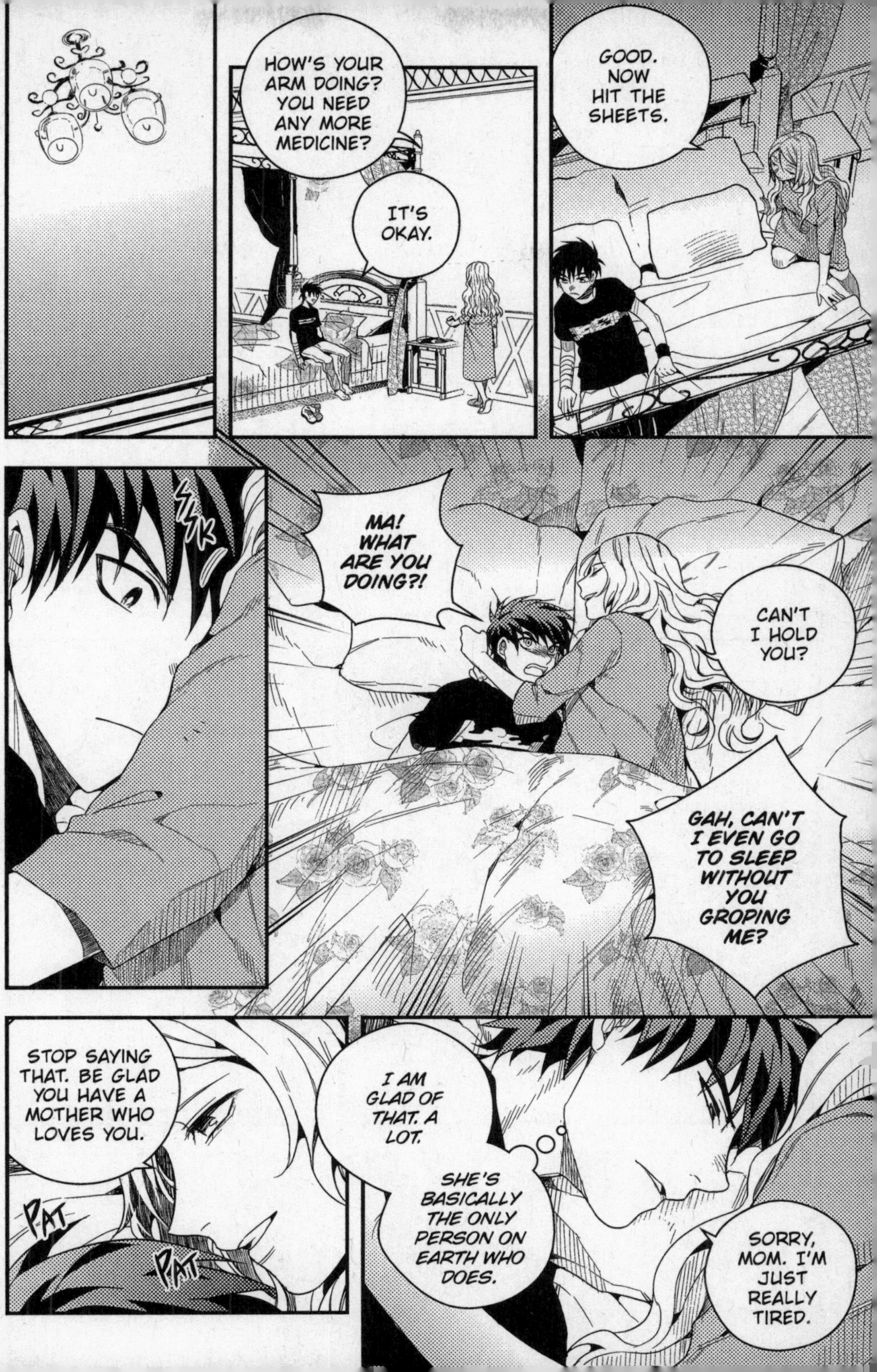
HOW'S YOUR ARM DOING? YOU NEED ANY MORE MEDICINE?
IT'S OKAY.
GOOD. NOW HIT THE SHEETS.
MA! WHAT ARE YOU DOING?!
CAN'T I HOLD YOU?
GAH, CAN'T I EVEN GO TO SLEEP WITHOUT YOU GROPING ME?
STOP SAYING THAT. BE GLAD YOU HAVE A MOTHER WHO LOVES YOU.
PAT
PAT
I AM GLAD OF THAT. A LOT.
SHE'S BASICALLY THE ONLY PERSON ON EARTH WHO DOES.
SORRY, MOM. I'M JUST REALLY TIRED.

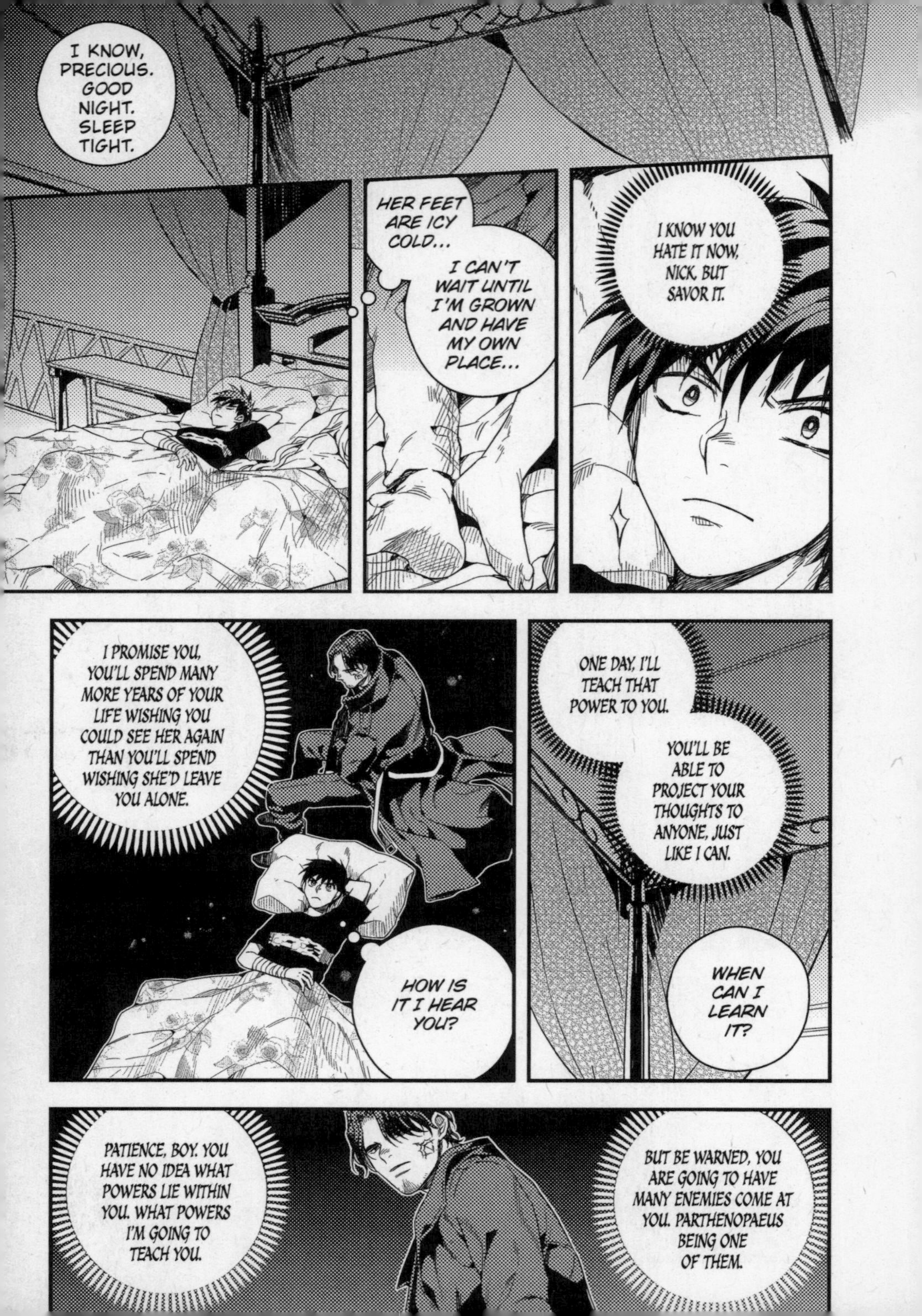
I KNOW, PRECIOUS. GOOD NIGHT. SLEEP TIGHT.
HER FEET ARE ICY COLD...
I CAN'T WAIT UNTIL I'M GROWN AND HAVE MY OWN PLACE...
I KNOW YOU HATE IT NOW, NICK, BUT SAVOR IT.
I PROMISE YOU, YOU'LL SPEND MANY MORE YEARS OF YOUR LIFE WISHING YOU COULD SEE HER AGAIN THAN YOU'LL SPEND WISHING SHE'D LEAVE YOU ALONE.
HOW IS IT I HEAR YOU?
ONE DAY, I'LL TEACH THAT POWER TO YOU.
YOU'LL BE ABLE TO PROJECT YOUR THOUGHTS TO ANYONE, JUST LIKE I CAN.
WHEN CAN I LEARN IT?
PATIENCE, BOY. YOU HAVE NO IDEA WHAT POWERS LIE WITHIN YOU. WHAT POWERS I'M GOING TO TEACH YOU.
BUT BE WARNED, YOU ARE GOING TO HAVE MANY ENEMIES COME AT YOU. PARTHENOPAEUS BEING ONE OF THEM.

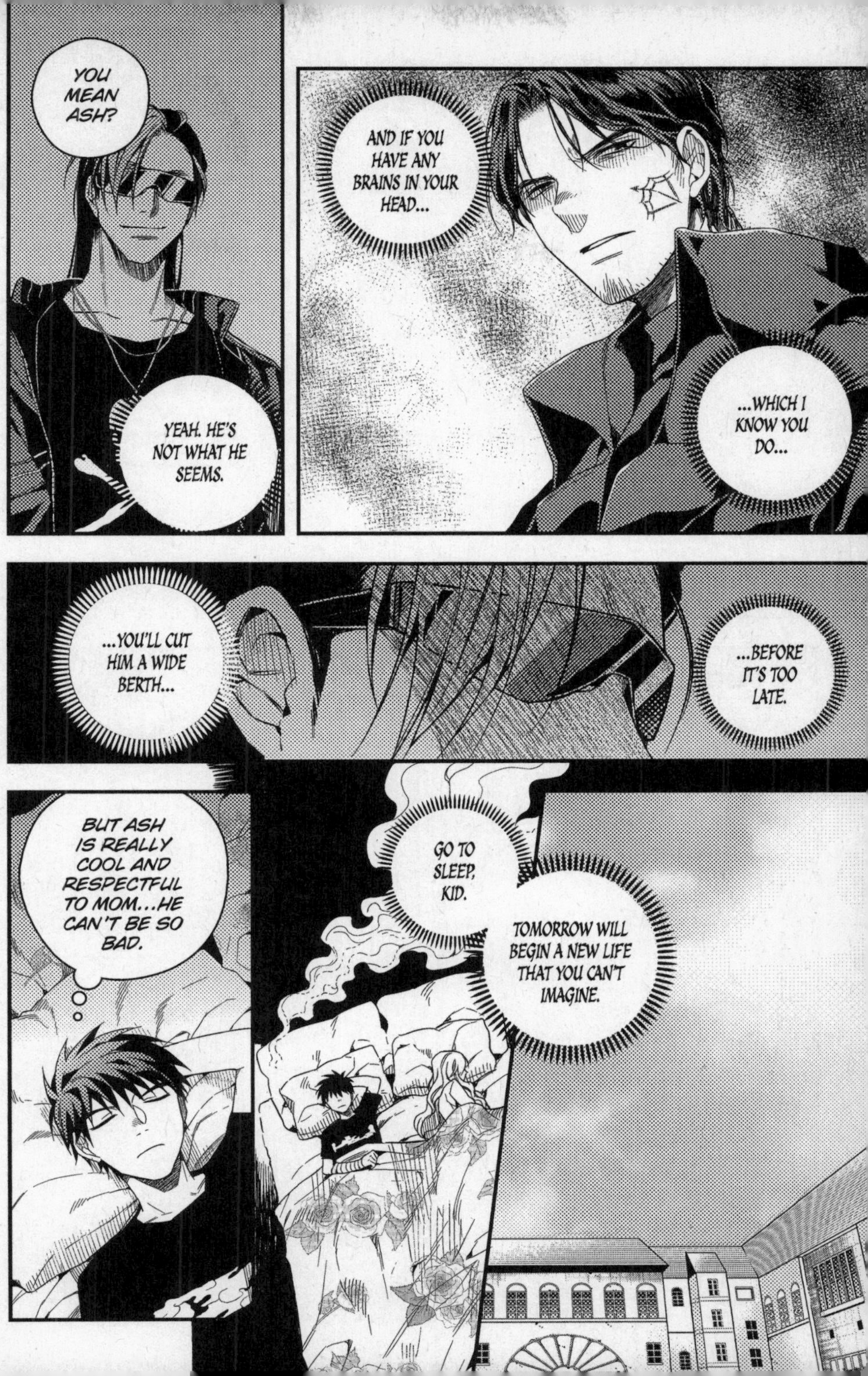
YOU MEAN ASH?
YEAH. HE'S NOT WHAT HE SEEMS.
AND IF YOU HAVE ANY BRAINS IN YOUR HEAD...
...WHICH I KNOW YOU DO...
...YOU'LL CUT HIM A WIDE BERTH...
...BEFORE IT'S TOO LATE.
BUT ASH IS REALLY COOL AND RESPECTFUL TO MOM...HE CAN'T BE SO BAD.
GO TO SLEEP, KID.
TOMORROW WILL BEGIN A NEW LIFE THAT YOU CAN'T IMAGINE.

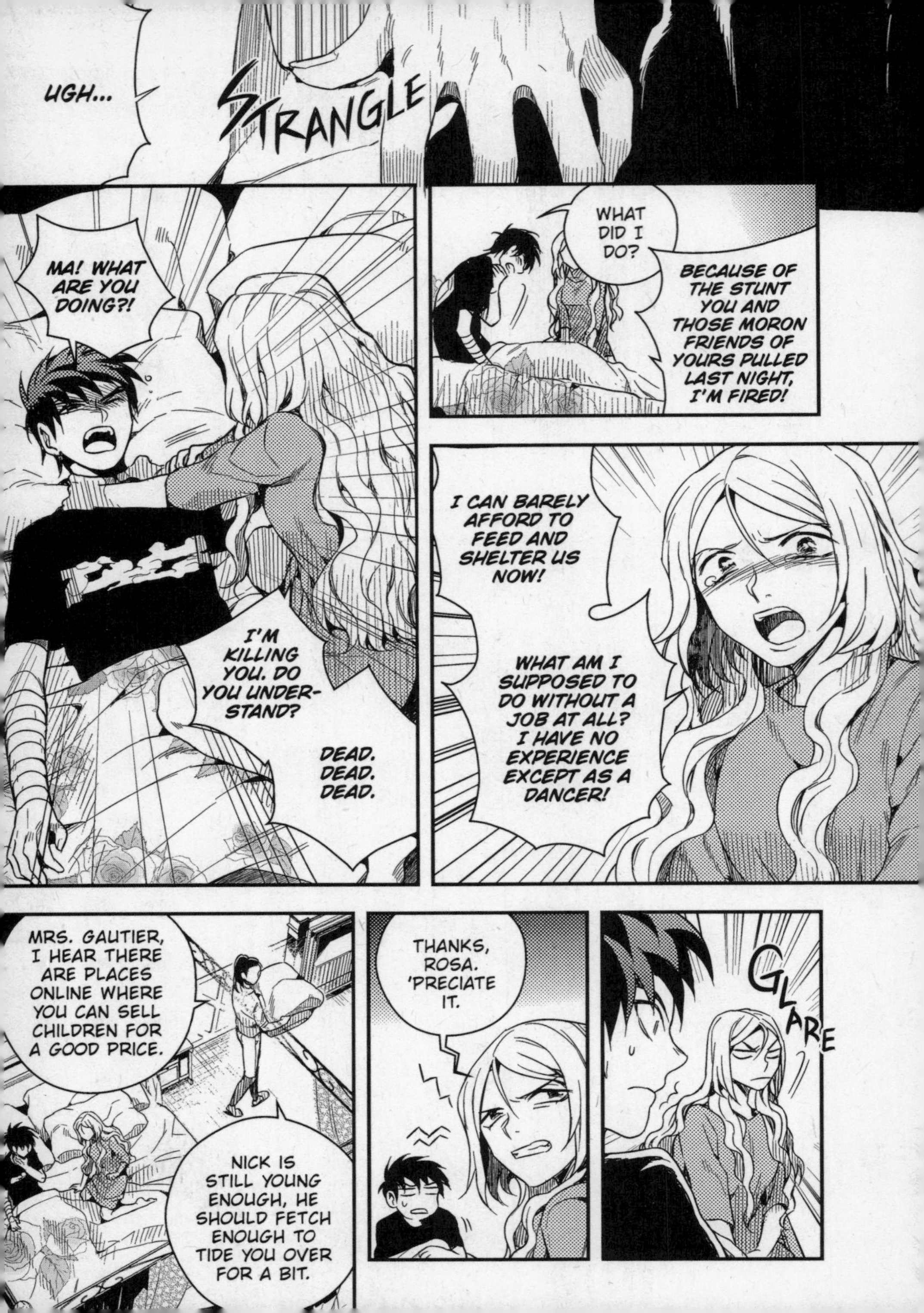
UGH...
STRANGLE
MA! WHAT ARE YOU DOING?!
I'M KILLING YOU. DO YOU UNDER-STAND?
DEAD. DEAD. DEAD.
WHAT DID I DO?
BECAUSE OF THE STUNT YOU AND THOSE MORON FRIENDS OF YOURS PULLED LAST NIGHT, I'M FIRED!
I CAN BARELY AFFORD TO FEED AND SHELTER US NOW!
WHAT AM I SUPPOSED TO DO WITHOUT A JOB AT ALL? I HAVE NO EXPERIENCE EXCEPT AS A DANCER!
MRS. GAUTIER, I HEAR THERE ARE PLACES ONLINE WHERE YOU CAN SELL CHILDREN FOR A GOOD PRICE.
NICK IS STILL YOUNG ENOUGH, HE SHOULD FETCH ENOUGH TO TIDE YOU OVER FOR A BIT.
THANKS, ROSA. 'PRECIATE IT.
GLARE

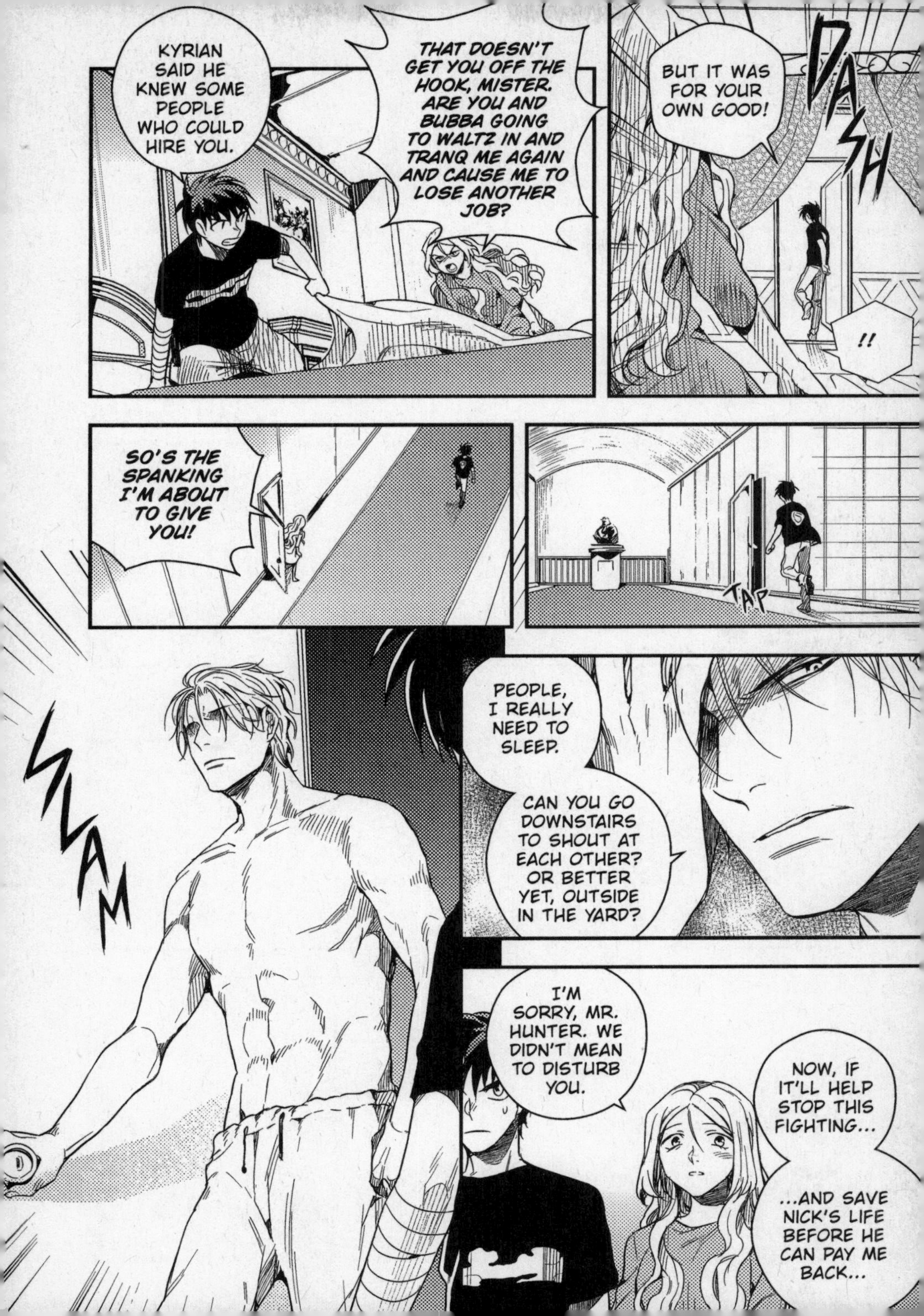
KYRIAN SAID HE KNEW SOME PEOPLE WHO COULD HIRE YOU.
THAT DOESN'T GET YOU OFF THE HOOK, MISTER. ARE YOU AND BUBBA GOING TO WALTZ IN AND TRANQ ME AGAIN AND CAUSE ME TO LOSE ANOTHER JOB?
BUT IT WAS FOR YOUR OWN GOOD!
DASH
!!
SO'S THE SPANKING I'M ABOUT TO GIVE YOU!
TAP
SLAM
PEOPLE, I REALLY NEED TO SLEEP.
CAN YOU GO DOWNSTAIRS TO SHOUT AT EACH OTHER? OR BETTER YET, OUTSIDE IN THE YARD?
I'M SORRY, MR. HUNTER. WE DIDN'T MEAN TO DISTURB YOU.
NOW, IF IT'LL HELP STOP THIS FIGHTING...
...AND SAVE NICK'S LIFE BEFORE HE CAN PAY ME BACK...

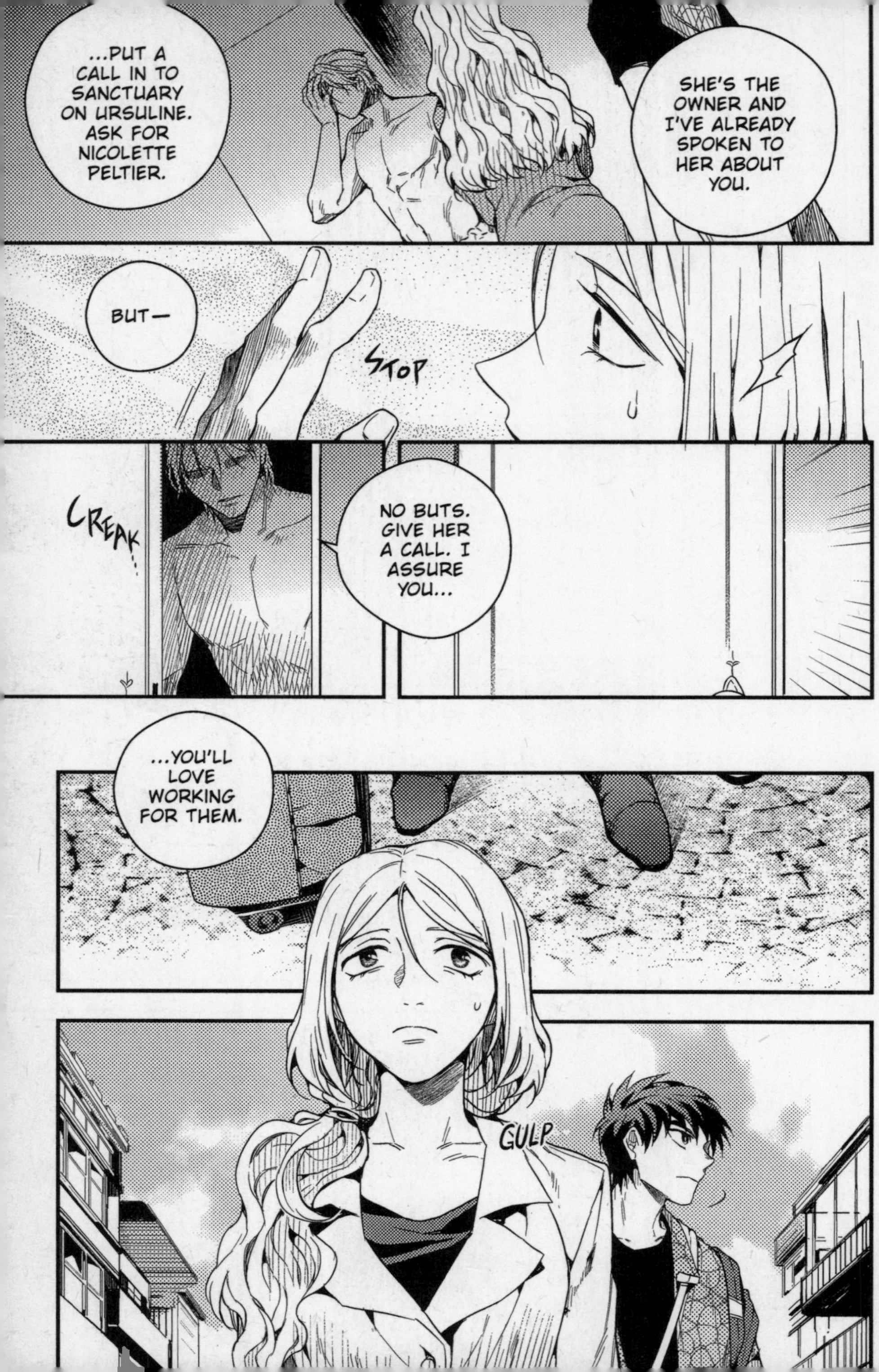
...PUT A CALL IN TO SANCTUARY ON URSULINE. ASK FOR NICOLETTE PELTIER.
SHE'S THE OWNER AND I'VE ALREADY SPOKEN TO HER ABOUT YOU.
BUT—
STOP
CREAK...
NO BUTS. GIVE HER A CALL. I ASSURE YOU...
...YOU'LL LOVE WORKING FOR THEM.
GULP

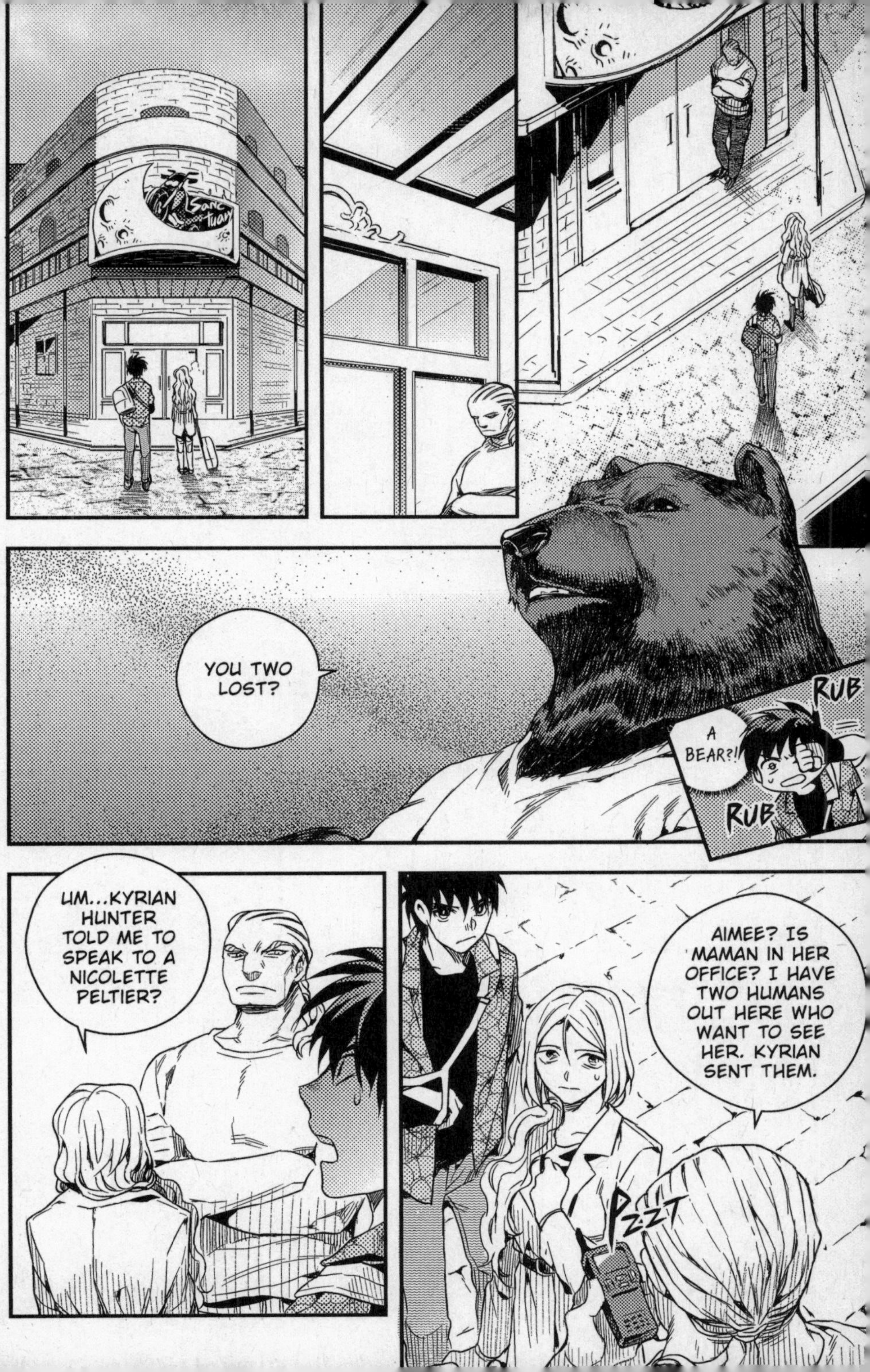
YOU TWO LOST?
RUB
A BEAR?!
RUB
UM...KYRIAN HUNTER TOLD ME TO SPEAK TO A NICOLETTE PELTIER?
AIMEE? IS MAMAN IN HER OFFICE? I HAVE TWO HUMANS OUT HERE WHO WANT TO SEE HER. KYRIAN SENT THEM.
PZZT

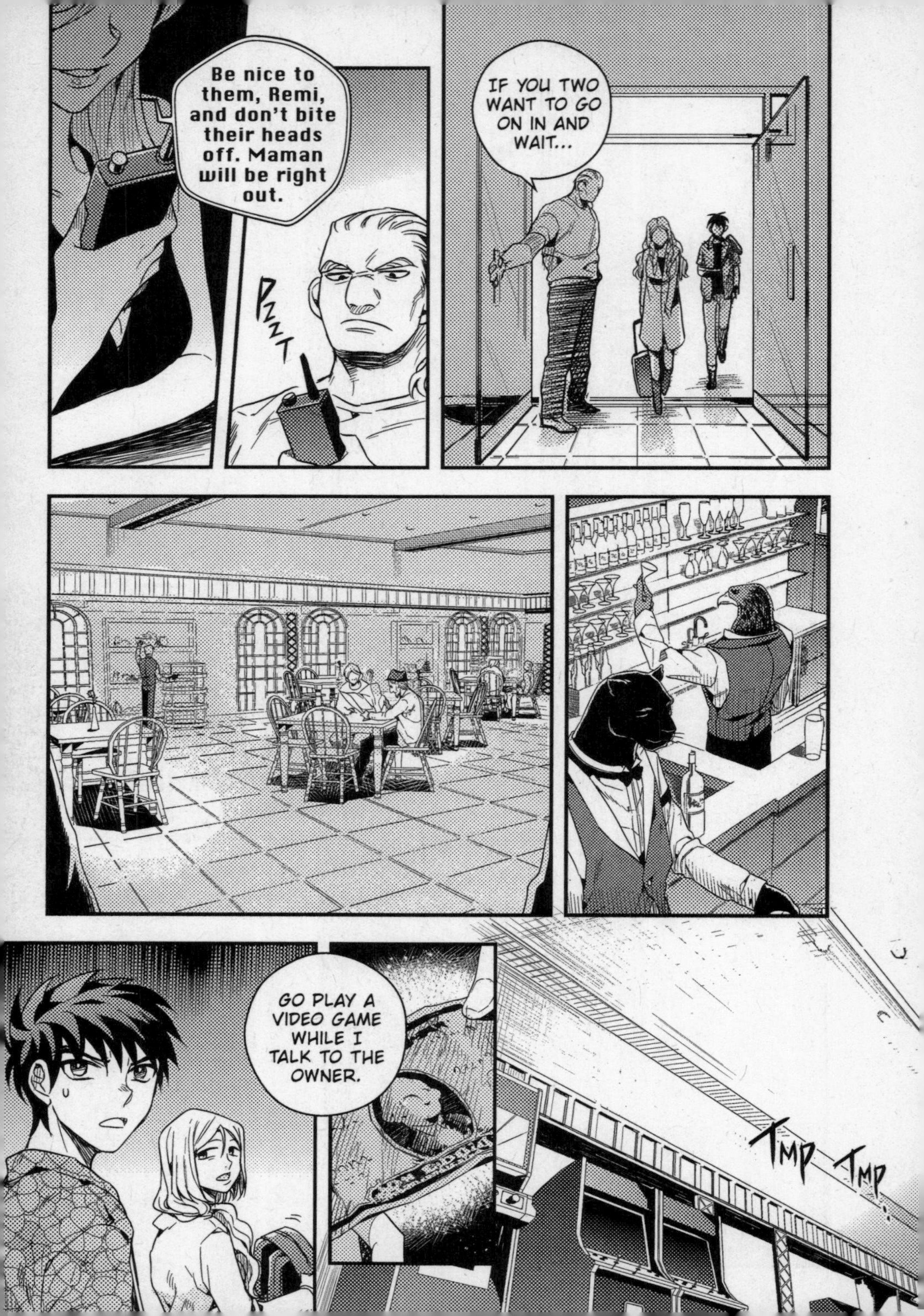
Be nice to them, Remi, and don't bite their heads off. Maman will be right out.
PZZT
IF YOU TWO WANT TO GO ON IN AND WAIT...
GO PLAY A VIDEO GAME WHILE I TALK TO THE OWNER.
TMP TMP

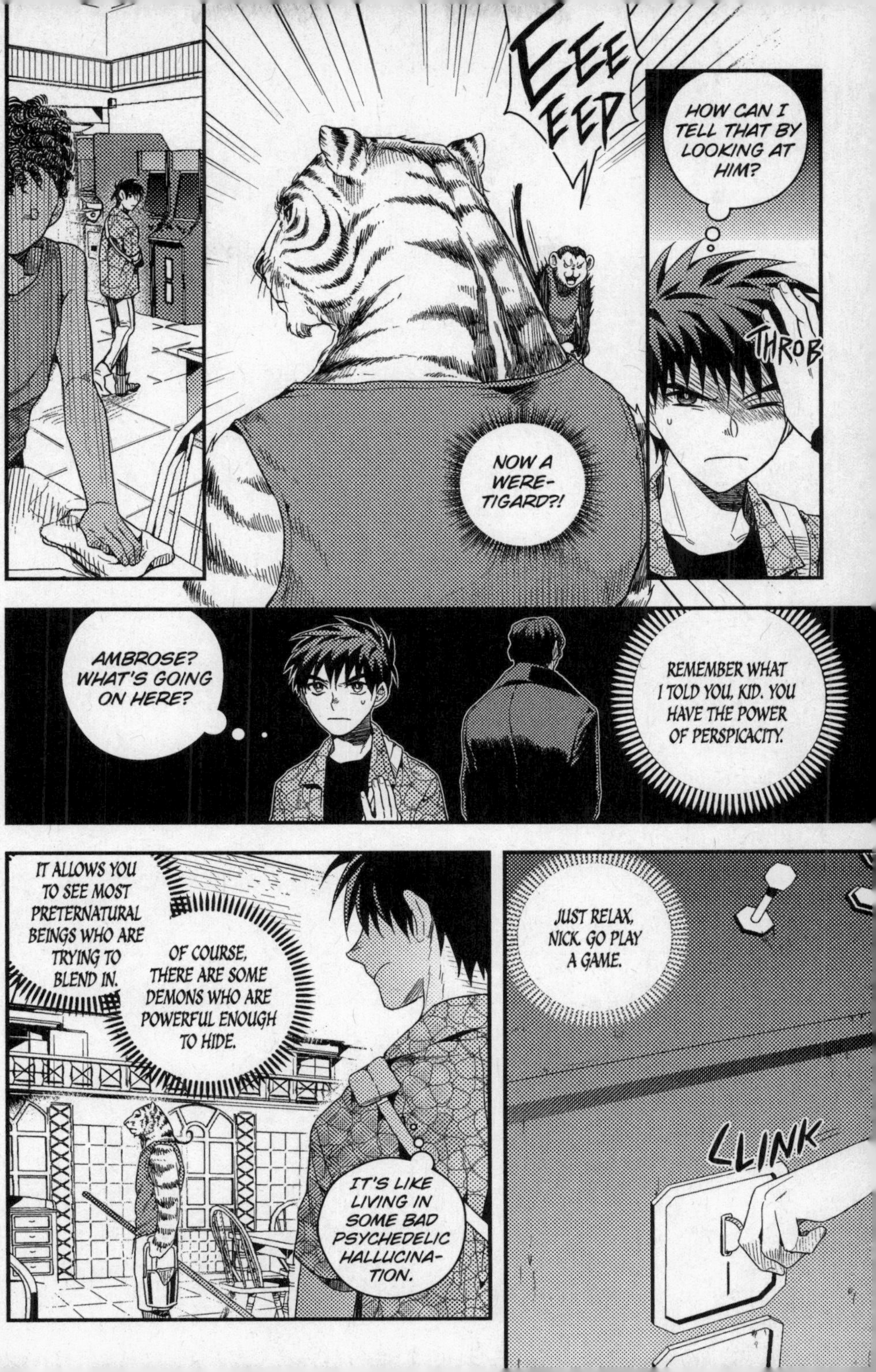
EEEEEP
HOW CAN I TELL THAT BY LOOKING AT HIM?
THROB
NOW A WERE-TIGARD?!
AMBROSE? WHAT'S GOING ON HERE?
REMEMBER WHAT I TOLD YOU, KID. YOU HAVE THE POWER OF PERSPICACITY.
IT ALLOWS YOU TO SEE MOST PRETERNATURAL BEINGS WHO ARE TRYING TO BLEND IN.
OF COURSE, THERE ARE SOME DEMONS WHO ARE POWERFUL ENOUGH TO HIDE.
IT'S LIKE LIVING IN SOME BAD PSYCHEDELIC HALLUCINA-TION.
JUST RELAX, NICK. GO PLAY A GAME.
CLINK

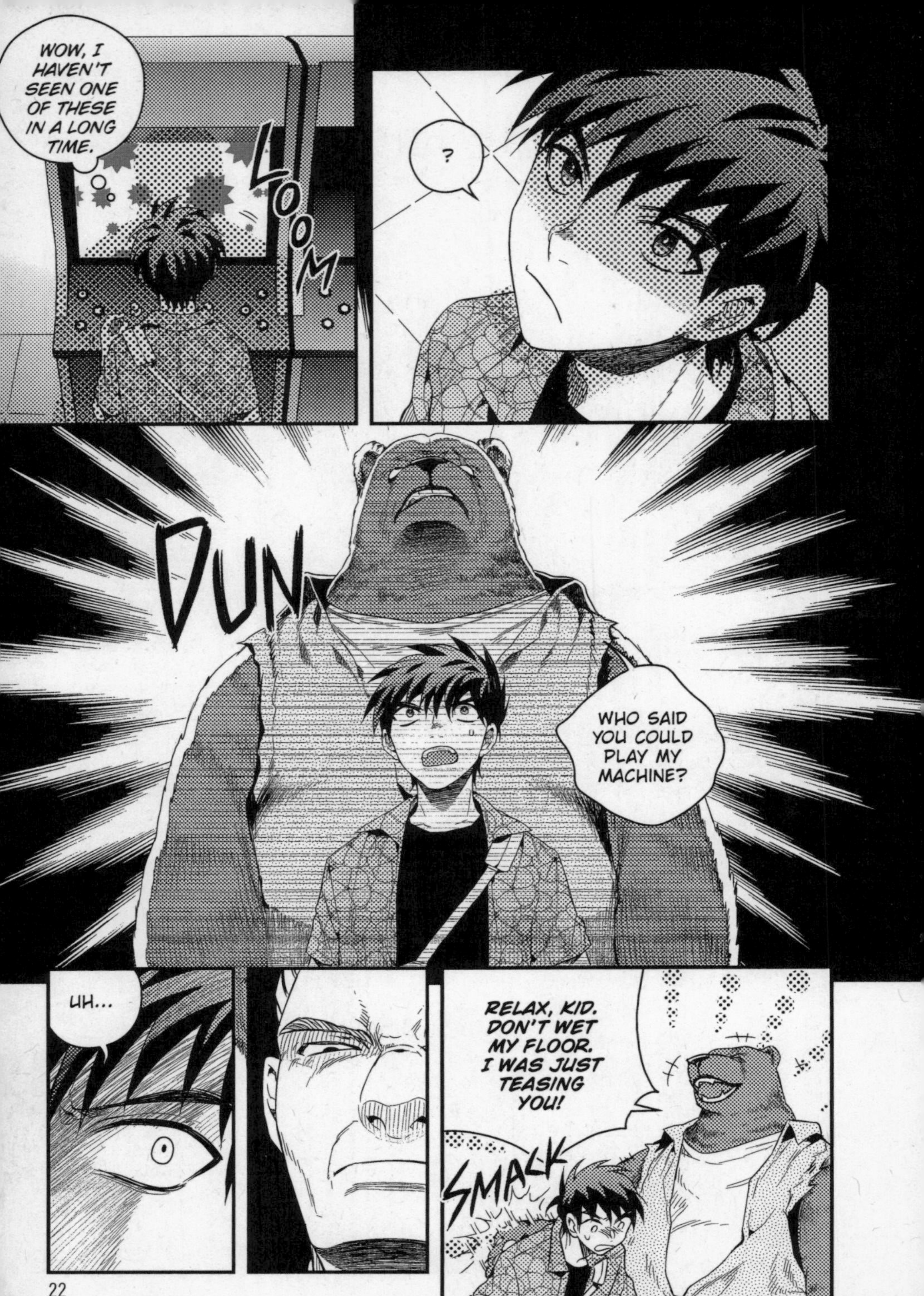
WOW, I HAVEN'T SEEN ONE OF THESE IN A LONG TIME.
LOOOM
?
DUN
WHO SAID YOU COULD PLAY MY MACHINE?
UH...
RELAX, KID. DON'T WET MY FLOOR. I WAS JUST TEASING YOU!
SMACK

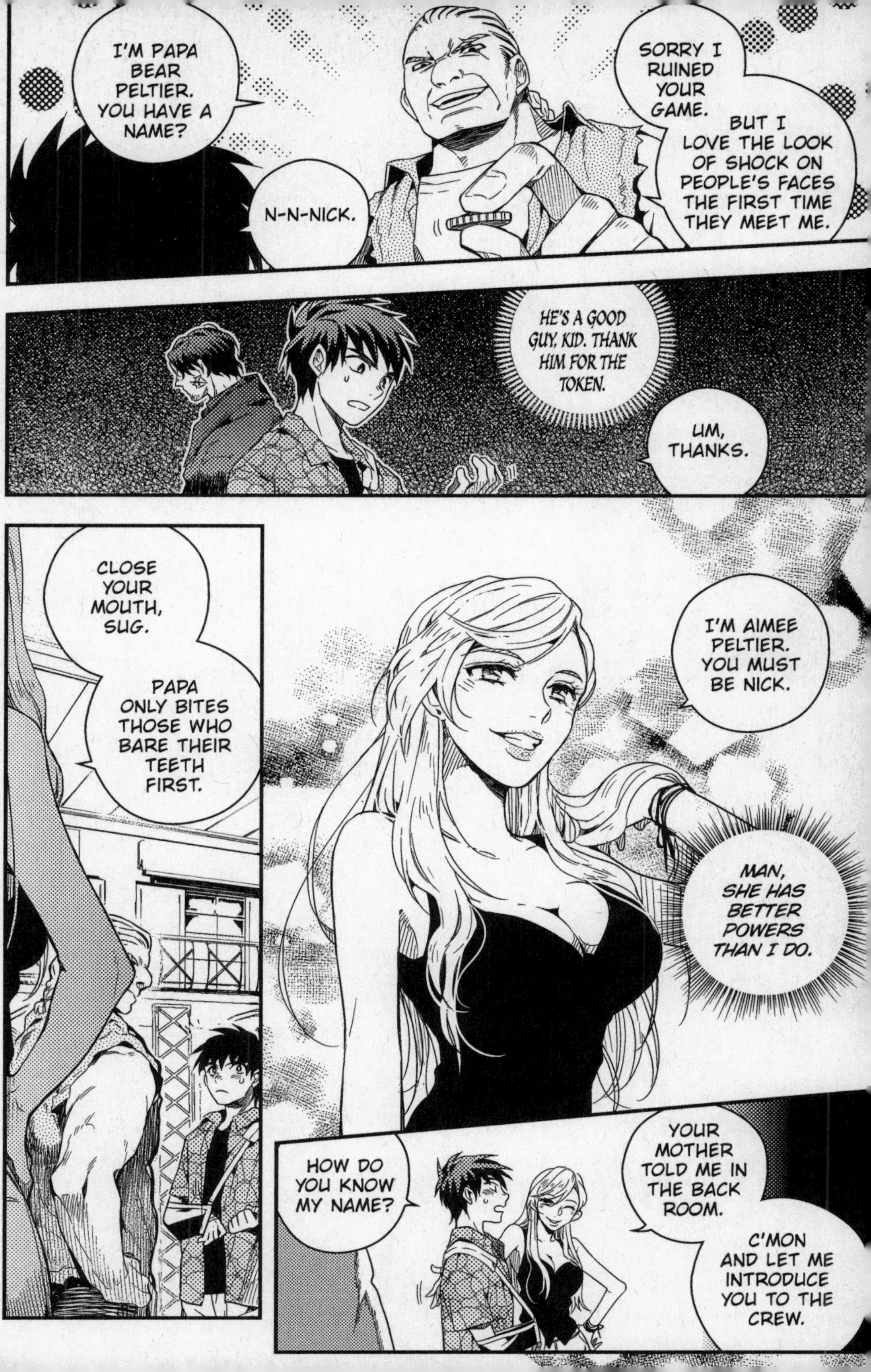
I'M PAPA BEAR PELTIER. YOU HAVE A NAME?
SORRY I RUINED YOUR GAME.
BUT I LOVE THE LOOK OF SHOCK ON PEOPLE'S FACES THE FIRST TIME THEY MEET ME.
N-N-NICK.
HE'S A GOOD GUY, KID. THANK HIM FOR THE TOKEN.
UM, THANKS.
CLOSE YOUR MOUTH, SUG.
PAPA ONLY BITES THOSE WHO BARE THEIR TEETH FIRST.
I'M AIMEE PELTIER. YOU MUST BE NICK.
MAN, SHE HAS BETTER POWERS THAN I DO.
HOW DO YOU KNOW MY NAME?
YOUR MOTHER TOLD ME IN THE BACK ROOM.
C'MON AND LET ME INTRODUCE YOU TO THE CREW.

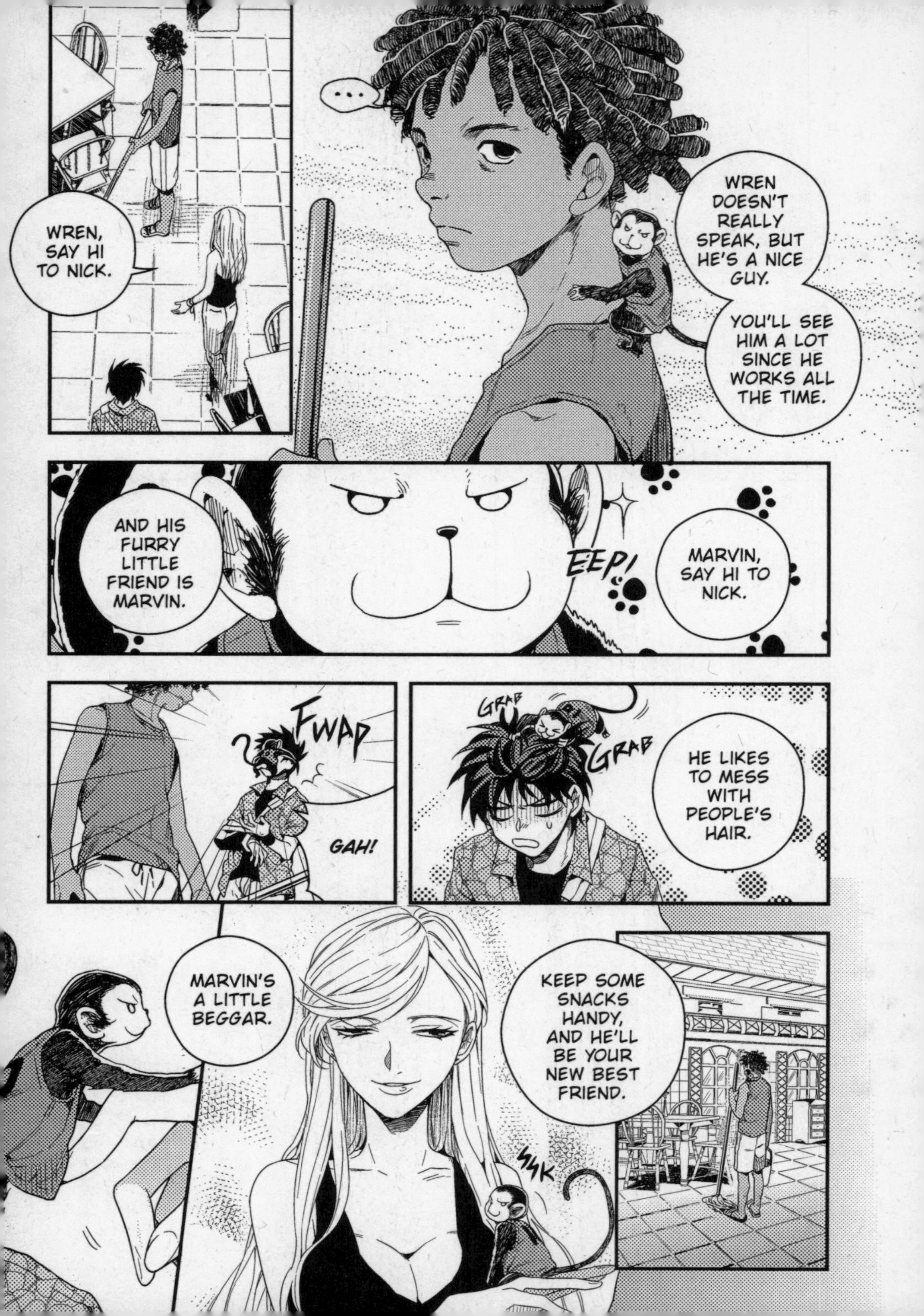
WREN, SAY HI TO NICK.
...
WREN DOESN'T REALLY SPEAK, BUT HE'S A NICE GUY.
YOU'LL SEE HIM A LOT SINCE HE WORKS ALL THE TIME.
AND HIS FURRY LITTLE FRIEND IS MARVIN.
EEP!
MARVIN, SAY HI TO NICK.
FWAP
GAH!
GRAB
GRAB
HE LIKES TO MESS WITH PEOPLE'S HAIR.
MARVIN'S A LITTLE BEGGAR.
KEEP SOME SNACKS HANDY, AND HE'LL BE YOUR NEW BEST FRIEND.
SSK

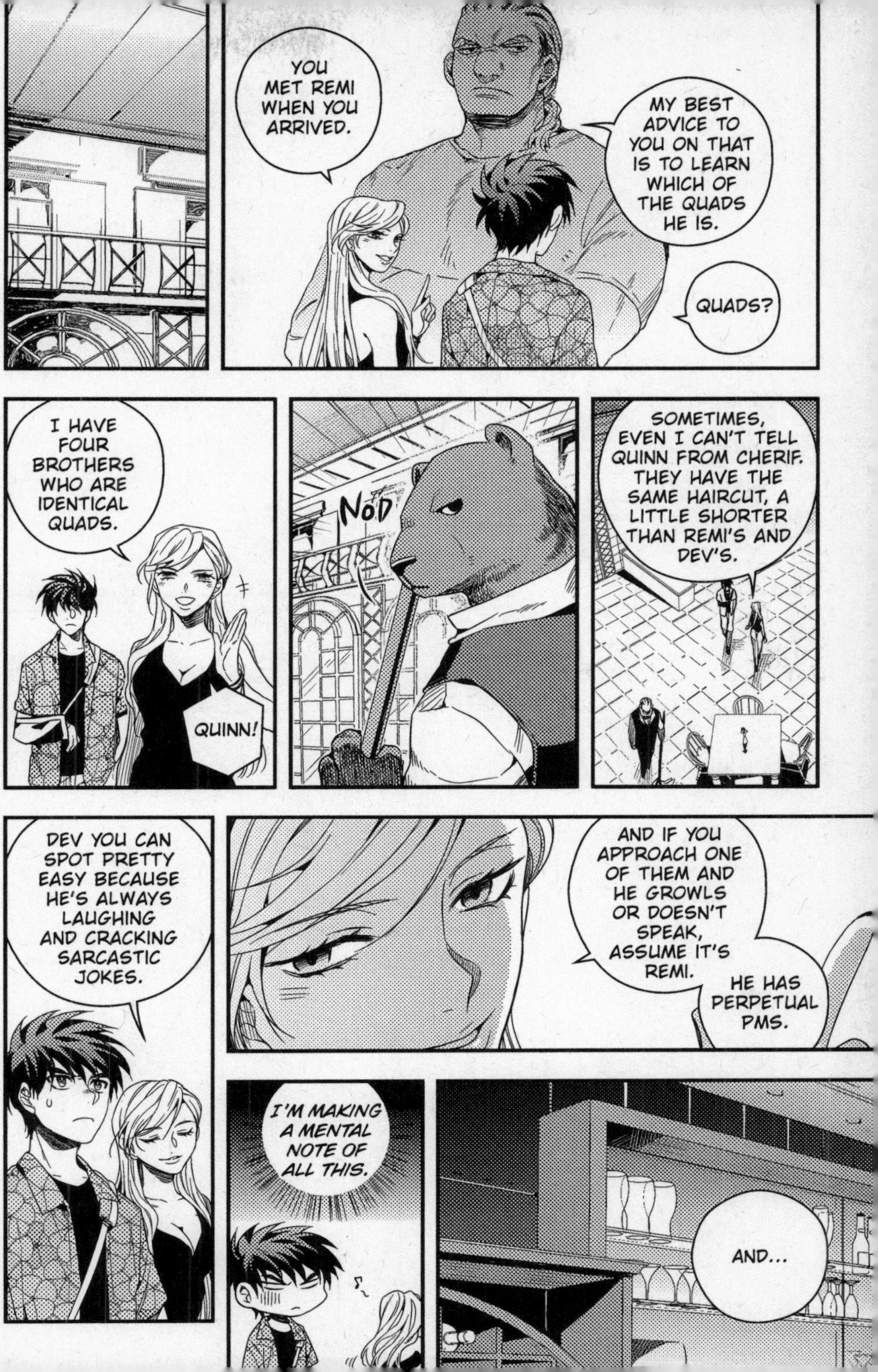
YOU MET REMI WHEN YOU ARRIVED.
MY BEST ADVICE TO YOU ON THAT IS TO LEARN WHICH OF THE QUADS HE IS.
QUADS?
I HAVE FOUR BROTHERS WHO ARE IDENTICAL QUADS.
QUINN!
NOD
SOMETIMES, EVEN I CAN'T TELL QUINN FROM CHERIF. THEY HAVE THE SAME HAIRCUT, A LITTLE SHORTER THAN REMI'S AND DEV'S.
DEV YOU CAN SPOT PRETTY EASY BECAUSE HE'S ALWAYS LAUGHING AND CRACKING SARCASTIC JOKES.
AND IF YOU APPROACH ONE OF THEM AND HE GROWLS OR DOESN'T SPEAK, ASSUME IT'S REMI.
HE HAS PERPETUAL PMS.
I'M MAKING A MENTAL NOTE OF ALL THIS.
AND...

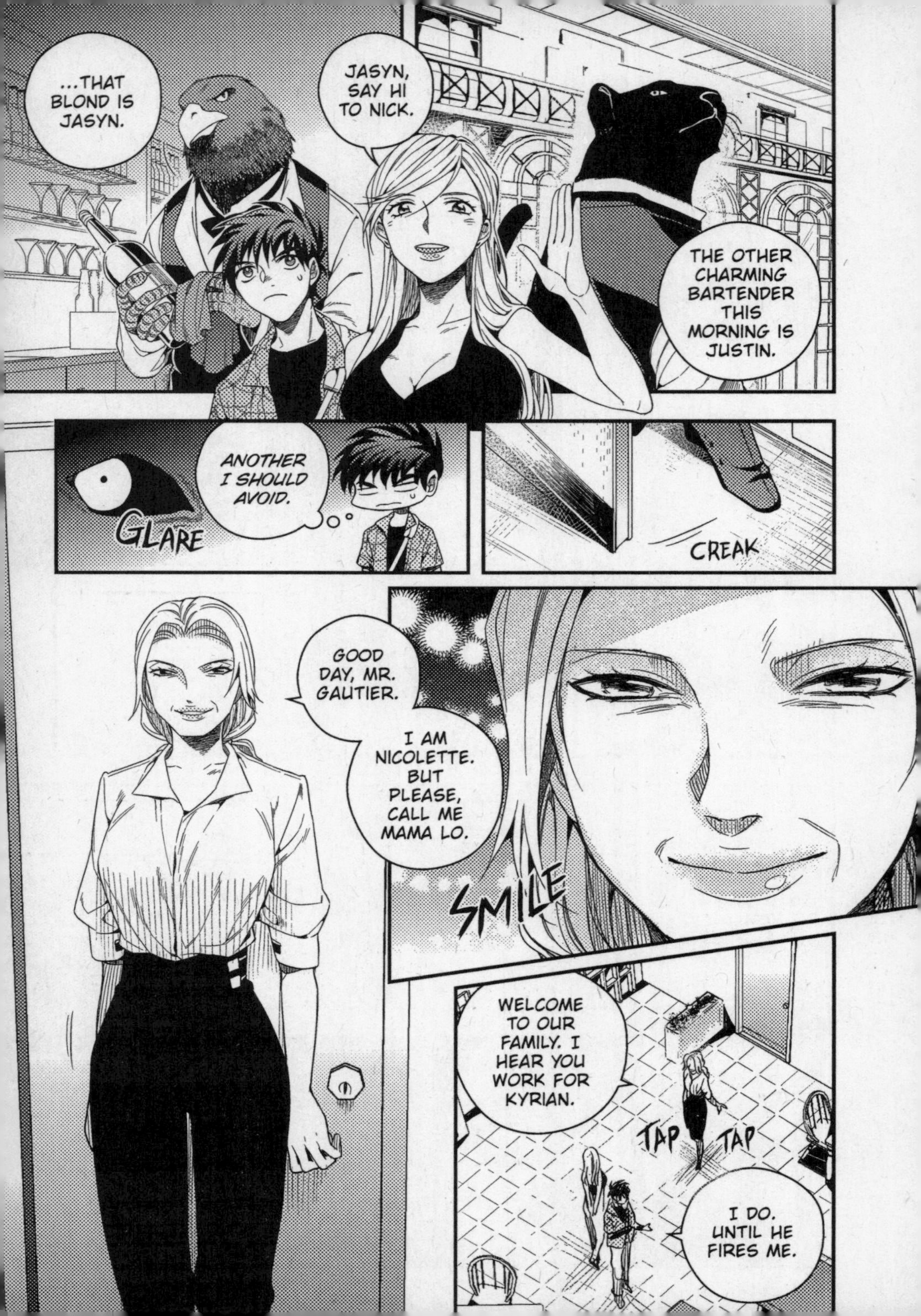

...THAT BLOND IS JASYN.
JASYN, SAY HI TO NICK.
THE OTHER CHARMING BARTENDER THIS MORNING IS JUSTIN.
GLARE
ANOTHER I SHOULD AVOID.
CREAK
GOOD DAY, MR. GAUTIER.
I AM NICOLETTE. BUT PLEASE, CALL ME MAMA LO.
SMILE
WELCOME TO OUR FAMILY. I HEAR YOU WORK FOR KYRIAN.
TAP TAP
I DO. UNTIL HE FIRES ME.

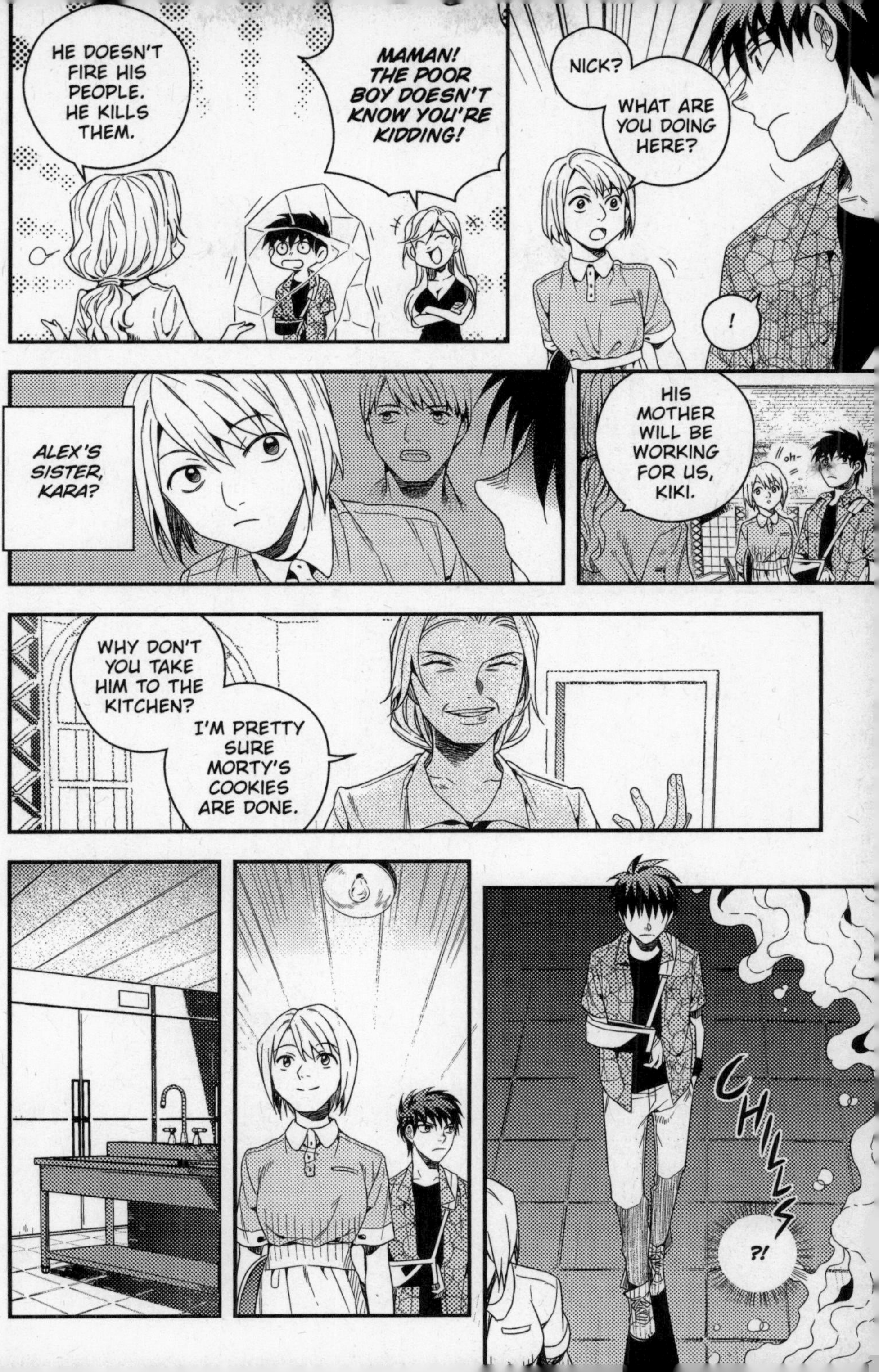
HE DOESN'T FIRE HIS PEOPLE. HE KILLS THEM.
MAMAN! THE POOR BOY DOESN'T KNOW YOU'RE KIDDING!
NICK?
WHAT ARE YOU DOING HERE?
!
ALEX'S SISTER, KARA?
HIS MOTHER WILL BE WORKING FOR US, KIKI.
oh-
WHY DON'T YOU TAKE HIM TO THE KITCHEN?
I'M PRETTY SURE MORTY'S COOKIES ARE DONE.
CHILLS
?!

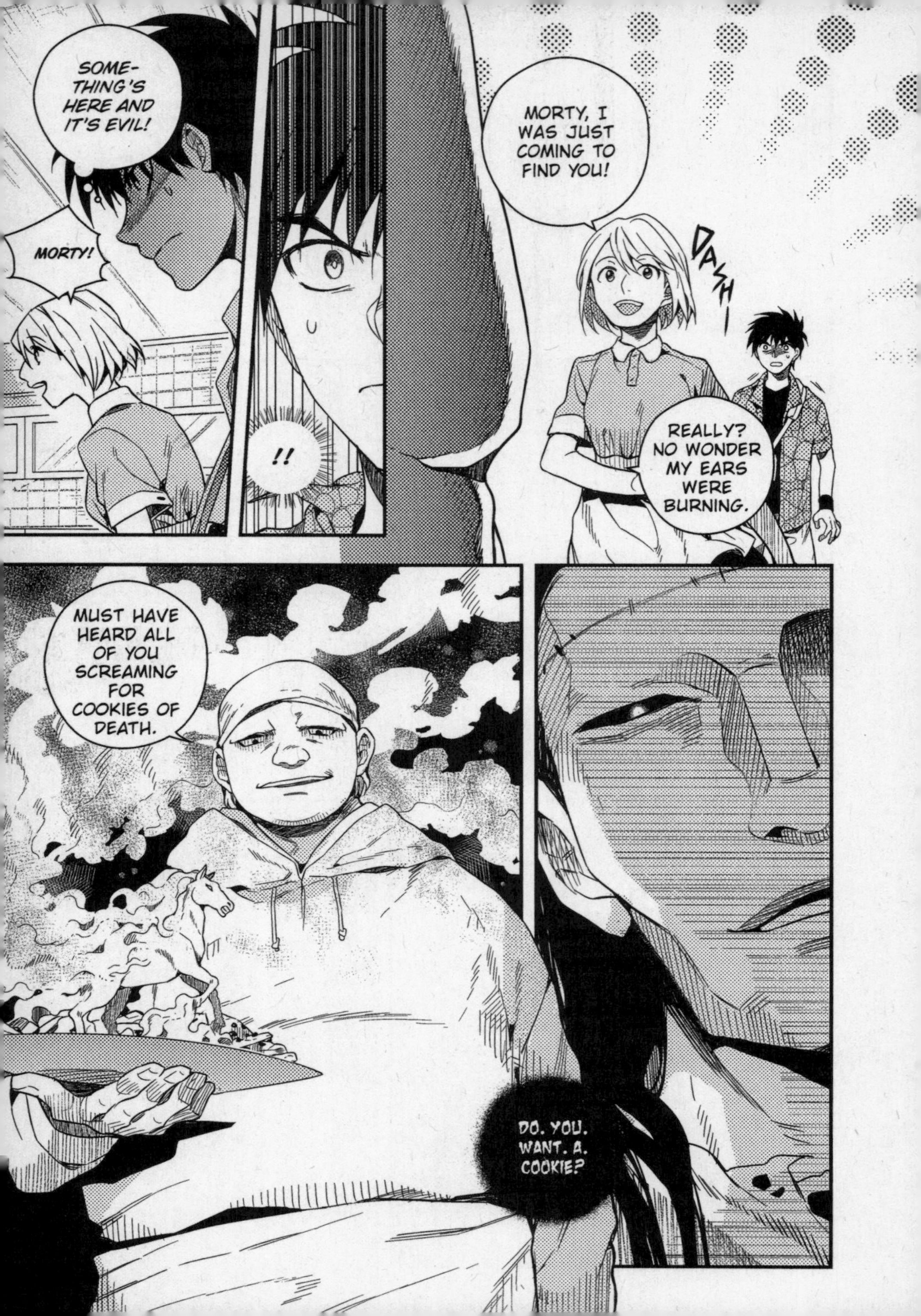
SOME-THING'S HERE AND IT'S EVIL!
MORTY!
!!
MORTY, I WAS JUST COMING TO FIND YOU!
DASH
REALLY? NO WONDER MY EARS WERE BURNING.
MUST HAVE HEARD ALL OF YOU SCREAMING FOR COOKIES OF DEATH.
DO. YOU. WANT. A. COOKIE?

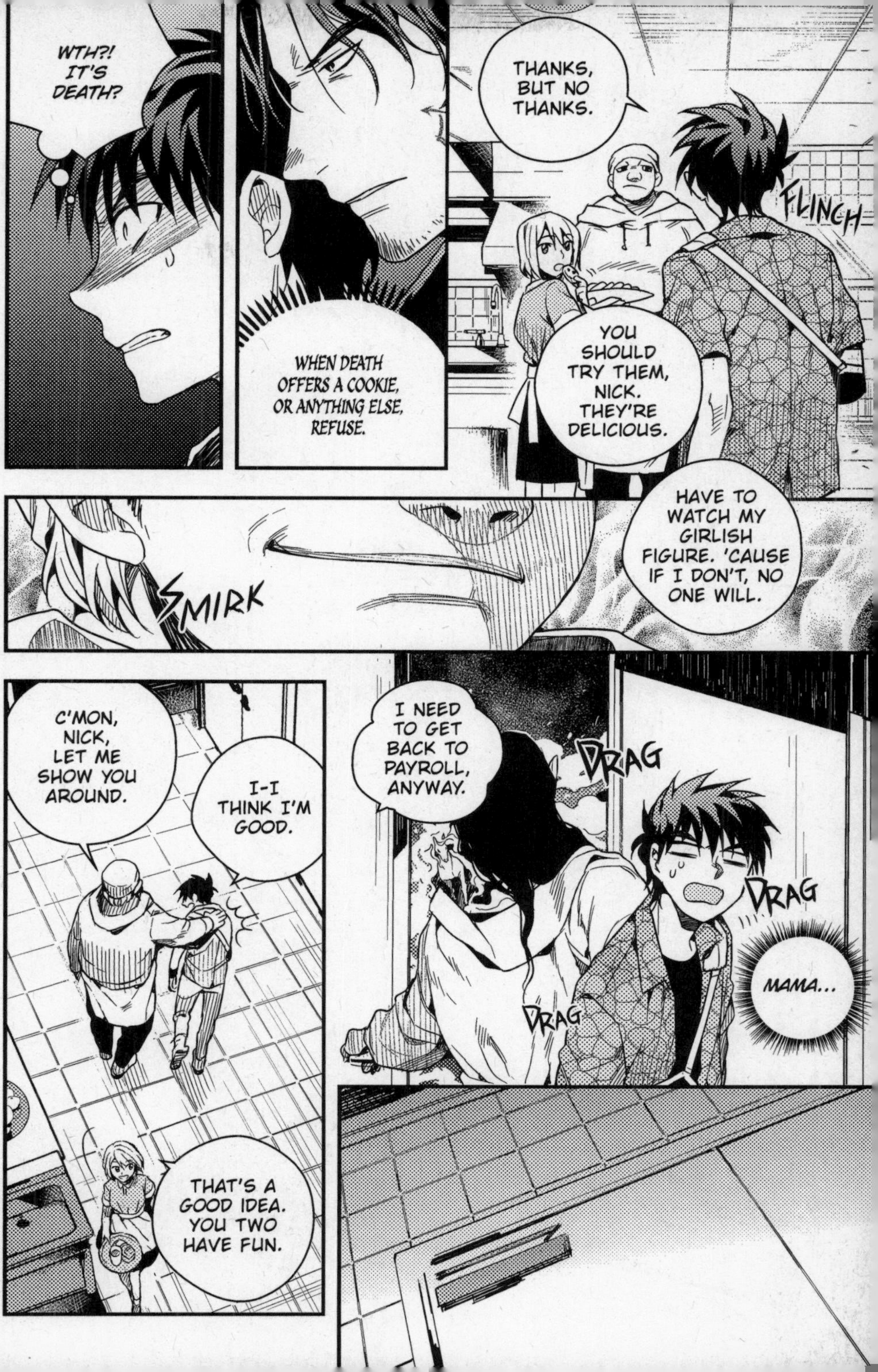
WTH?! IT'S DEATH?
WHEN DEATH OFFERS A COOKIE, OR ANYTHING ELSE, REFUSE.
THANKS, BUT NO THANKS.
FLINCH
YOU SHOULD TRY THEM, NICK. THEY'RE DELICIOUS.
SMIRK
HAVE TO WATCH MY GIRLISH FIGURE. 'CAUSE IF I DON'T, NO ONE WILL.
C'MON, NICK, LET ME SHOW YOU AROUND.
I-I THINK I'M GOOD.
THAT'S A GOOD IDEA. YOU TWO HAVE FUN.
I NEED TO GET BACK TO PAYROLL, ANYWAY.
DRAG
DRAG
DRAG
MAMA...

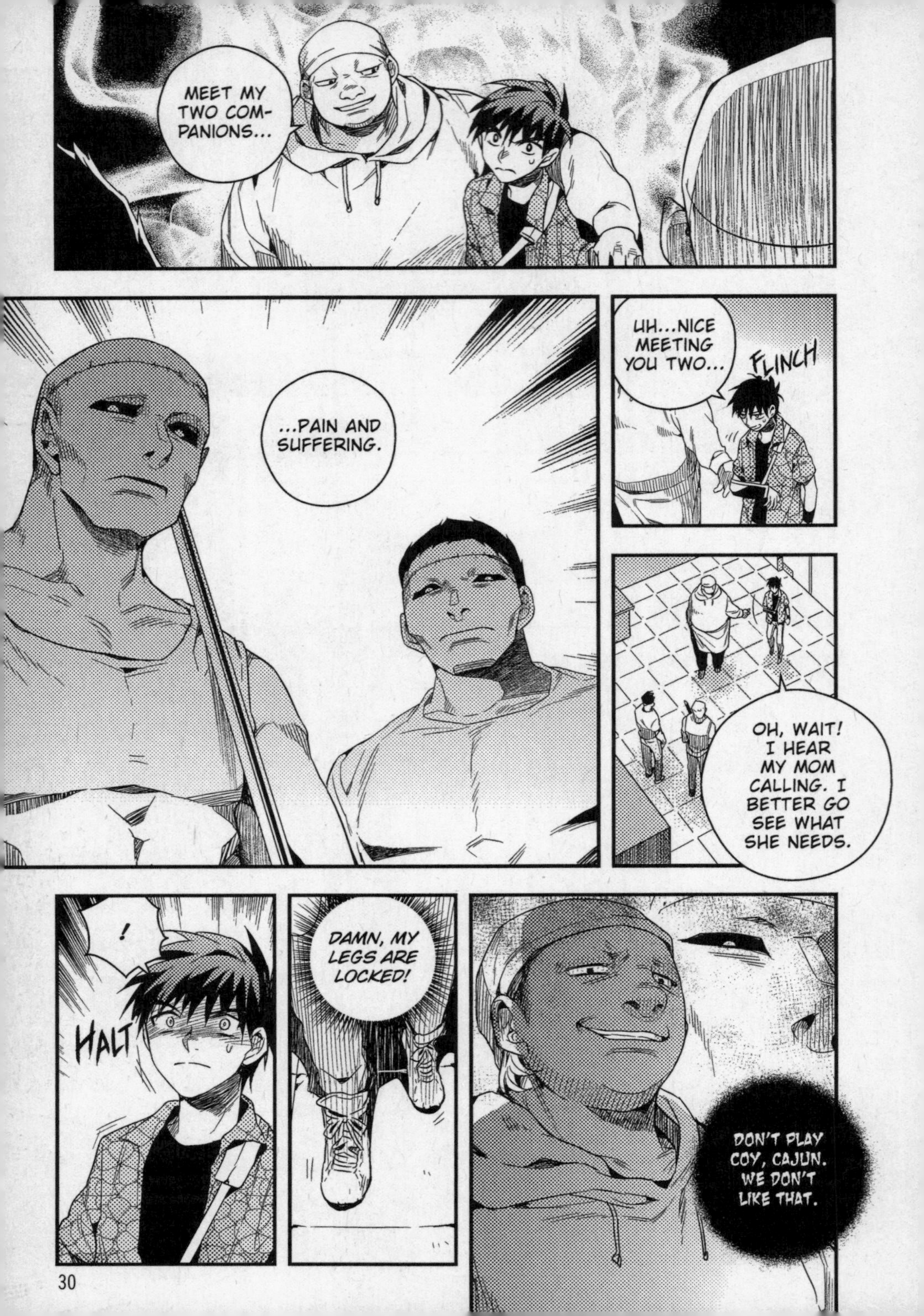
MEET MY TWO COMPANIONS...
...PAIN AND SUFFERING.
UH...NICE MEETING YOU TWO...
FLINCH
OH, WAIT! I HEAR MY MOM CALLING. I BETTER GO SEE WHAT SHE NEEDS.
!
HALT
DAMN, MY LEGS ARE LOCKED!
DON'T PLAY COY, CAJUN. WE DON'T LIKE THAT.

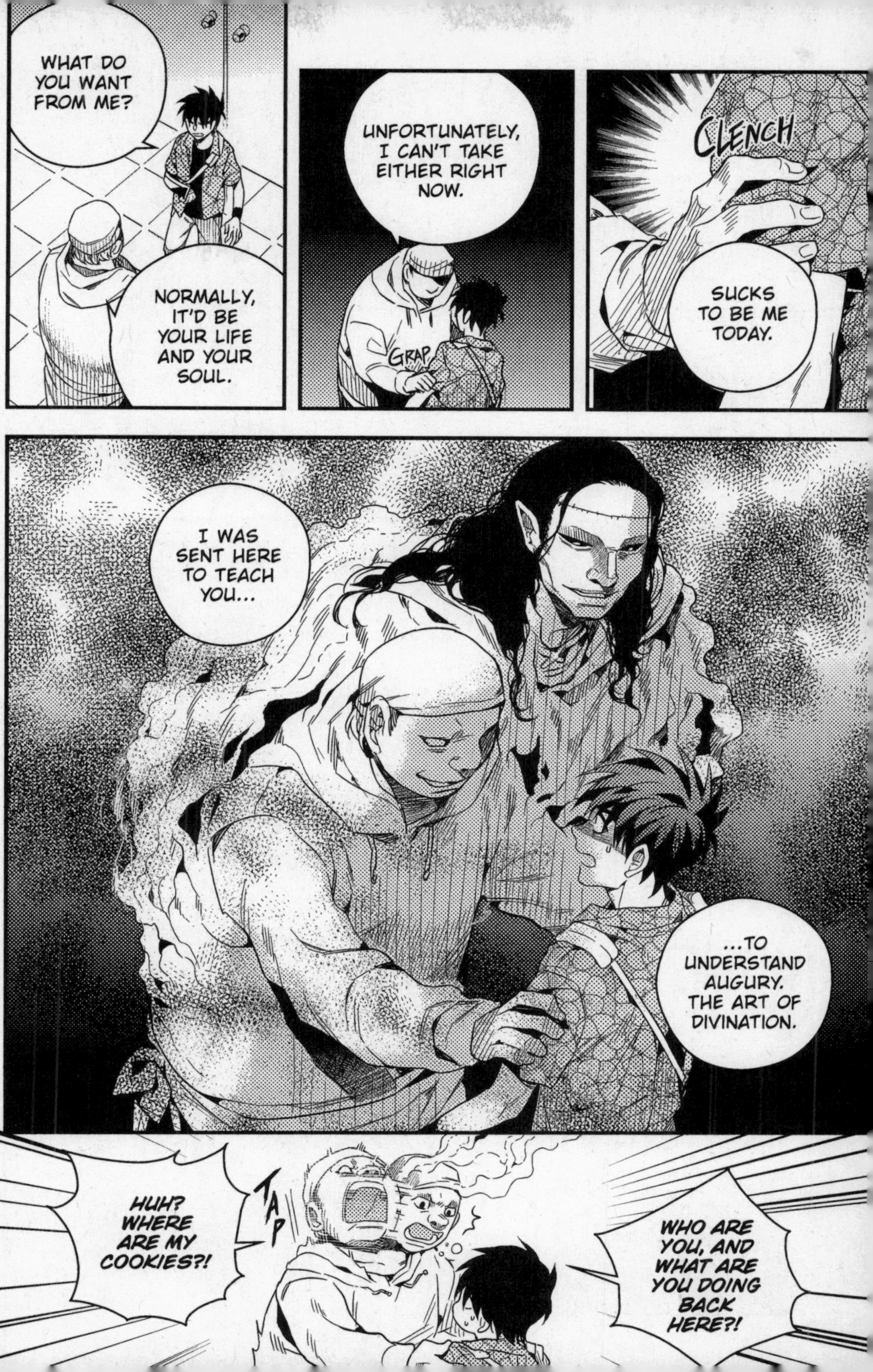
WHAT DO YOU WANT FROM ME?
NORMALLY, IT'D BE YOUR LIFE AND YOUR SOUL.
UNFORTUNATELY, I CAN'T TAKE EITHER RIGHT NOW.
GRAP
CLENCH
SUCKS TO BE ME TODAY.
I WAS SENT HERE TO TEACH YOU...
...TO UNDERSTAND AUGURY. THE ART OF DIVINATION.
HUH? WHERE ARE MY COOKIES?!
TAP
WHO ARE YOU, AND WHAT ARE YOU DOING BACK HERE?!

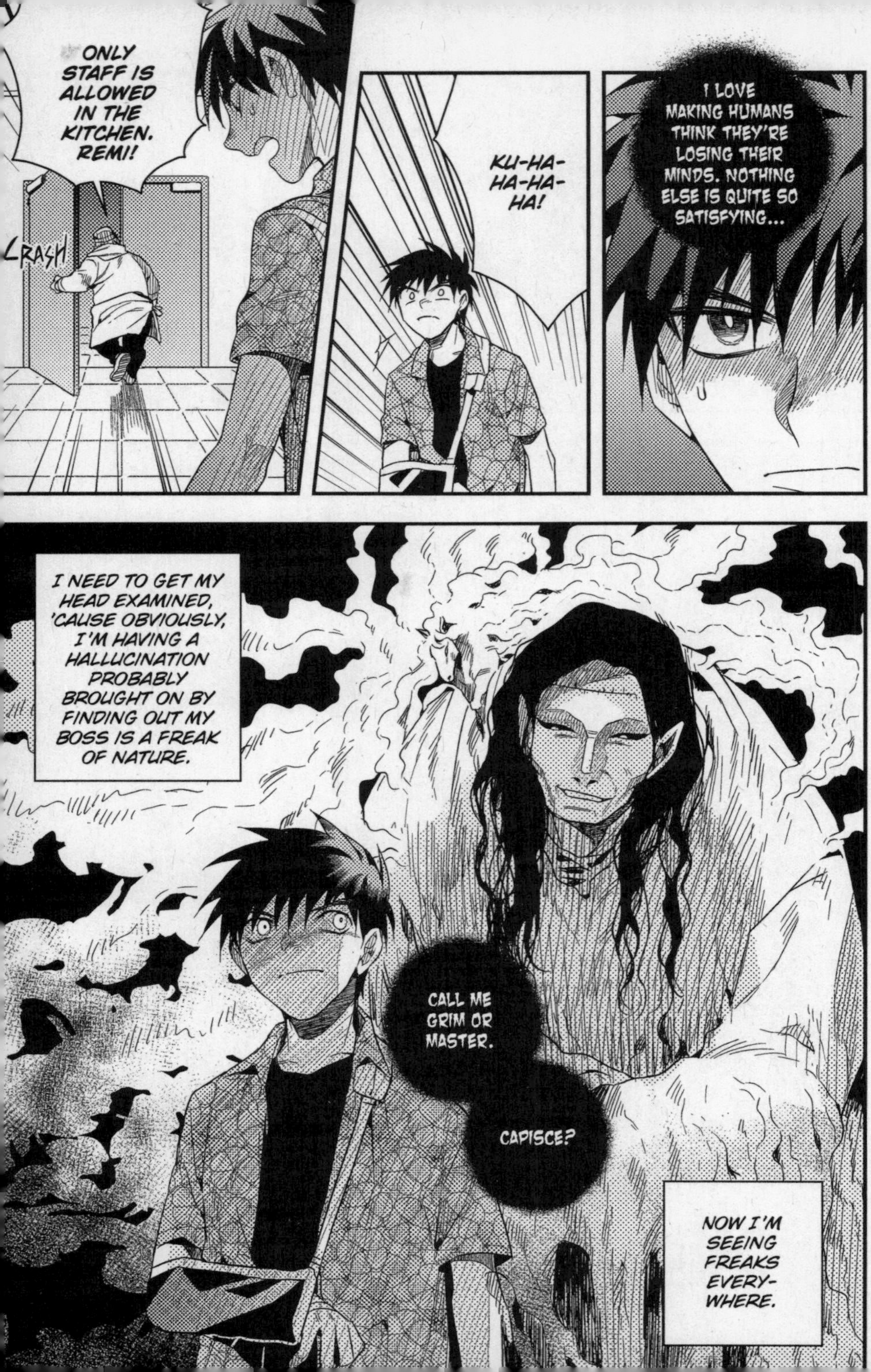

ONLY STAFF IS ALLOWED IN THE KITCHEN. REMI!
CRASH
KU-HA-HA-HA-HA!
I LOVE MAKING HUMANS THINK THEY'RE LOSING THEIR MINDS. NOTHING ELSE IS QUITE SO SATISFYING...
I NEED TO GET MY HEAD EXAMINED, 'CAUSE OBVIOUSLY, I'M HAVING A HALLUCINATION PROBABLY BROUGHT ON BY FINDING OUT MY BOSS IS A FREAK OF NATURE.
CALL ME GRIM OR MASTER.
CAPISCE?
NOW I'M SEEING FREAKS EVERY-WHERE.

THE DARK-HUNTERS: INFINITY

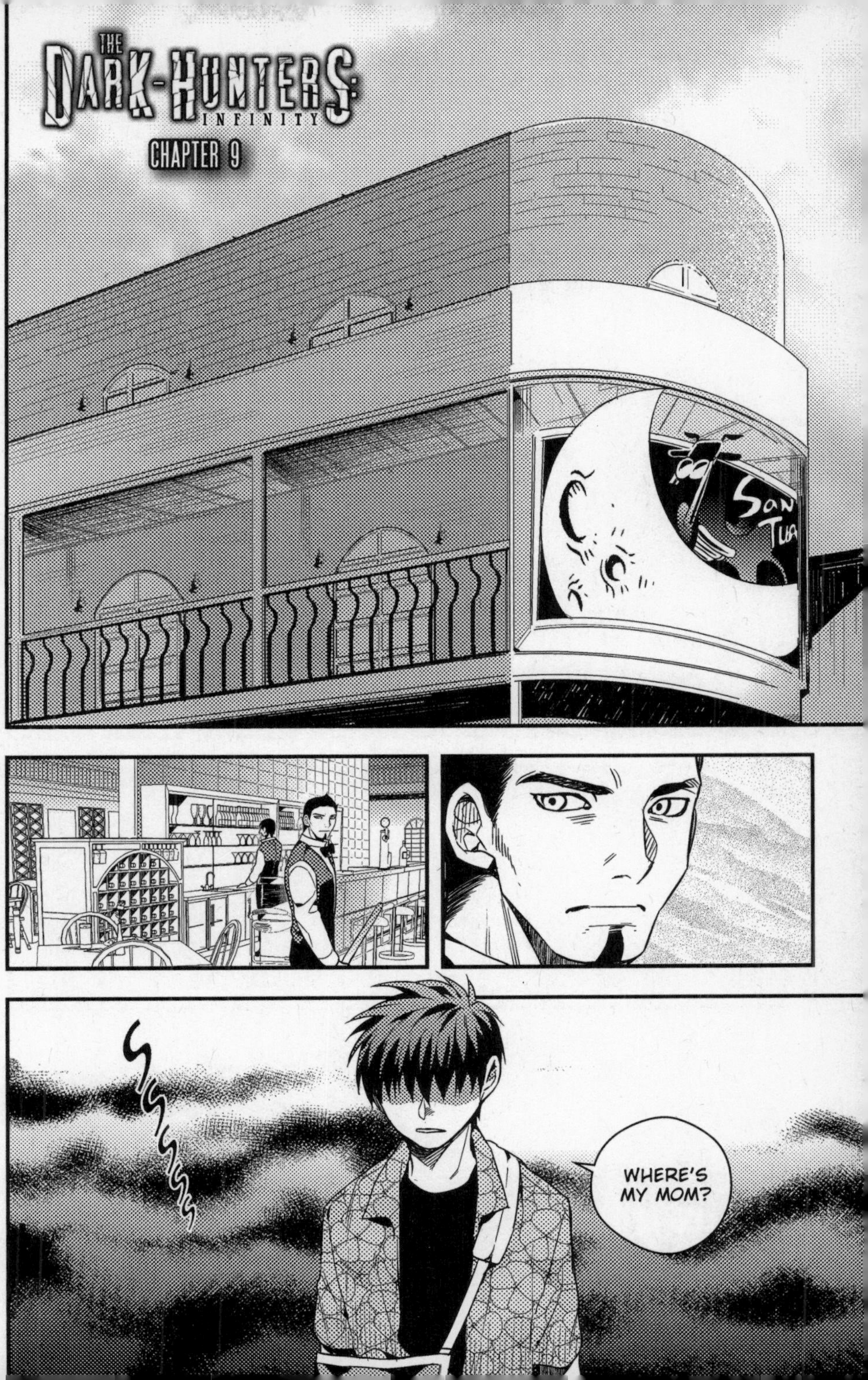
THE DARK-HUNTERS: INFINITY
CHAPTER 9
WHERE'S MY MOM?

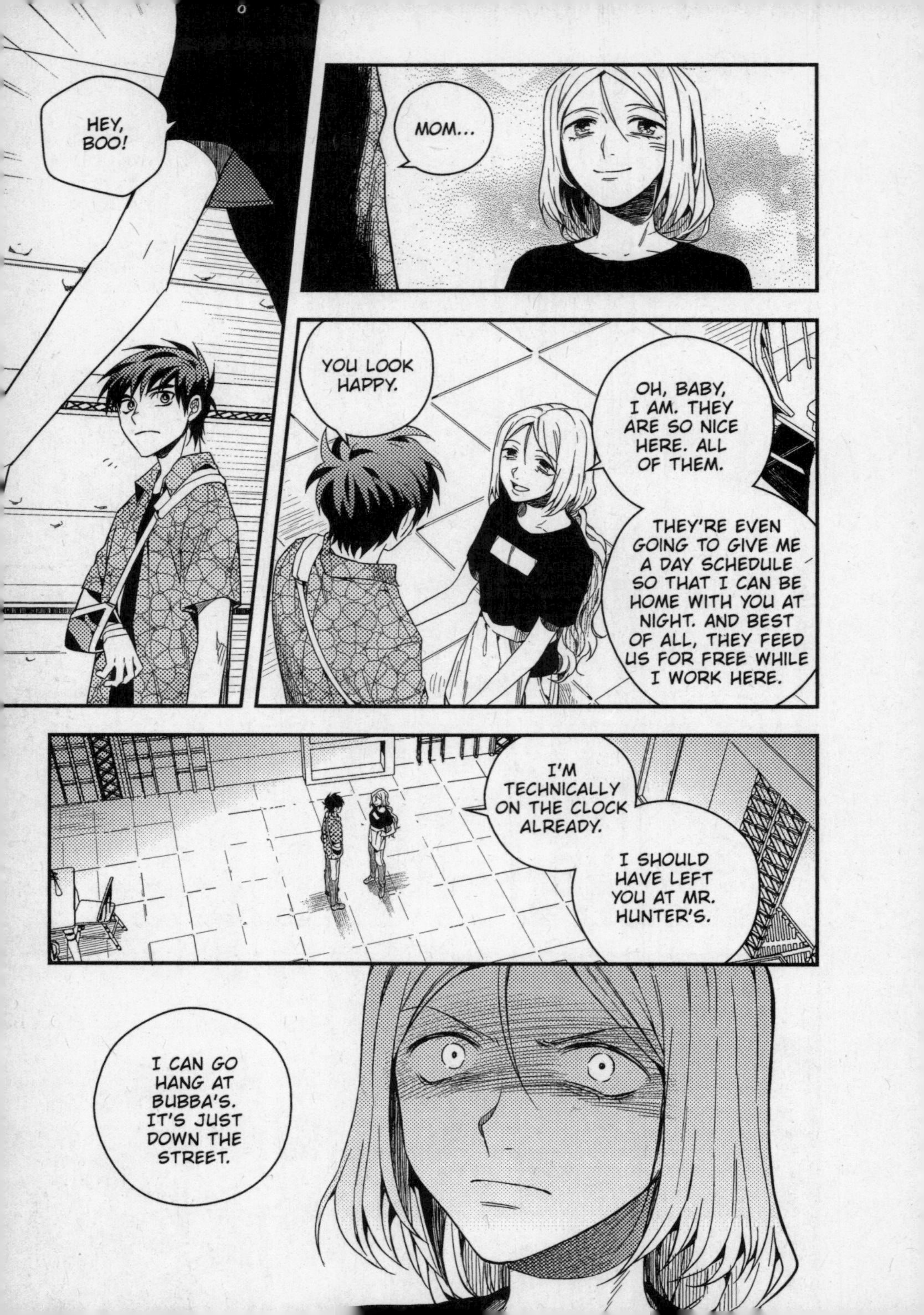
HEY, BOO!
MOM...
YOU LOOK HAPPY.
OH, BABY, I AM. THEY ARE SO NICE HERE. ALL OF THEM.
THEY'RE EVEN GOING TO GIVE ME A DAY SCHEDULE SO THAT I CAN BE HOME WITH YOU AT NIGHT. AND BEST OF ALL, THEY FEED US FOR FREE WHILE I WORK HERE.
I'M TECHNICALLY ON THE CLOCK ALREADY.
I SHOULD HAVE LEFT YOU AT MR. HUNTER'S.
I CAN GO HANG AT BUBBA'S. IT'S JUST DOWN THE STREET.

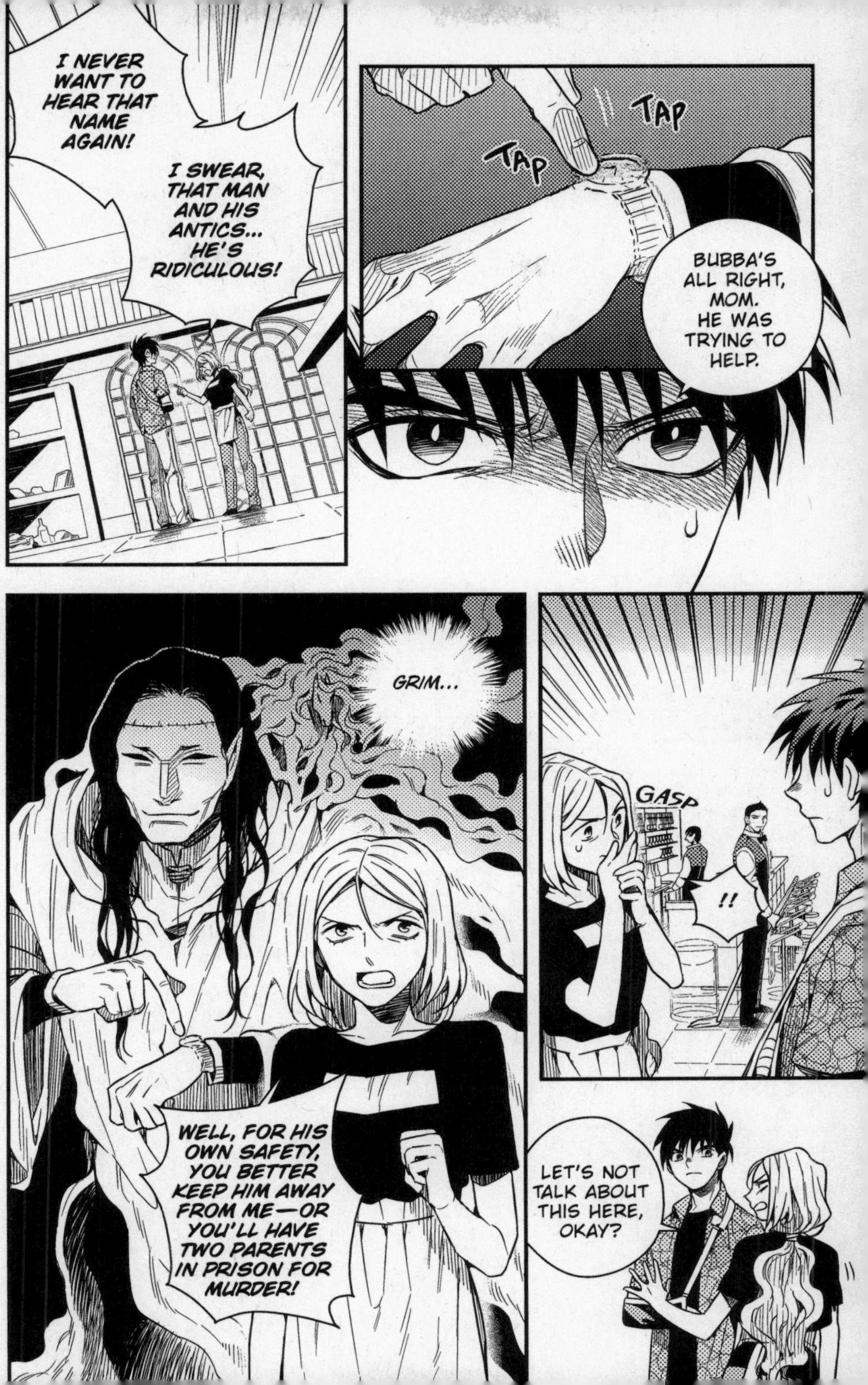
I NEVER WANT TO HEAR THAT NAME AGAIN!
I SWEAR, THAT MAN AND HIS ANTICS... HE'S RIDICULOUS!
TAP
TAP
BUBBA'S ALL RIGHT, MOM. HE WAS TRYING TO HELP.
GRIM...
WELL, FOR HIS OWN SAFETY, YOU BETTER KEEP HIM AWAY FROM ME—OR YOU'LL HAVE TWO PARENTS IN PRISON FOR MURDER!
GASP
!!
LET'S NOT TALK ABOUT THIS HERE, OKAY?

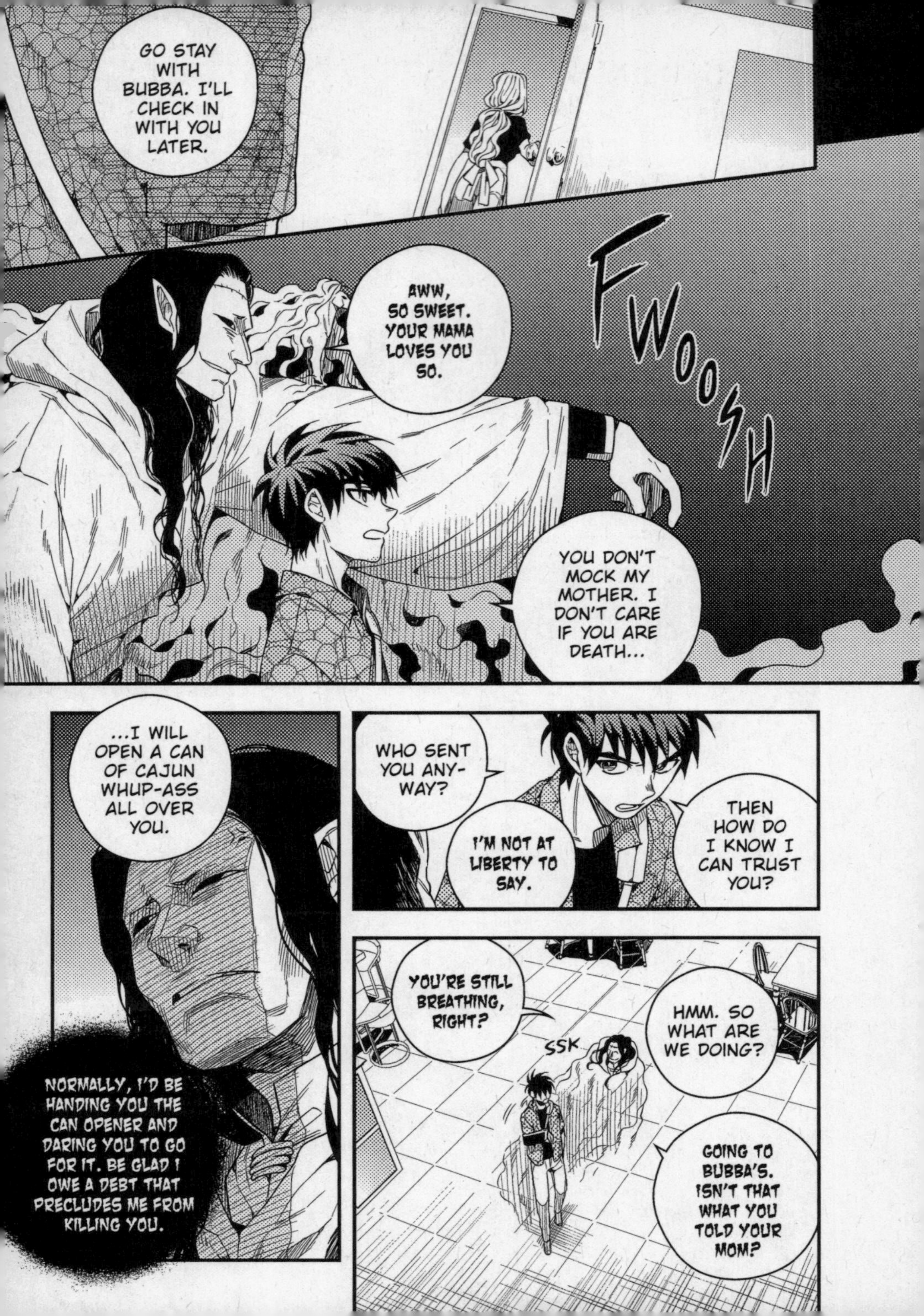
GO STAY WITH BUBBA. I'LL CHECK IN WITH YOU LATER.
FWOOSH
AWW, SO SWEET. YOUR MAMA LOVES YOU SO.
YOU DON'T MOCK MY MOTHER. I DON'T CARE IF YOU ARE DEATH...
...I WILL OPEN A CAN OF CAJUN WHUP-ASS ALL OVER YOU.
NORMALLY, I'D BE HANDING YOU THE CAN OPENER AND DARING YOU TO GO FOR IT. BE GLAD I OWE A DEBT THAT PRECLUDES ME FROM KILLING YOU.
WHO SENT YOU ANYWAY?
I'M NOT AT LIBERTY TO SAY.
THEN HOW DO I KNOW I CAN TRUST YOU?
YOU'RE STILL BREATHING, RIGHT?
SSK
HMM. SO WHAT ARE WE DOING?
GOING TO BUBBA'S. ISN'T THAT WHAT YOU TOLD YOUR MOM?

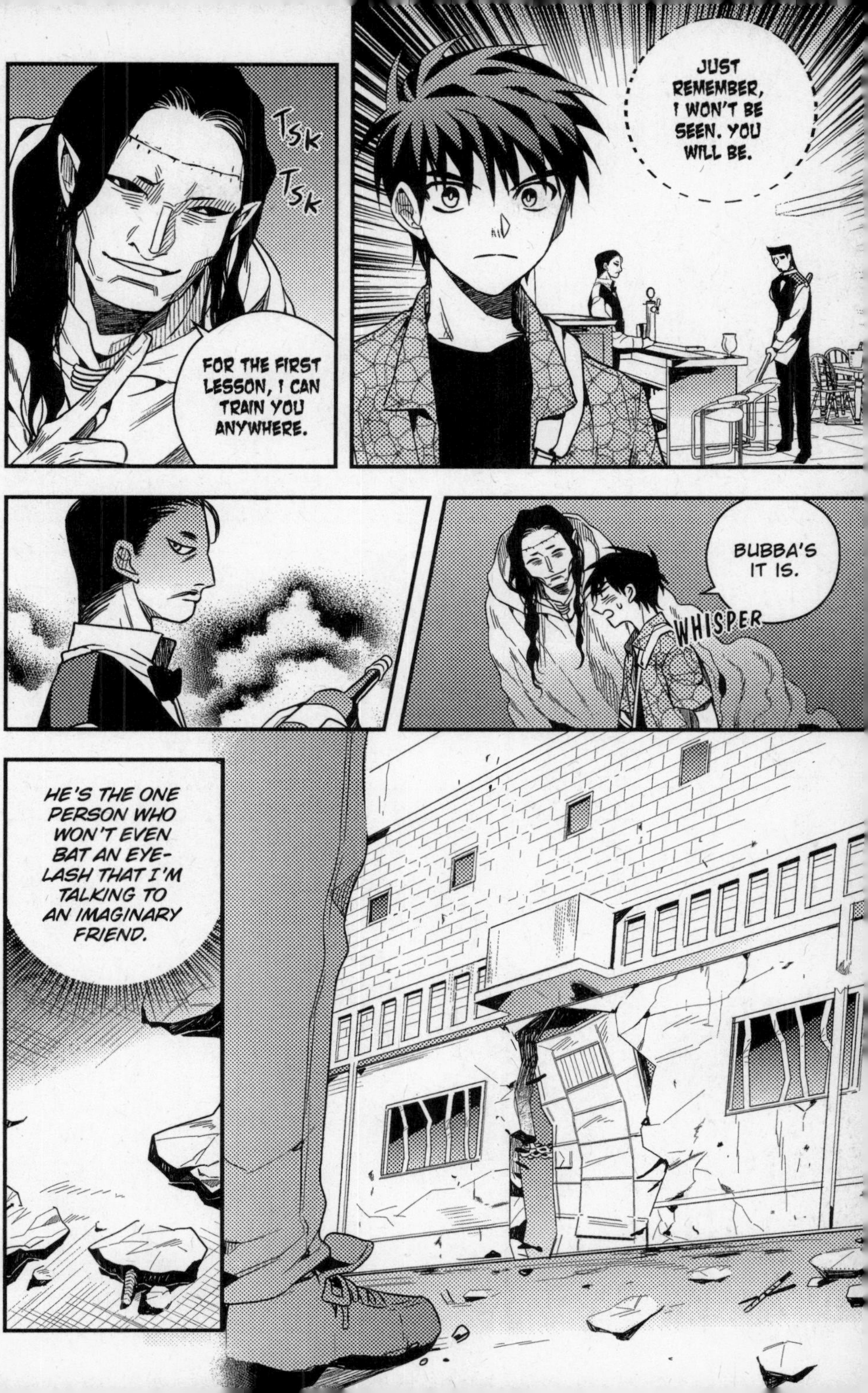
JUST REMEMBER, I WON'T BE SEEN. YOU WILL BE.
TSK TSK
FOR THE FIRST LESSON, I CAN TRAIN YOU ANYWHERE.
BUBBA'S IT IS.
WHISPER
HE'S THE ONE PERSON WHO WON'T EVEN BAT AN EYE-LASH THAT I'M TALKING TO AN IMAGINARY FRIEND.

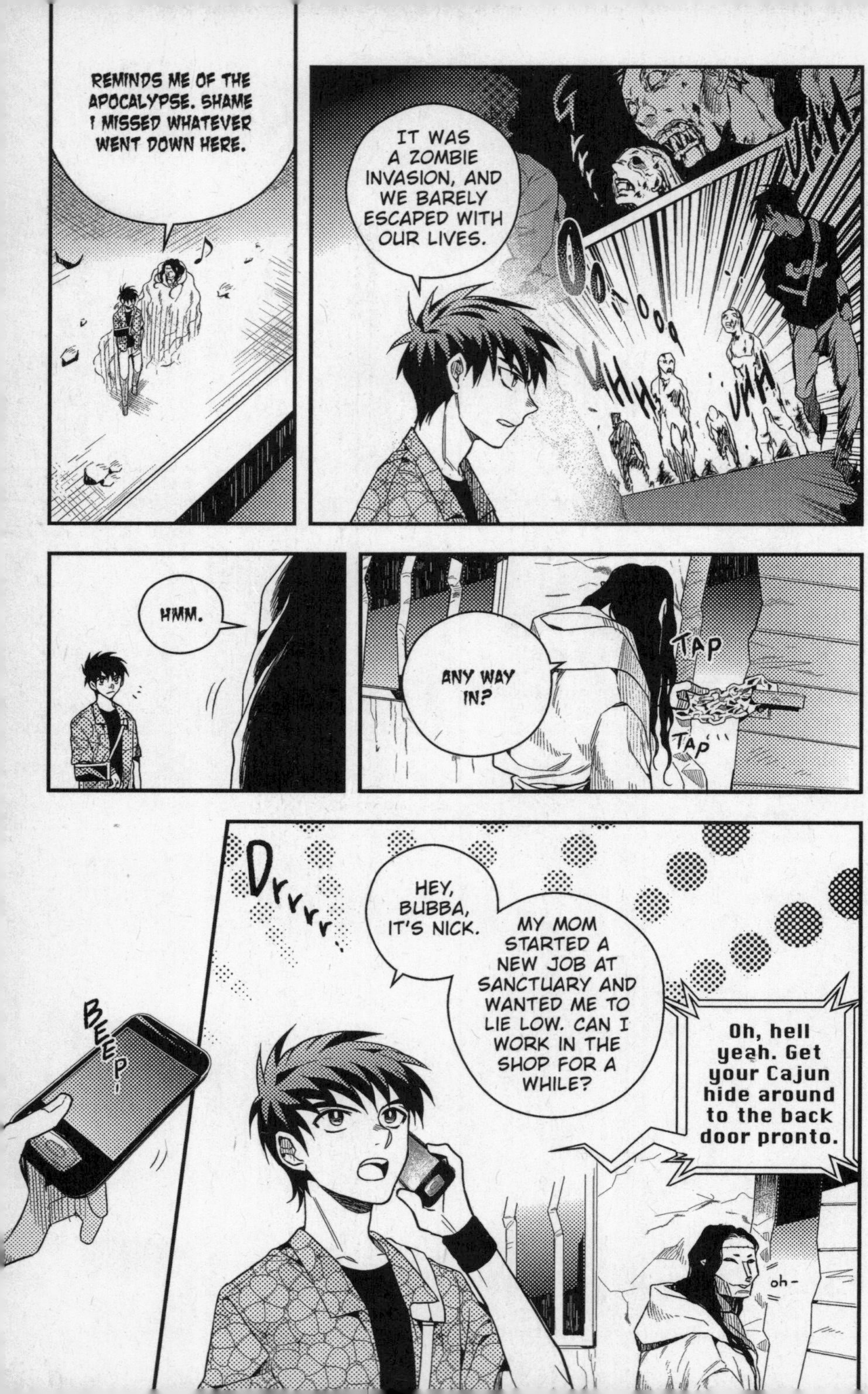
REMINDS ME OF THE APOCALYPSE. SHAME I MISSED WHATEVER WENT DOWN HERE.
IT WAS A ZOMBIE INVASION, AND WE BARELY ESCAPED WITH OUR LIVES.
HMM.
ANY WAY IN?
TAP
TAP
Drrrr.
HEY, BUBBA, IT'S NICK.
MY MOM STARTED A NEW JOB AT SANCTUARY AND WANTED ME TO LIE LOW. CAN I WORK IN THE SHOP FOR A WHILE?
BEEP!
Oh, hell yeah. Get your Cajun hide around to the back door pronto.
oh-

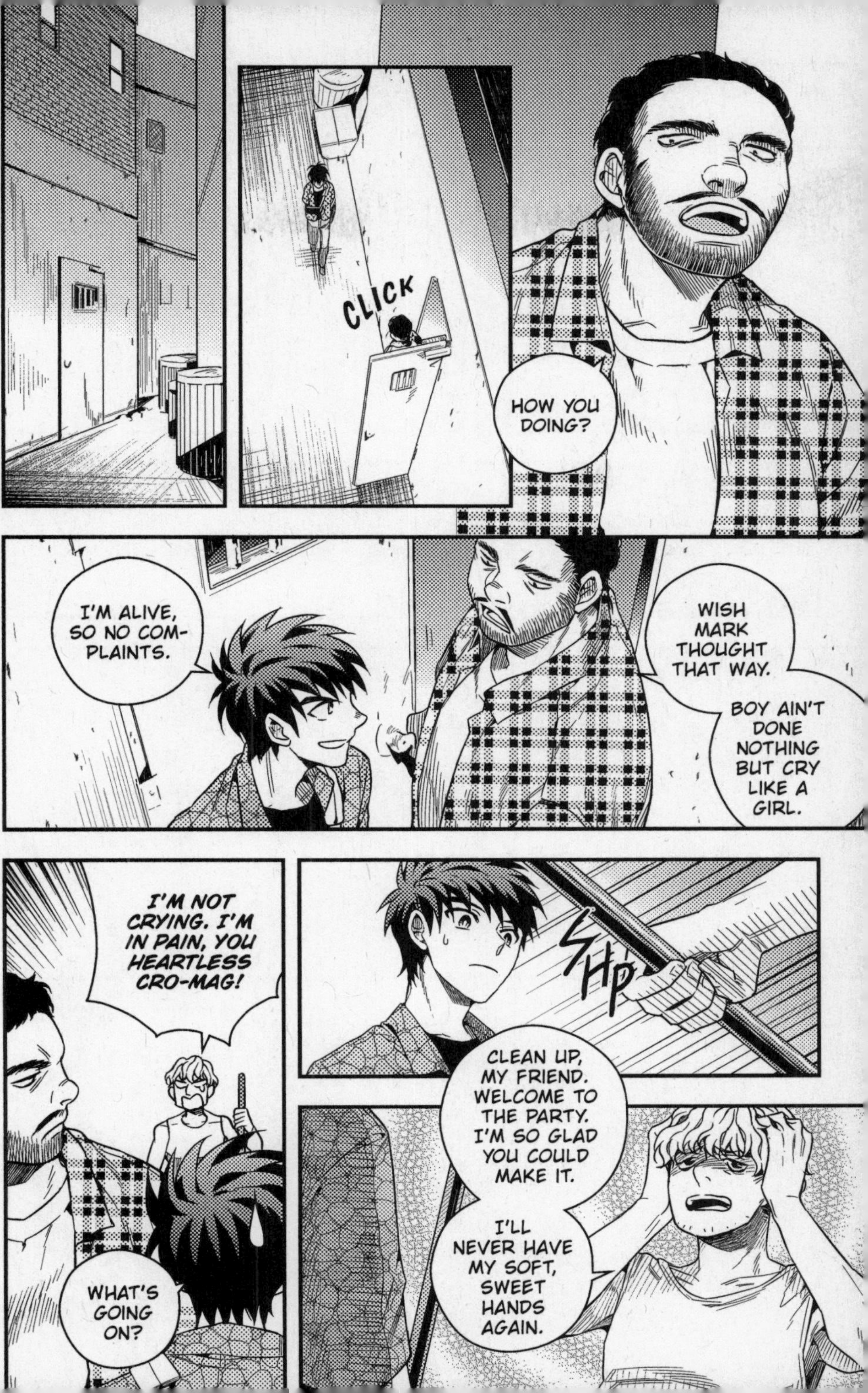
CLICK
HOW YOU DOING?
I'M ALIVE, SO NO COM-PLAINTS.
WISH MARK THOUGHT THAT WAY.
BOY AIN'T DONE NOTHING BUT CRY LIKE A GIRL.
I'M NOT CRYING. I'M IN PAIN, YOU HEARTLESS CRO-MAG!
WHAT'S GOING ON?
SHP
CLEAN UP, MY FRIEND. WELCOME TO THE PARTY. I'M SO GLAD YOU COULD MAKE IT.
I'LL NEVER HAVE MY SOFT, SWEET HANDS AGAIN.

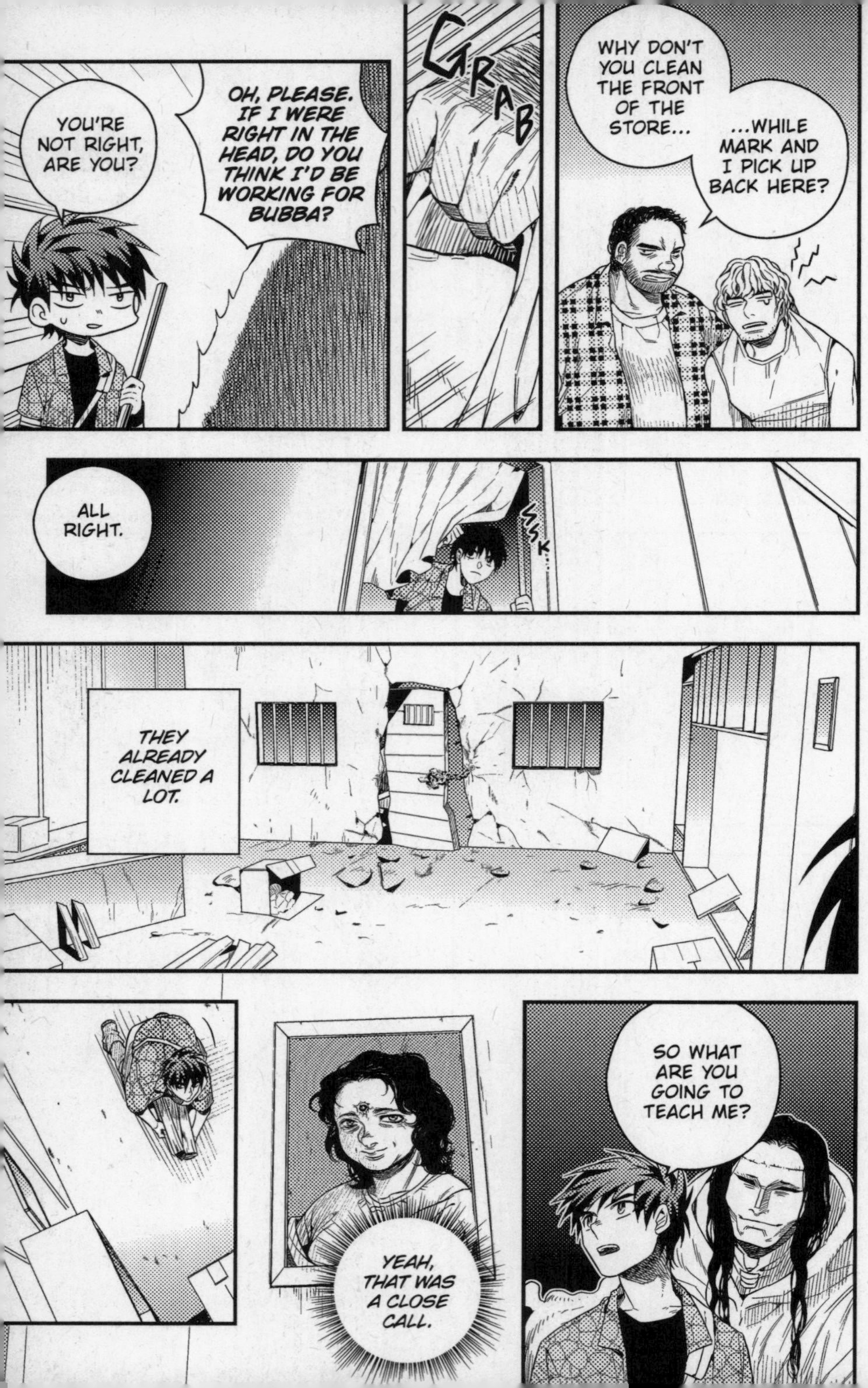
YOU'RE NOT RIGHT, ARE YOU?
OH, PLEASE. IF I WERE RIGHT IN THE HEAD, DO YOU THINK I'D BE WORKING FOR BUBBA?
GRAB
WHY DON'T YOU CLEAN THE FRONT OF THE STORE...
...WHILE MARK AND I PICK UP BACK HERE?
ALL RIGHT.
SSSK
THEY ALREADY CLEANED A LOT.
YEAH, THAT WAS A CLOSE CALL.
SO WHAT ARE YOU GOING TO TEACH ME?

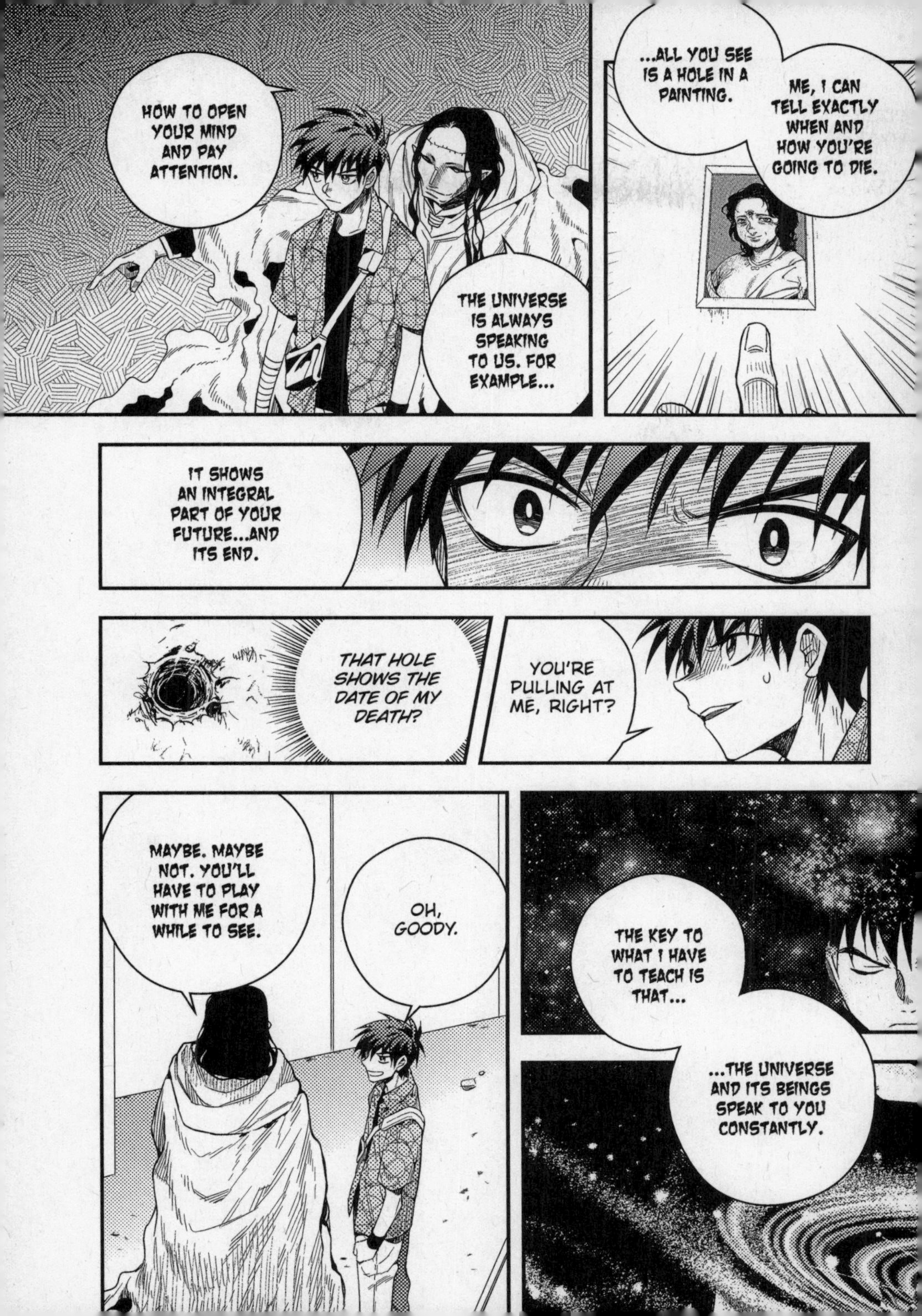
HOW TO OPEN YOUR MIND AND PAY ATTENTION.
THE UNIVERSE IS ALWAYS SPEAKING TO US. FOR EXAMPLE...
...ALL YOU SEE IS A HOLE IN A PAINTING.
ME, I CAN TELL EXACTLY WHEN AND HOW YOU'RE GOING TO DIE.
IT SHOWS AN INTEGRAL PART OF YOUR FUTURE...AND ITS END.
THAT HOLE SHOWS THE DATE OF MY DEATH?
YOU'RE PULLING AT ME, RIGHT?
MAYBE. MAYBE NOT. YOU'LL HAVE TO PLAY WITH ME FOR A WHILE TO SEE.
OH, GOODY.
THE KEY TO WHAT I HAVE TO TEACH IS THAT...
...THE UNIVERSE AND ITS BEINGS SPEAK TO YOU CONSTANTLY.

AND THE POWER OF DIVINATION IS A WAY FOR YOU TO LISTEN TO THE WARNINGS THE UNIVERSE GIVES.

SNAP

?!

FWIP

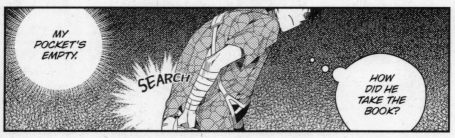

MY POCKET'S EMPTY.

SEARCH

HOW DID HE TAKE THE BOOK?

THIS PUPPY BARKS LOUDLY. GUARD IT WITH YOUR LIFE, BECAUSE IN THE RIGHT HANDS, IT IS YOUR LIFE AND YOUR DEATH.

BUMP

IN FACT, GUARD EVERY POSSESSION YOU HAVE. EVERY STRAY HAIR. EVERY PARTICLE OF SKIN AND CLOTHING.

YOU'RE SPECIAL, KID, IN WAYS YOU CAN'T CONCEIVE. AND YOU WILL HAVE TO GUARD YOUR BACK EVERY SECOND YOU WANT TO KEEP BREATHING.

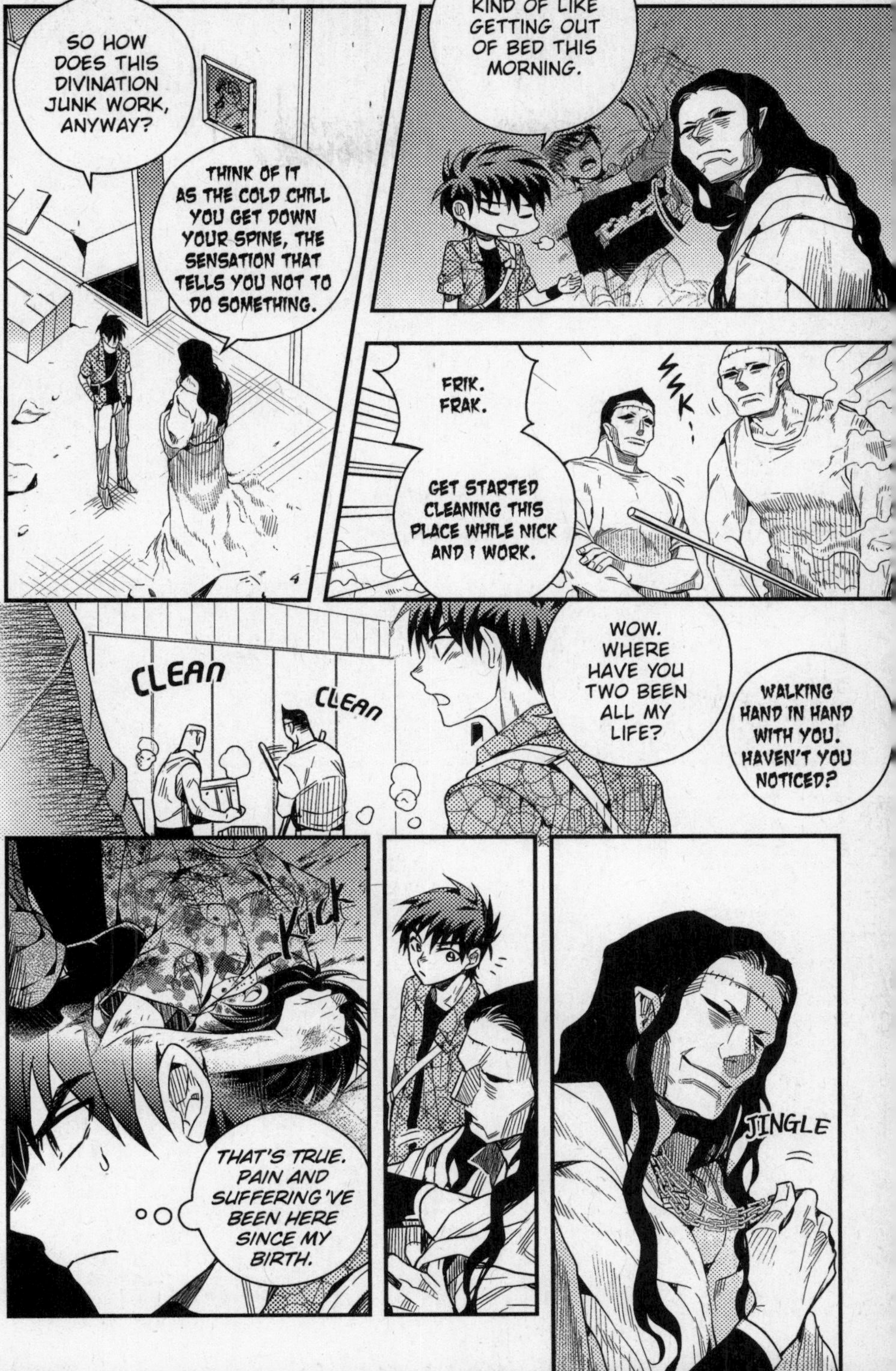

SO HOW DOES THIS DIVINATION JUNK WORK, ANYWAY?
THINK OF IT AS THE COLD CHILL YOU GET DOWN YOUR SPINE, THE SENSATION THAT TELLS YOU NOT TO DO SOMETHING.
KIND OF LIKE GETTING OUT OF BED THIS MORNING.
FRIK. FRAK.
GET STARTED CLEANING THIS PLACE WHILE NICK AND I WORK.
CLEAN
CLEAN
WOW. WHERE HAVE YOU TWO BEEN ALL MY LIFE?
WALKING HAND IN HAND WITH YOU. HAVEN'T YOU NOTICED?
KICK
THAT'S TRUE. PAIN AND SUFFERING'VE BEEN HERE SINCE MY BIRTH.
JINGLE

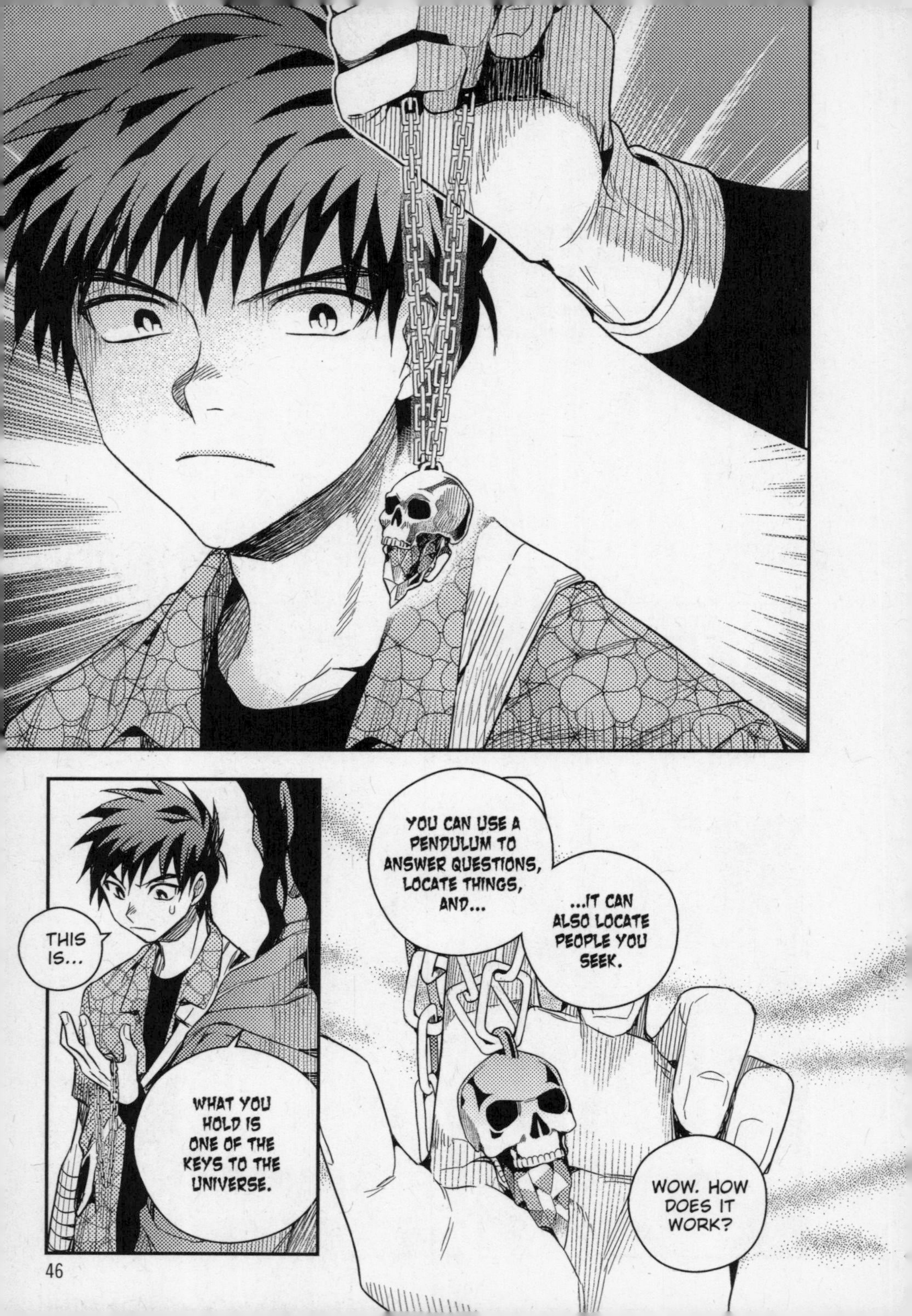
YOU CAN USE A PENDULUM TO ANSWER QUESTIONS, LOCATE THINGS, AND...
...IT CAN ALSO LOCATE PEOPLE YOU SEEK.
THIS IS...
WHAT YOU HOLD IS ONE OF THE KEYS TO THE UNIVERSE.
WOW. HOW DOES IT WORK?

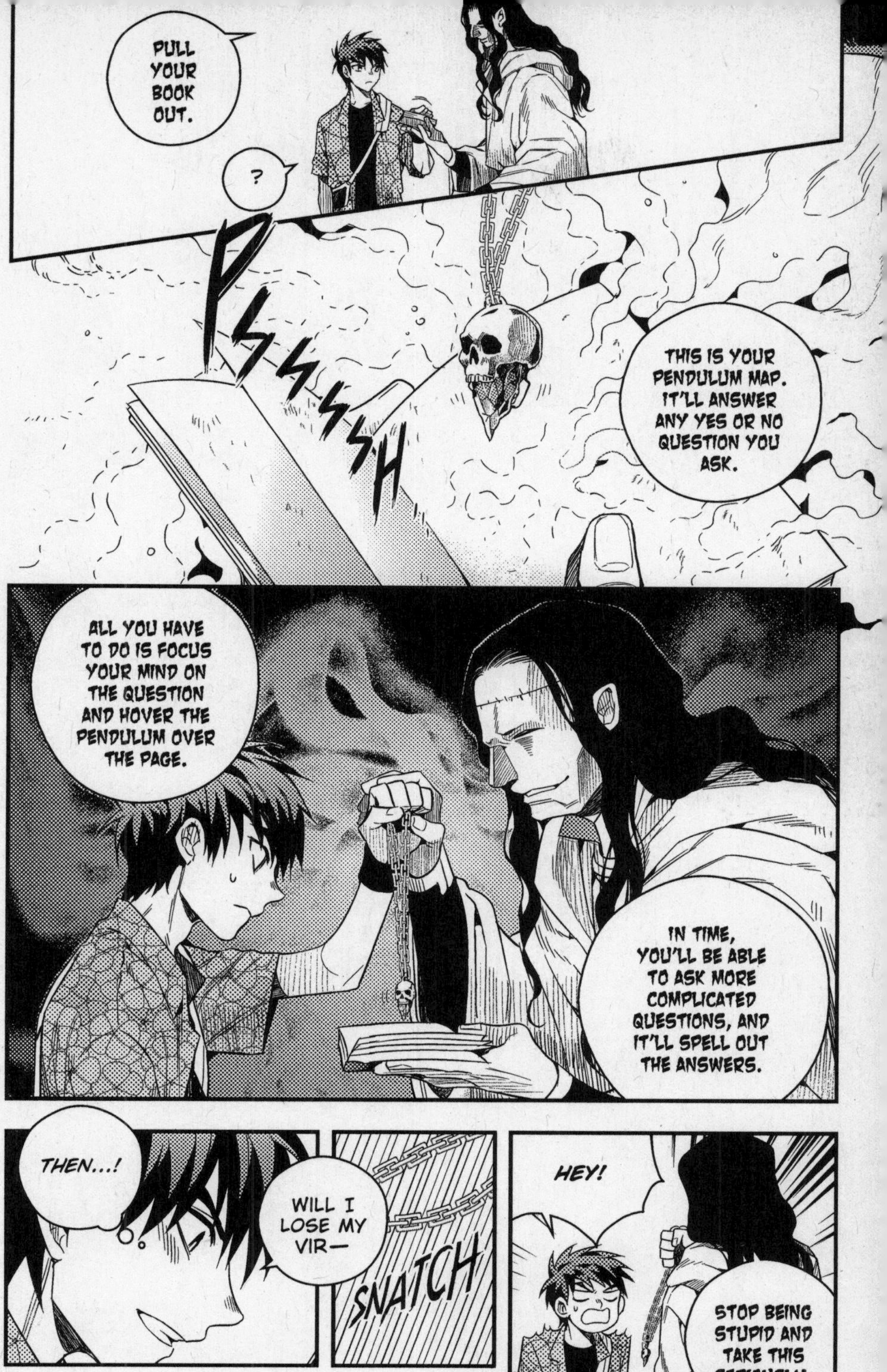
PULL YOUR BOOK OUT.
?
PSSSSSH
THIS IS YOUR PENDULUM MAP. IT'LL ANSWER ANY YES OR NO QUESTION YOU ASK.
ALL YOU HAVE TO DO IS FOCUS YOUR MIND ON THE QUESTION AND HOVER THE PENDULUM OVER THE PAGE.
IN TIME, YOU'LL BE ABLE TO ASK MORE COMPLICATED QUESTIONS, AND IT'LL SPELL OUT THE ANSWERS.
THEN...!
WILL I LOSE MY VIR—
SNATCH
HEY!
STOP BEING STUPID AND TAKE THIS SERIOUSLY.

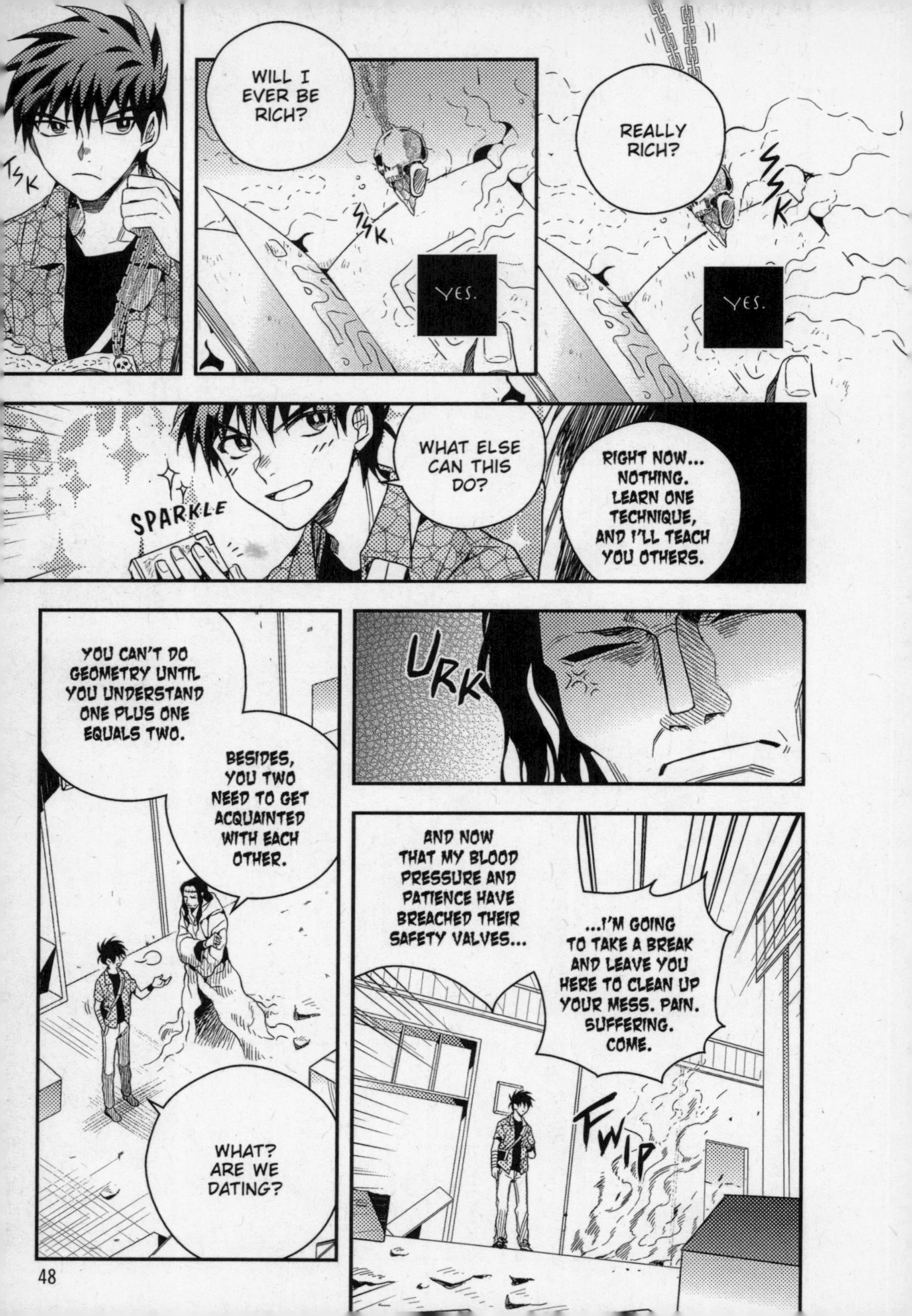
TSK
WILL I EVER BE RICH?
SSK
YES.
REALLY RICH?
SSK
YES.
SPARKLE
WHAT ELSE CAN THIS DO?
RIGHT NOW... NOTHING. LEARN ONE TECHNIQUE, AND I'LL TEACH YOU OTHERS.
URK
YOU CAN'T DO GEOMETRY UNTIL YOU UNDERSTAND ONE PLUS ONE EQUALS TWO.
BESIDES, YOU TWO NEED TO GET ACQUAINTED WITH EACH OTHER.
WHAT? ARE WE DATING?
AND NOW THAT MY BLOOD PRESSURE AND PATIENCE HAVE BREACHED THEIR SAFETY VALVES...
...I'M GOING TO TAKE A BREAK AND LEAVE YOU HERE TO CLEAN UP YOUR MESS. PAIN. SUFFERING. COME.
FWIP

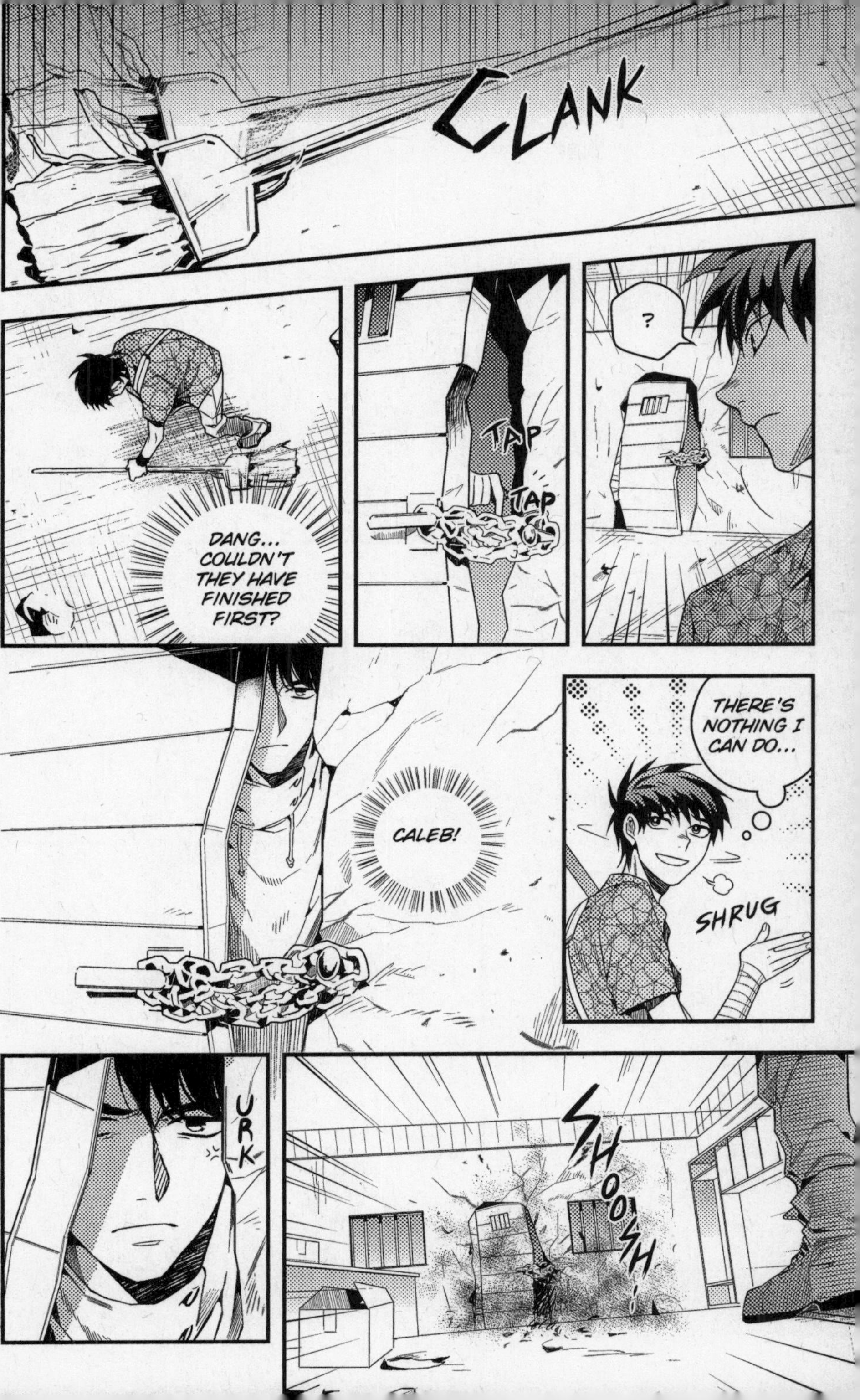
CLANK
DANG... COULDN'T THEY HAVE FINISHED FIRST?
TAP
TAP
?
CALEB!
THERE'S NOTHING I CAN DO...
SHRUG
URK
SHOOSH!

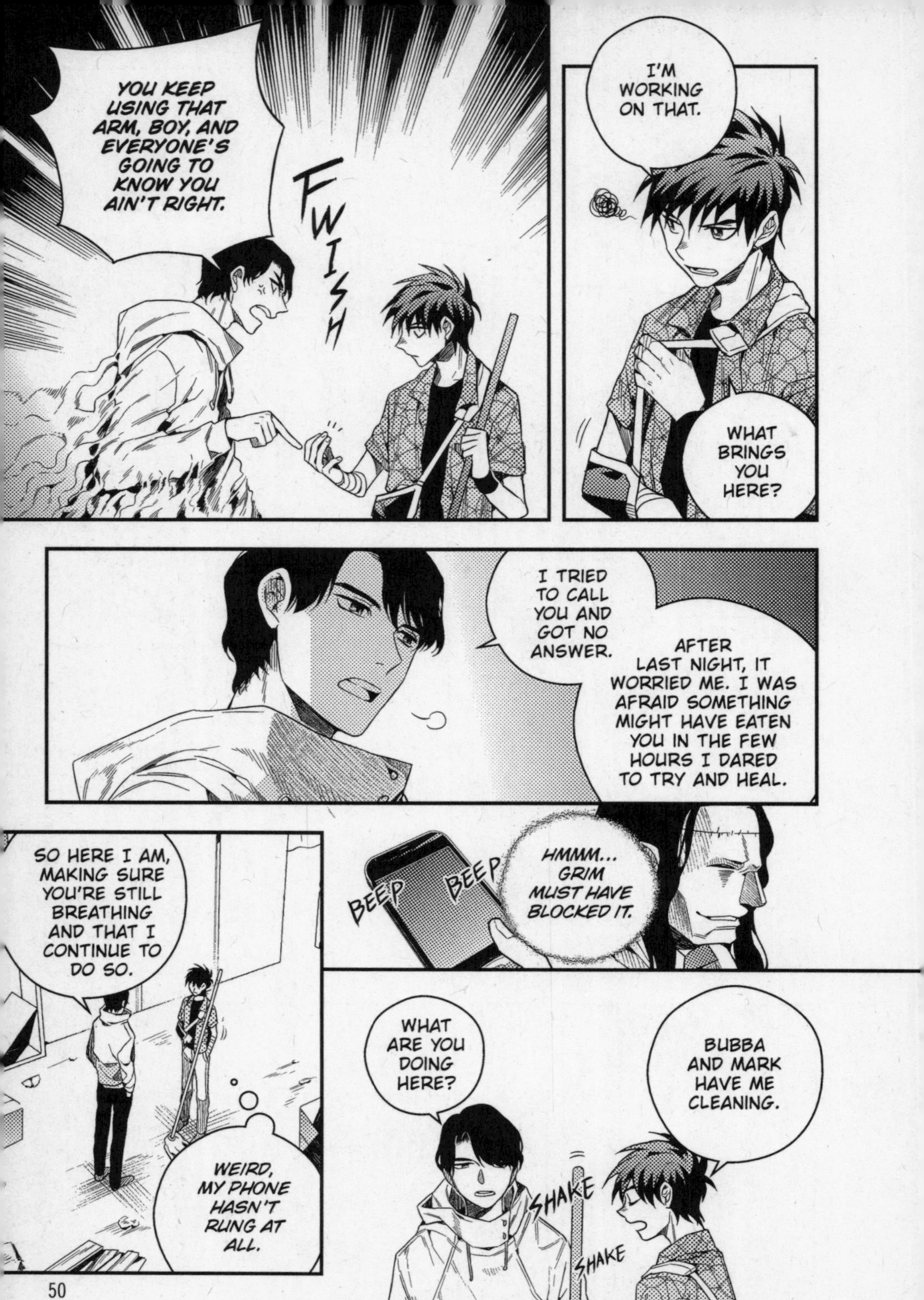

YOU KEEP USING THAT ARM, BOY, AND EVERYONE'S GOING TO KNOW YOU AIN'T RIGHT.
FWISH
I'M WORKING ON THAT.
WHAT BRINGS YOU HERE?
I TRIED TO CALL YOU AND GOT NO ANSWER.
AFTER LAST NIGHT, IT WORRIED ME. I WAS AFRAID SOMETHING MIGHT HAVE EATEN YOU IN THE FEW HOURS I DARED TO TRY AND HEAL.
BEEP BEEP
HMMM... GRIM MUST HAVE BLOCKED IT.
SO HERE I AM, MAKING SURE YOU'RE STILL BREATHING AND THAT I CONTINUE TO DO SO.
WEIRD, MY PHONE HASN'T RUNG AT ALL.
WHAT ARE YOU DOING HERE?
BUBBA AND MARK HAVE ME CLEANING.
SHAKE
SHAKE

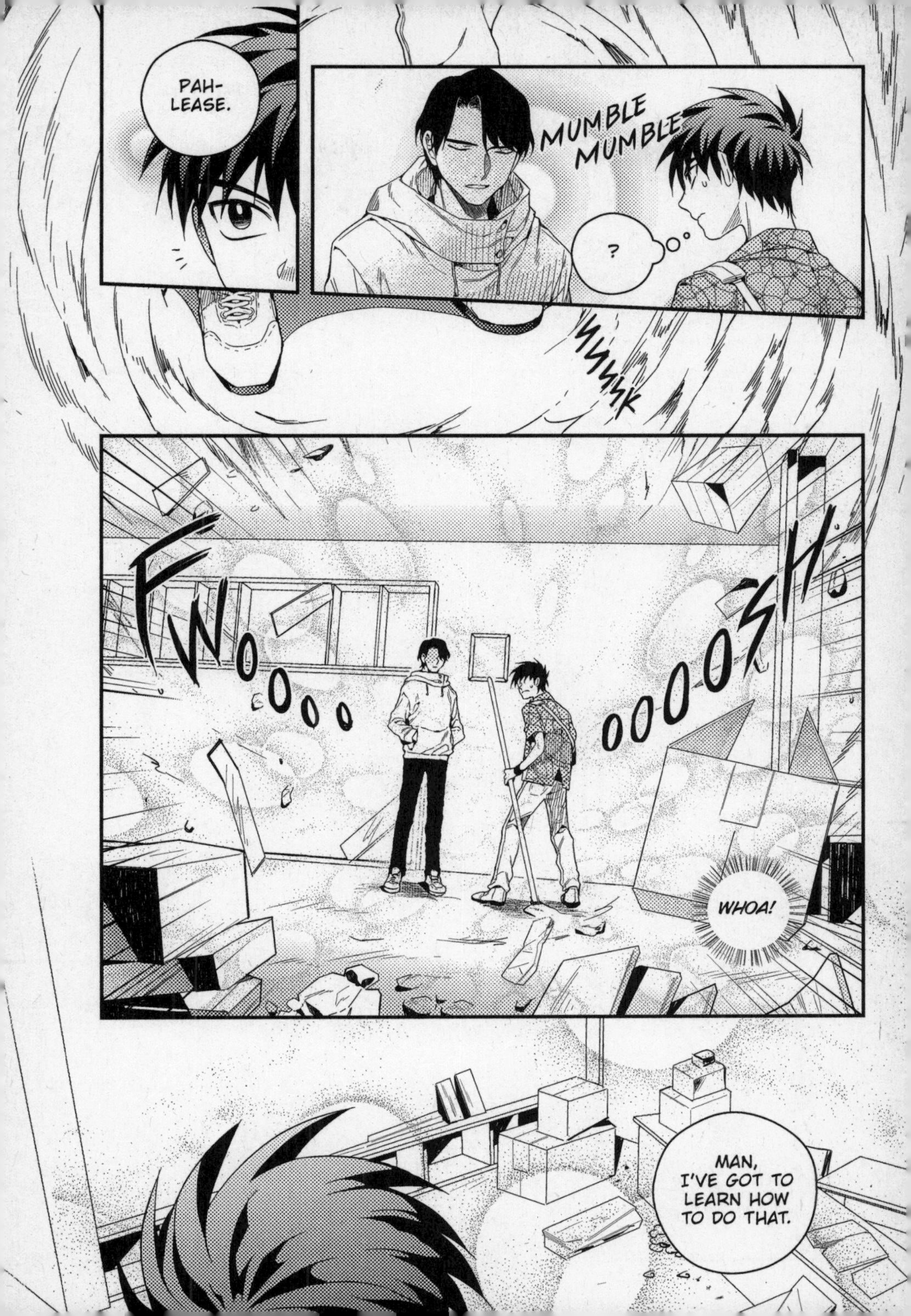
PAH-
LEASE.
MUMBLE
MUMBLE
?
VWWWK
FWOOOO OOOOOSH
WHOA!
MAN,
I'VE GOT TO
LEARN HOW
TO DO THAT.

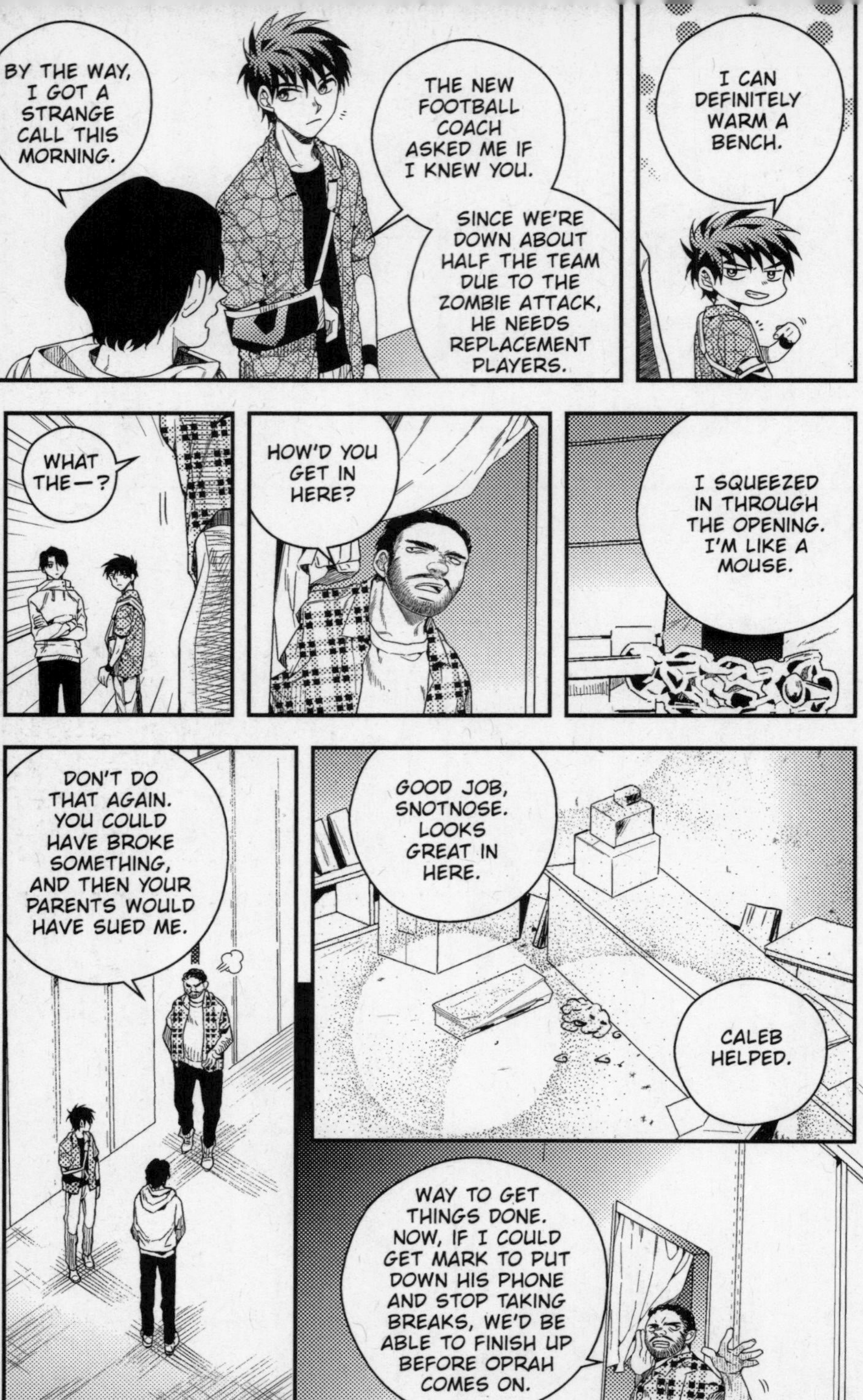
BY THE WAY, I GOT A STRANGE CALL THIS MORNING.
THE NEW FOOTBALL COACH ASKED ME IF I KNEW YOU.
SINCE WE'RE DOWN ABOUT HALF THE TEAM DUE TO THE ZOMBIE ATTACK, HE NEEDS REPLACEMENT PLAYERS.
I CAN DEFINITELY WARM A BENCH.
WHAT THE—?
HOW'D YOU GET IN HERE?
I SQUEEZED IN THROUGH THE OPENING. I'M LIKE A MOUSE.
DON'T DO THAT AGAIN. YOU COULD HAVE BROKE SOMETHING, AND THEN YOUR PARENTS WOULD HAVE SUED ME.
GOOD JOB, SNOTNOSE. LOOKS GREAT IN HERE.
CALEB HELPED.
WAY TO GET THINGS DONE. NOW, IF I COULD GET MARK TO PUT DOWN HIS PHONE AND STOP TAKING BREAKS, WE'D BE ABLE TO FINISH UP BEFORE OPRAH COMES ON.

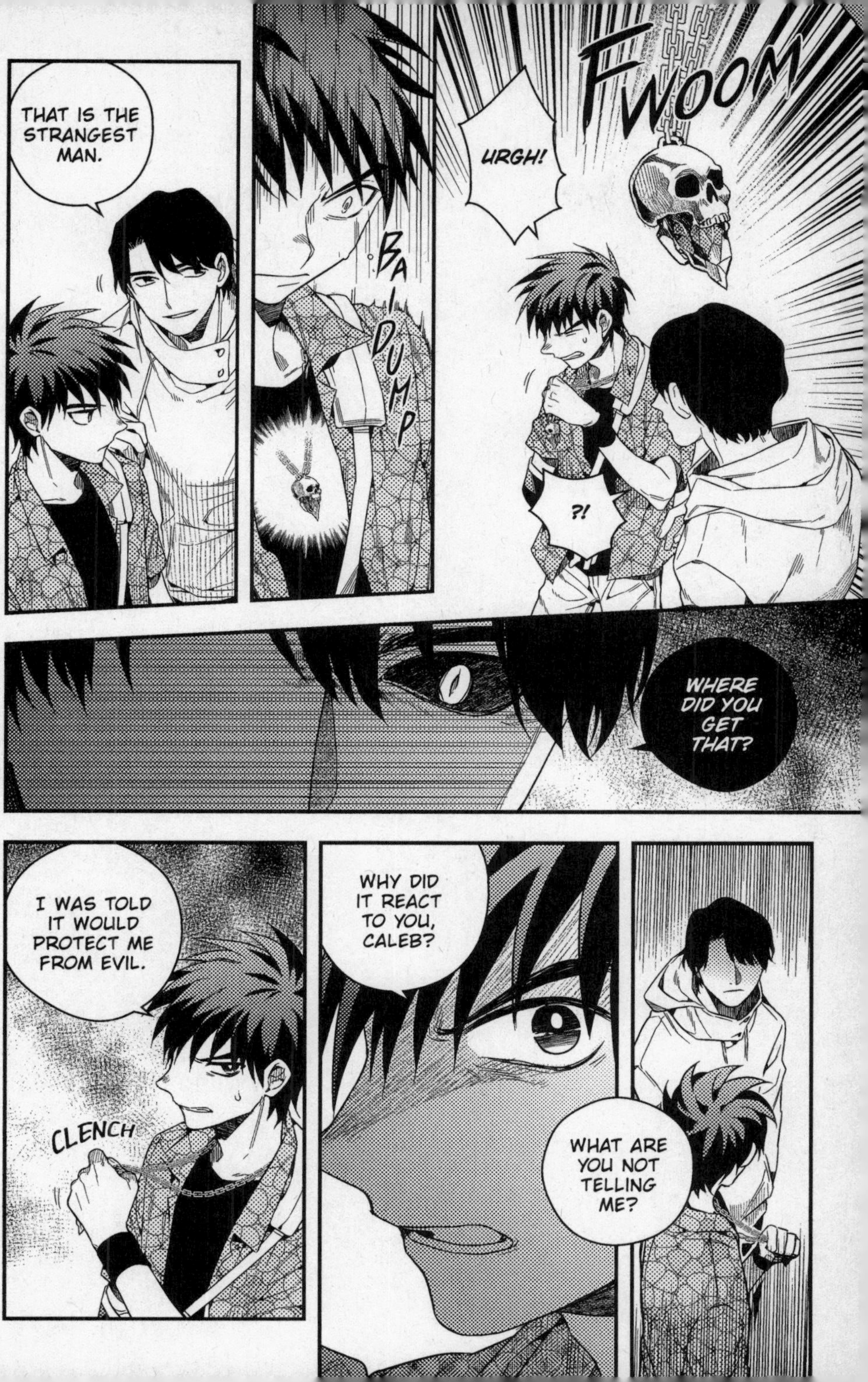
THAT IS THE STRANGEST MAN.
BA-DUMP
URGH!
FWOOM
?!
WHERE DID YOU GET THAT?
I WAS TOLD IT WOULD PROTECT ME FROM EVIL.
CLENCH
WHY DID IT REACT TO YOU, CALEB?
WHAT ARE YOU NOT TELLING ME?

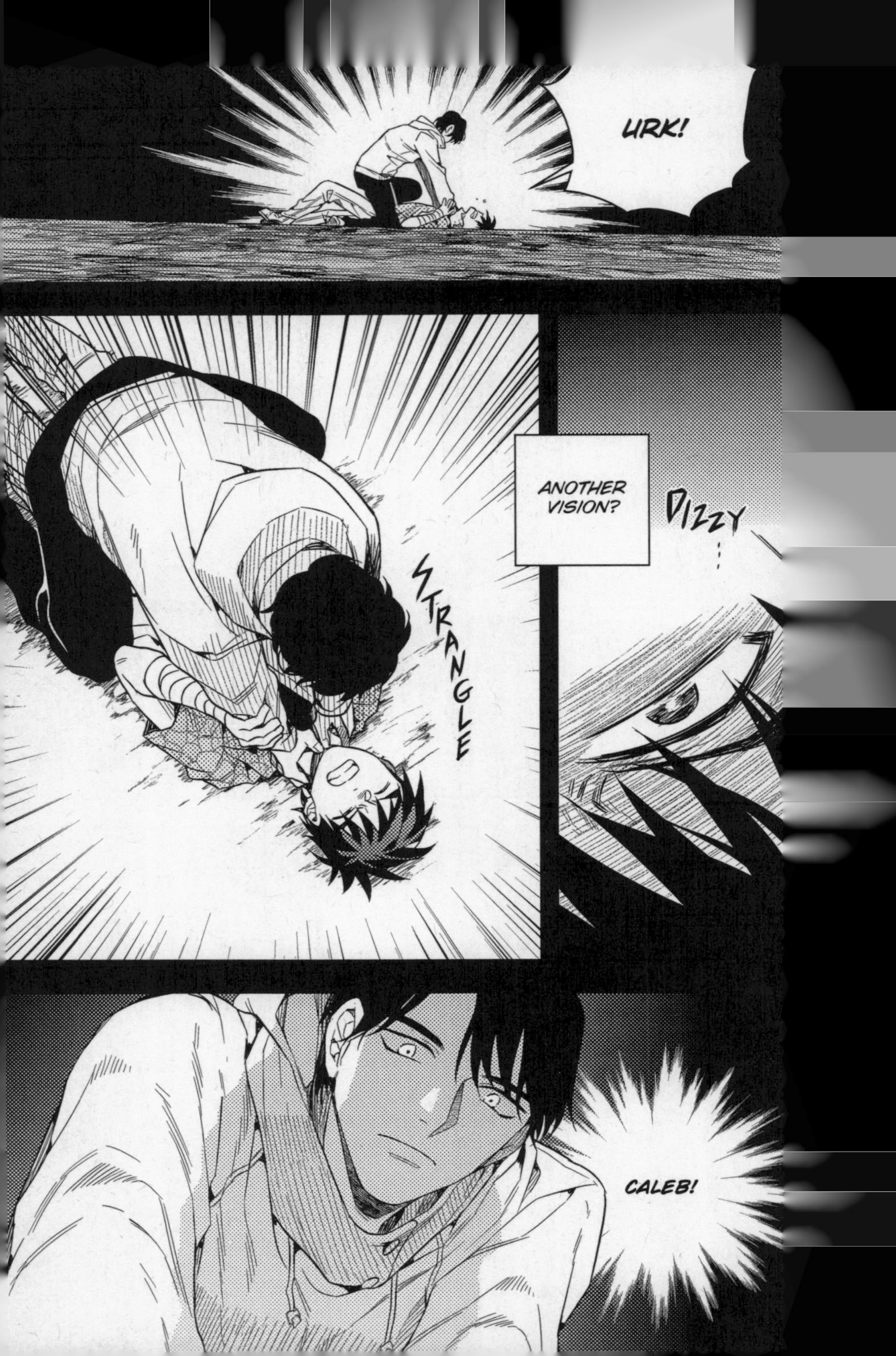
URK!
ANOTHER VISION?
DIZZY
STRANGLE
CALEB!

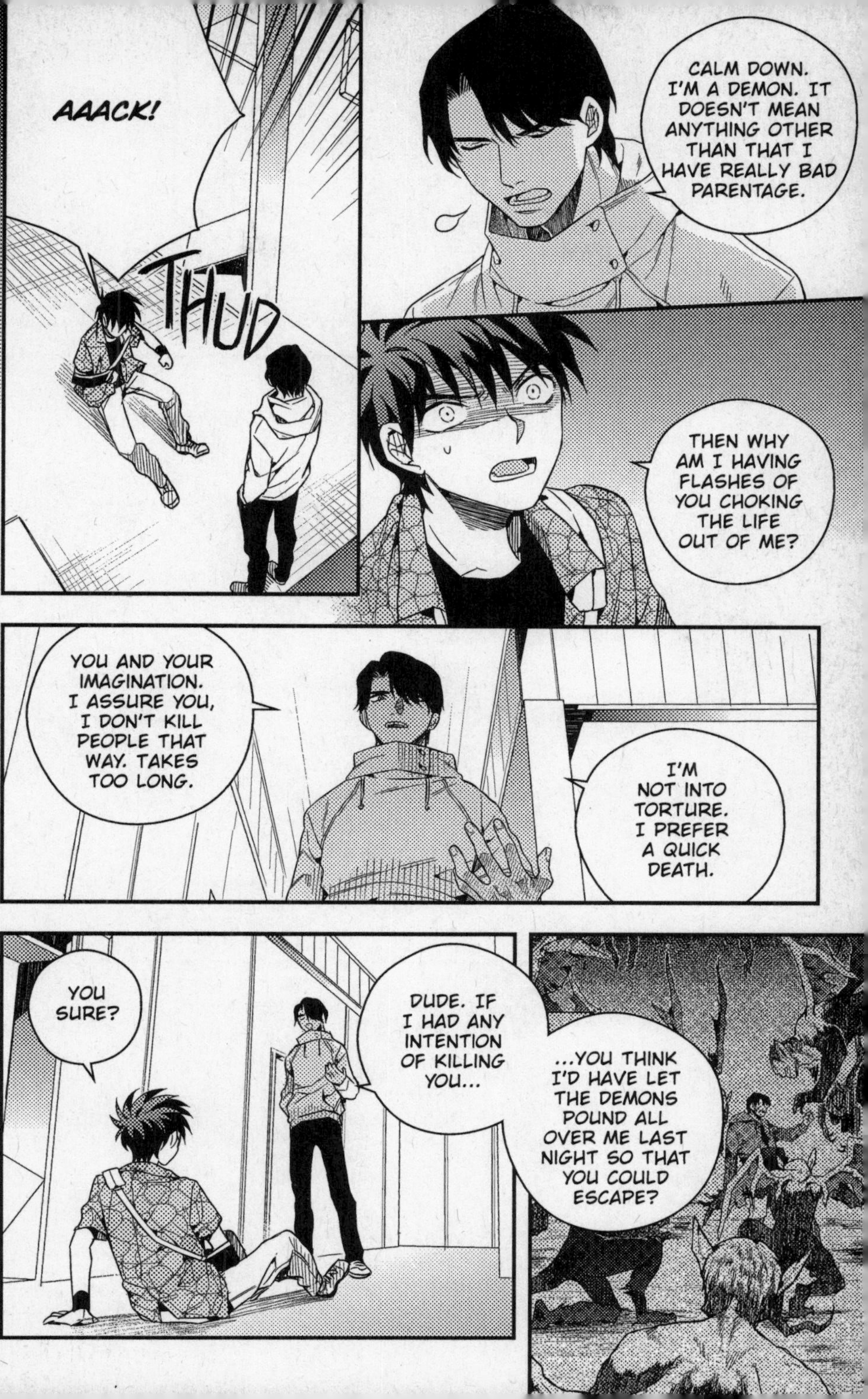
AAACK!
THUD
CALM DOWN. I'M A DEMON. IT DOESN'T MEAN ANYTHING OTHER THAN THAT I HAVE REALLY BAD PARENTAGE.
THEN WHY AM I HAVING FLASHES OF YOU CHOKING THE LIFE OUT OF ME?
YOU AND YOUR IMAGINATION. I ASSURE YOU, I DON'T KILL PEOPLE THAT WAY. TAKES TOO LONG.
I'M NOT INTO TORTURE. I PREFER A QUICK DEATH.
YOU SURE?
DUDE. IF I HAD ANY INTENTION OF KILLING YOU...
...YOU THINK I'D HAVE LET THE DEMONS POUND ALL OVER ME LAST NIGHT SO THAT YOU COULD ESCAPE?

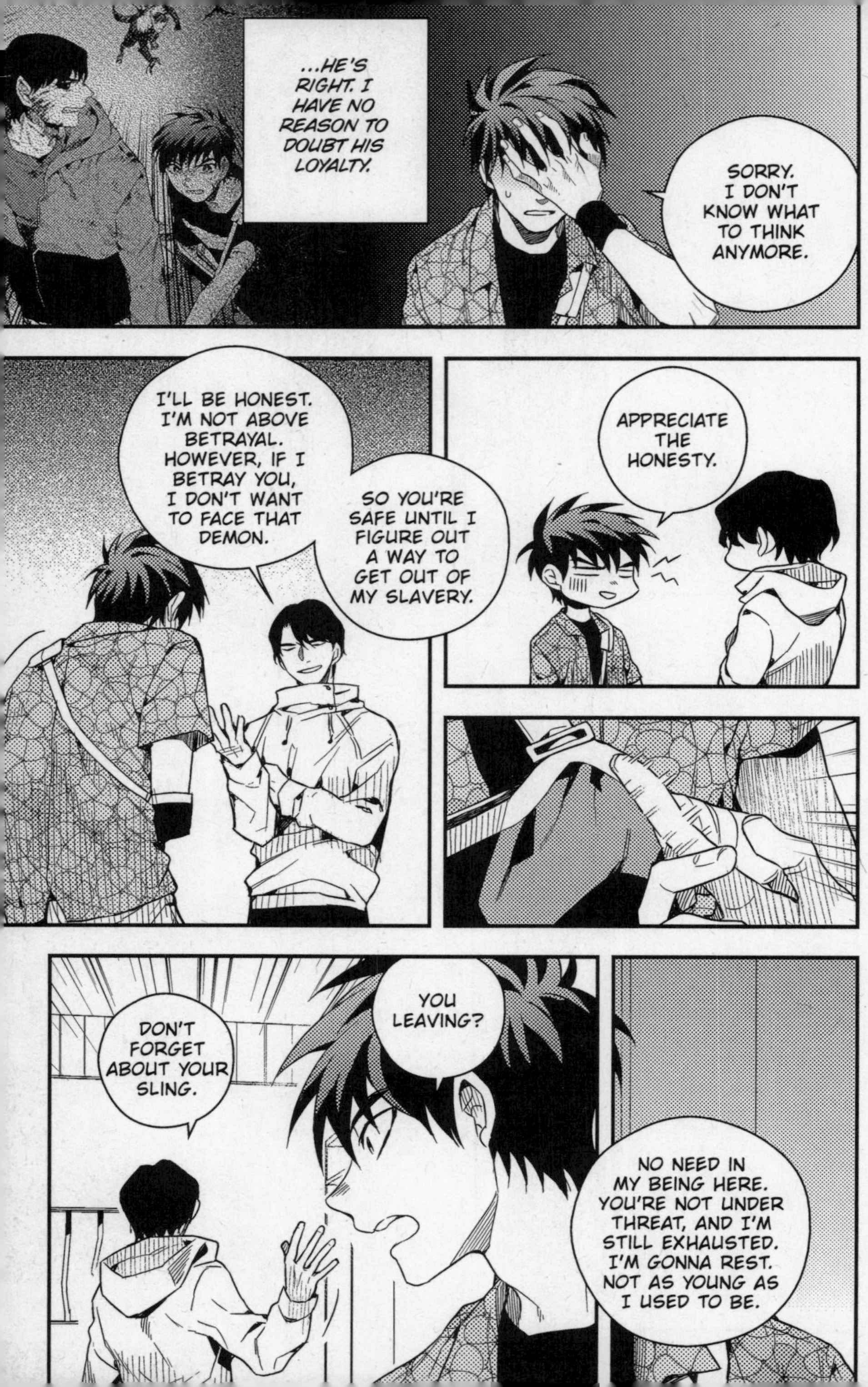
...HE'S RIGHT. I HAVE NO REASON TO DOUBT HIS LOYALTY.
SORRY. I DON'T KNOW WHAT TO THINK ANYMORE.
I'LL BE HONEST. I'M NOT ABOVE BETRAYAL. HOWEVER, IF I BETRAY YOU, I DON'T WANT TO FACE THAT DEMON.
SO YOU'RE SAFE UNTIL I FIGURE OUT A WAY TO GET OUT OF MY SLAVERY.
APPRECIATE THE HONESTY.
DON'T FORGET ABOUT YOUR SLING.
YOU LEAVING?
NO NEED IN MY BEING HERE. YOU'RE NOT UNDER THREAT, AND I'M STILL EXHAUSTED. I'M GONNA REST. NOT AS YOUNG AS I USED TO BE.

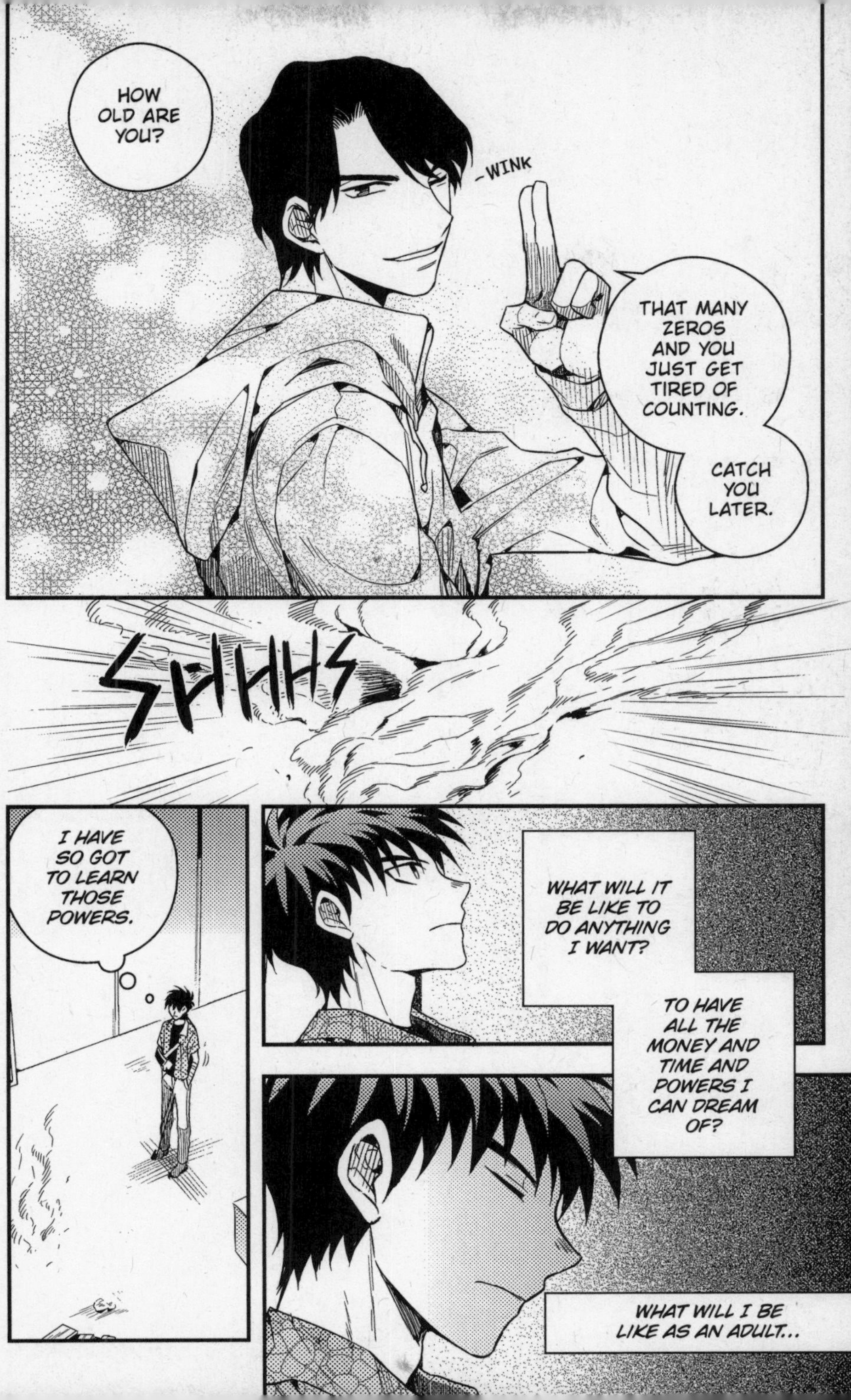
HOW OLD ARE YOU?
-WINK
THAT MANY ZEROS AND YOU JUST GET TIRED OF COUNTING.
CATCH YOU LATER.
SHHHS
I HAVE SO GOT TO LEARN THOSE POWERS.
WHAT WILL IT BE LIKE TO DO ANYTHING I WANT?
TO HAVE ALL THE MONEY AND TIME AND POWERS I CAN DREAM OF?
WHAT WILL I BE LIKE AS AN ADULT...

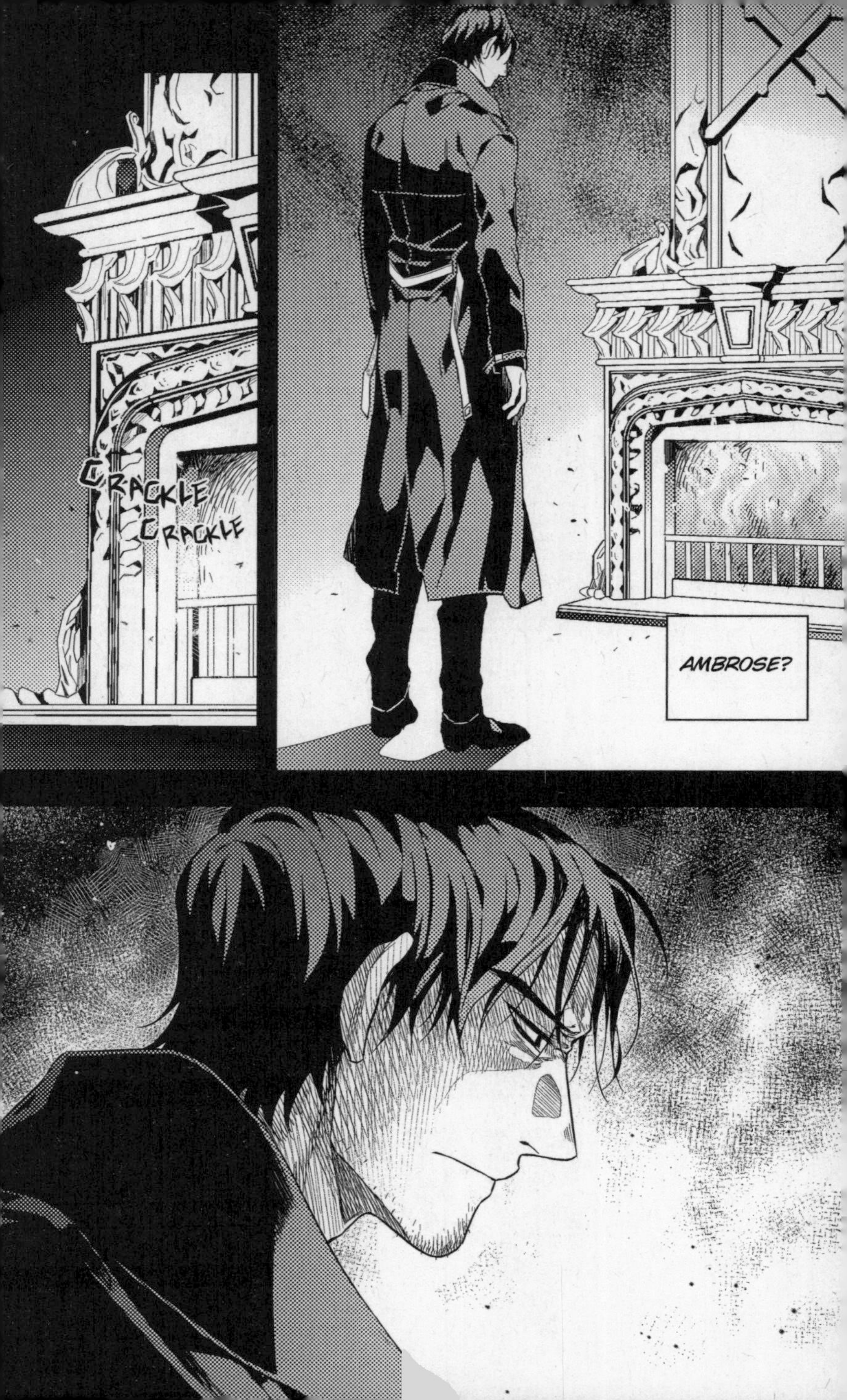
CRACKLE
CRACKLE
AMBROSE?

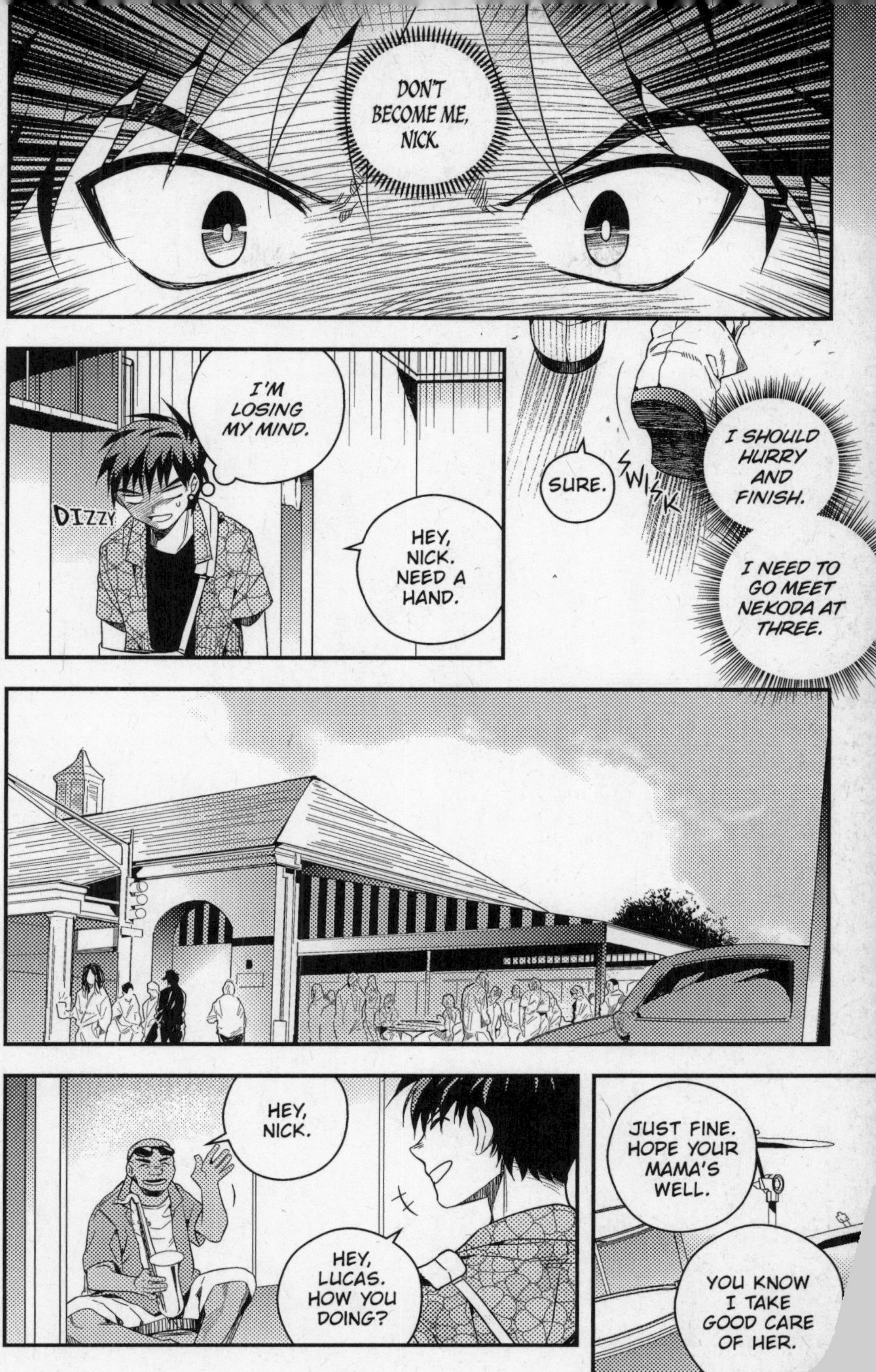
DON'T BECOME ME, NICK.
I'M LOSING MY MIND.
DIZZY
HEY, NICK. NEED A HAND.
SURE.
SWISK
I SHOULD HURRY AND FINISH.
I NEED TO GO MEET NEKODA AT THREE.
HEY, NICK.
HEY, LUCAS. HOW YOU DOING?
JUST FINE. HOPE YOUR MAMA'S WELL.
YOU KNOW I TAKE GOOD CARE OF HER.

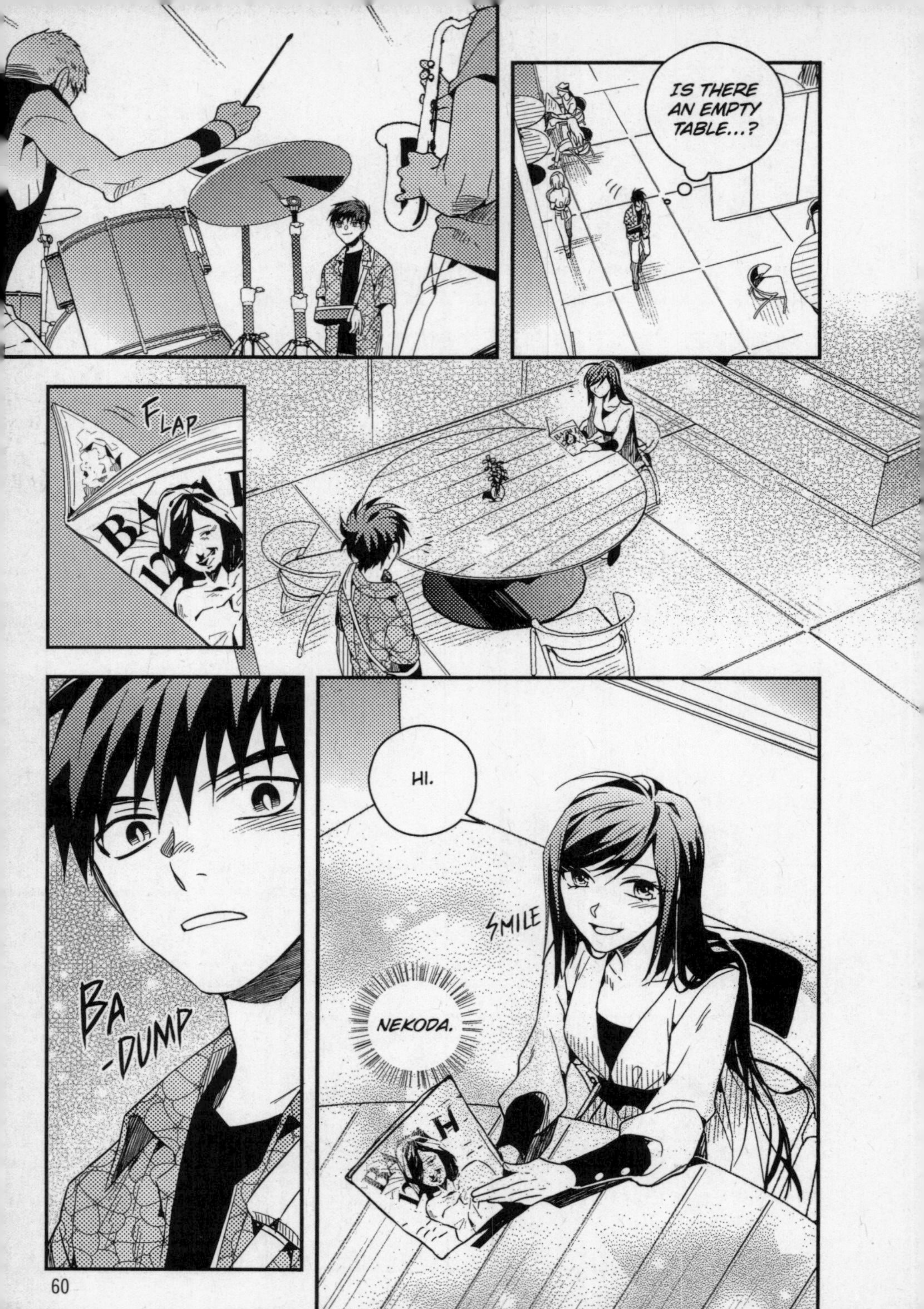
IS THERE AN EMPTY TABLE...?
FLAP
HI.
NEKODA.
SMILE
BA-DUMP

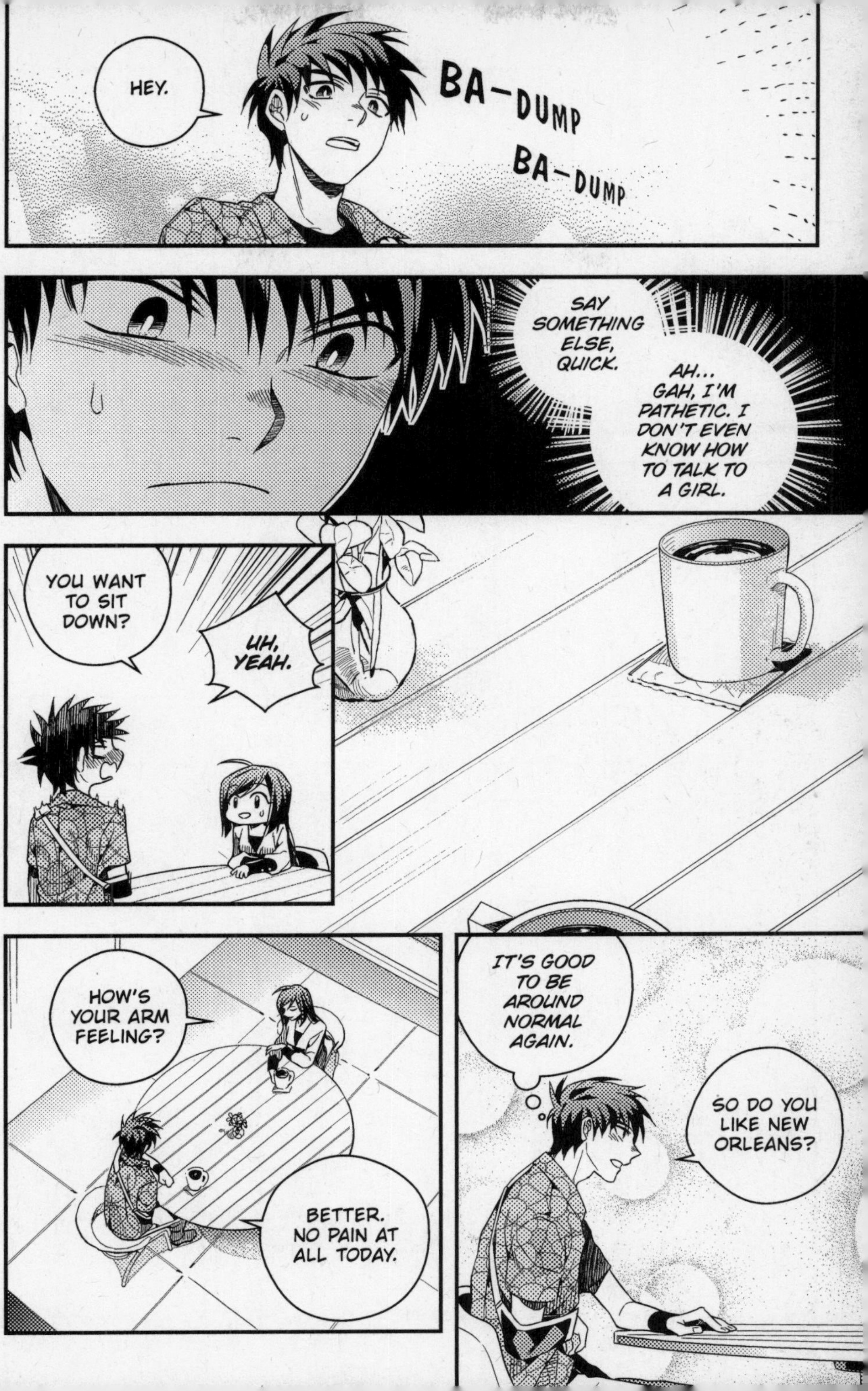
HEY.
BA-DUMP
BA-DUMP
SAY SOMETHING ELSE, QUICK.
AH... GAH, I'M PATHETIC. I DON'T EVEN KNOW HOW TO TALK TO A GIRL.
YOU WANT TO SIT DOWN?
UH, YEAH.
HOW'S YOUR ARM FEELING?
BETTER. NO PAIN AT ALL TODAY.
IT'S GOOD TO BE AROUND NORMAL AGAIN.
SO DO YOU LIKE NEW ORLEANS?

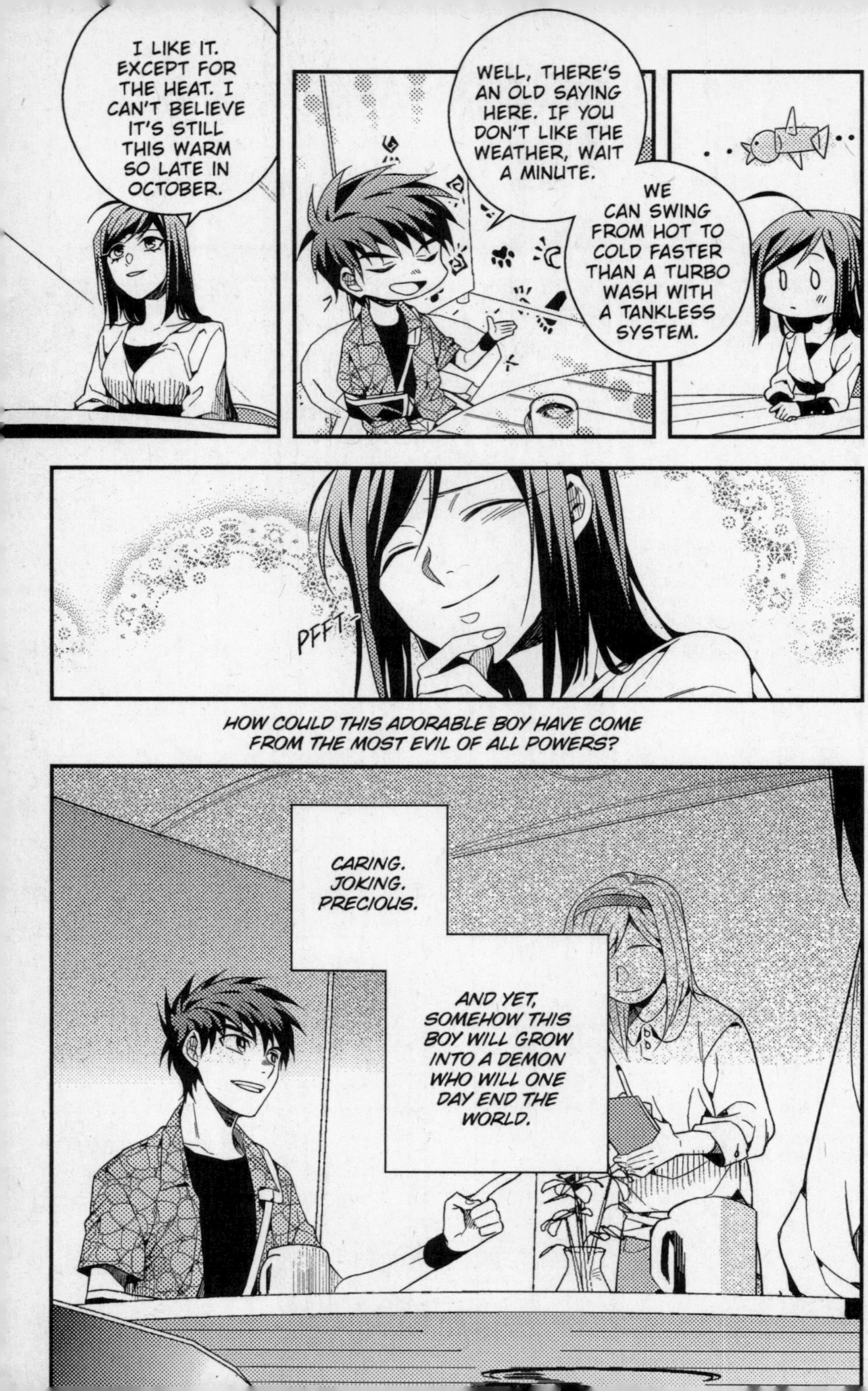
I LIKE IT. EXCEPT FOR THE HEAT. I CAN'T BELIEVE IT'S STILL THIS WARM SO LATE IN OCTOBER.
WELL, THERE'S AN OLD SAYING HERE. IF YOU DON'T LIKE THE WEATHER, WAIT A MINUTE.
WE CAN SWING FROM HOT TO COLD FASTER THAN A TURBO WASH WITH A TANKLESS SYSTEM.
PFFT
HOW COULD THIS ADORABLE BOY HAVE COME FROM THE MOST EVIL OF ALL POWERS?
CARING. JOKING. PRECIOUS.
AND YET, SOMEHOW THIS BOY WILL GROW INTO A DEMON WHO WILL ONE DAY END THE WORLD.

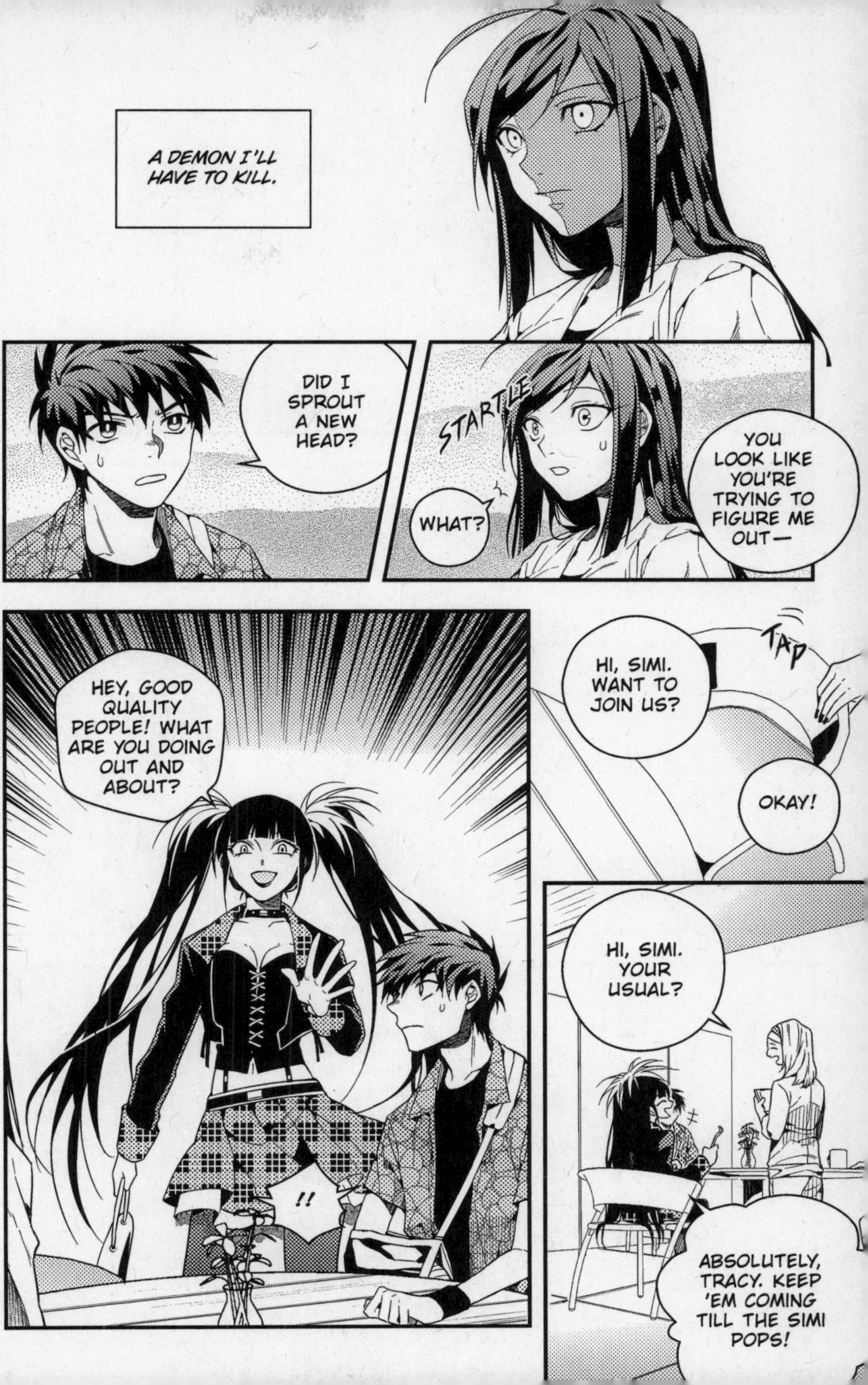
A DEMON I'LL HAVE TO KILL.
DID I SPROUT A NEW HEAD?
STARTLE
WHAT?
YOU LOOK LIKE YOU'RE TRYING TO FIGURE ME OUT—
TAP
HI, SIMI. WANT TO JOIN US?
OKAY!
HEY, GOOD QUALITY PEOPLE! WHAT ARE YOU DOING OUT AND ABOUT?
!!
HI, SIMI. YOUR USUAL?
ABSOLUTELY, TRACY. KEEP 'EM COMING TILL THE SIMI POPS!

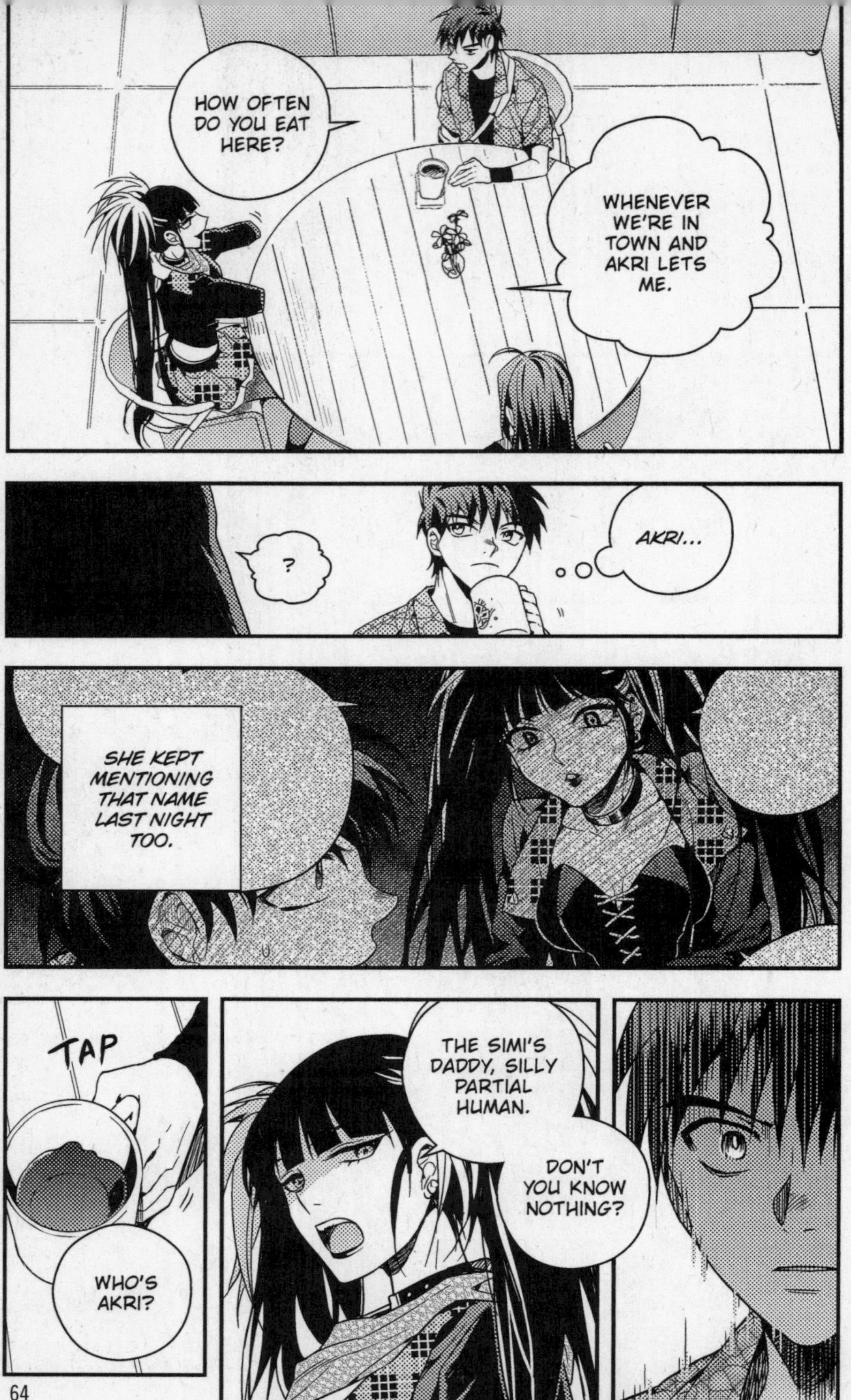
HOW OFTEN DO YOU EAT HERE?
WHENEVER WE'RE IN TOWN AND AKRI LETS ME.
AKRI...
?
SHE KEPT MENTIONING THAT NAME LAST NIGHT TOO.
TAP
WHO'S AKRI?
THE SIMI'S DADDY, SILLY PARTIAL HUMAN.
DON'T YOU KNOW NOTHING?

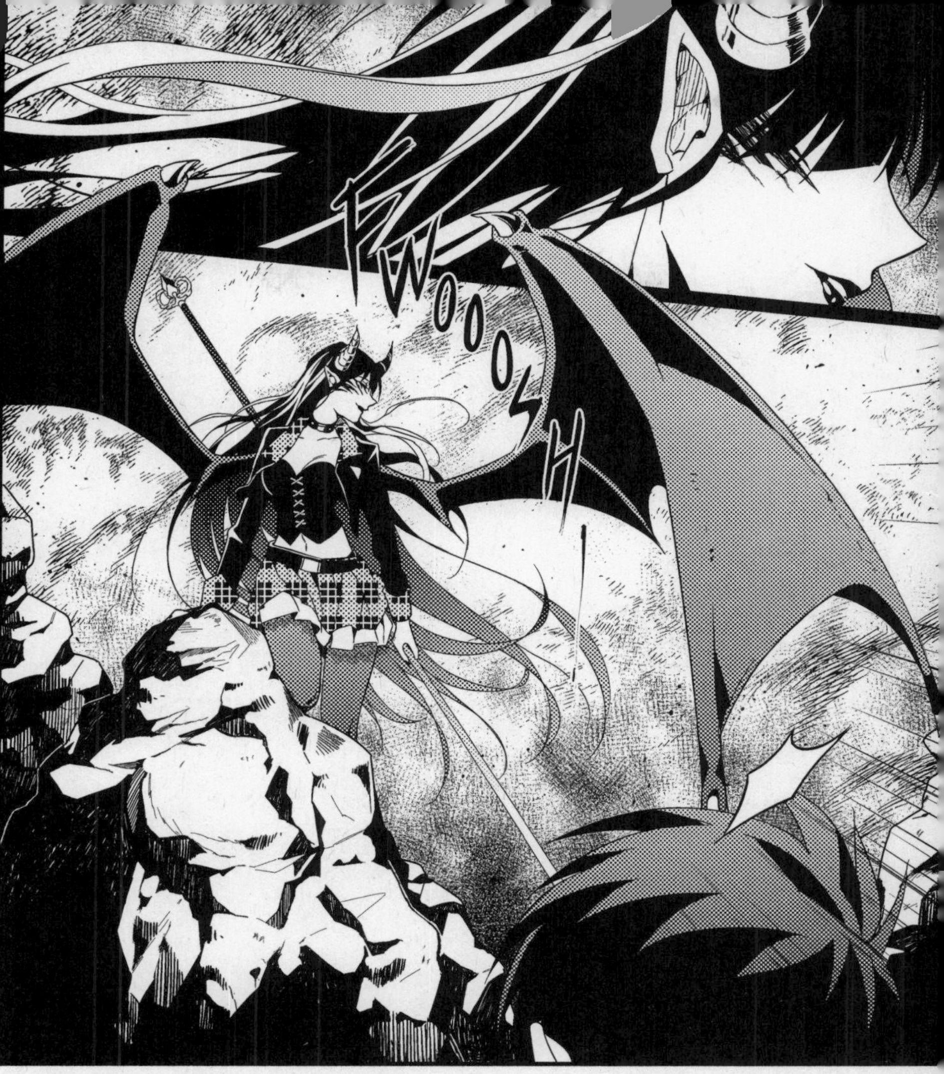
FWOOOSH

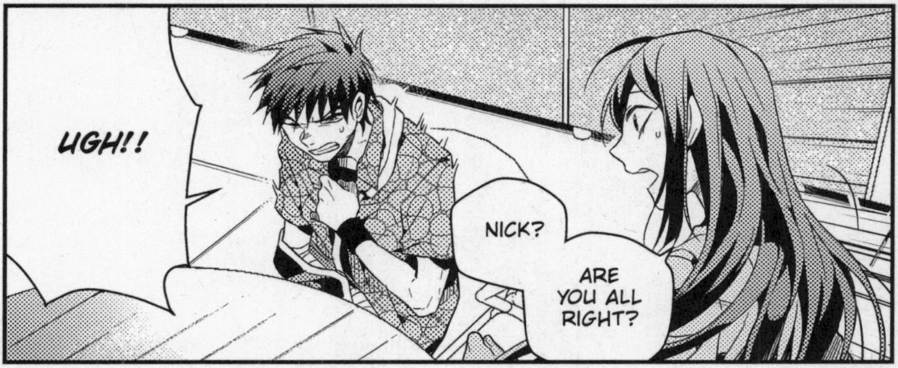
UGH!!
NICK?
ARE YOU ALL RIGHT?

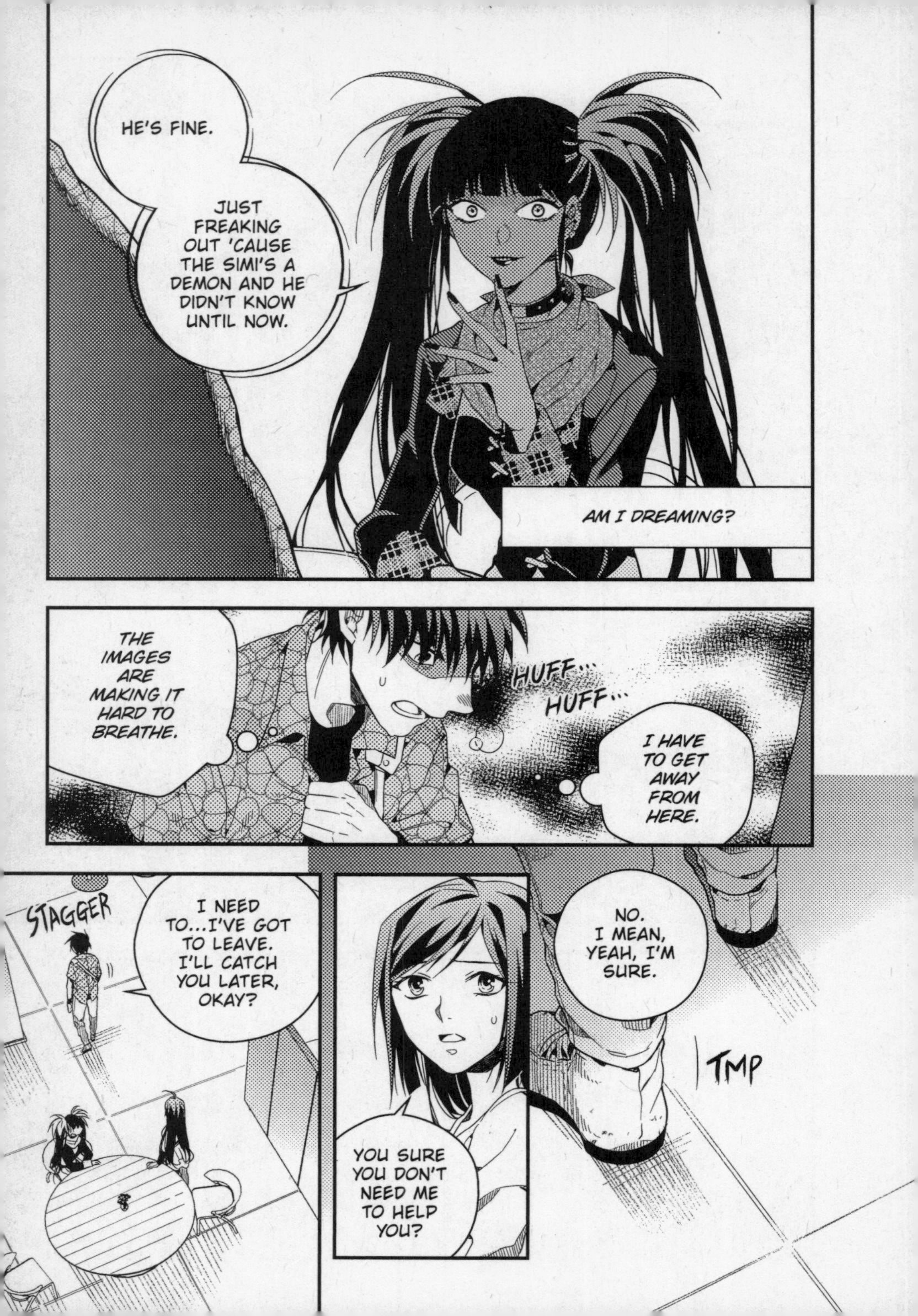
HE'S FINE.
JUST FREAKING OUT 'CAUSE THE SIMI'S A DEMON AND HE DIDN'T KNOW UNTIL NOW.
AM I DREAMING?
THE IMAGES ARE MAKING IT HARD TO BREATHE.
HUFF... HUFF...
I HAVE TO GET AWAY FROM HERE.
TMP
NO. I MEAN, YEAH, I'M SURE.
YOU SURE YOU DON'T NEED ME TO HELP YOU?
I NEED TO...I'VE GOT TO LEAVE. I'LL CATCH YOU LATER, OKAY?
STAGGER

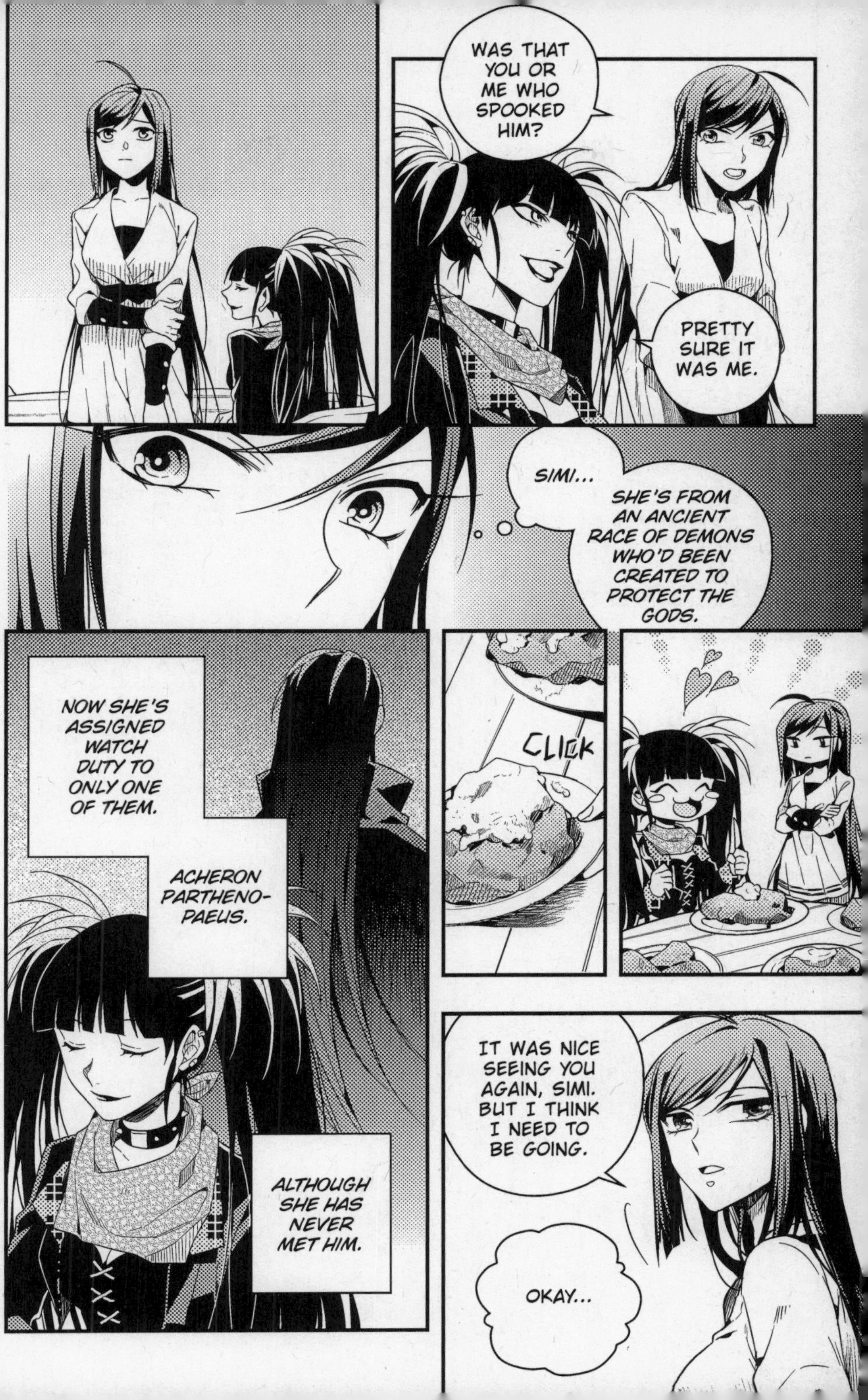
WAS THAT YOU OR ME WHO SPOOKED HIM?
PRETTY SURE IT WAS ME.
SIMI...
SHE'S FROM AN ANCIENT RACE OF DEMONS WHO'D BEEN CREATED TO PROTECT THE GODS.
NOW SHE'S ASSIGNED WATCH DUTY TO ONLY ONE OF THEM.
ACHERON PARTHENO-PAEUS.
ALTHOUGH SHE HAS NEVER MET HIM.
CLICK
IT WAS NICE SEEING YOU AGAIN, SIMI. BUT I THINK I NEED TO BE GOING.
OKAY...

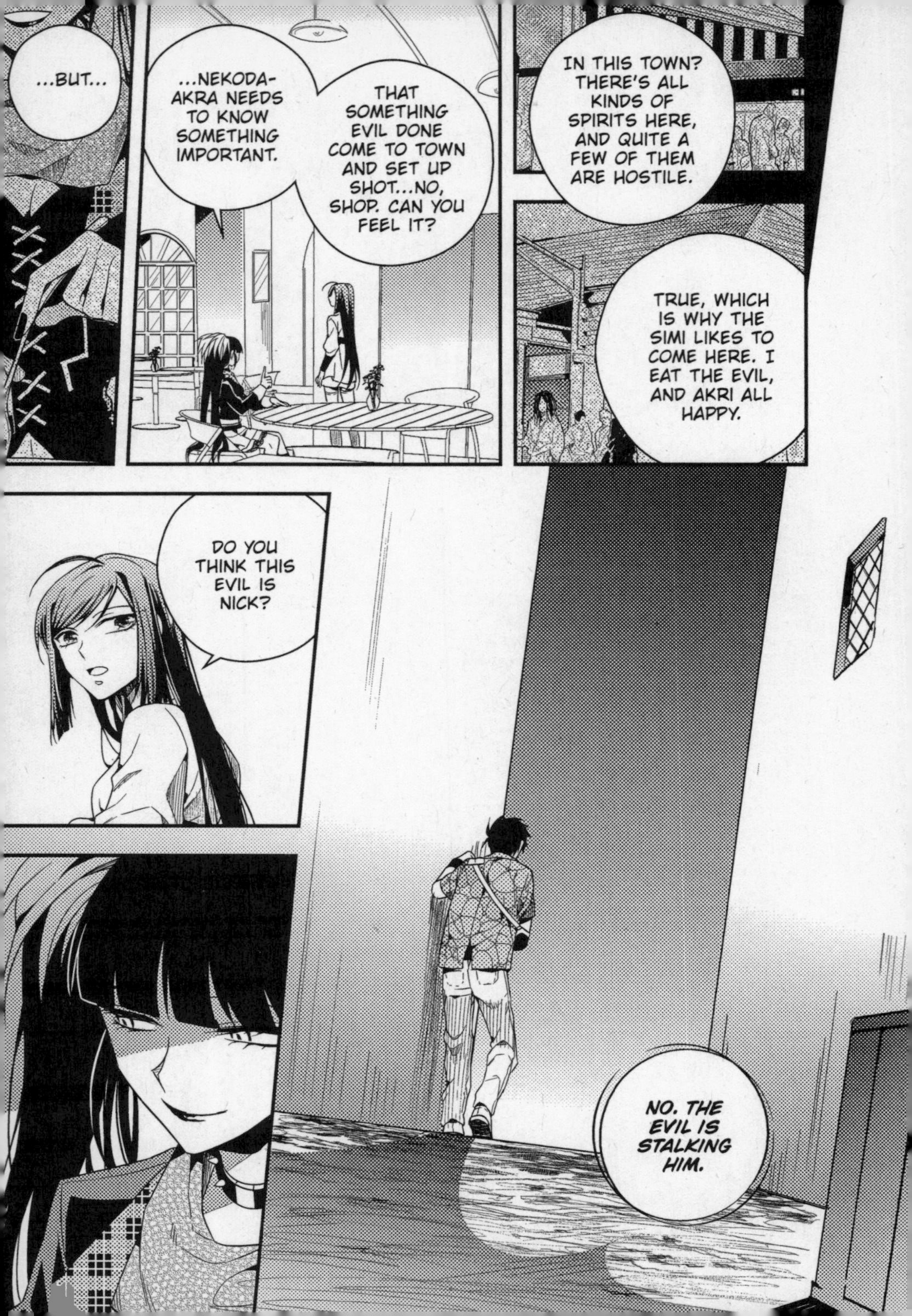
...BUT...
...NEKODA-AKRA NEEDS TO KNOW SOMETHING IMPORTANT.
THAT SOMETHING EVIL DONE COME TO TOWN AND SET UP SHOT...NO, SHOP. CAN YOU FEEL IT?
IN THIS TOWN? THERE'S ALL KINDS OF SPIRITS HERE, AND QUITE A FEW OF THEM ARE HOSTILE.
TRUE, WHICH IS WHY THE SIMI LIKES TO COME HERE. I EAT THE EVIL, AND AKRI ALL HAPPY.
DO YOU THINK THIS EVIL IS NICK?
NO. THE EVIL IS STALKING HIM.

THE DARK-HUNTERS: INFINITY

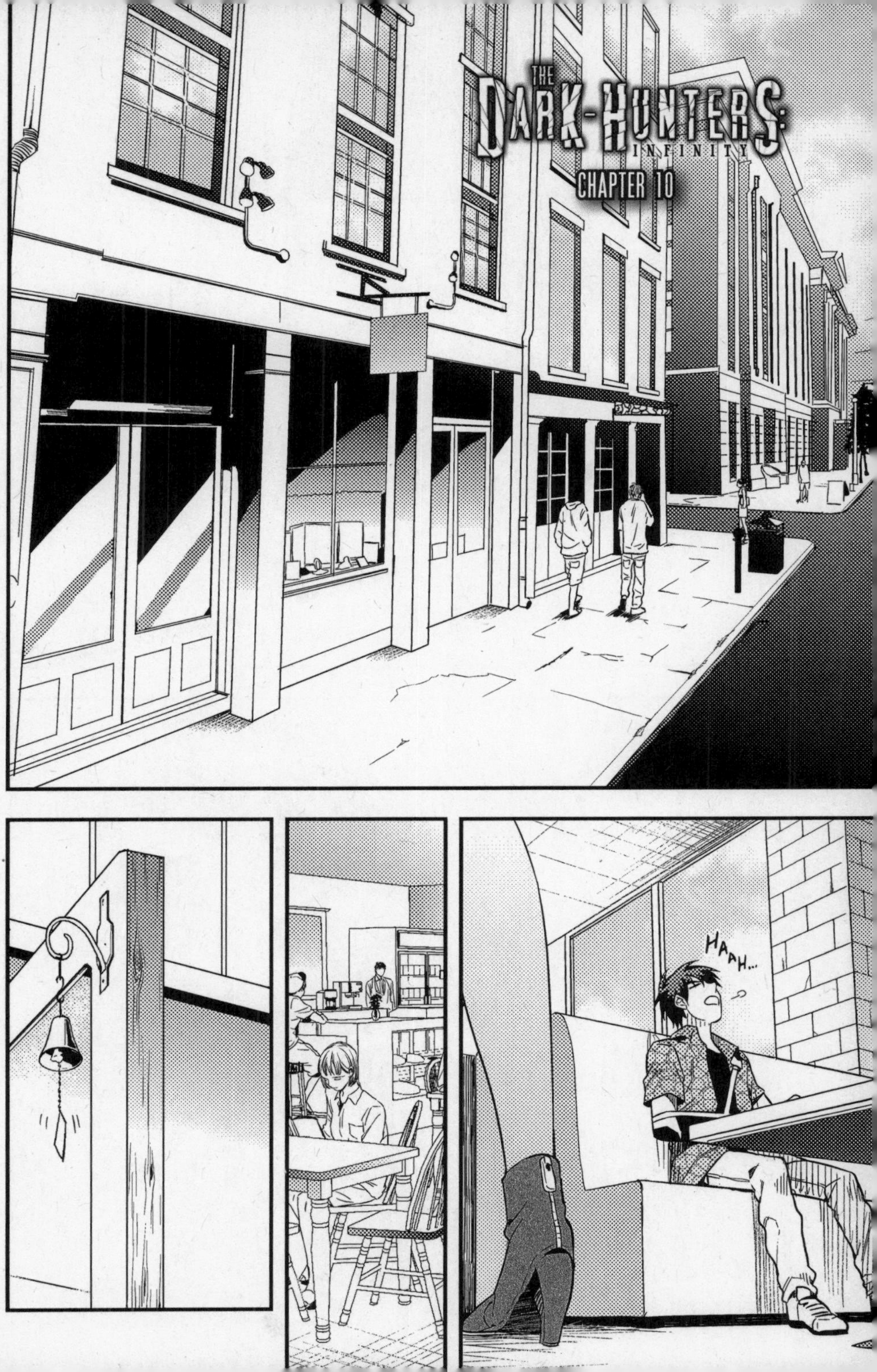
THE DARK-HUNTERS: INFINITY
CHAPTER 10
HAAH...

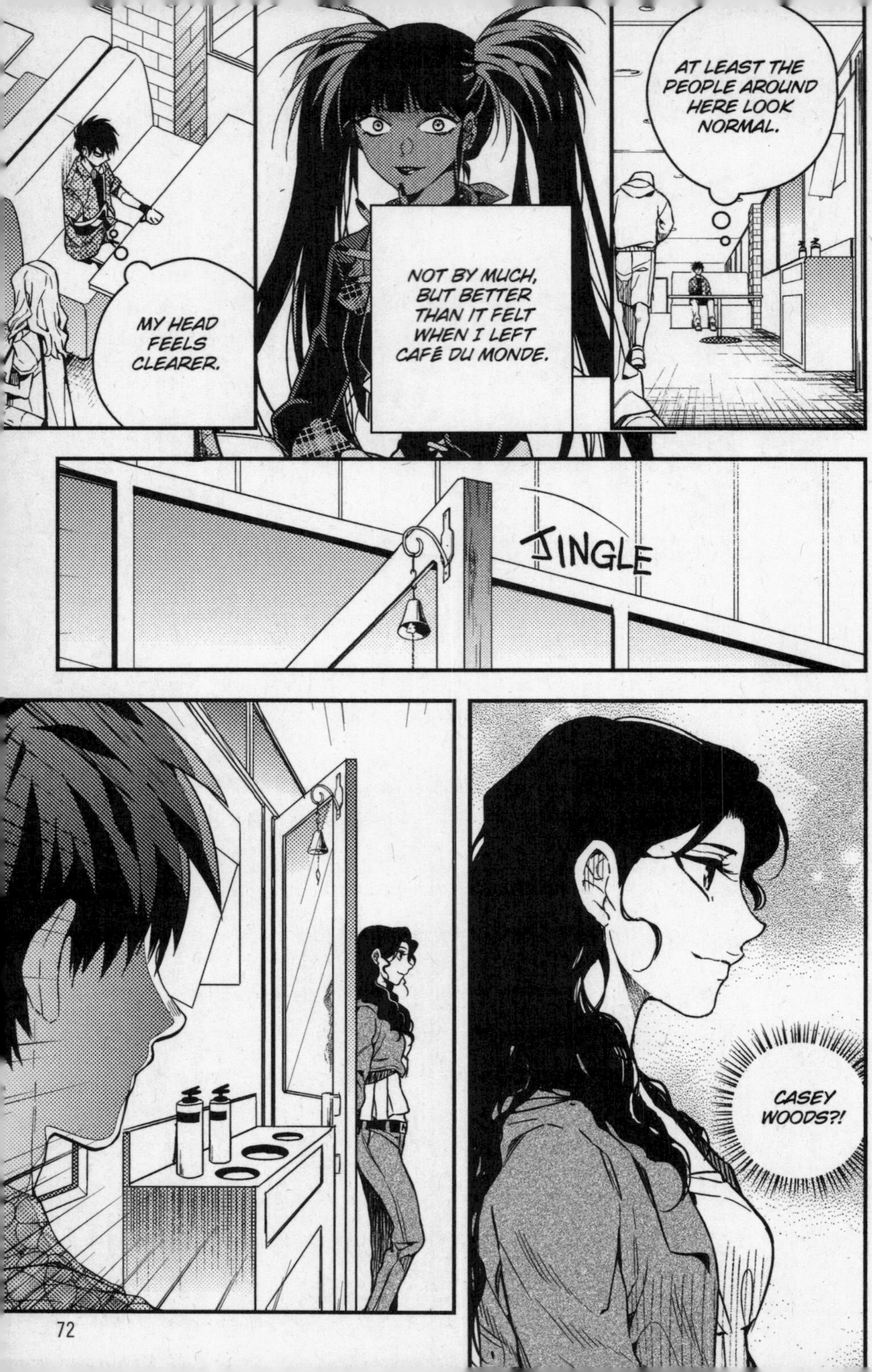
MY HEAD FEELS CLEARER.
NOT BY MUCH, BUT BETTER THAN IT FELT WHEN I LEFT CAFÉ DU MONDE.
AT LEAST THE PEOPLE AROUND HERE LOOK NORMAL.
JINGLE
CASEY WOODS?!

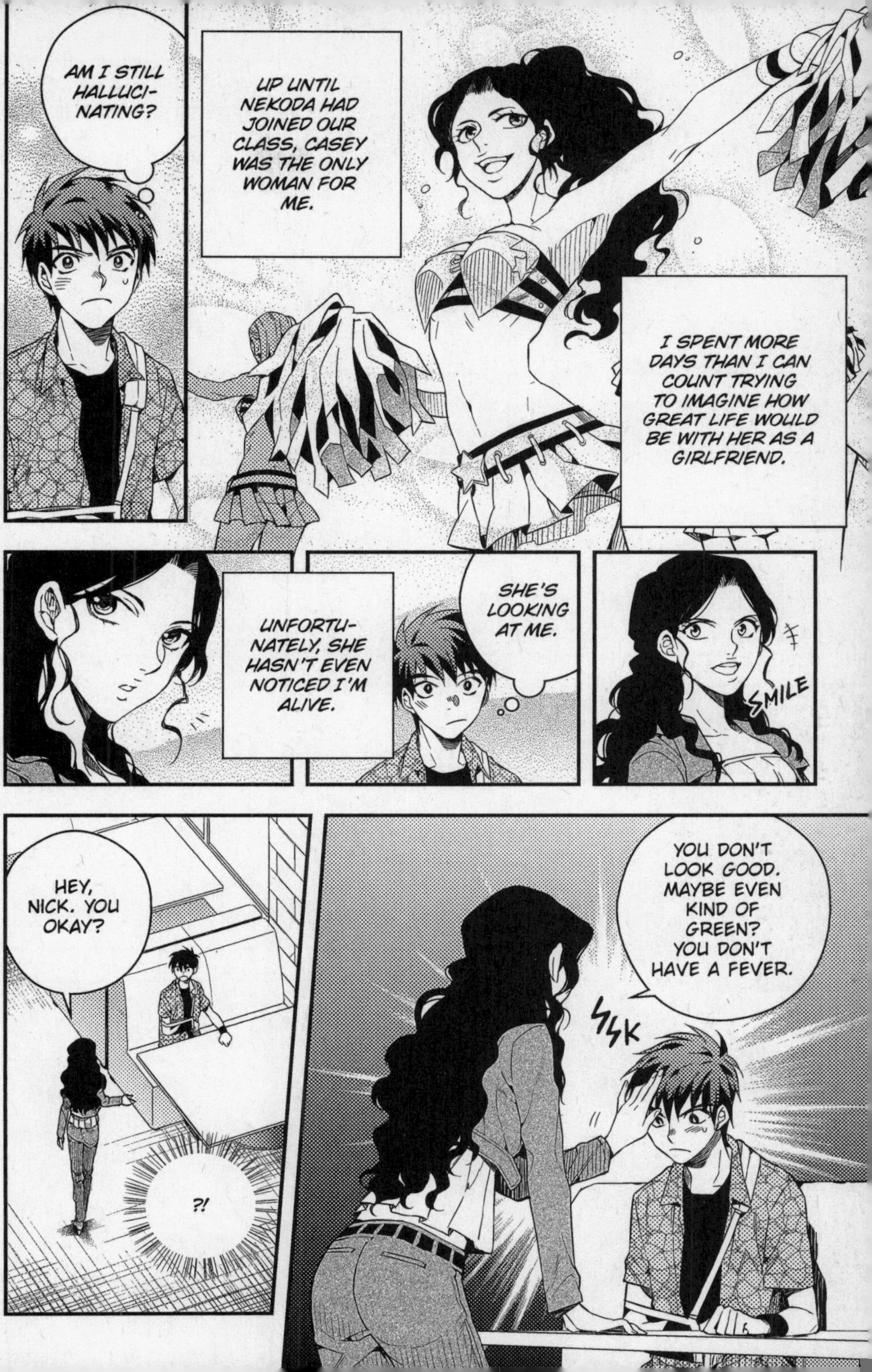
AM I STILL HALLUCI-NATING?
UP UNTIL NEKODA HAD JOINED OUR CLASS, CASEY WAS THE ONLY WOMAN FOR ME.
I SPENT MORE DAYS THAN I CAN COUNT TRYING TO IMAGINE HOW GREAT LIFE WOULD BE WITH HER AS A GIRLFRIEND.
UNFORTU-NATELY, SHE HASN'T EVEN NOTICED I'M ALIVE.
SHE'S LOOKING AT ME.
SMILE
HEY, NICK. YOU OKAY?
?!
YOU DON'T LOOK GOOD. MAYBE EVEN KIND OF GREEN? YOU DON'T HAVE A FEVER.
SSK

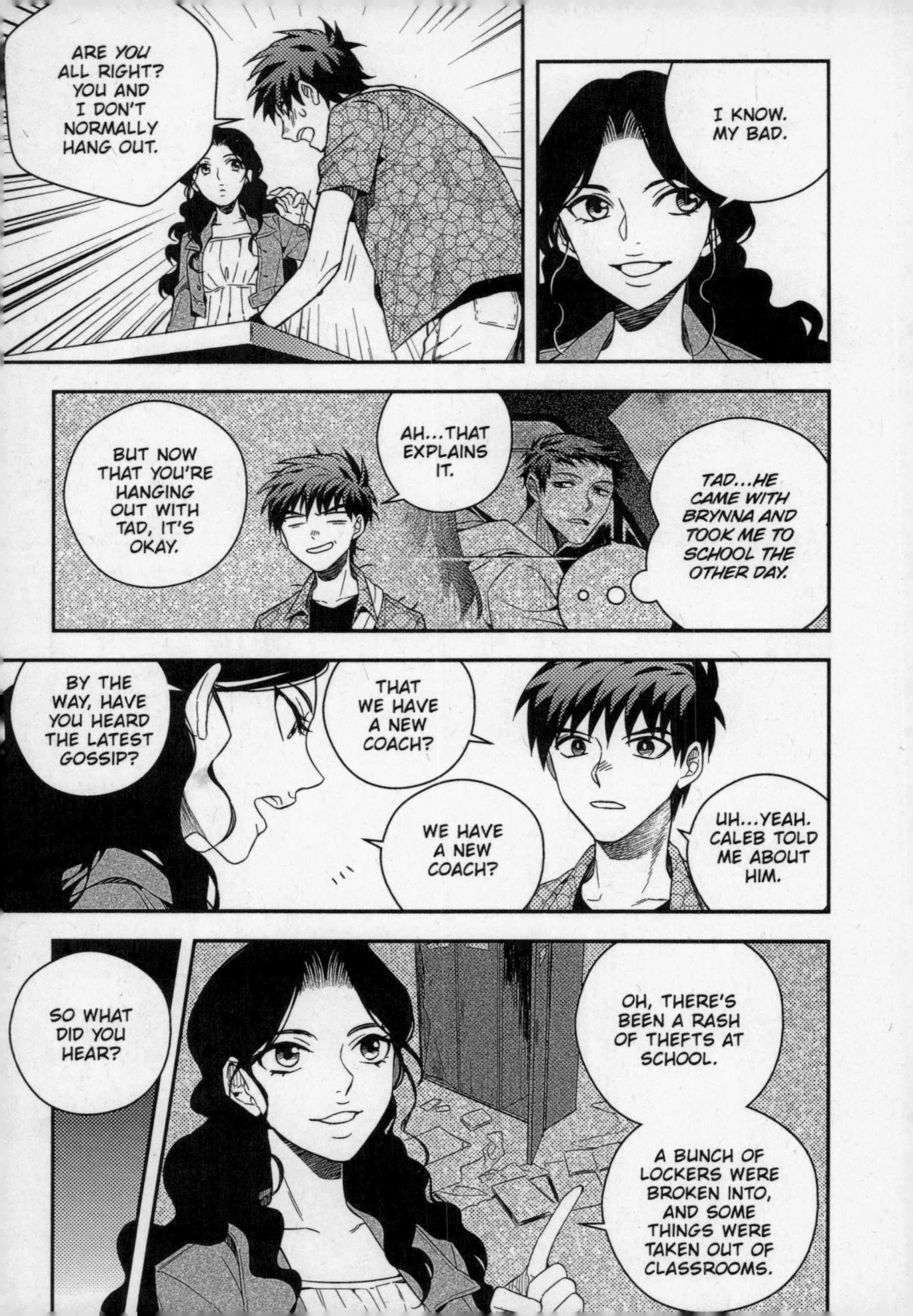
ARE YOU ALL RIGHT? YOU AND I DON'T NORMALLY HANG OUT.
I KNOW. MY BAD.
BUT NOW THAT YOU'RE HANGING OUT WITH TAD, IT'S OKAY.
AH...THAT EXPLAINS IT.
TAD...HE CAME WITH BRYNNA AND TOOK ME TO SCHOOL THE OTHER DAY.
BY THE WAY, HAVE YOU HEARD THE LATEST GOSSIP?
THAT WE HAVE A NEW COACH?
WE HAVE A NEW COACH?
UH...YEAH. CALEB TOLD ME ABOUT HIM.
SO WHAT DID YOU HEAR?
OH, THERE'S BEEN A RASH OF THEFTS AT SCHOOL.
A BUNCH OF LOCKERS WERE BROKEN INTO, AND SOME THINGS WERE TAKEN OUT OF CLASSROOMS.

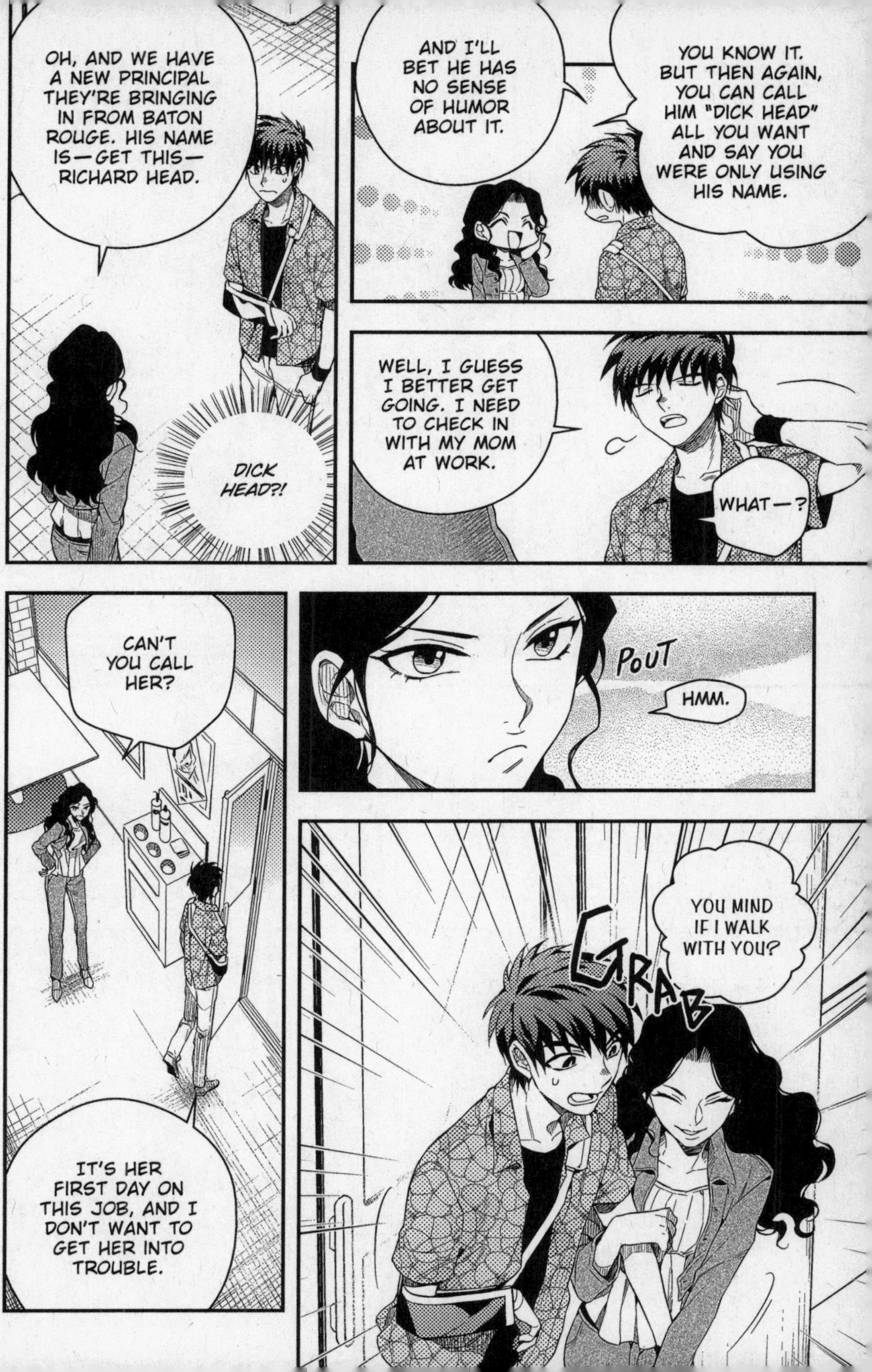
OH, AND WE HAVE A NEW PRINCIPAL THEY'RE BRINGING IN FROM BATON ROUGE. HIS NAME IS—GET THIS—RICHARD HEAD.
DICK HEAD?!
AND I'LL BET HE HAS NO SENSE OF HUMOR ABOUT IT.
YOU KNOW IT. BUT THEN AGAIN, YOU CAN CALL HIM "DICK HEAD" ALL YOU WANT AND SAY YOU WERE ONLY USING HIS NAME.
WELL, I GUESS I BETTER GET GOING. I NEED TO CHECK IN WITH MY MOM AT WORK.
WHAT—?
CAN'T YOU CALL HER?
IT'S HER FIRST DAY ON THIS JOB, AND I DON'T WANT TO GET HER INTO TROUBLE.
POUT
HMM.
YOU MIND IF I WALK WITH YOU?
GRAB

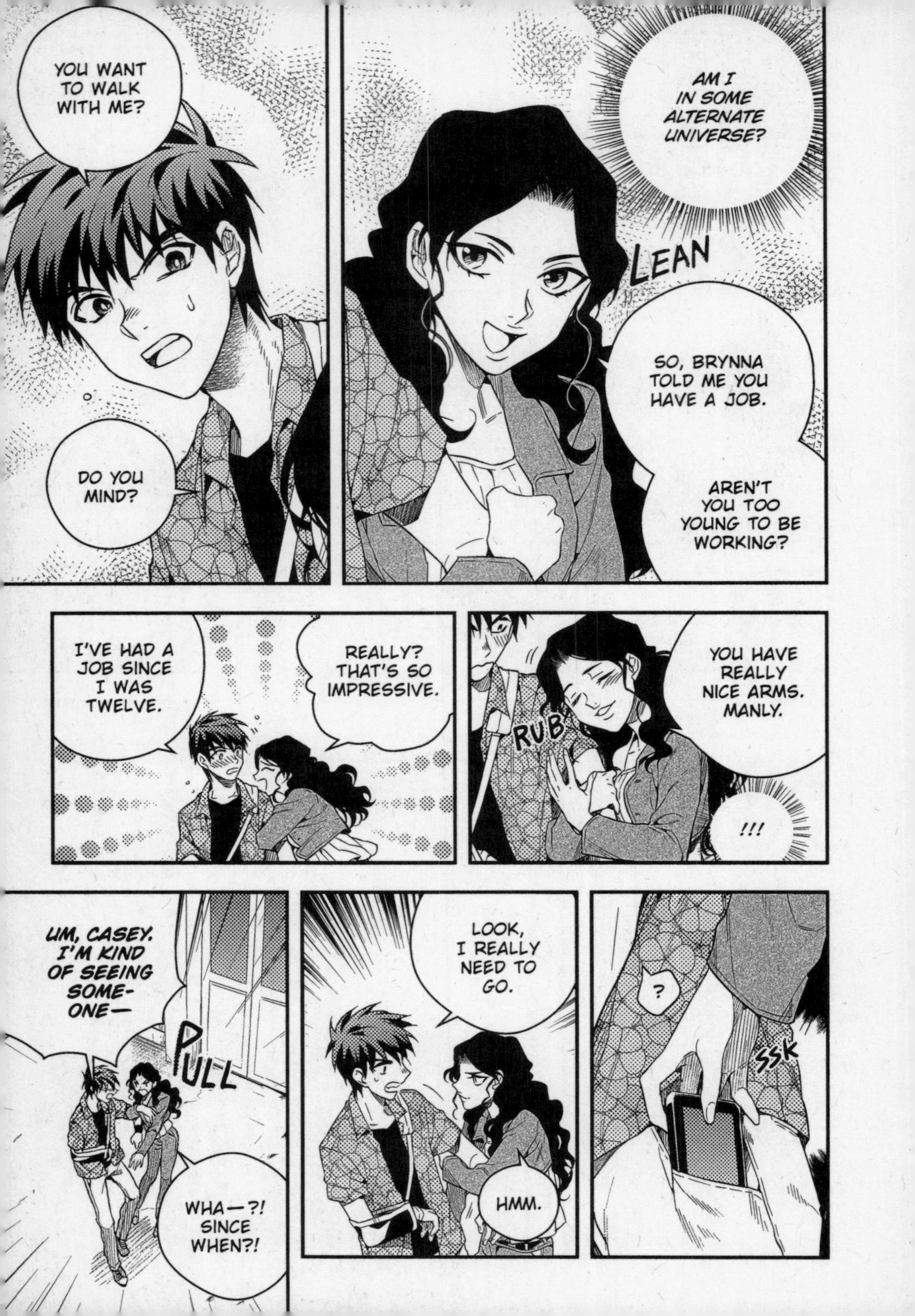
YOU WANT TO WALK WITH ME?
DO YOU MIND?
AM I IN SOME ALTERNATE UNIVERSE?
LEAN
SO, BRYNNA TOLD ME YOU HAVE A JOB.
AREN'T YOU TOO YOUNG TO BE WORKING?
I'VE HAD A JOB SINCE I WAS TWELVE.
REALLY? THAT'S SO IMPRESSIVE.
YOU HAVE REALLY NICE ARMS. MANLY.
RUB
!!!
UM, CASEY. I'M KIND OF SEEING SOME-ONE—
PULL
WHA—?! SINCE WHEN?!
LOOK, I REALLY NEED TO GO.
HMM.
?
SSK

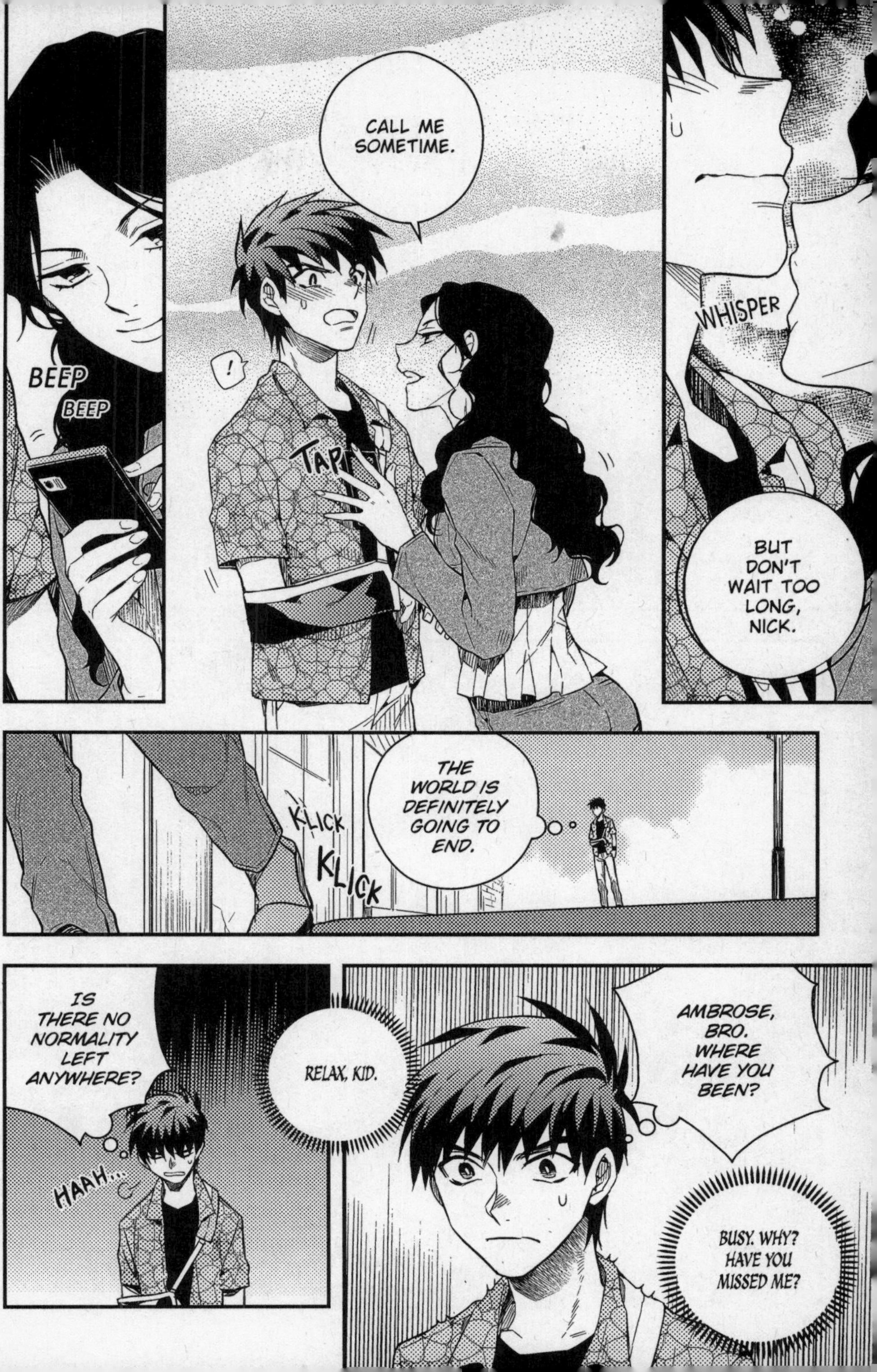
CALL ME SOMETIME.
!
BEEP
BEEP
TAP
WHISPER
BUT DON'T WAIT TOO LONG, NICK.
KLICK
KLICK
THE WORLD IS DEFINITELY GOING TO END.
IS THERE NO NORMALITY LEFT ANYWHERE?
HAAH...
RELAX, KID.
AMBROSE, BRO. WHERE HAVE YOU BEEN?
BUSY. WHY? HAVE YOU MISSED ME?

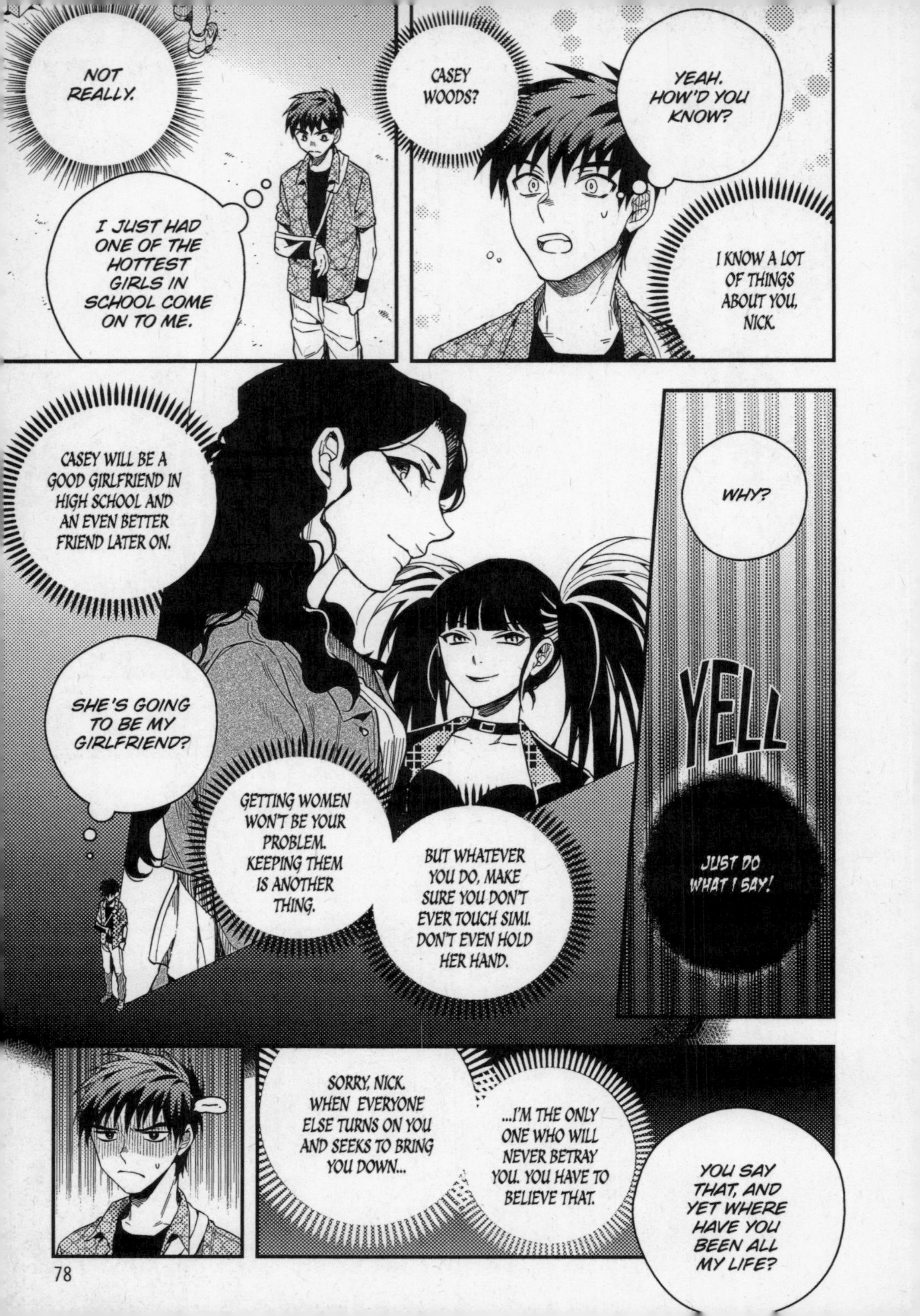

NOT REALLY.
I JUST HAD ONE OF THE HOTTEST GIRLS IN SCHOOL COME ON TO ME.
CASEY WOODS?
YEAH. HOW'D YOU KNOW?
I KNOW A LOT OF THINGS ABOUT YOU, NICK.
CASEY WILL BE A GOOD GIRLFRIEND IN HIGH SCHOOL AND AN EVEN BETTER FRIEND LATER ON.
SHE'S GOING TO BE MY GIRLFRIEND?
GETTING WOMEN WON'T BE YOUR PROBLEM. KEEPING THEM IS ANOTHER THING.
BUT WHATEVER YOU DO, MAKE SURE YOU DON'T EVER TOUCH SIMI. DON'T EVEN HOLD HER HAND.
WHY?
YELL
JUST DO WHAT I SAY!
SORRY, NICK. WHEN EVERYONE ELSE TURNS ON YOU AND SEEKS TO BRING YOU DOWN...
...I'M THE ONLY ONE WHO WILL NEVER BETRAY YOU. YOU HAVE TO BELIEVE THAT.
YOU SAY THAT, AND YET WHERE HAVE YOU BEEN ALL MY LIFE?

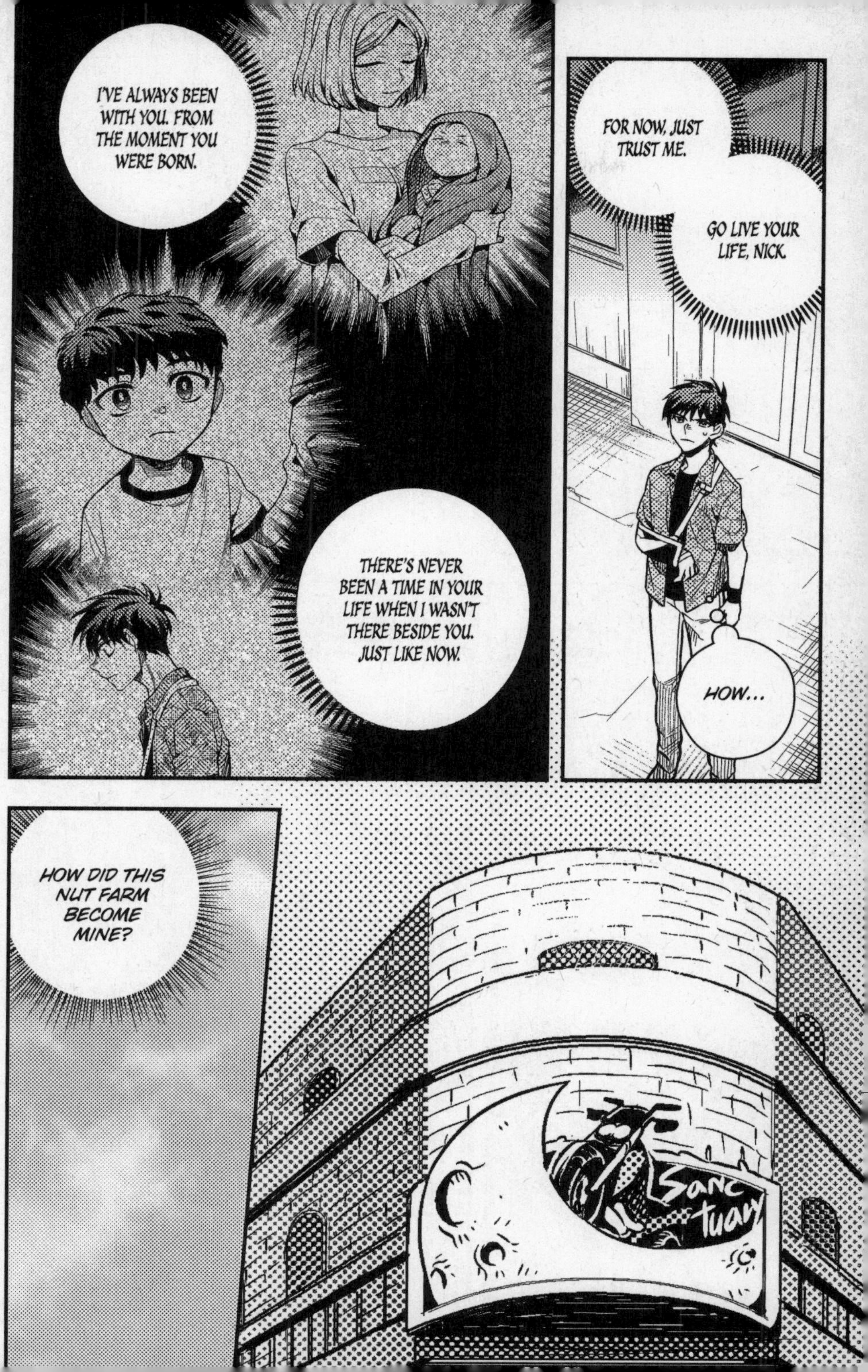
I'VE ALWAYS BEEN WITH YOU. FROM THE MOMENT YOU WERE BORN.
THERE'S NEVER BEEN A TIME IN YOUR LIFE WHEN I WASN'T THERE BESIDE YOU. JUST LIKE NOW.
FOR NOW, JUST TRUST ME.
GO LIVE YOUR LIFE, NICK.
HOW...
HOW DID THIS NUT FARM BECOME MINE?
Sanctuary

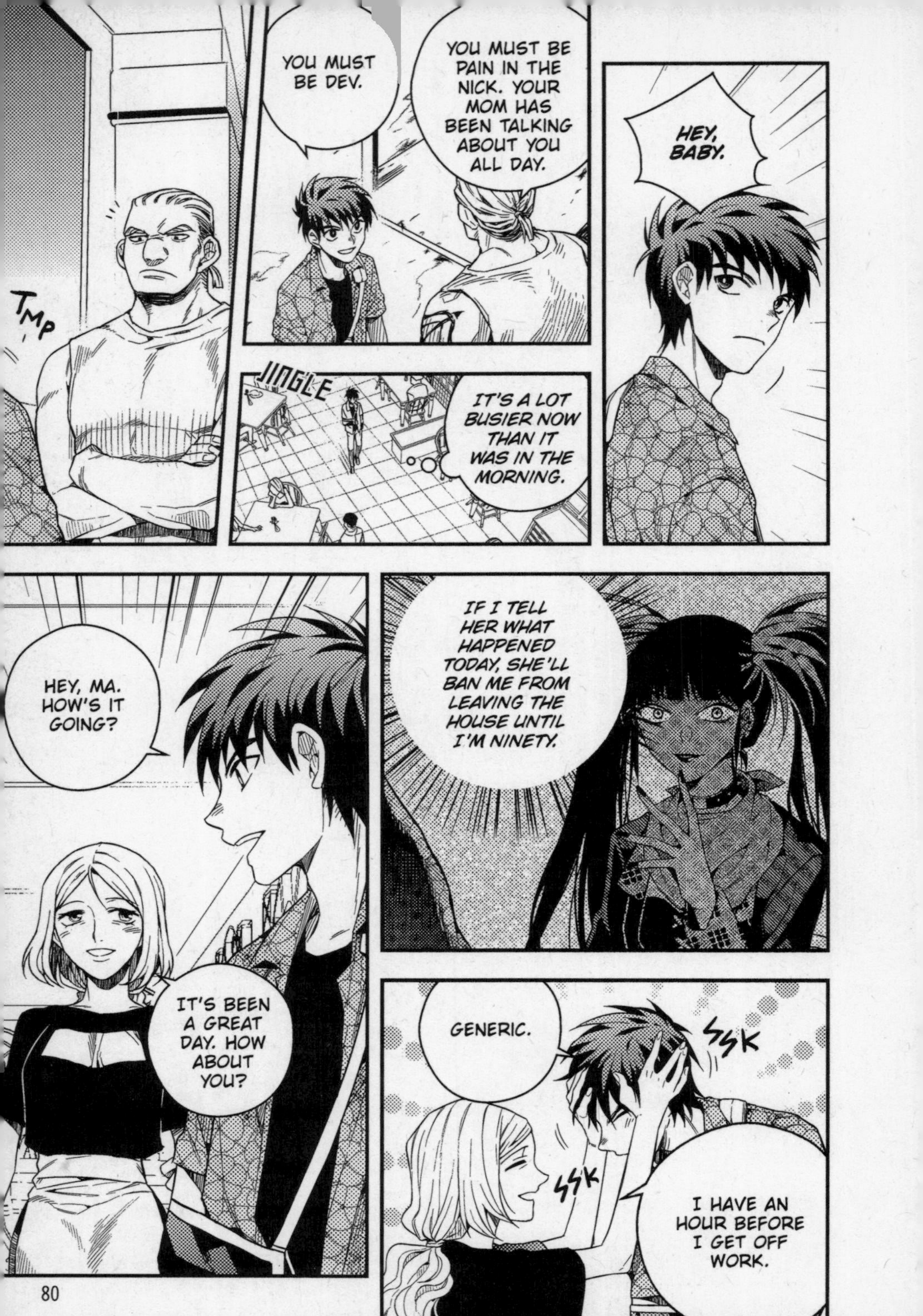
YOU MUST BE DEV.
YOU MUST BE PAIN IN THE NICK. YOUR MOM HAS BEEN TALKING ABOUT YOU ALL DAY.
TMP
HEY, BABY.
JINGLE
IT'S A LOT BUSIER NOW THAN IT WAS IN THE MORNING.
HEY, MA. HOW'S IT GOING?
IF I TELL HER WHAT HAPPENED TODAY, SHE'LL BAN ME FROM LEAVING THE HOUSE UNTIL I'M NINETY.
IT'S BEEN A GREAT DAY. HOW ABOUT YOU?
GENERIC.
SSK
SSK
I HAVE AN HOUR BEFORE I GET OFF WORK.

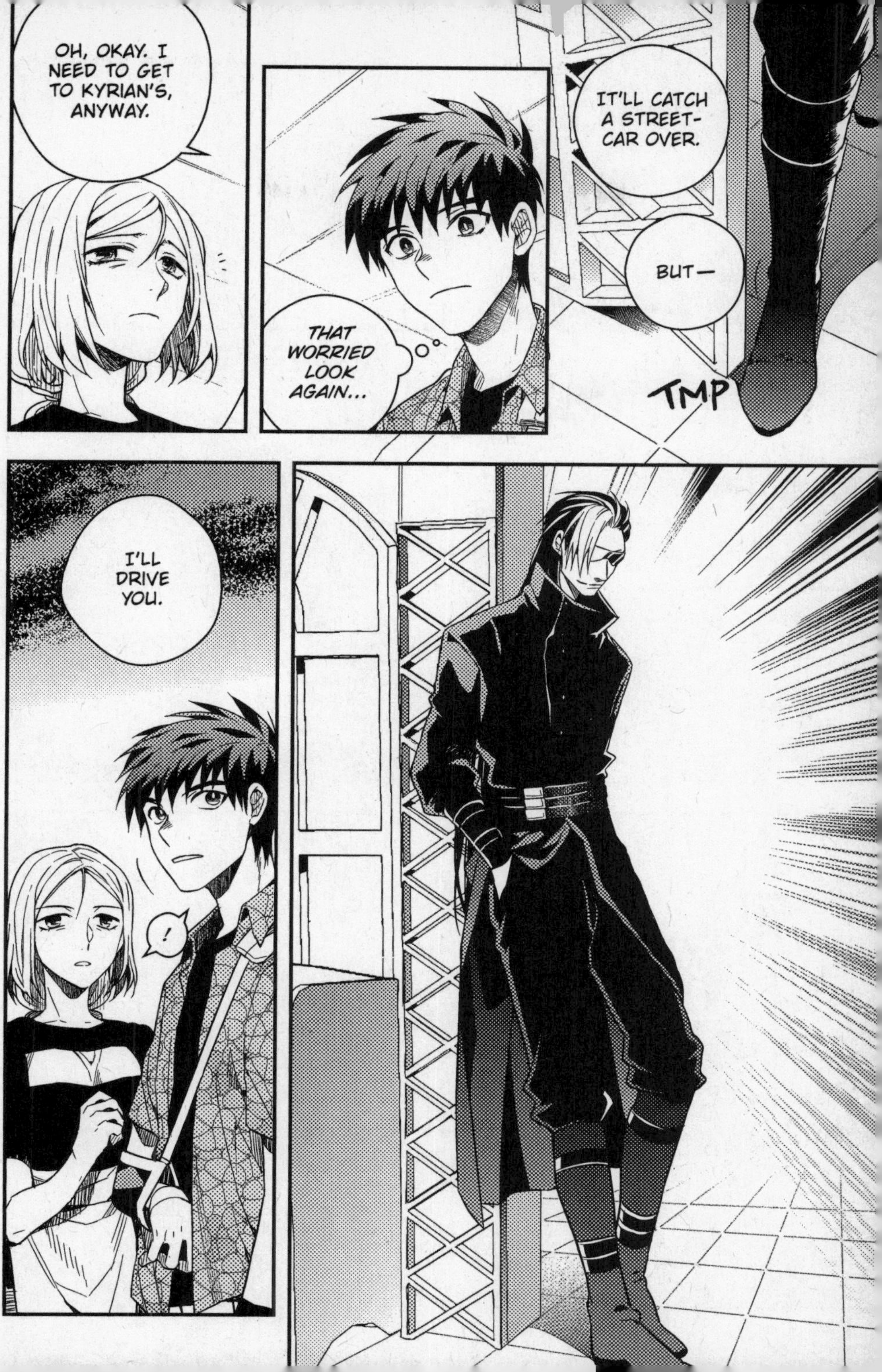
OH, OKAY. I NEED TO GET TO KYRIAN'S, ANYWAY.
THAT WORRIED LOOK AGAIN...
IT'LL CATCH A STREET-CAR OVER.
BUT—
TMP
I'LL DRIVE YOU.
!

ACHERON!

KYRIAN SAID YOU HAVE FANGS. DO YOU?

IS IT IMPORTANT?

MAYBE.

WOW. YOU ARE GOOD AT HIDING THEM.

SO HAVE YOU EVER DRUNK BLOOD?

WHAT DID THE TWO OF YOU TALK ABOUT?

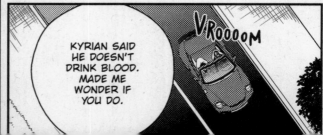

KYRIAN SAID HE DOESN'T DRINK BLOOD. MADE ME WONDER IF YOU DO.

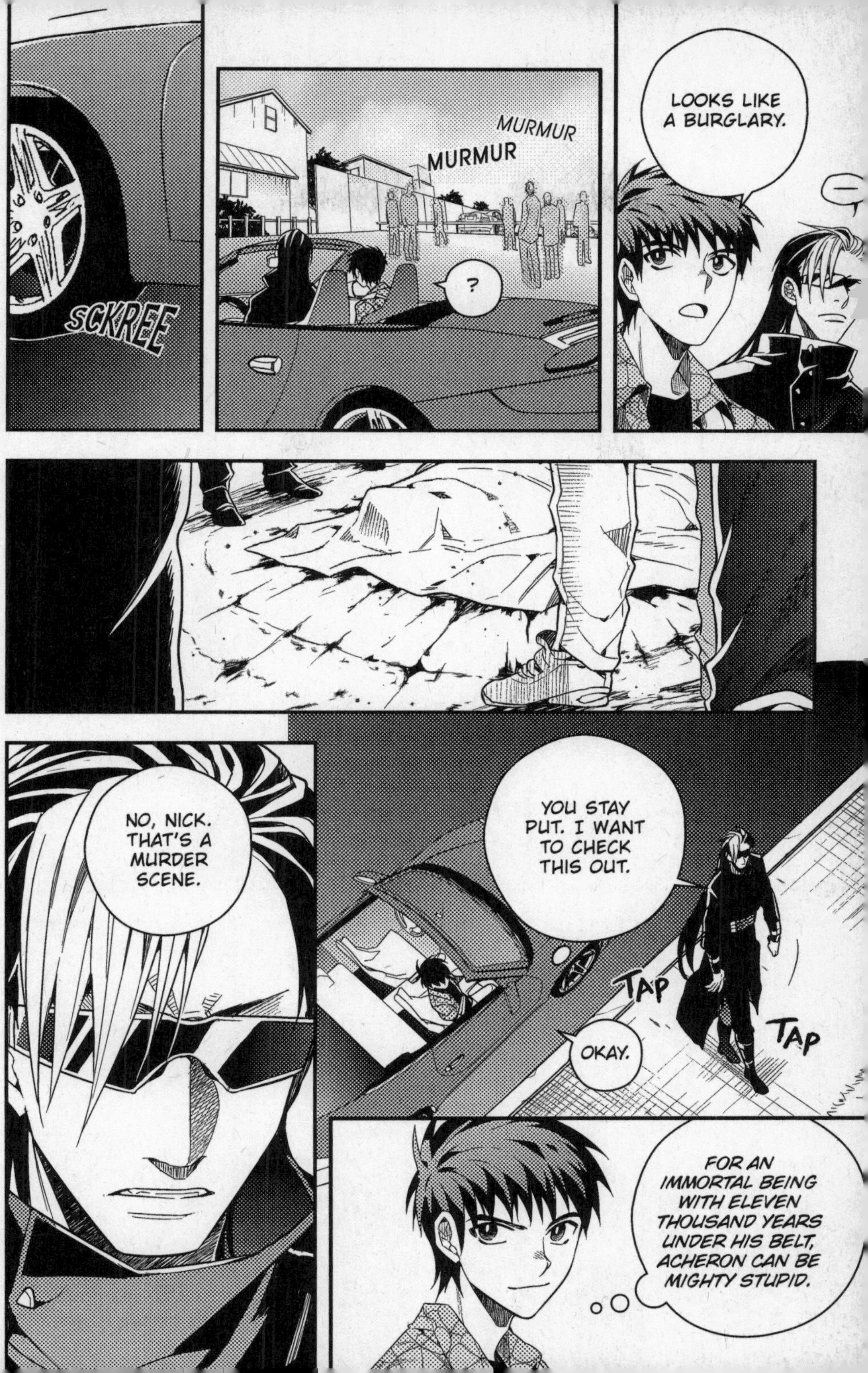
SCKREE
MURMUR
MURMUR
?
LOOKS LIKE A BURGLARY.
NO, NICK. THAT'S A MURDER SCENE.
YOU STAY PUT. I WANT TO CHECK THIS OUT.
OKAY.
TAP
TAP
FOR AN IMMORTAL BEING WITH ELEVEN THOUSAND YEARS UNDER HIS BELT, ACHERON CAN BE MIGHTY STUPID.

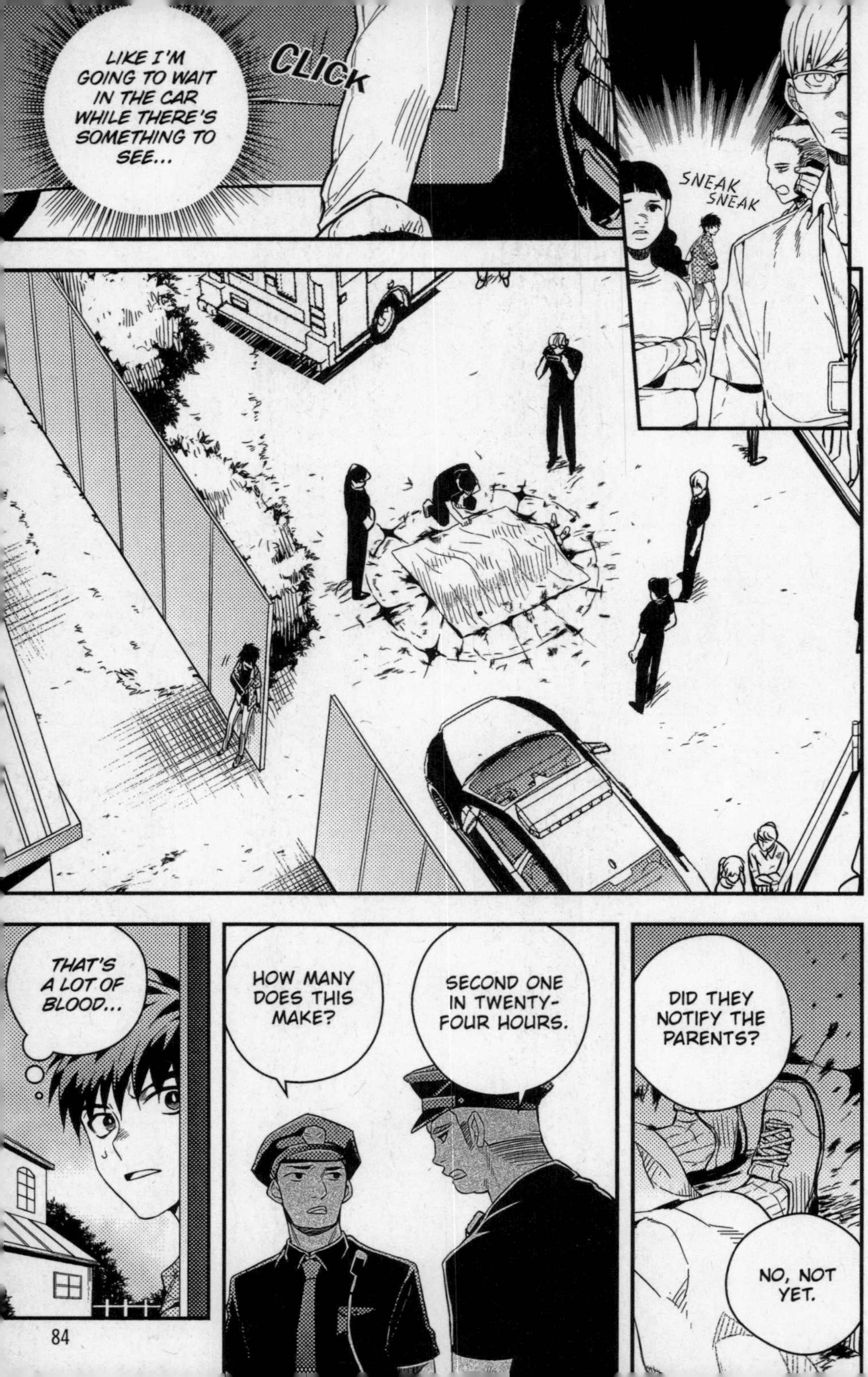
LIKE I'M GOING TO WAIT IN THE CAR WHILE THERE'S SOMETHING TO SEE...
CLICK
SNEAK SNEAK
THAT'S A LOT OF BLOOD...
HOW MANY DOES THIS MAKE?
SECOND ONE IN TWENTY-FOUR HOURS.
DID THEY NOTIFY THE PARENTS?
NO, NOT YET.

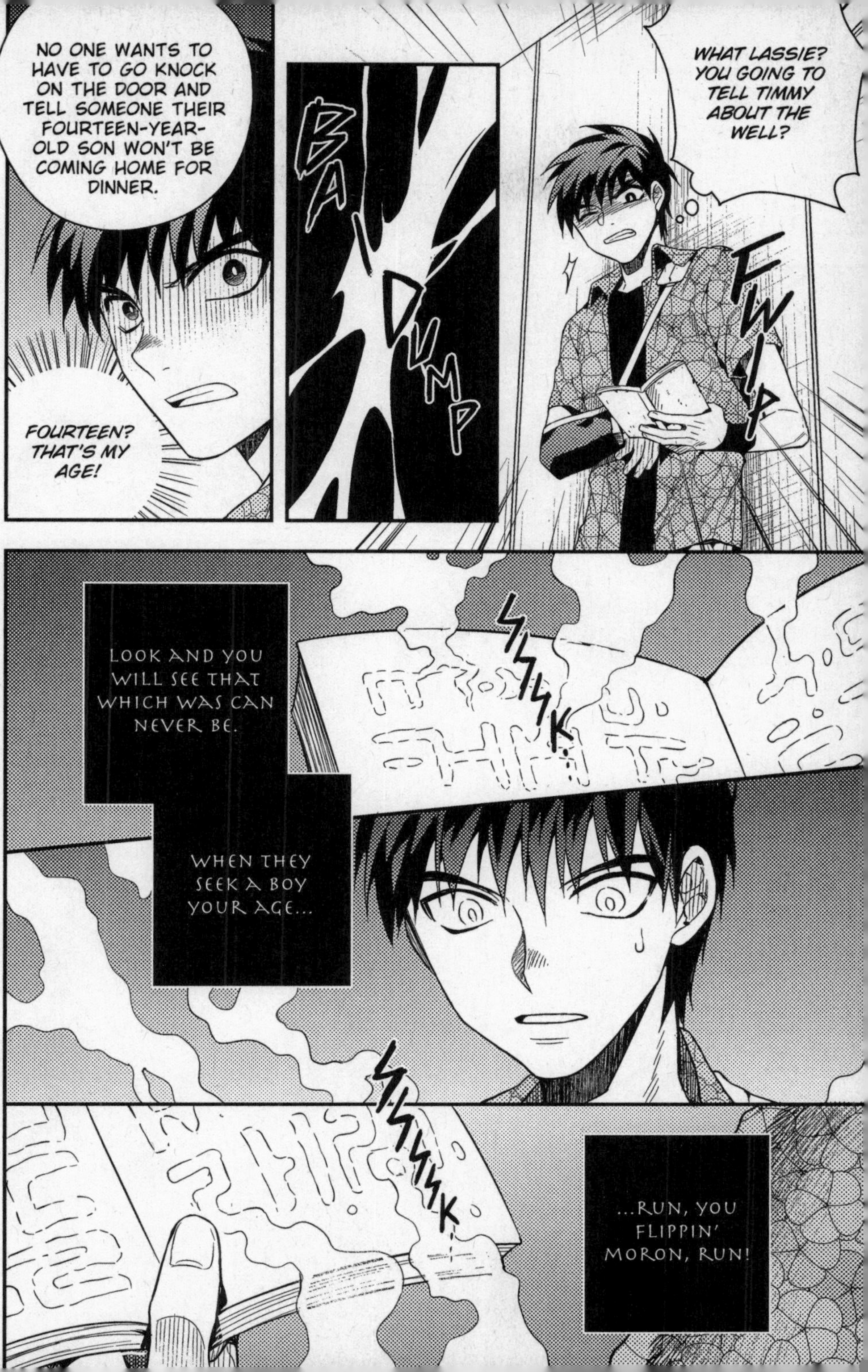
NO ONE WANTS TO HAVE TO GO KNOCK ON THE DOOR AND TELL SOMEONE THEIR FOURTEEN-YEAR-OLD SON WON'T BE COMING HOME FOR DINNER.
FOURTEEN? THAT'S MY AGE!
BA DUMP
WHAT LASSIE? YOU GOING TO TELL TIMMY ABOUT THE WELL?
FWIP
LOOK AND YOU WILL SEE THAT WHICH WAS CAN NEVER BE.
SSSK
WHEN THEY SEEK A BOY YOUR AGE...
SSSSK
...RUN, YOU FLIPPIN' MORON, RUN!

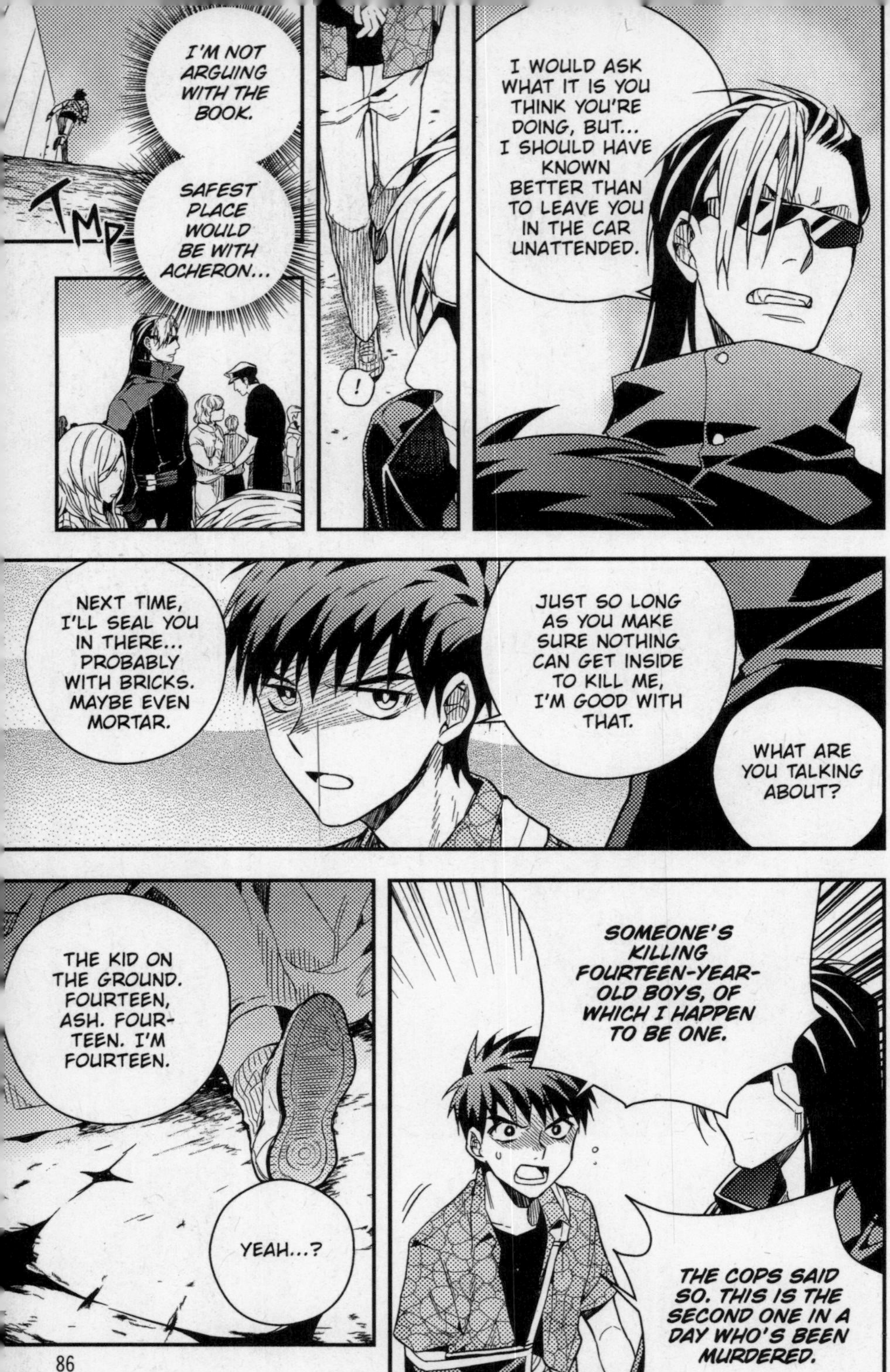

I'M NOT ARGUING WITH THE BOOK.
SAFEST PLACE WOULD BE WITH ACHERON...
TMP
!
I WOULD ASK WHAT IT IS YOU THINK YOU'RE DOING, BUT... I SHOULD HAVE KNOWN BETTER THAN TO LEAVE YOU IN THE CAR UNATTENDED.
NEXT TIME, I'LL SEAL YOU IN THERE... PROBABLY WITH BRICKS. MAYBE EVEN MORTAR.
JUST SO LONG AS YOU MAKE SURE NOTHING CAN GET INSIDE TO KILL ME, I'M GOOD WITH THAT.
WHAT ARE YOU TALKING ABOUT?
THE KID ON THE GROUND. FOURTEEN, ASH. FOUR-TEEN. I'M FOURTEEN.
YEAH...?
SOMEONE'S KILLING FOURTEEN-YEAR-OLD BOYS, OF WHICH I HAPPEN TO BE ONE.
THE COPS SAID SO. THIS IS THE SECOND ONE IN A DAY WHO'S BEEN MURDERED.

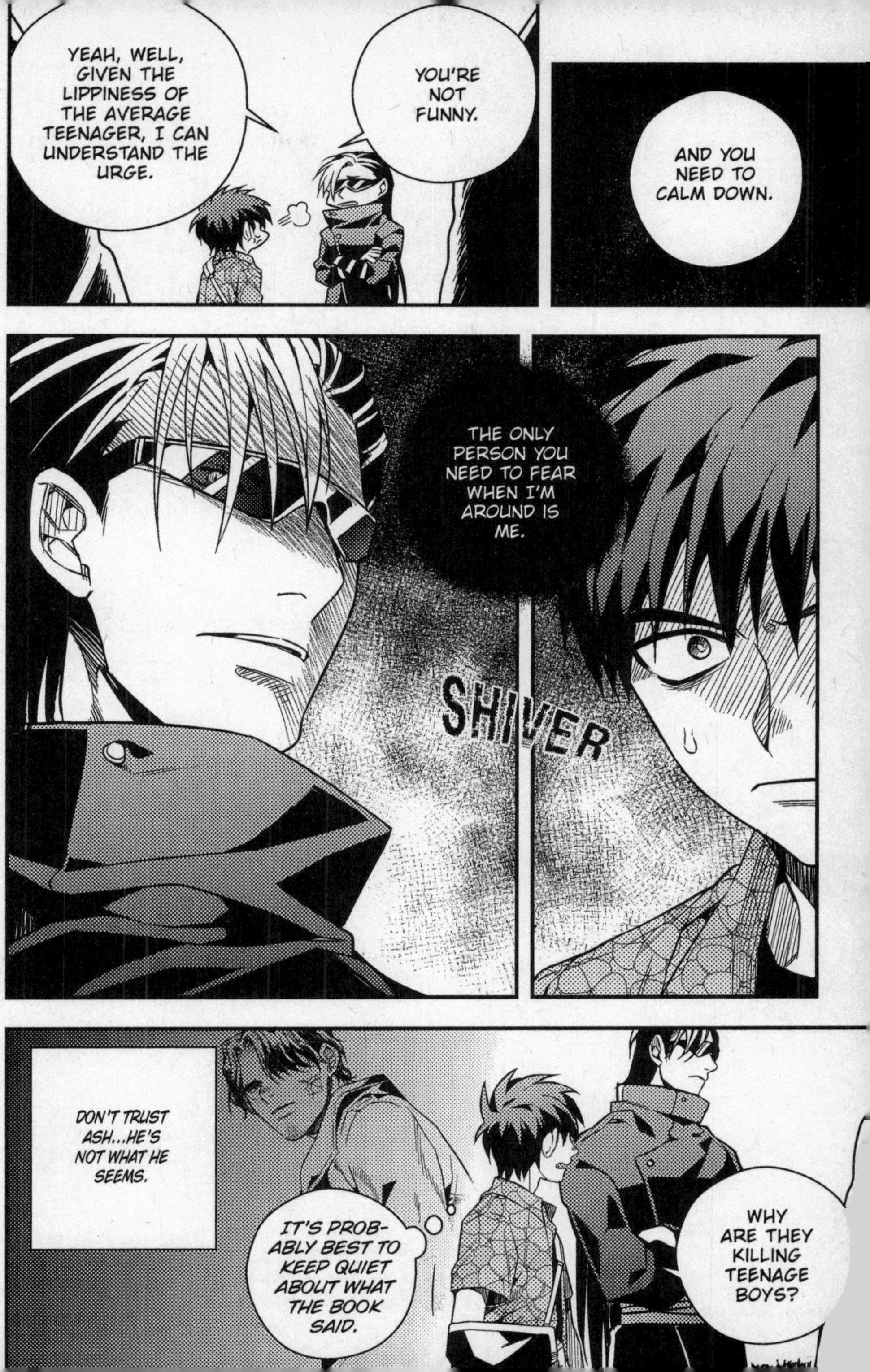
YEAH, WELL, GIVEN THE LIPPINESS OF THE AVERAGE TEENAGER, I CAN UNDERSTAND THE URGE.
YOU'RE NOT FUNNY.
AND YOU NEED TO CALM DOWN.
THE ONLY PERSON YOU NEED TO FEAR WHEN I'M AROUND IS ME.
SHIVER
DON'T TRUST ASH...HE'S NOT WHAT HE SEEMS.
IT'S PROBABLY BEST TO KEEP QUIET ABOUT WHAT THE BOOK SAID.
WHY ARE THEY KILLING TEENAGE BOYS?

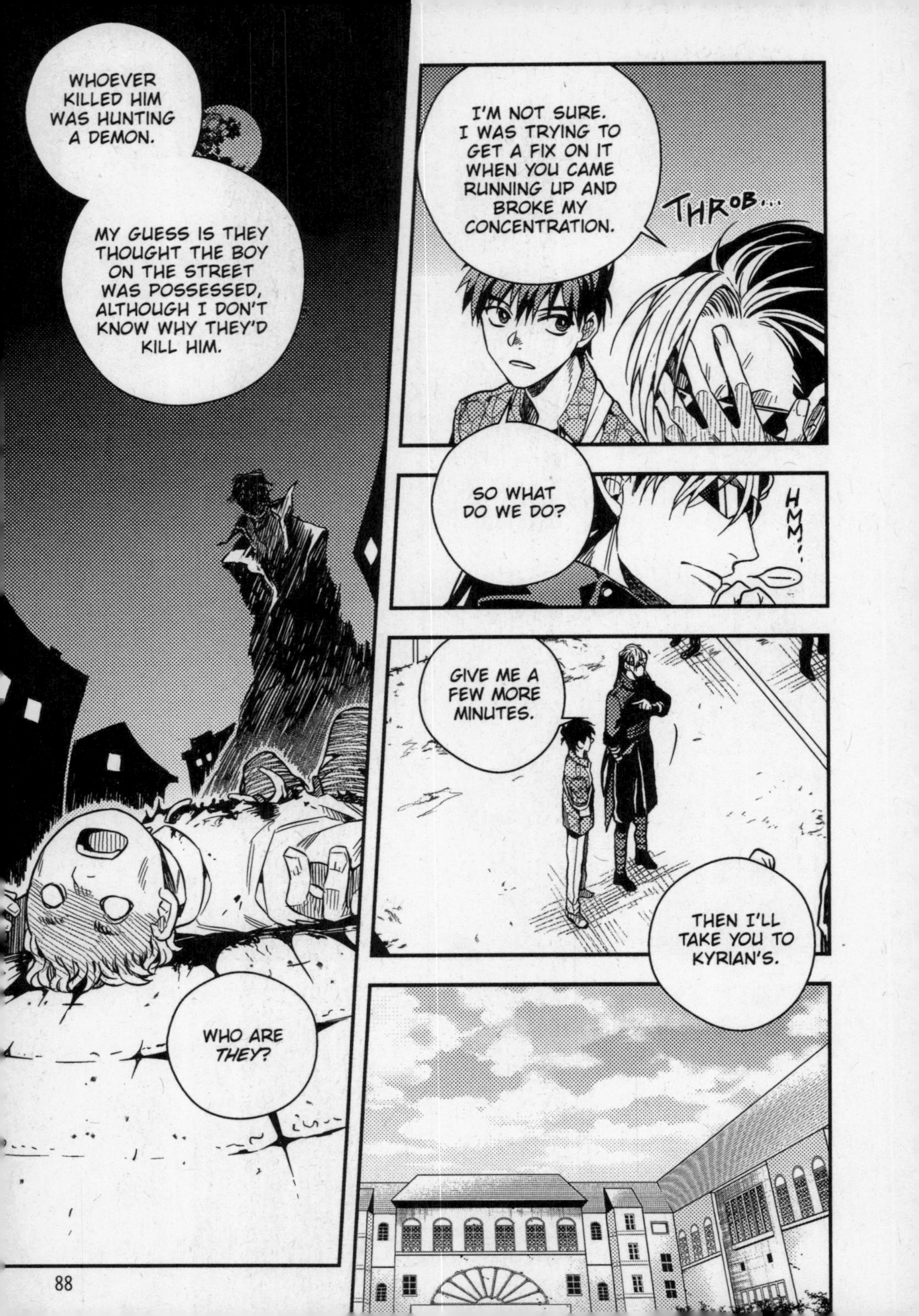
WHOEVER KILLED HIM WAS HUNTING A DEMON.
MY GUESS IS THEY THOUGHT THE BOY ON THE STREET WAS POSSESSED, ALTHOUGH I DON'T KNOW WHY THEY'D KILL HIM.
WHO ARE *THEY?*
I'M NOT SURE. I WAS TRYING TO GET A FIX ON IT WHEN YOU CAME RUNNING UP AND BROKE MY CONCENTRATION.
THROB...
SO WHAT DO WE DO?
HMM
GIVE ME A FEW MORE MINUTES.
THEN I'LL TAKE YOU TO KYRIAN'S.

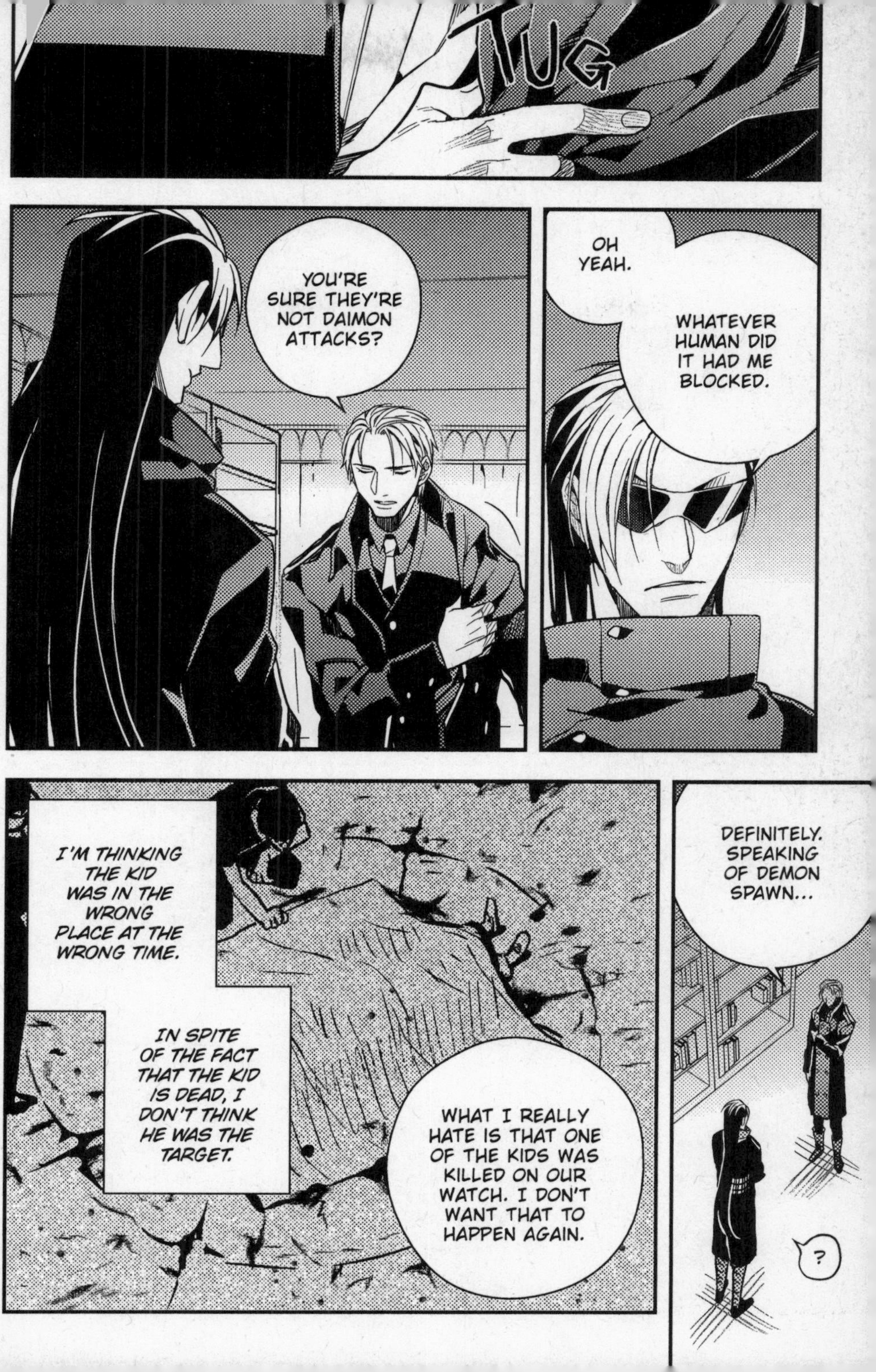
TUG
YOU'RE SURE THEY'RE NOT DAIMON ATTACKS?
OH YEAH.
WHATEVER HUMAN DID IT HAD ME BLOCKED.
I'M THINKING THE KID WAS IN THE WRONG PLACE AT THE WRONG TIME.
IN SPITE OF THE FACT THAT THE KID IS DEAD, I DON'T THINK HE WAS THE TARGET.
WHAT I REALLY HATE IS THAT ONE OF THE KIDS WAS KILLED ON OUR WATCH. I DON'T WANT THAT TO HAPPEN AGAIN.
DEFINITELY. SPEAKING OF DEMON SPAWN...
?

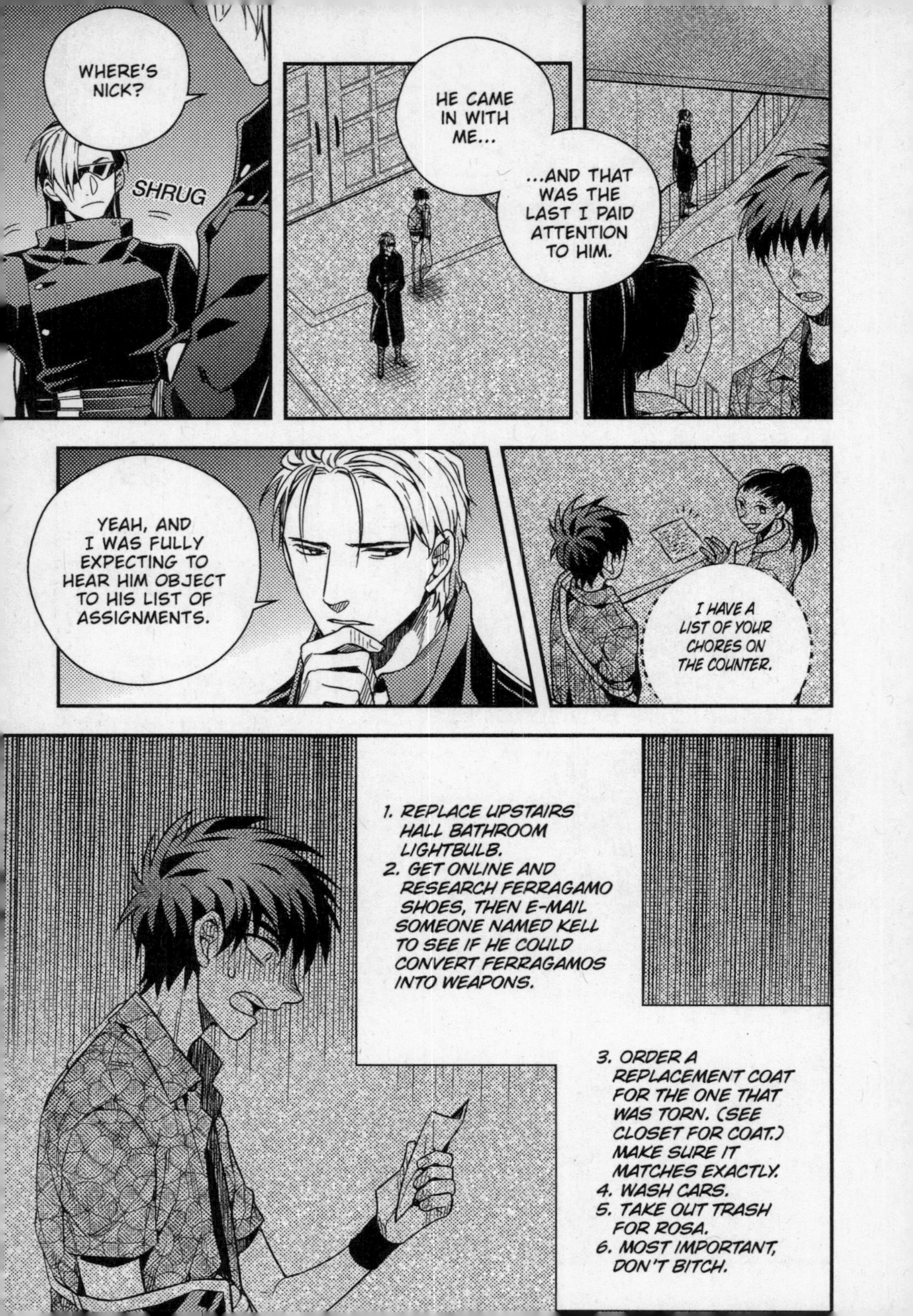

WHERE'S NICK?
SHRUG
HE CAME IN WITH ME...
...AND THAT WAS THE LAST I PAID ATTENTION TO HIM.
YEAH, AND I WAS FULLY EXPECTING TO HEAR HIM OBJECT TO HIS LIST OF ASSIGNMENTS.
I HAVE A LIST OF YOUR CHORES ON THE COUNTER.
1. REPLACE UPSTAIRS HALL BATHROOM LIGHTBULB.
2. GET ONLINE AND RESEARCH FERRAGAMO SHOES, THEN E-MAIL SOMEONE NAMED KELL TO SEE IF HE COULD CONVERT FERRAGAMOS INTO WEAPONS.
3. ORDER A REPLACEMENT COAT FOR THE ONE THAT WAS TORN. (SEE CLOSET FOR COAT.) MAKE SURE IT MATCHES EXACTLY.
4. WASH CARS.
5. TAKE OUT TRASH FOR ROSA.
6. MOST IMPORTANT, DON'T BITCH.

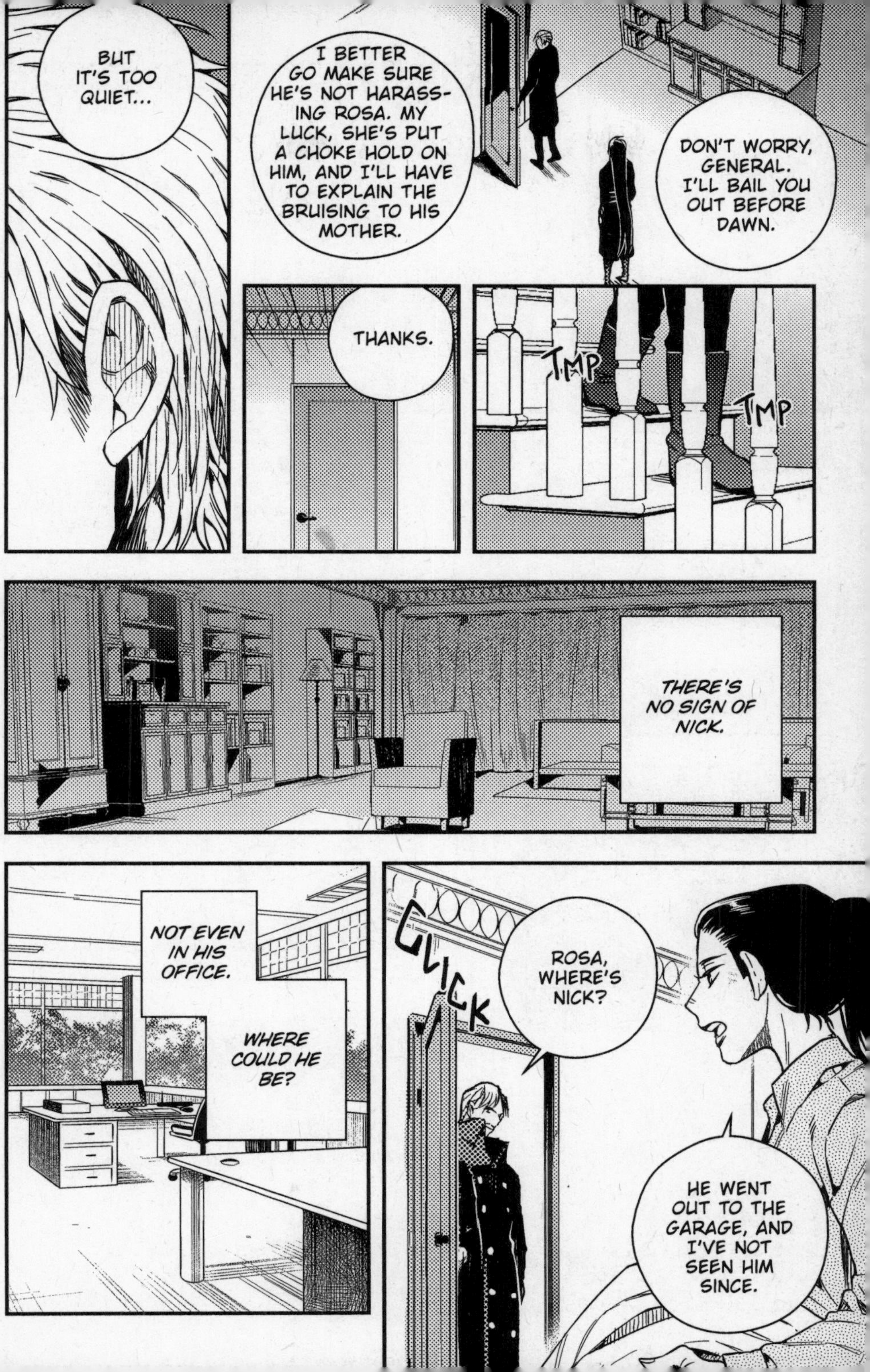

BUT IT'S TOO QUIET...
I BETTER GO MAKE SURE HE'S NOT HARASS-ING ROSA. MY LUCK, SHE'S PUT A CHOKE HOLD ON HIM, AND I'LL HAVE TO EXPLAIN THE BRUISING TO HIS MOTHER.
DON'T WORRY, GENERAL. I'LL BAIL YOU OUT BEFORE DAWN.
THANKS.
TMP
TMP
THERE'S NO SIGN OF NICK.
NOT EVEN IN HIS OFFICE.
WHERE COULD HE BE?
CLICK
ROSA, WHERE'S NICK?
HE WENT OUT TO THE GARAGE, AND I'VE NOT SEEN HIM SINCE.

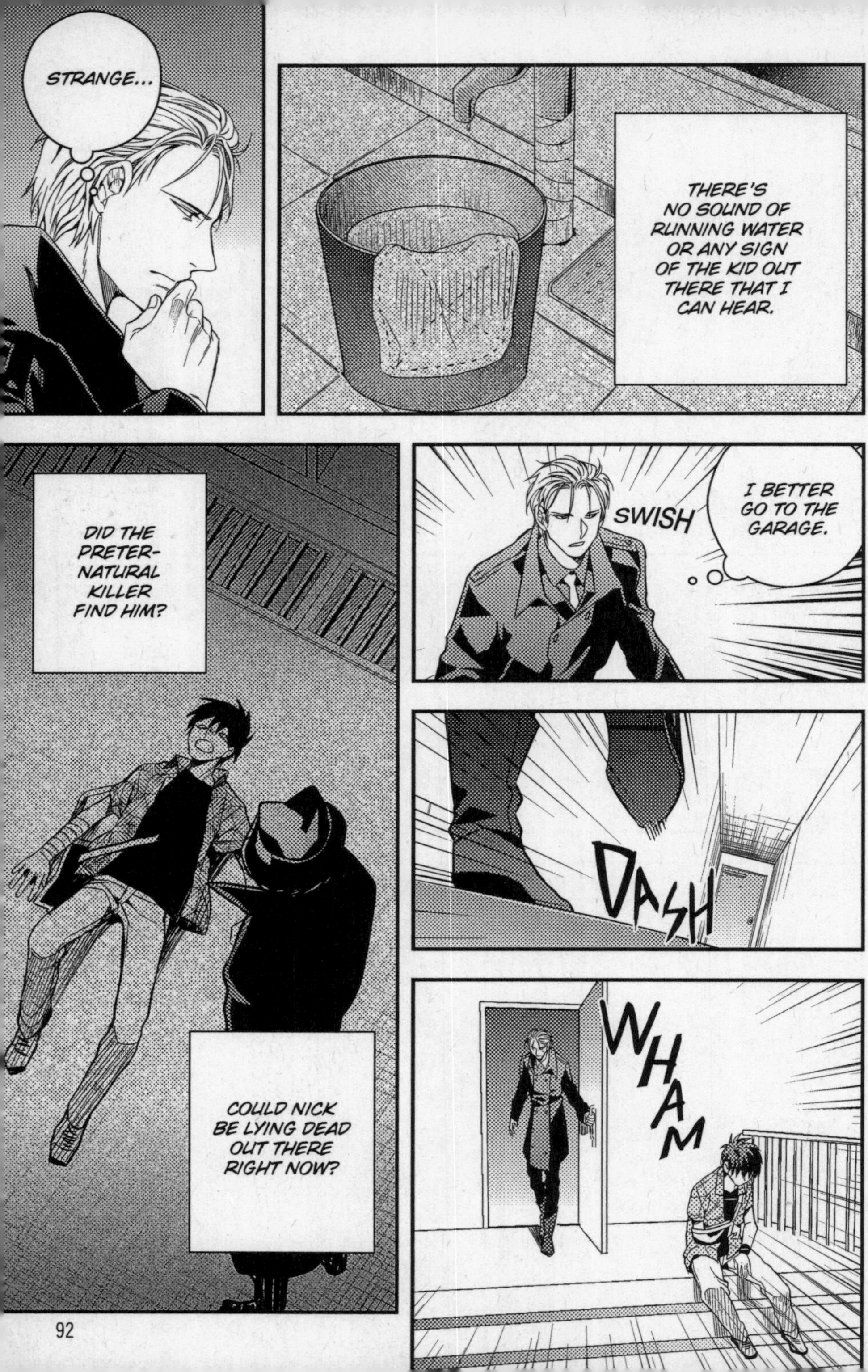
STRANGE...
THERE'S NO SOUND OF RUNNING WATER OR ANY SIGN OF THE KID OUT THERE THAT I CAN HEAR.
DID THE PRETER-NATURAL KILLER FIND HIM?
COULD NICK BE LYING DEAD OUT THERE RIGHT NOW?
SWISH
I BETTER GO TO THE GARAGE.
DASH
WHAM

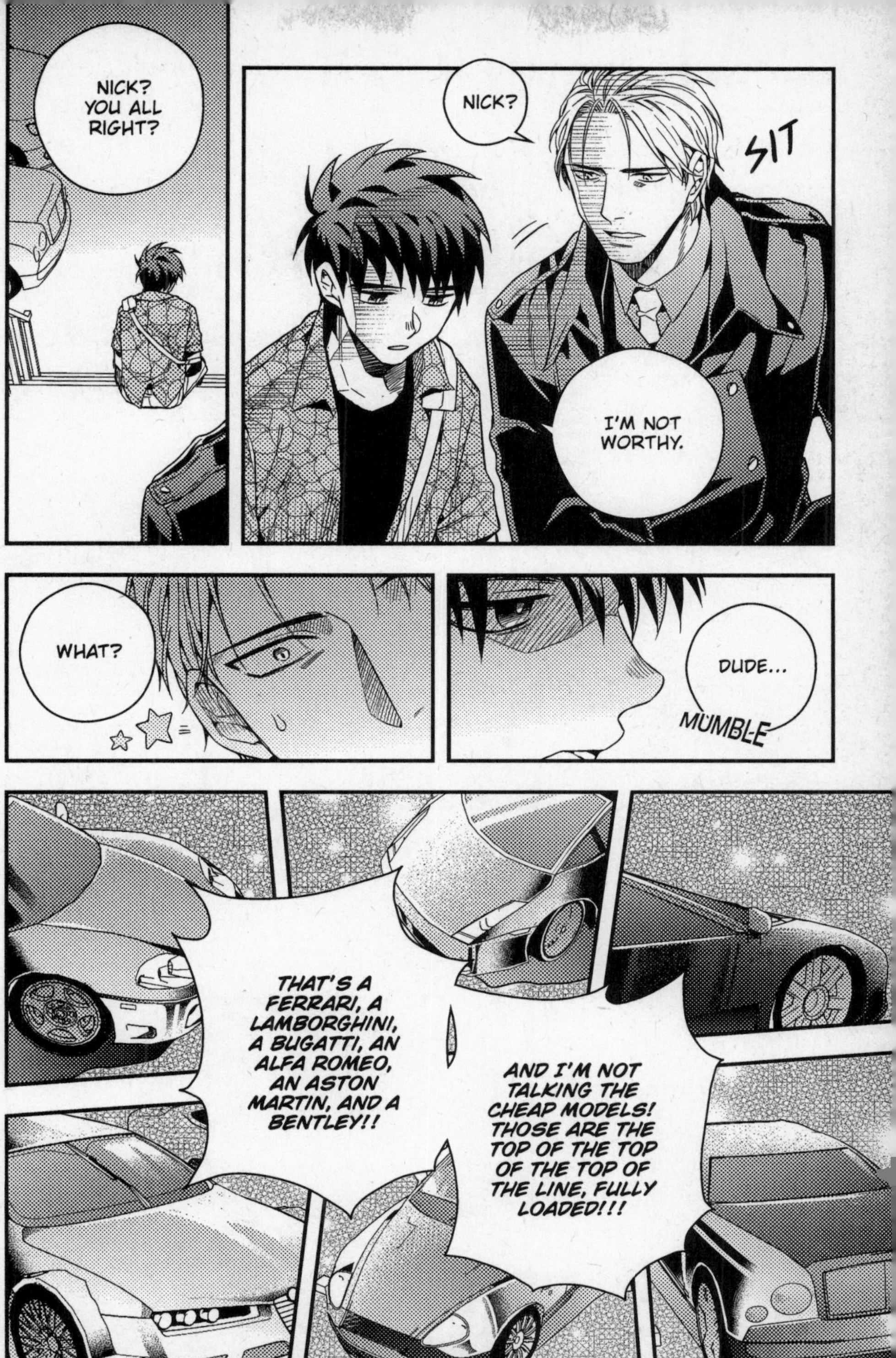
NICK? YOU ALL RIGHT?
NICK?
SIT
I'M NOT WORTHY.
WHAT?
DUDE...
MUMBLE
THAT'S A FERRARI, A LAMBORGHINI, A BUGATTI, AN ALFA ROMEO, AN ASTON MARTIN, AND A BENTLEY!!
AND I'M NOT TALKING THE CHEAP MODELS! THOSE ARE THE TOP OF THE TOP OF THE TOP OF THE LINE, FULLY LOADED!!!

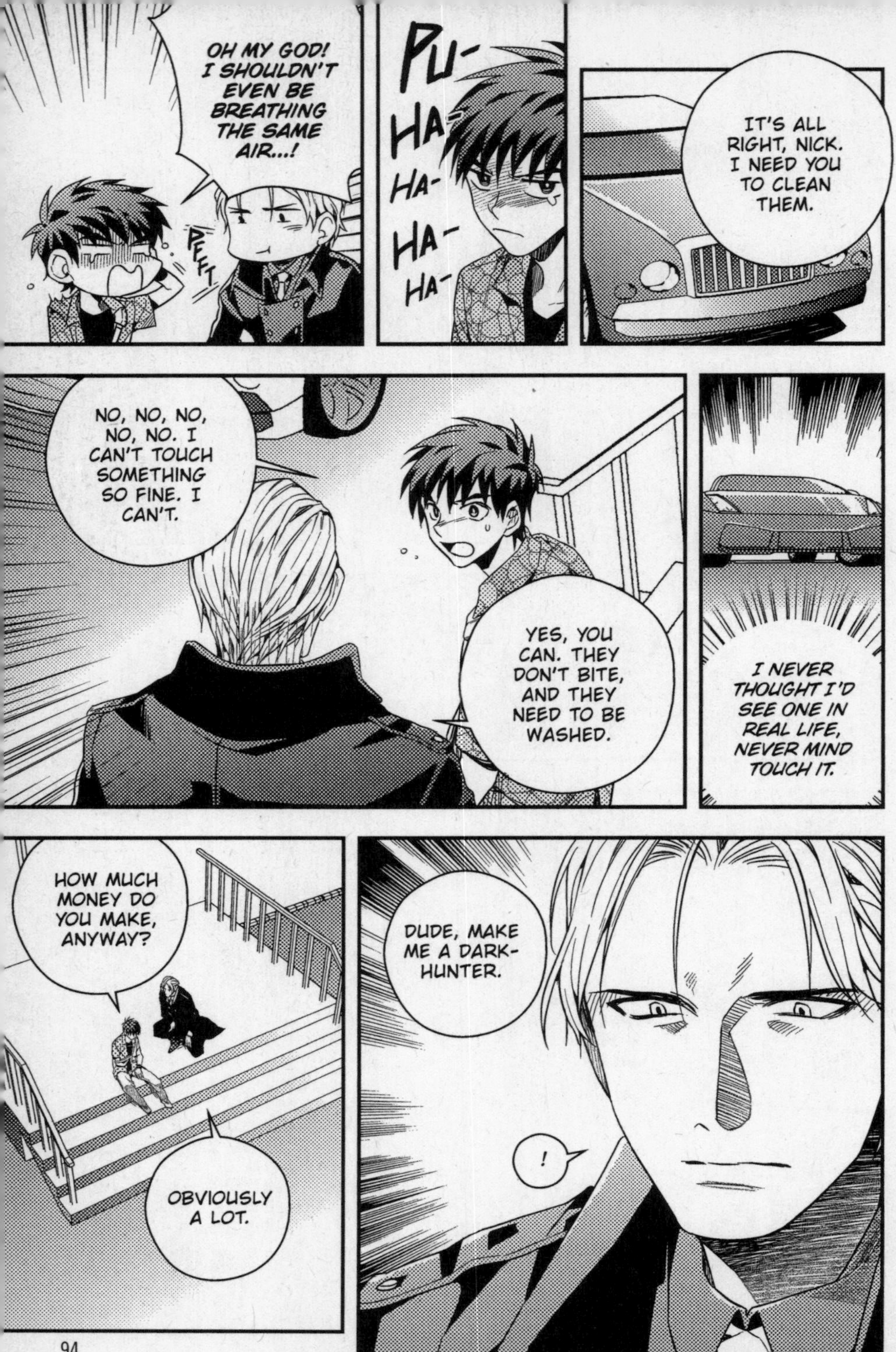
OH MY GOD! I SHOULDN'T EVEN BE BREATHING THE SAME AIR...!
PFFFT
PU-HA-HA-HA-HA-
IT'S ALL RIGHT, NICK. I NEED YOU TO CLEAN THEM.
NO, NO, NO, NO, NO. I CAN'T TOUCH SOMETHING SO FINE. I CAN'T.
YES, YOU CAN. THEY DON'T BITE, AND THEY NEED TO BE WASHED.
I NEVER THOUGHT I'D SEE ONE IN REAL LIFE, NEVER MIND TOUCH IT.
HOW MUCH MONEY DO YOU MAKE, ANYWAY?
OBVIOUSLY A LOT.
DUDE, MAKE ME A DARK-HUNTER.
!

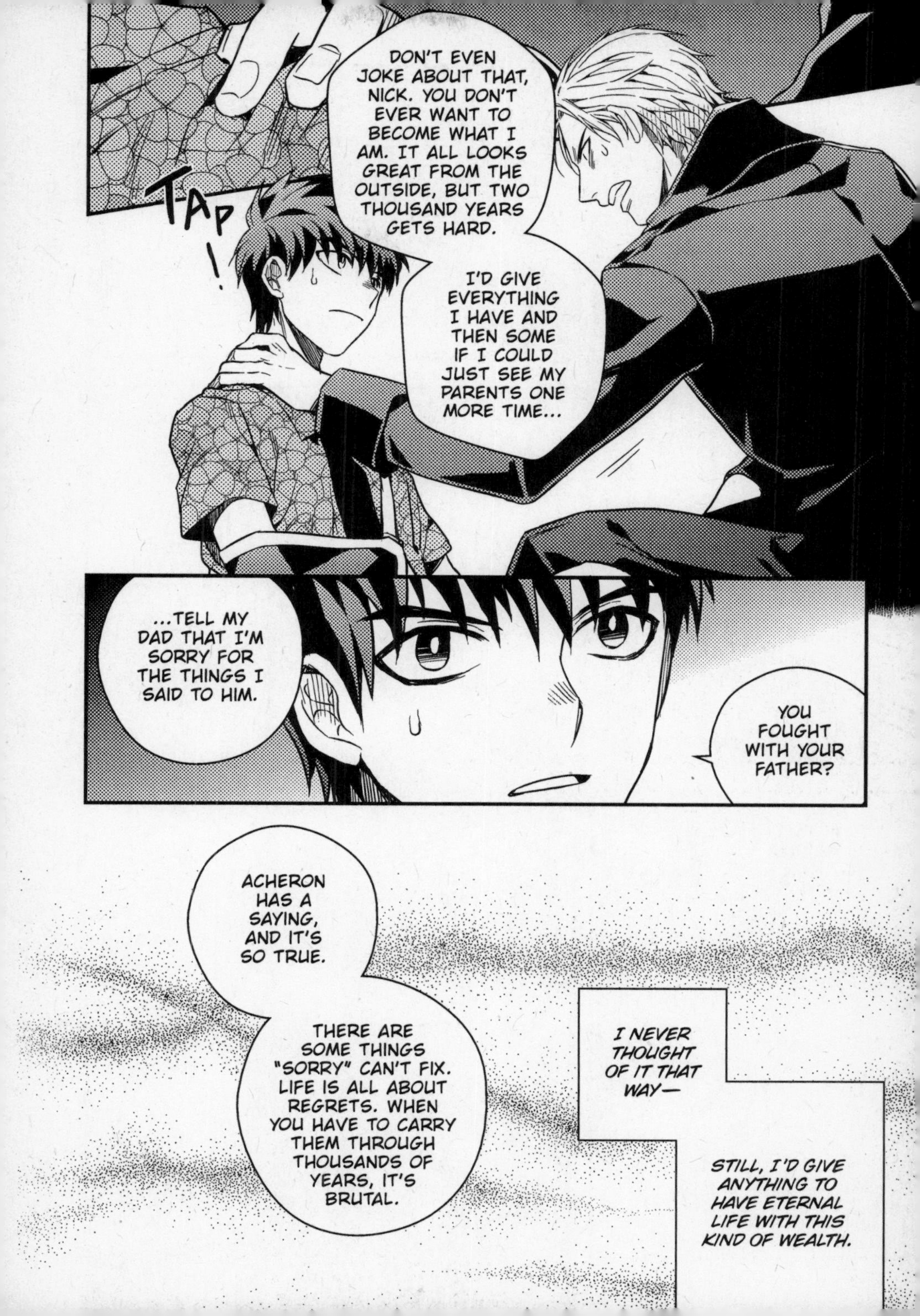

DON'T EVEN JOKE ABOUT THAT, NICK. YOU DON'T EVER WANT TO BECOME WHAT I AM. IT ALL LOOKS GREAT FROM THE OUTSIDE, BUT TWO THOUSAND YEARS GETS HARD.
TAP
!
I'D GIVE EVERYTHING I HAVE AND THEN SOME IF I COULD JUST SEE MY PARENTS ONE MORE TIME...
...TELL MY DAD THAT I'M SORRY FOR THE THINGS I SAID TO HIM.
YOU FOUGHT WITH YOUR FATHER?
ACHERON HAS A SAYING, AND IT'S SO TRUE.
THERE ARE SOME THINGS "SORRY" CAN'T FIX. LIFE IS ALL ABOUT REGRETS. WHEN YOU HAVE TO CARRY THEM THROUGH THOUSANDS OF YEARS, IT'S BRUTAL.
I NEVER THOUGHT OF IT THAT WAY—
STILL, I'D GIVE ANYTHING TO HAVE ETERNAL LIFE WITH THIS KIND OF WEALTH.

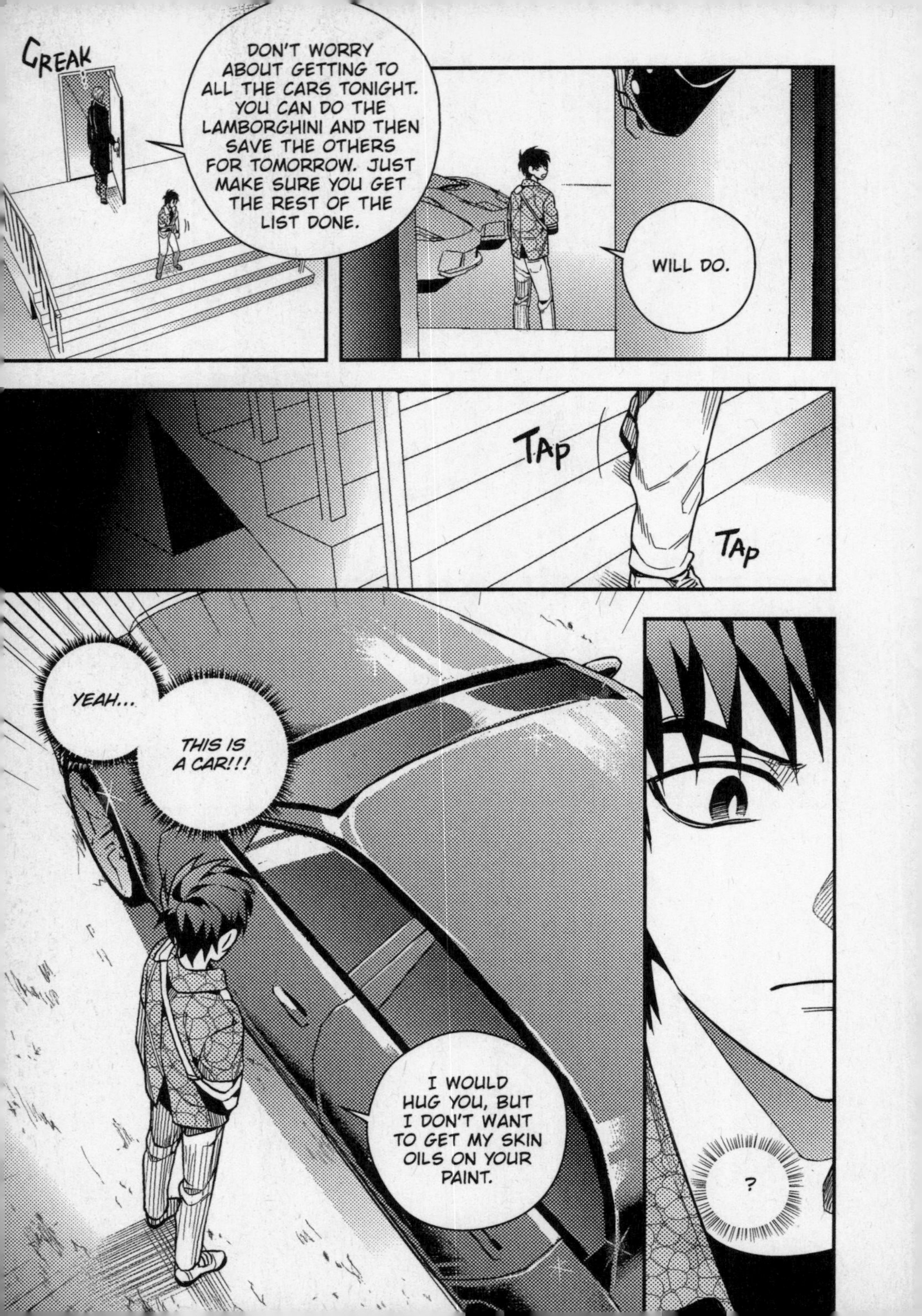
CREAK
DON'T WORRY ABOUT GETTING TO ALL THE CARS TONIGHT. YOU CAN DO THE LAMBORGHINI AND THEN SAVE THE OTHERS FOR TOMORROW. JUST MAKE SURE YOU GET THE REST OF THE LIST DONE.
WILL DO.
TAP
TAP
YEAH...
THIS IS A CAR!!!
I WOULD HUG YOU, BUT I DON'T WANT TO GET MY SKIN OILS ON YOUR PAINT.
?

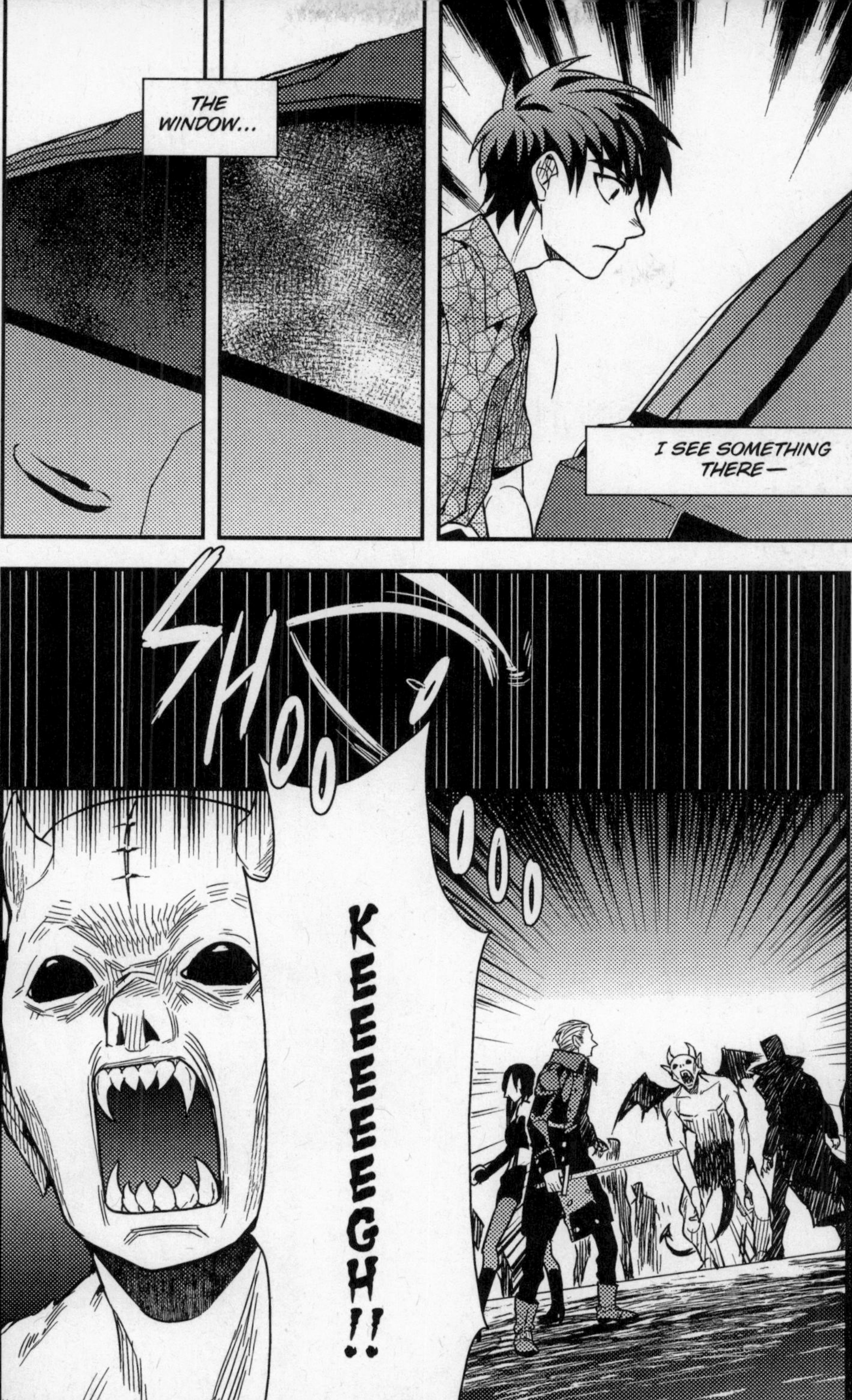
THE WINDOW...
I SEE SOMETHING THERE—
SHOOOOOOOO
KEEEEEEEGH!!

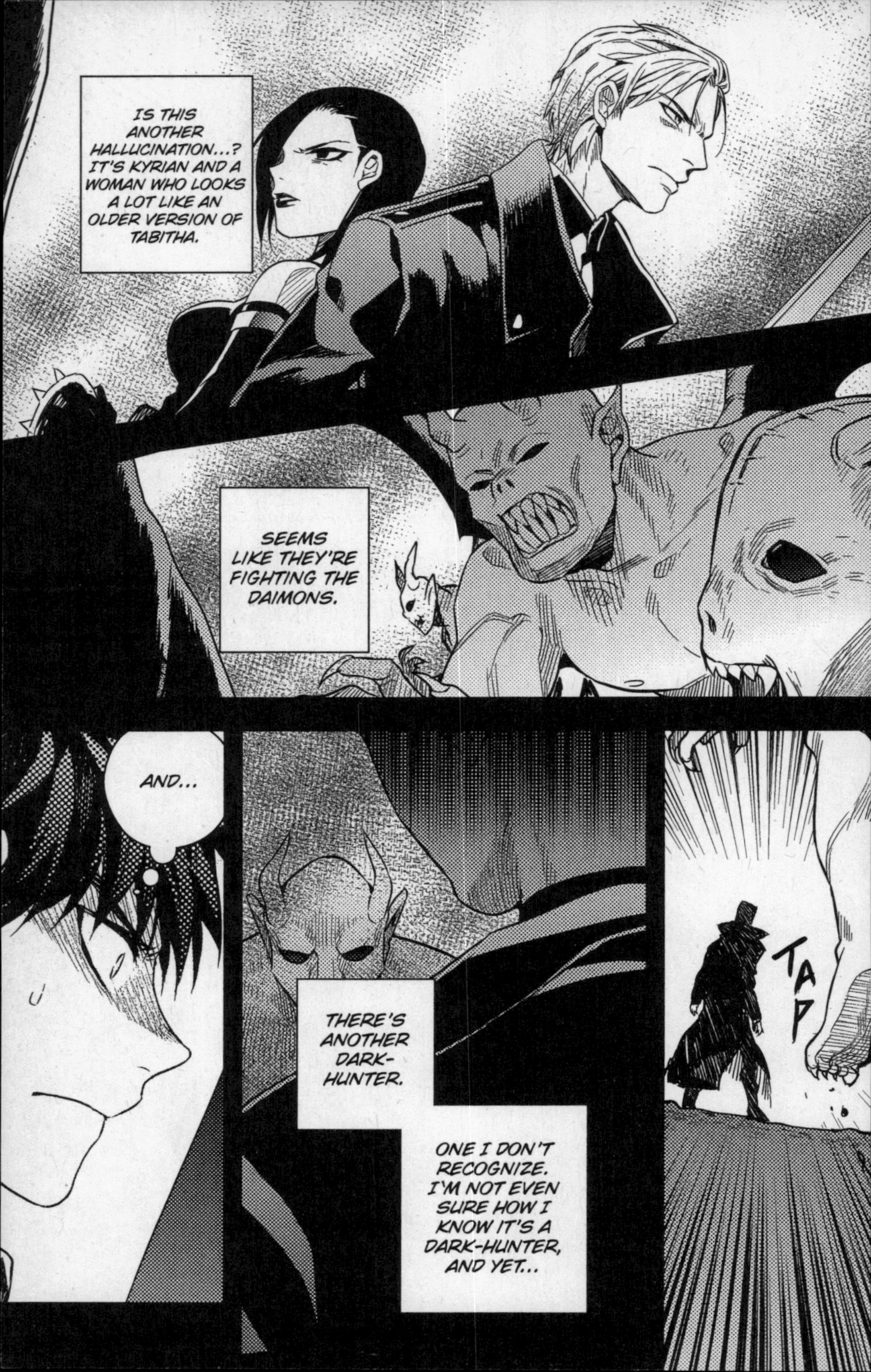
IS THIS ANOTHER HALLUCINATION...? IT'S KYRIAN AND A WOMAN WHO LOOKS A LOT LIKE AN OLDER VERSION OF TABITHA.
SEEMS LIKE THEY'RE FIGHTING THE DAIMONS.
AND...
TAP
TAP
THERE'S ANOTHER DARK-HUNTER.
ONE I DON'T RECOGNIZE. I'M NOT EVEN SURE HOW I KNOW IT'S A DARK-HUNTER, AND YET...

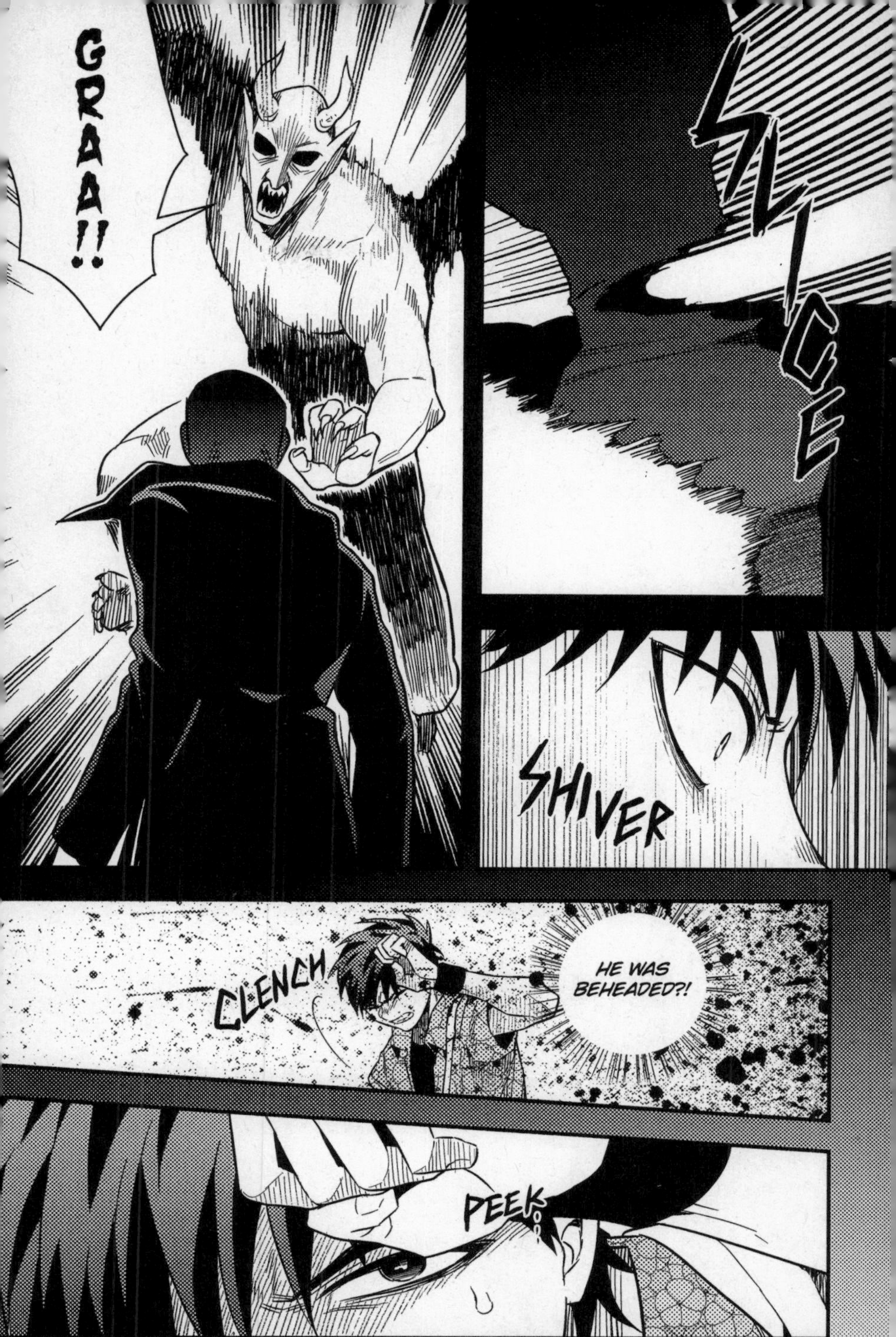
SLICE
GRAA!!
SHIVER
HE WAS BEHEADED?!
CLENCH
PEEK...

IS
THAT...

...ME?!

YOU
SHAP
NEVE
BEW
SIO
NO
SMA
W S
OR

THE DARK-HUNTERS:
INFINITY

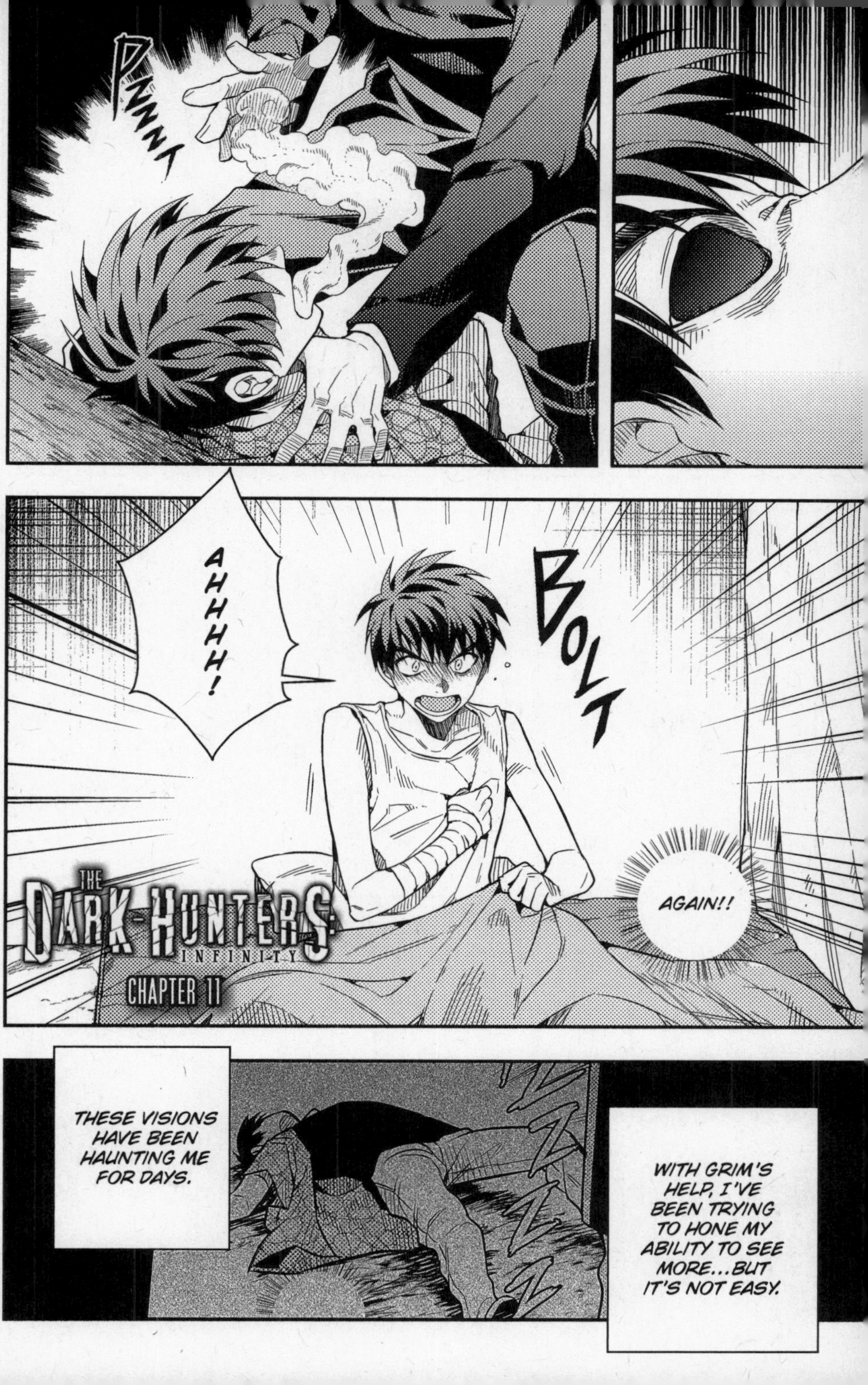
PNNNT
AHHHH!
BOLT
AGAIN!!
THE DARK-HUNTERS: INFINITY
CHAPTER 11
THESE VISIONS HAVE BEEN HAUNTING ME FOR DAYS.
WITH GRIM'S HELP, I'VE BEEN TRYING TO HONE MY ABILITY TO SEE MORE...BUT IT'S NOT EASY.

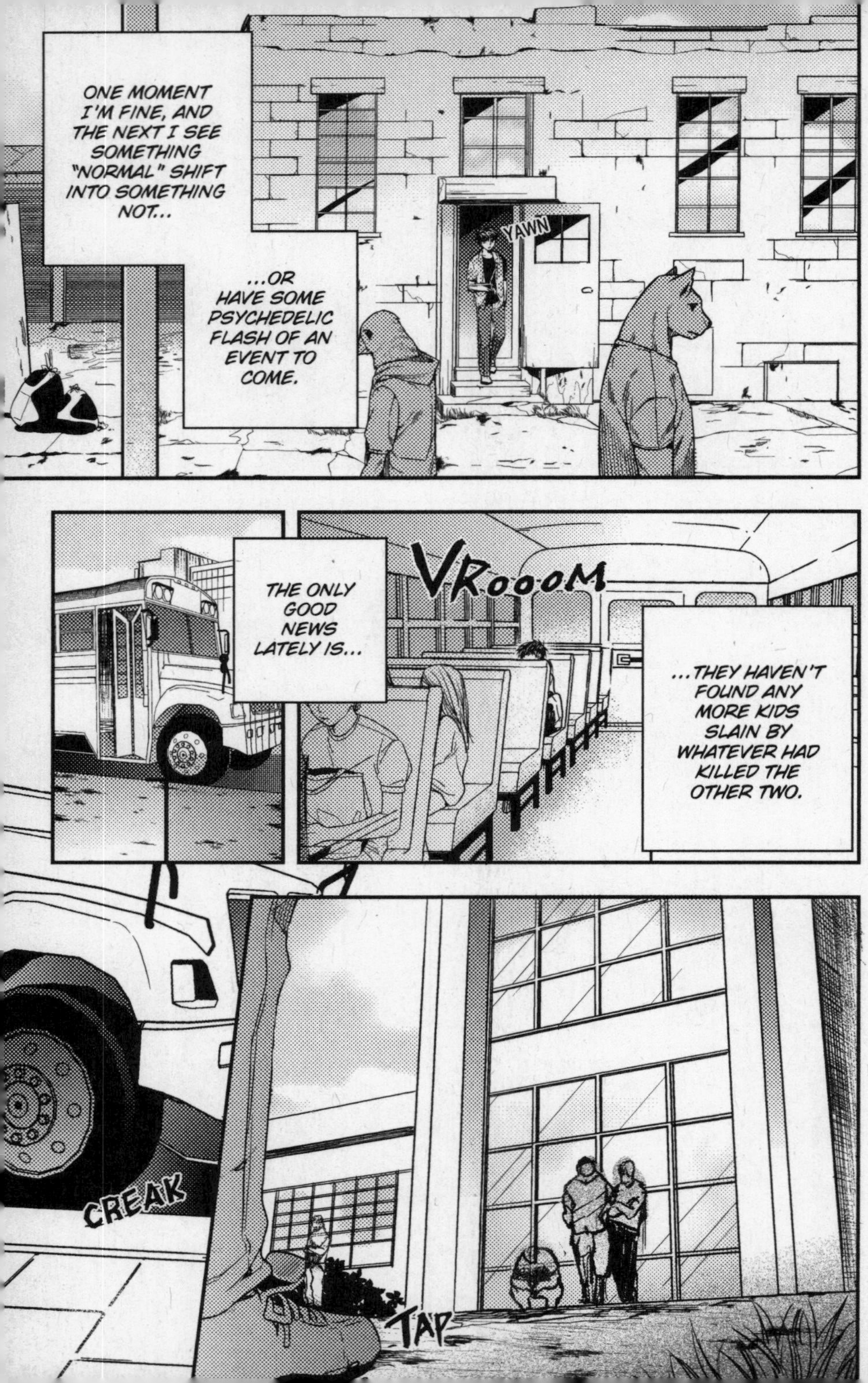
ONE MOMENT I'M FINE, AND THE NEXT I SEE SOMETHING "NORMAL" SHIFT INTO SOMETHING NOT...
YAWN
...OR HAVE SOME PSYCHEDELIC FLASH OF AN EVENT TO COME.
THE ONLY GOOD NEWS LATELY IS...
VROOOM
...THEY HAVEN'T FOUND ANY MORE KIDS SLAIN BY WHATEVER HAD KILLED THE OTHER TWO.
CREAK
TAP

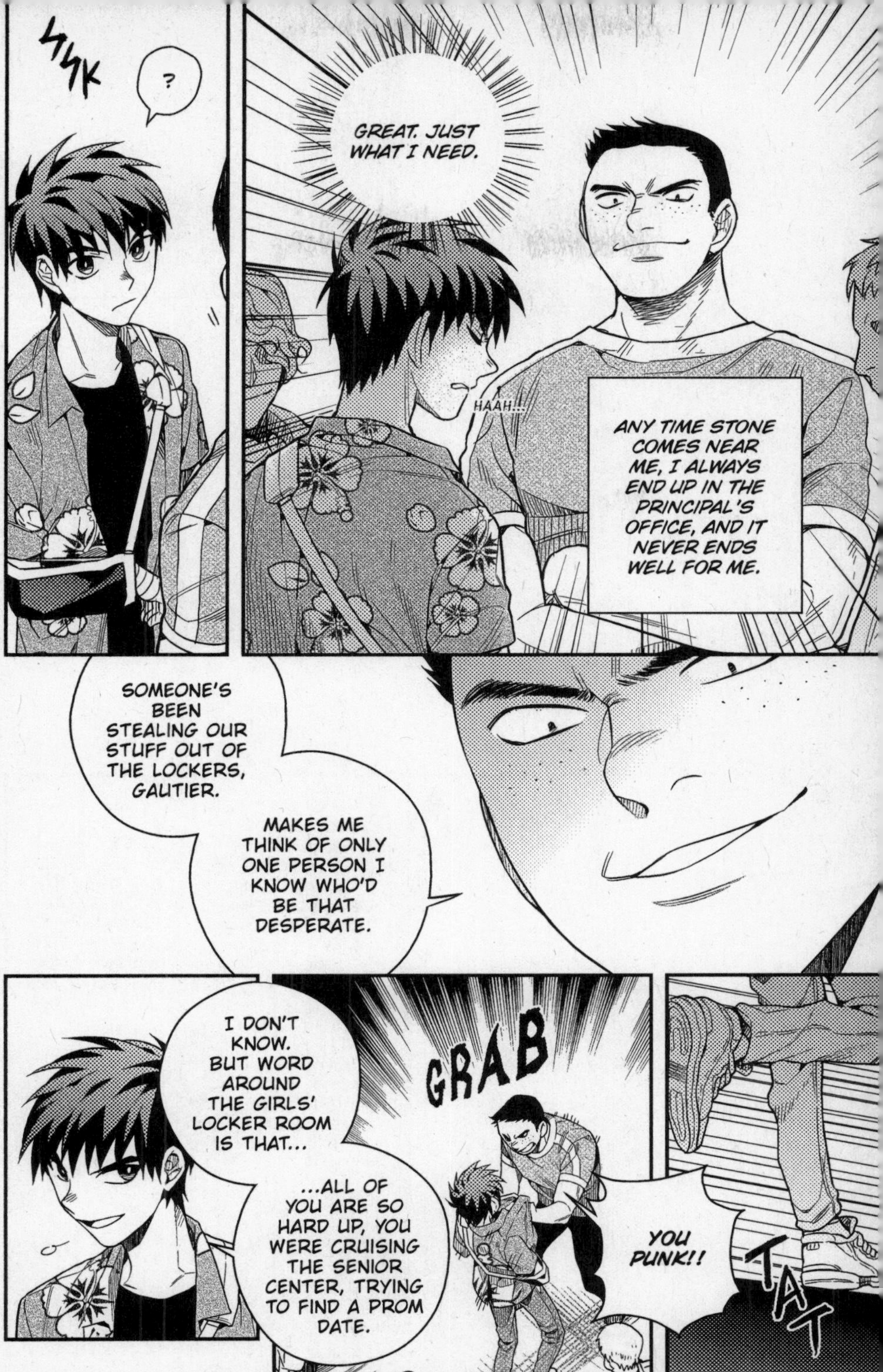
SNIK
?
GREAT. JUST WHAT I NEED.
HAAH...
ANY TIME STONE COMES NEAR ME, I ALWAYS END UP IN THE PRINCIPAL'S OFFICE, AND IT NEVER ENDS WELL FOR ME.
SOMEONE'S BEEN STEALING OUR STUFF OUT OF THE LOCKERS, GAUTIER.
MAKES ME THINK OF ONLY ONE PERSON I KNOW WHO'D BE THAT DESPERATE.
I DON'T KNOW. BUT WORD AROUND THE GIRLS' LOCKER ROOM IS THAT...
...ALL OF YOU ARE SO HARD UP, YOU WERE CRUISING THE SENIOR CENTER, TRYING TO FIND A PROM DATE.
GRAB
YOU PUNK!!
TAT

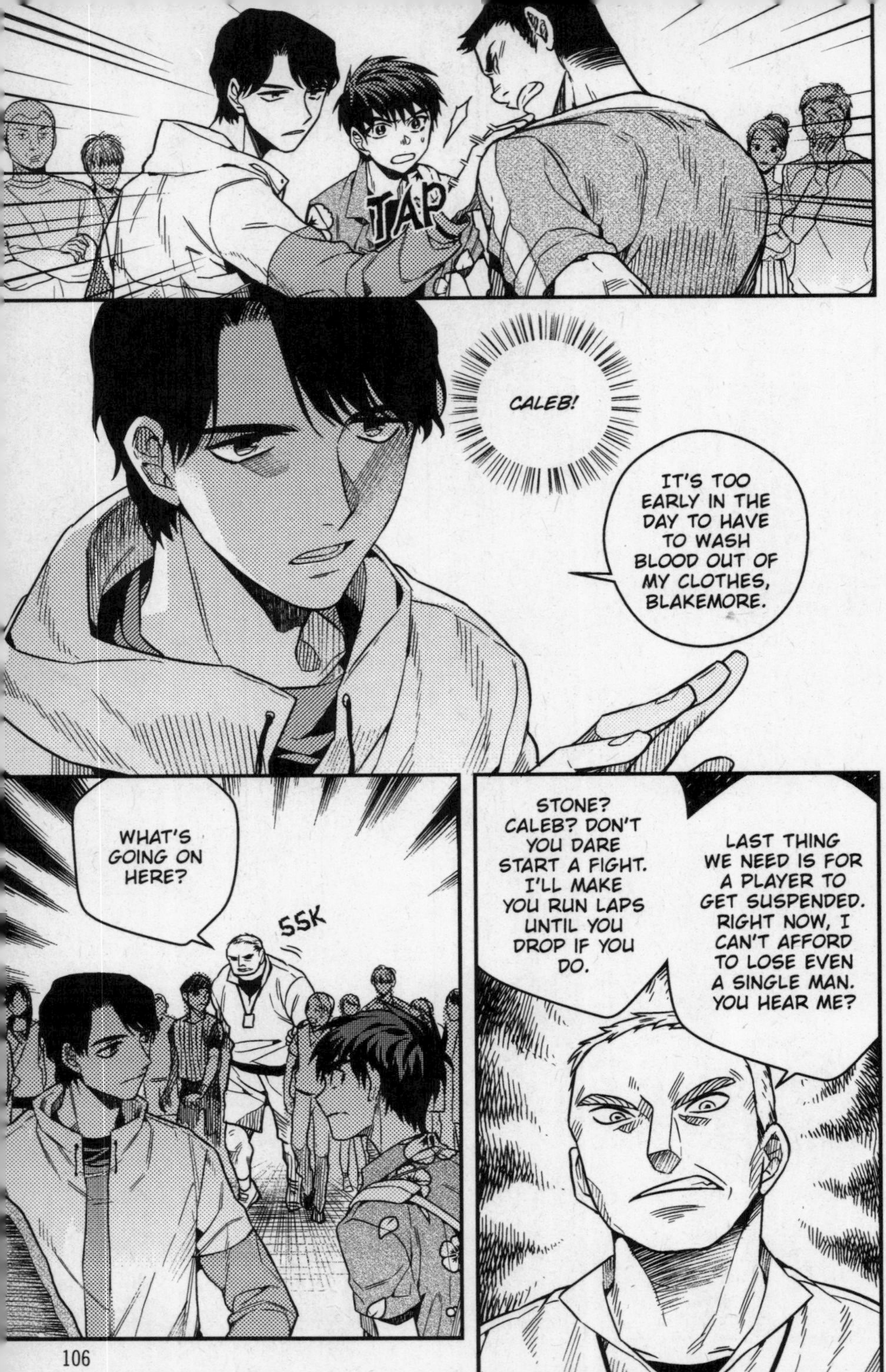
TAP
CALEB!
IT'S TOO EARLY IN THE DAY TO HAVE TO WASH BLOOD OUT OF MY CLOTHES, BLAKEMORE.
WHAT'S GOING ON HERE?
SSK
STONE? CALEB? DON'T YOU DARE START A FIGHT. I'LL MAKE YOU RUN LAPS UNTIL YOU DROP IF YOU DO.
LAST THING WE NEED IS FOR A PLAYER TO GET SUSPENDED. RIGHT NOW, I CAN'T AFFORD TO LOSE EVEN A SINGLE MAN. YOU HEAR ME?

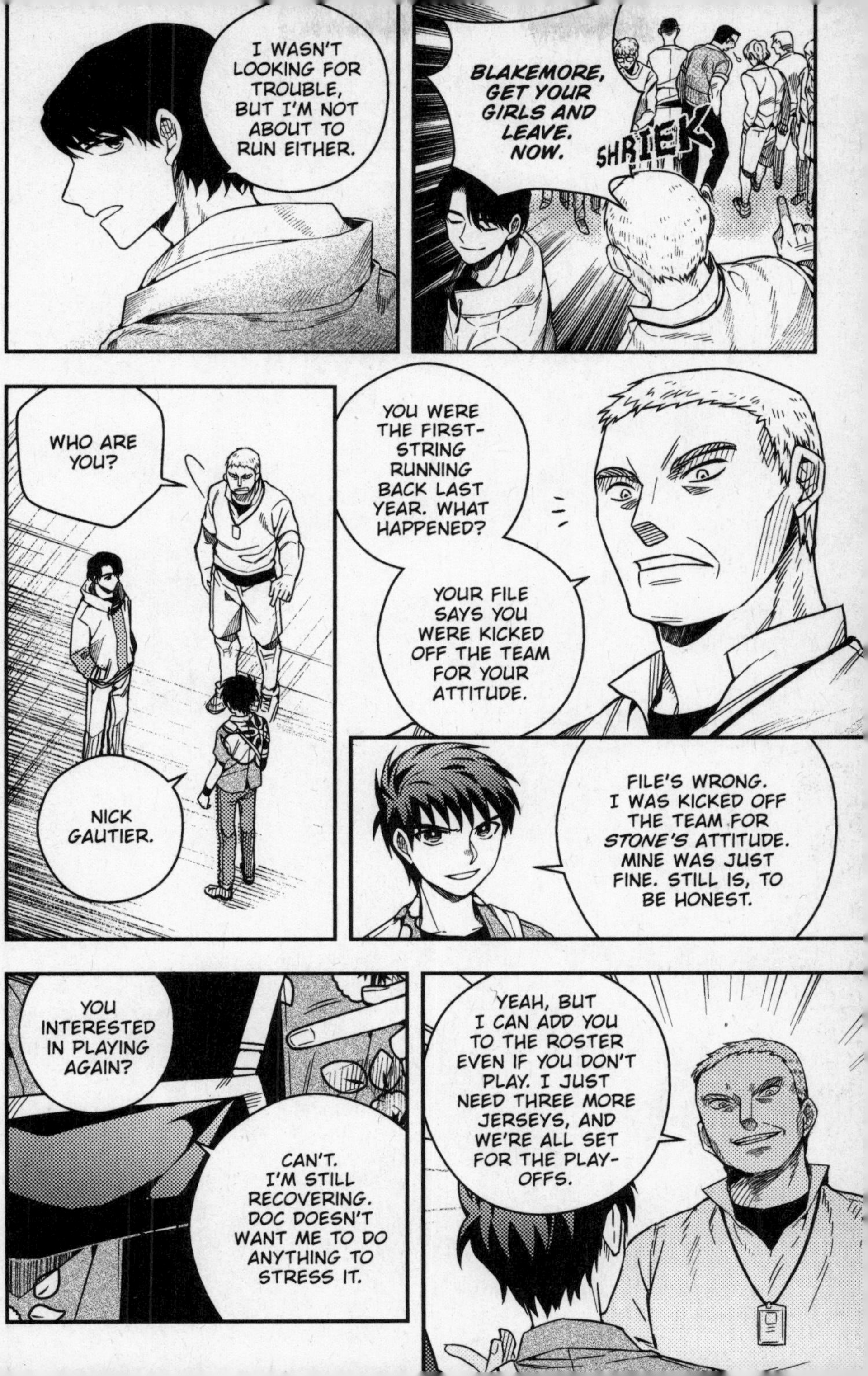
I WASN'T LOOKING FOR TROUBLE, BUT I'M NOT ABOUT TO RUN EITHER.
BLAKEMORE, GET YOUR GIRLS AND LEAVE. NOW.
SHRIEK
WHO ARE YOU?
NICK GAUTIER.
YOU WERE THE FIRST-STRING RUNNING BACK LAST YEAR. WHAT HAPPENED?
YOUR FILE SAYS YOU WERE KICKED OFF THE TEAM FOR YOUR ATTITUDE.
FILE'S WRONG. I WAS KICKED OFF THE TEAM FOR STONE'S ATTITUDE. MINE WAS JUST FINE. STILL IS, TO BE HONEST.
YOU INTERESTED IN PLAYING AGAIN?
CAN'T. I'M STILL RECOVERING. DOC DOESN'T WANT ME TO DO ANYTHING TO STRESS IT.
YEAH, BUT I CAN ADD YOU TO THE ROSTER EVEN IF YOU DON'T PLAY. I JUST NEED THREE MORE JERSEYS, AND WE'RE ALL SET FOR THE PLAY-OFFS.

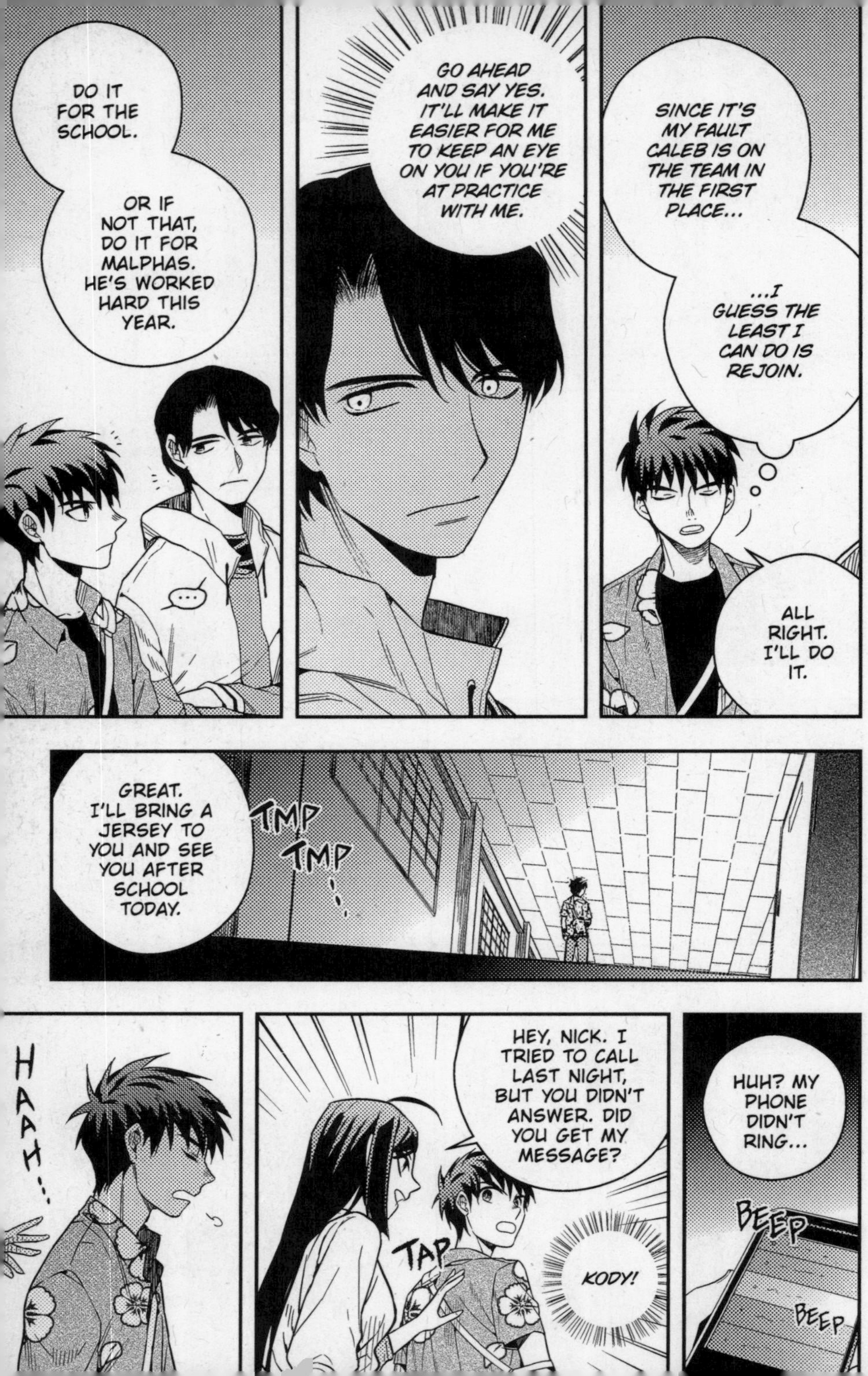
DO IT FOR THE SCHOOL.
OR IF NOT THAT, DO IT FOR MALPHAS. HE'S WORKED HARD THIS YEAR.
...
GO AHEAD AND SAY YES. IT'LL MAKE IT EASIER FOR ME TO KEEP AN EYE ON YOU IF YOU'RE AT PRACTICE WITH ME.
SINCE IT'S MY FAULT CALEB IS ON THE TEAM IN THE FIRST PLACE...
...I GUESS THE LEAST I CAN DO IS REJOIN.
ALL RIGHT. I'LL DO IT.
GREAT. I'LL BRING A JERSEY TO YOU AND SEE YOU AFTER SCHOOL TODAY.
TMP TMP
HAAH...
HEY, NICK. I TRIED TO CALL LAST NIGHT, BUT YOU DIDN'T ANSWER. DID YOU GET MY MESSAGE?
TAP
KODY!
HUH? MY PHONE DIDN'T RING...
BEEP
BEEP

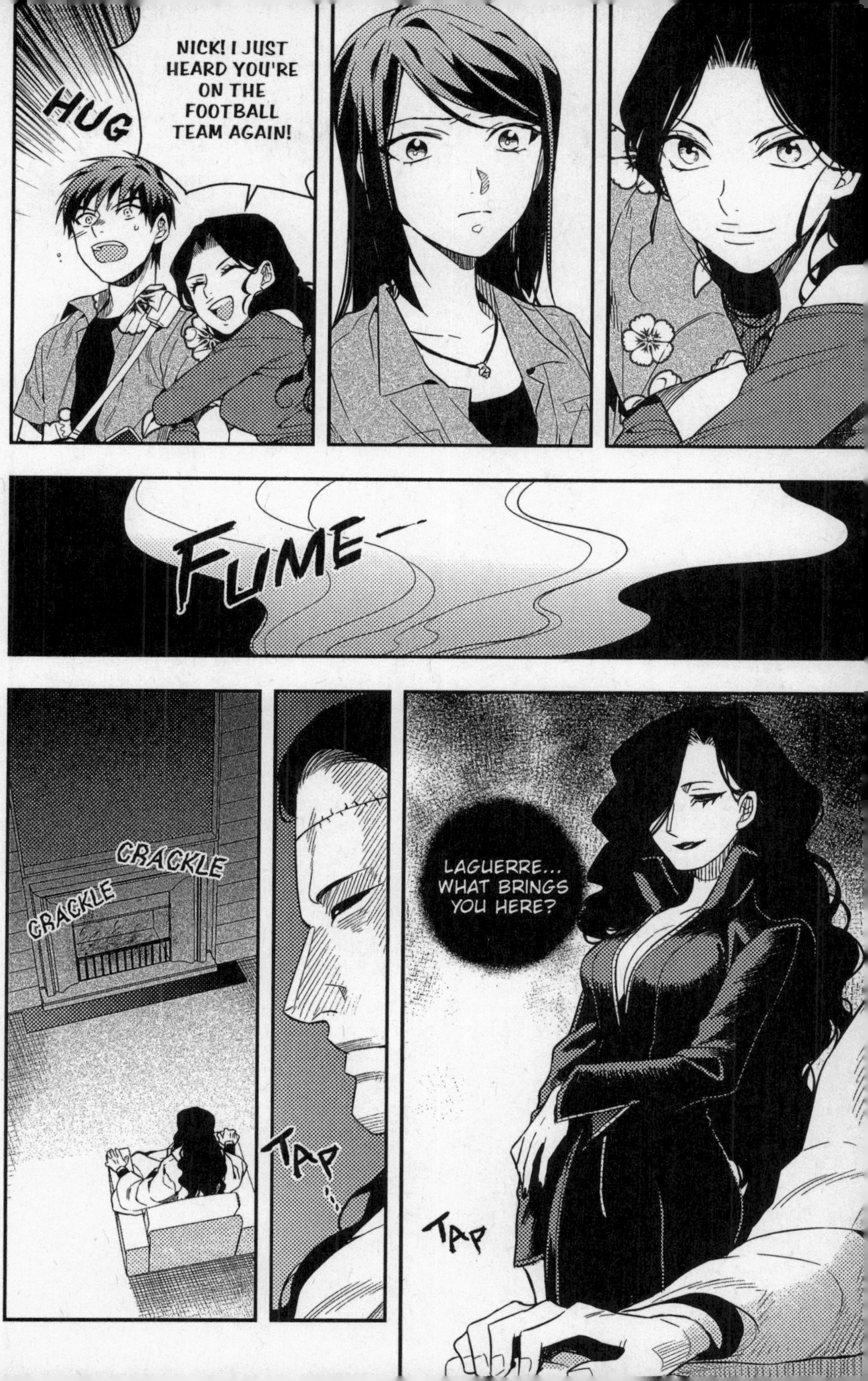
HUG
NICK! I JUST HEARD YOU'RE ON THE FOOTBALL TEAM AGAIN!
FUME
CRACKLE
CRACKLE
TAP
TAP
LAGUERRE... WHAT BRINGS YOU HERE?

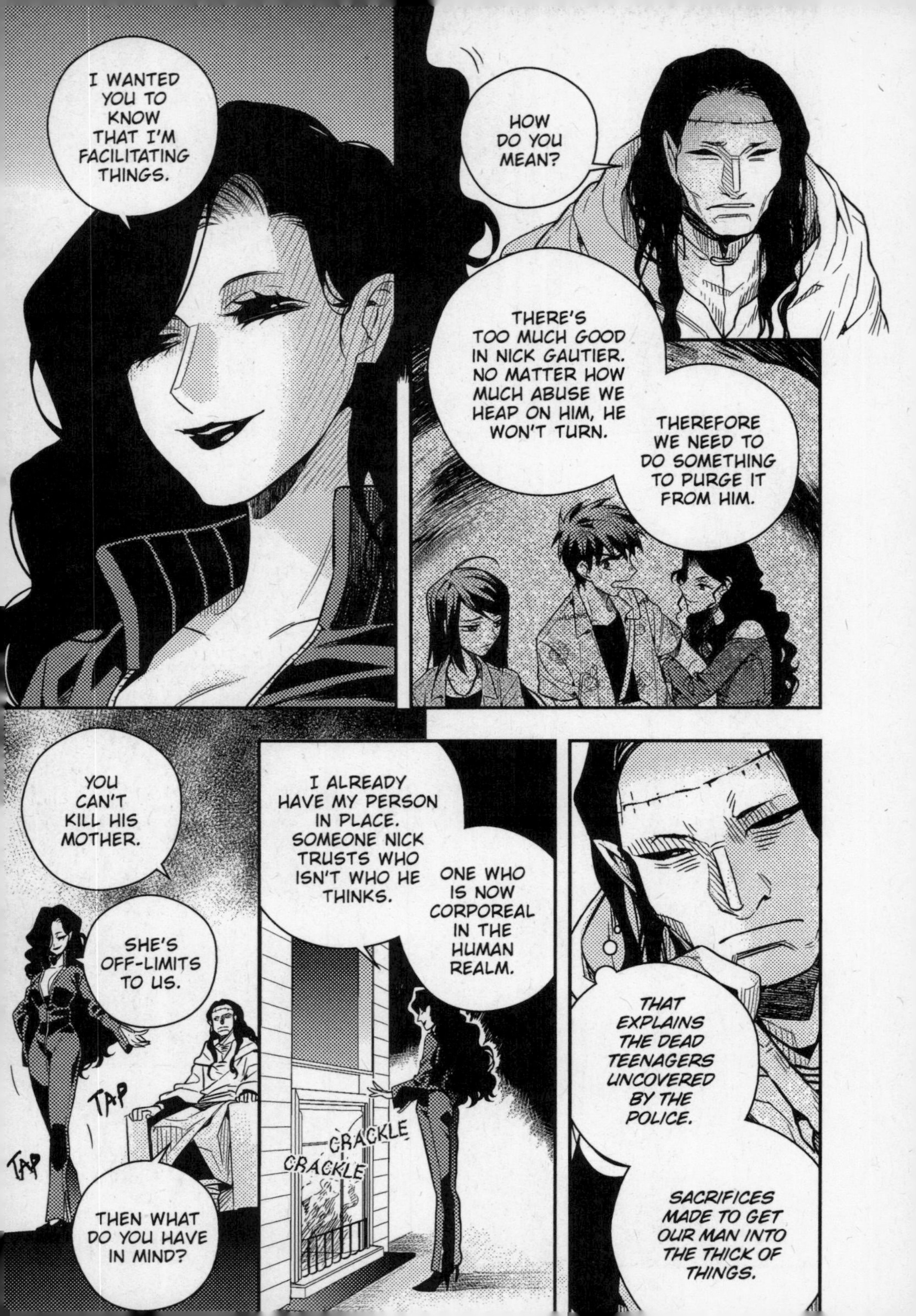
I WANTED YOU TO KNOW THAT I'M FACILITATING THINGS.
HOW DO YOU MEAN?
THERE'S TOO MUCH GOOD IN NICK GAUTIER. NO MATTER HOW MUCH ABUSE WE HEAP ON HIM, HE WON'T TURN.
THEREFORE WE NEED TO DO SOMETHING TO PURGE IT FROM HIM.
YOU CAN'T KILL HIS MOTHER.
SHE'S OFF-LIMITS TO US.
TAP
TAP
THEN WHAT DO YOU HAVE IN MIND?
I ALREADY HAVE MY PERSON IN PLACE. SOMEONE NICK TRUSTS WHO ISN'T WHO HE THINKS.
ONE WHO IS NOW CORPOREAL IN THE HUMAN REALM.
CRACKLE
CRACKLE
THAT EXPLAINS THE DEAD TEENAGERS UNCOVERED BY THE POLICE.
SACRIFICES MADE TO GET OUR MAN INTO THE THICK OF THINGS.

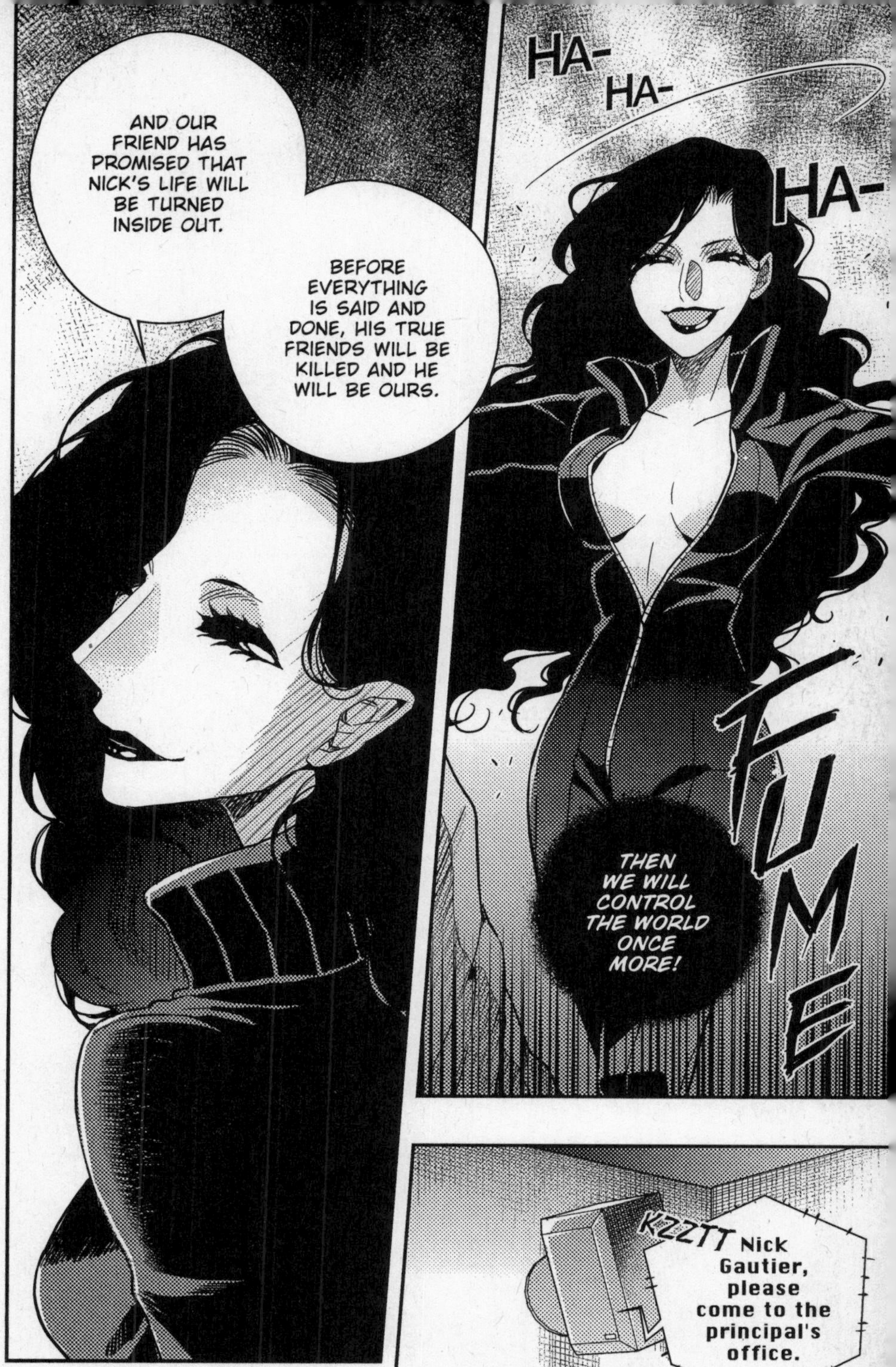
AND OUR FRIEND HAS PROMISED THAT NICK'S LIFE WILL BE TURNED INSIDE OUT.
BEFORE EVERYTHING IS SAID AND DONE, HIS TRUE FRIENDS WILL BE KILLED AND HE WILL BE OURS.
HA-
HA-
HA-
THEN WE WILL CONTROL THE WORLD ONCE MORE!
FUME
KZZTT
Nick Gautier, please come to the principal's office.

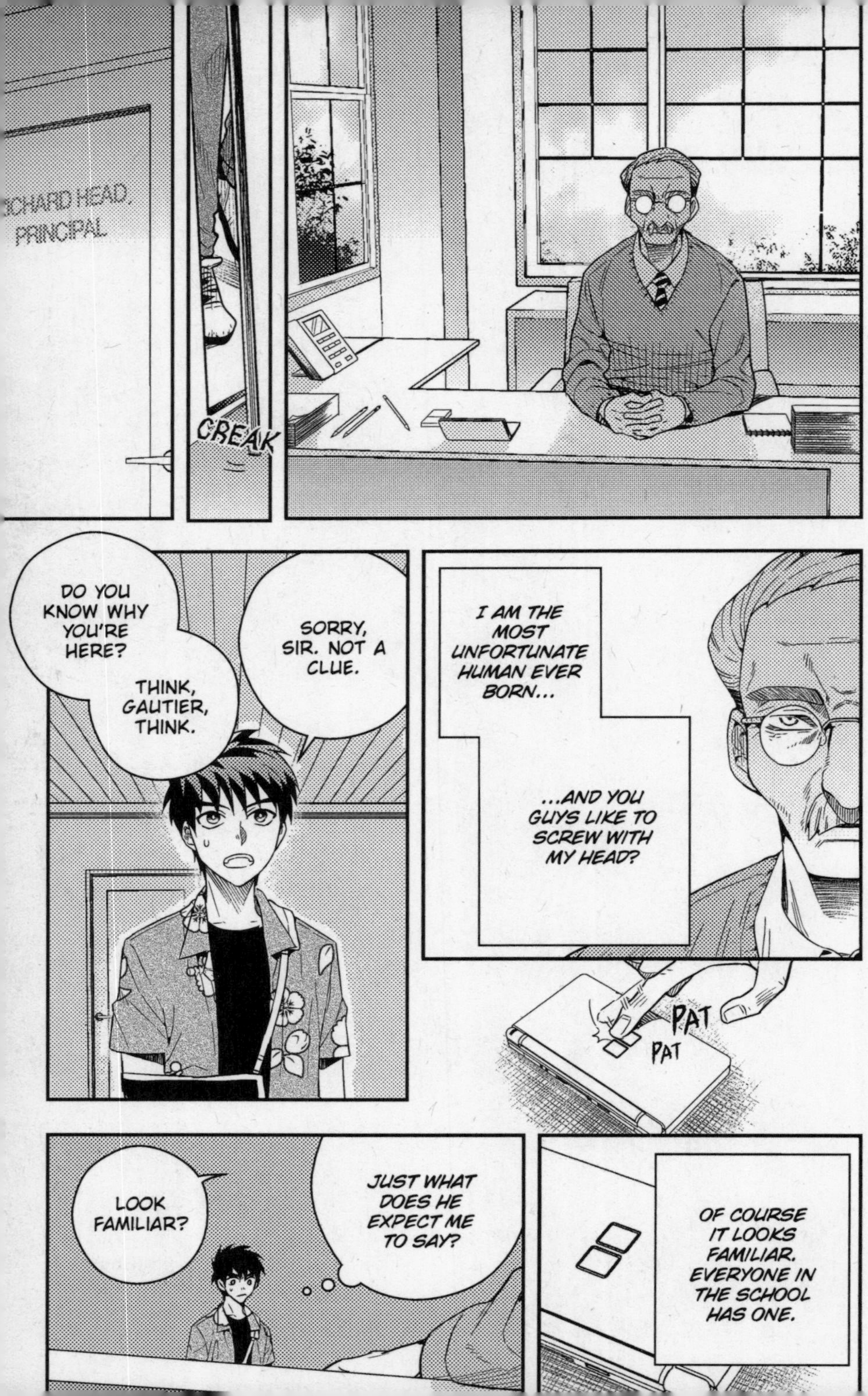

ICHARD HEAD,
PRINCIPAL
CREAK
DO YOU KNOW WHY YOU'RE HERE?
THINK, GAUTIER, THINK.
SORRY, SIR. NOT A CLUE.
I AM THE MOST UNFORTUNATE HUMAN EVER BORN...
...AND YOU GUYS LIKE TO SCREW WITH MY HEAD?
PAT
PAT
LOOK FAMILIAR?
JUST WHAT DOES HE EXPECT ME TO SAY?
OF COURSE IT LOOKS FAMILIAR. EVERYONE IN THE SCHOOL HAS ONE.

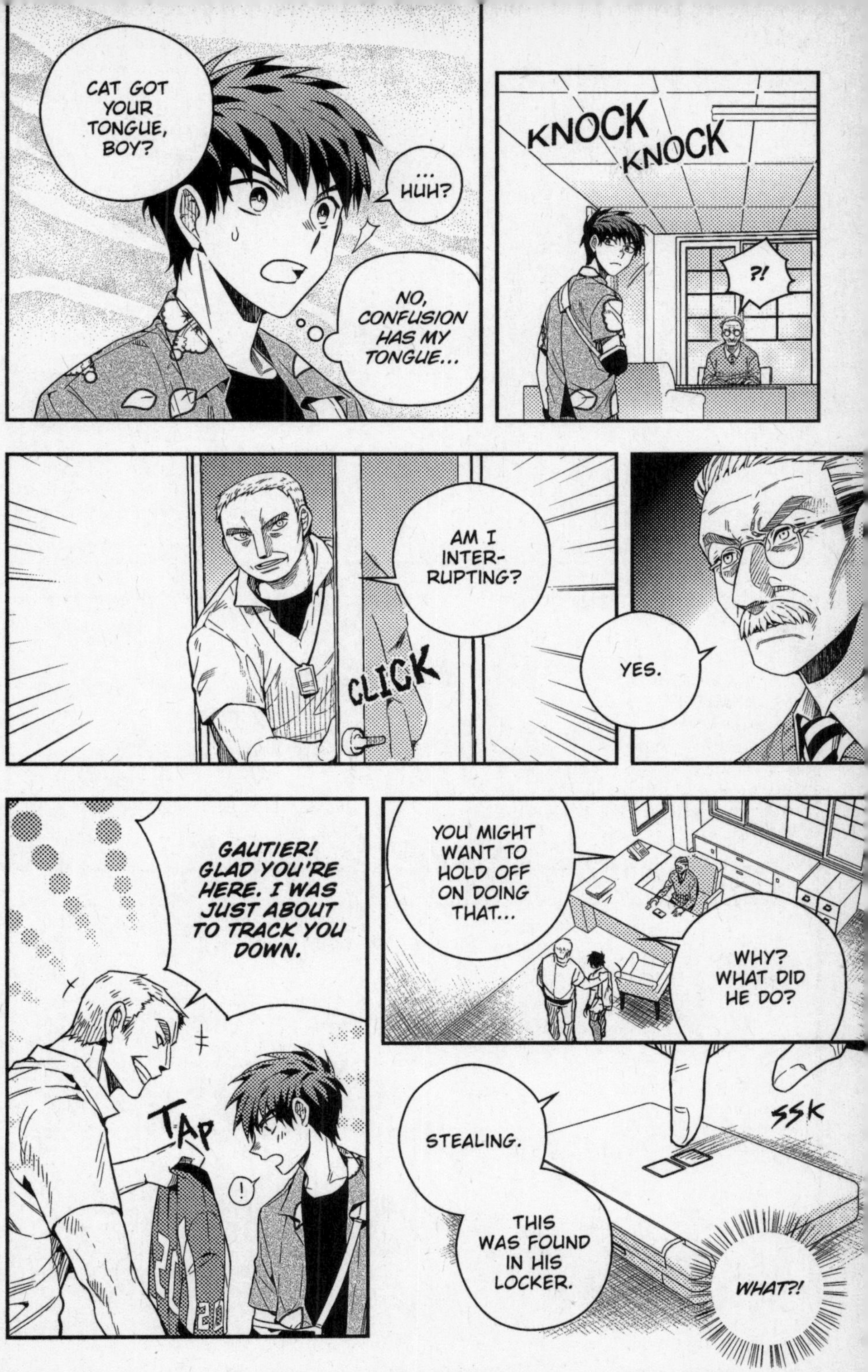
CAT GOT YOUR TONGUE, BOY?
... HUH?
NO, CONFUSION HAS MY TONGUE...
KNOCK KNOCK
?!
AM I INTER-RUPTING?
CLICK
YES.
GAUTIER! GLAD YOU'RE HERE. I WAS JUST ABOUT TO TRACK YOU DOWN.
TAP
!
YOU MIGHT WANT TO HOLD OFF ON DOING THAT...
WHY? WHAT DID HE DO?
STEALING.
SSK
THIS WAS FOUND IN HIS LOCKER.
WHAT?!

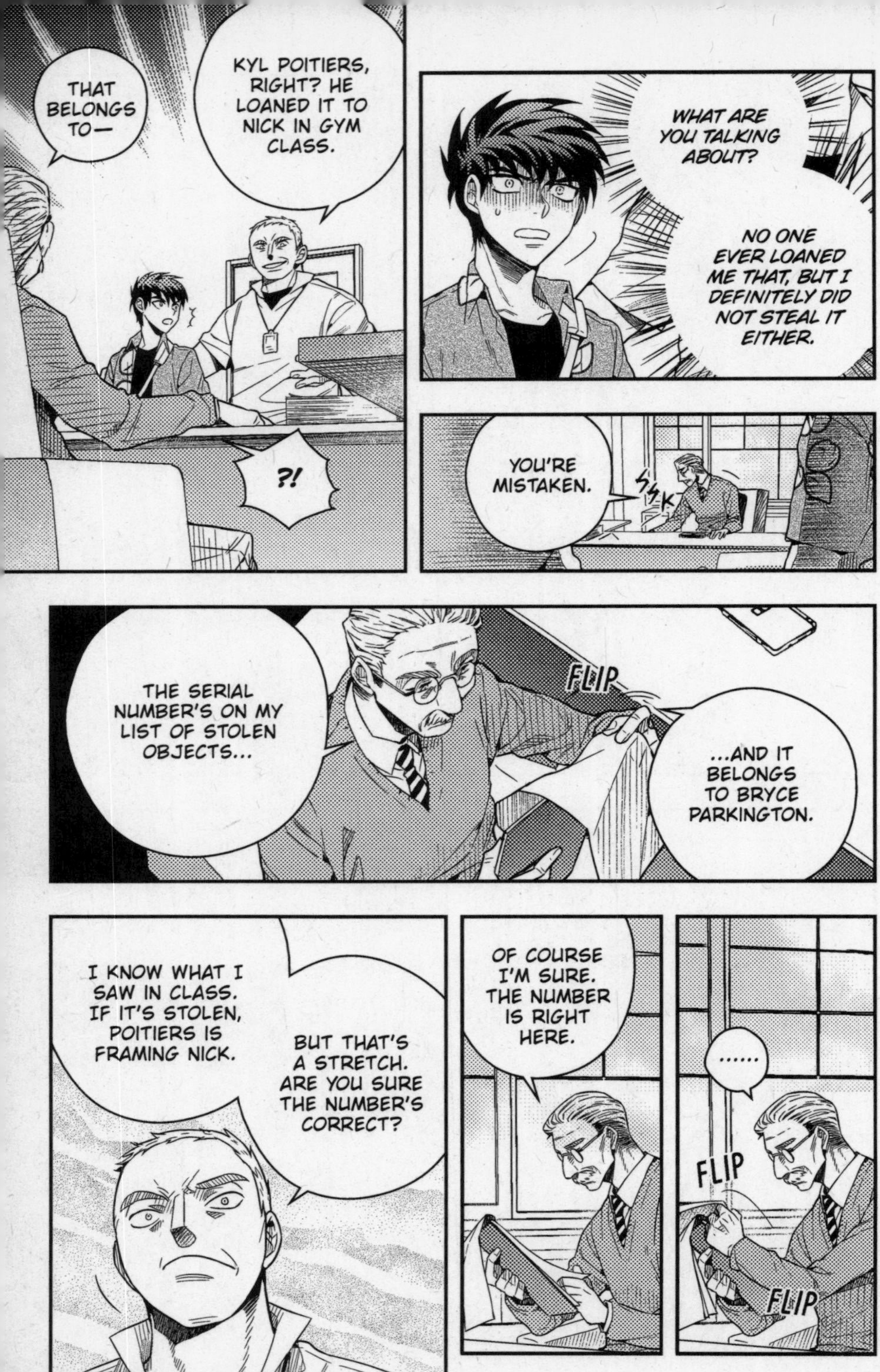
THAT BELONGS TO—
KYL POITIERS, RIGHT? HE LOANED IT TO NICK IN GYM CLASS.
?!
WHAT ARE YOU TALKING ABOUT?
NO ONE EVER LOANED ME THAT, BUT I DEFINITELY DID NOT STEAL IT EITHER.
YOU'RE MISTAKEN.
SHK
THE SERIAL NUMBER'S ON MY LIST OF STOLEN OBJECTS...
FLIP
...AND IT BELONGS TO BRYCE PARKINGTON.
I KNOW WHAT I SAW IN CLASS. IF IT'S STOLEN, POITIERS IS FRAMING NICK.
BUT THAT'S A STRETCH. ARE YOU SURE THE NUMBER'S CORRECT?
OF COURSE I'M SURE. THE NUMBER IS RIGHT HERE.
......
FLIP
FLIP

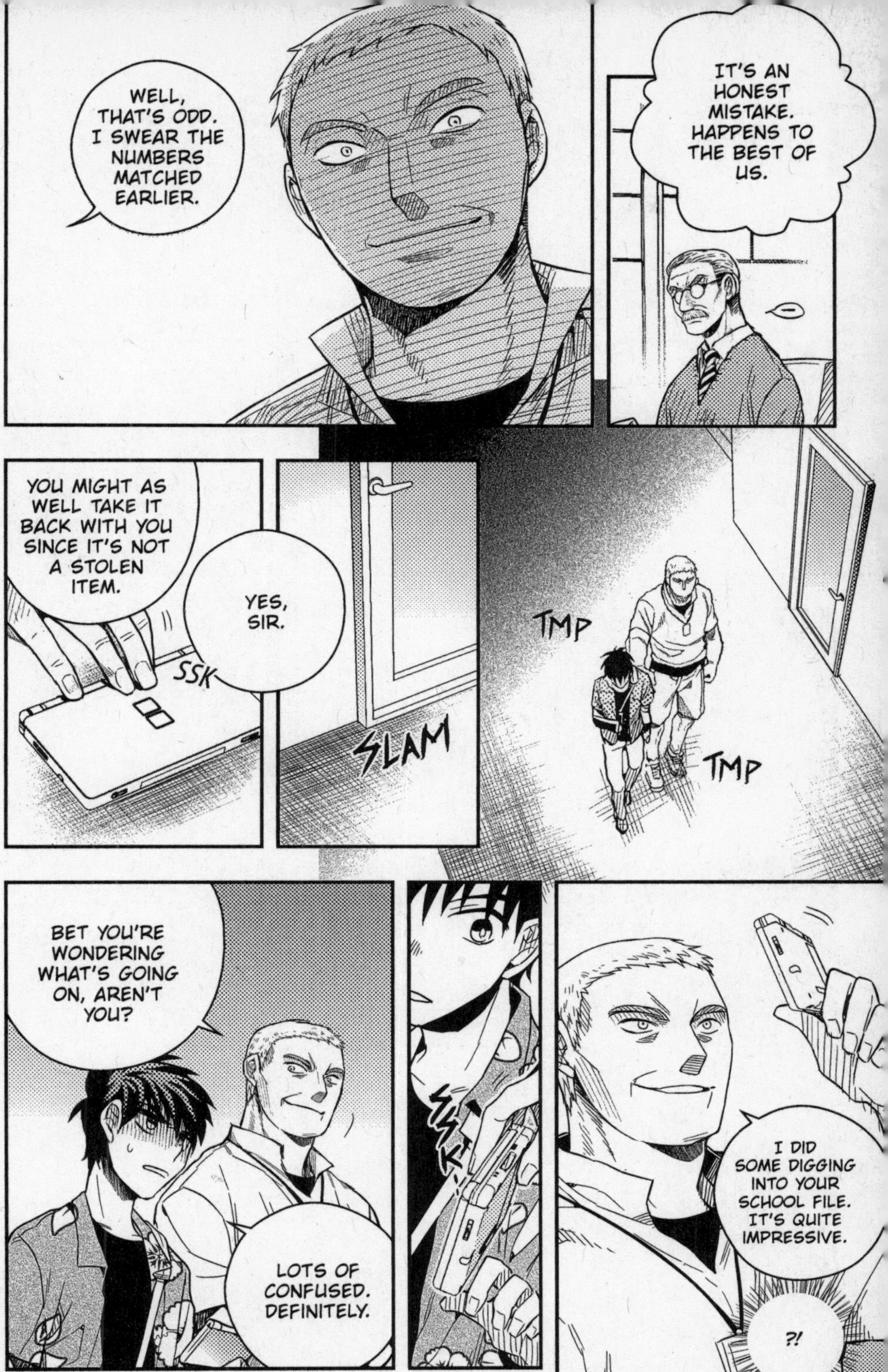
WELL, THAT'S ODD. I SWEAR THE NUMBERS MATCHED EARLIER.
IT'S AN HONEST MISTAKE. HAPPENS TO THE BEST OF US.
YOU MIGHT AS WELL TAKE IT BACK WITH YOU SINCE IT'S NOT A STOLEN ITEM.
YES, SIR.
SSK
SLAM
TMP
TMP
BET YOU'RE WONDERING WHAT'S GOING ON, AREN'T YOU?
LOTS OF CONFUSED. DEFINITELY.
SSK
I DID SOME DIGGING INTO YOUR SCHOOL FILE. IT'S QUITE IMPRESSIVE.
?!

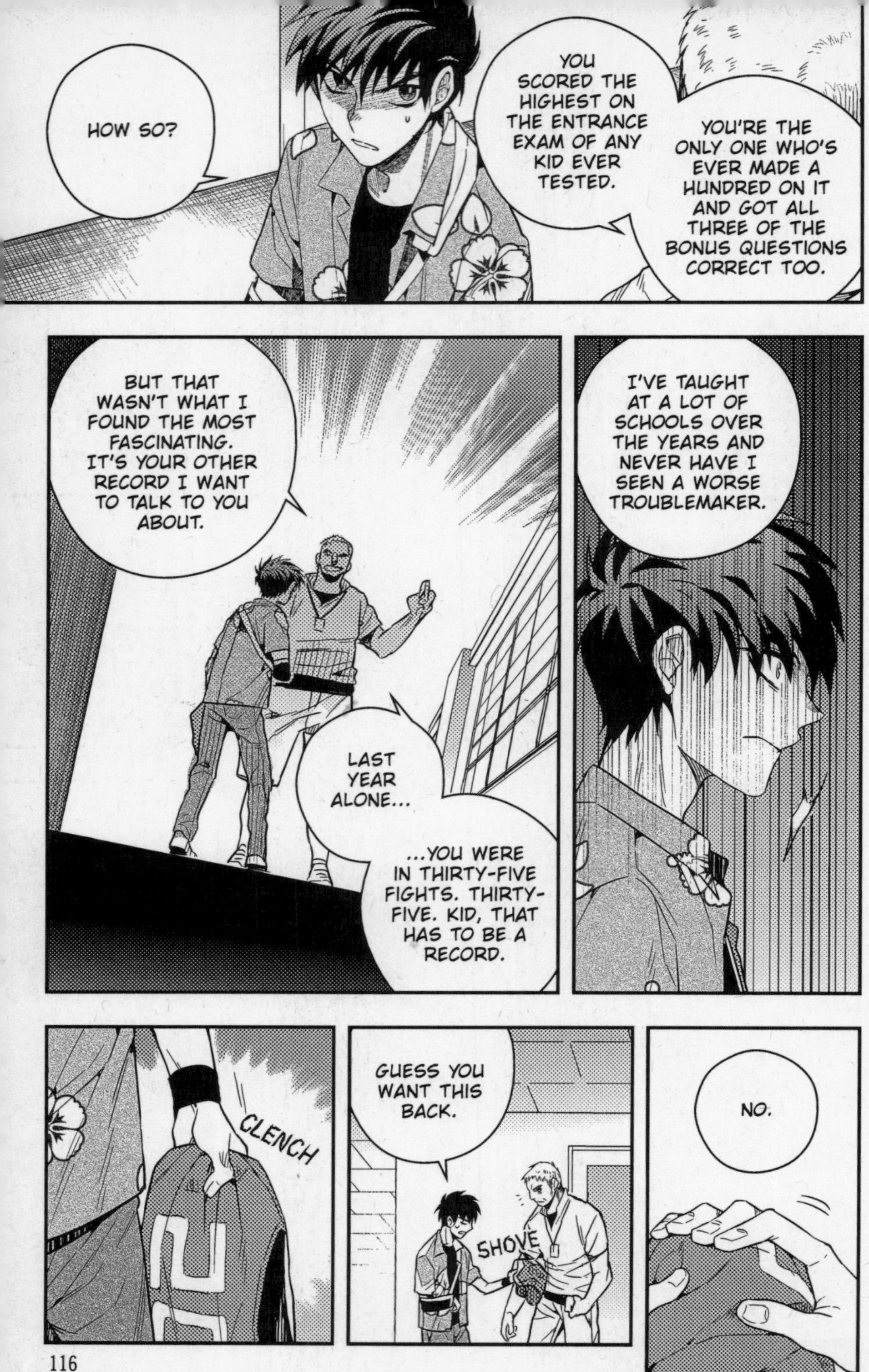
HOW SO?
YOU SCORED THE HIGHEST ON THE ENTRANCE EXAM OF ANY KID EVER TESTED.
YOU'RE THE ONLY ONE WHO'S EVER MADE A HUNDRED ON IT AND GOT ALL THREE OF THE BONUS QUESTIONS CORRECT TOO.
BUT THAT WASN'T WHAT I FOUND THE MOST FASCINATING. IT'S YOUR OTHER RECORD I WANT TO TALK TO YOU ABOUT.
LAST YEAR ALONE...
...YOU WERE IN THIRTY-FIVE FIGHTS. THIRTY-FIVE. KID, THAT HAS TO BE A RECORD.
I'VE TAUGHT AT A LOT OF SCHOOLS OVER THE YEARS AND NEVER HAVE I SEEN A WORSE TROUBLEMAKER.
CLENCH
GUESS YOU WANT THIS BACK.
SHOVE
NO.

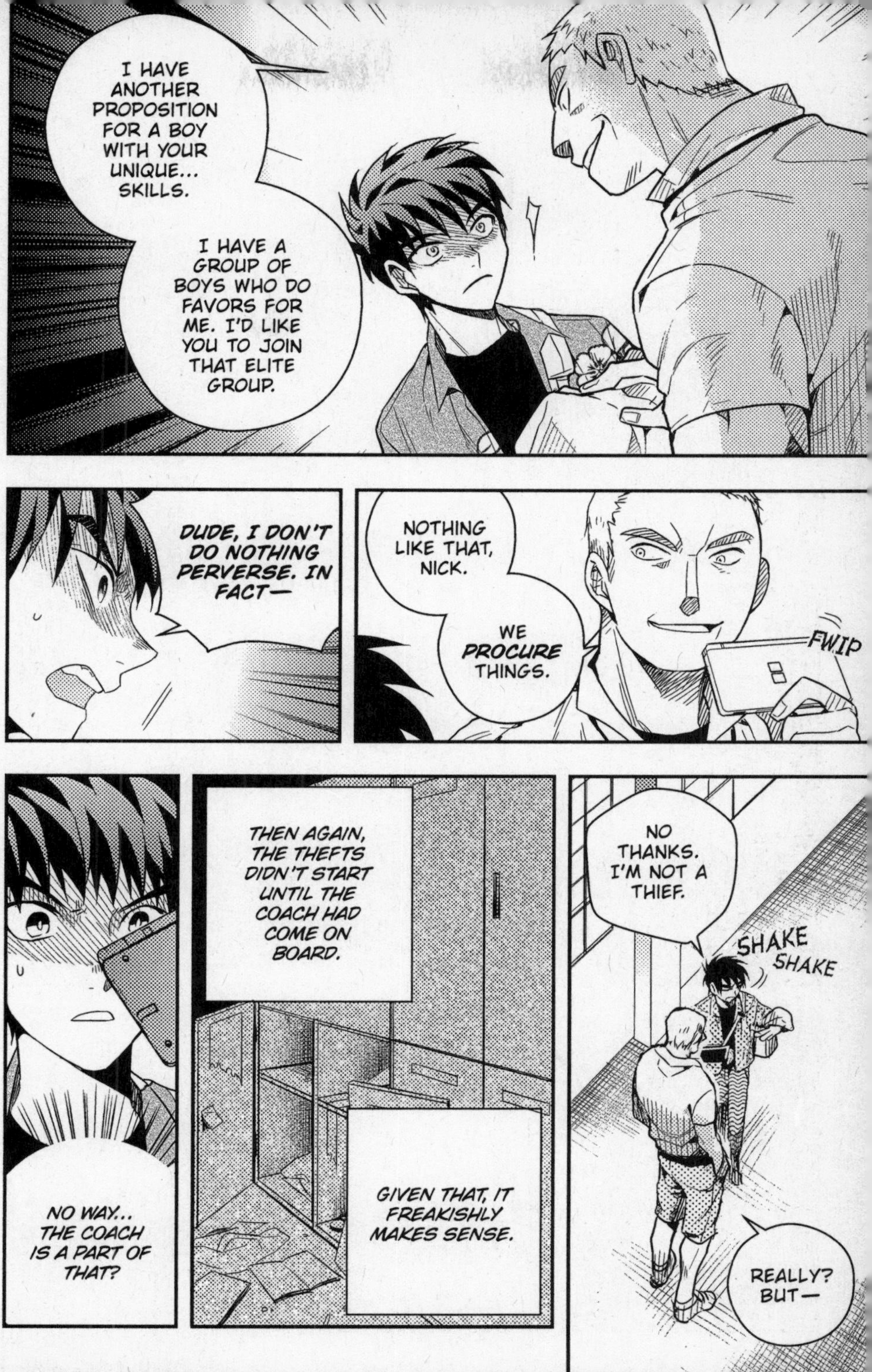
I HAVE ANOTHER PROPOSITION FOR A BOY WITH YOUR UNIQUE... SKILLS.
I HAVE A GROUP OF BOYS WHO DO FAVORS FOR ME. I'D LIKE YOU TO JOIN THAT ELITE GROUP.
DUDE, I DON'T DO NOTHING PERVERSE. IN FACT—
NOTHING LIKE THAT, NICK.
WE PROCURE THINGS.
FWIP
NO WAY... THE COACH IS A PART OF THAT?
THEN AGAIN, THE THEFTS DIDN'T START UNTIL THE COACH HAD COME ON BOARD.
GIVEN THAT, IT FREAKISHLY MAKES SENSE.
NO THANKS. I'M NOT A THIEF.
SHAKE SHAKE
REALLY? BUT—

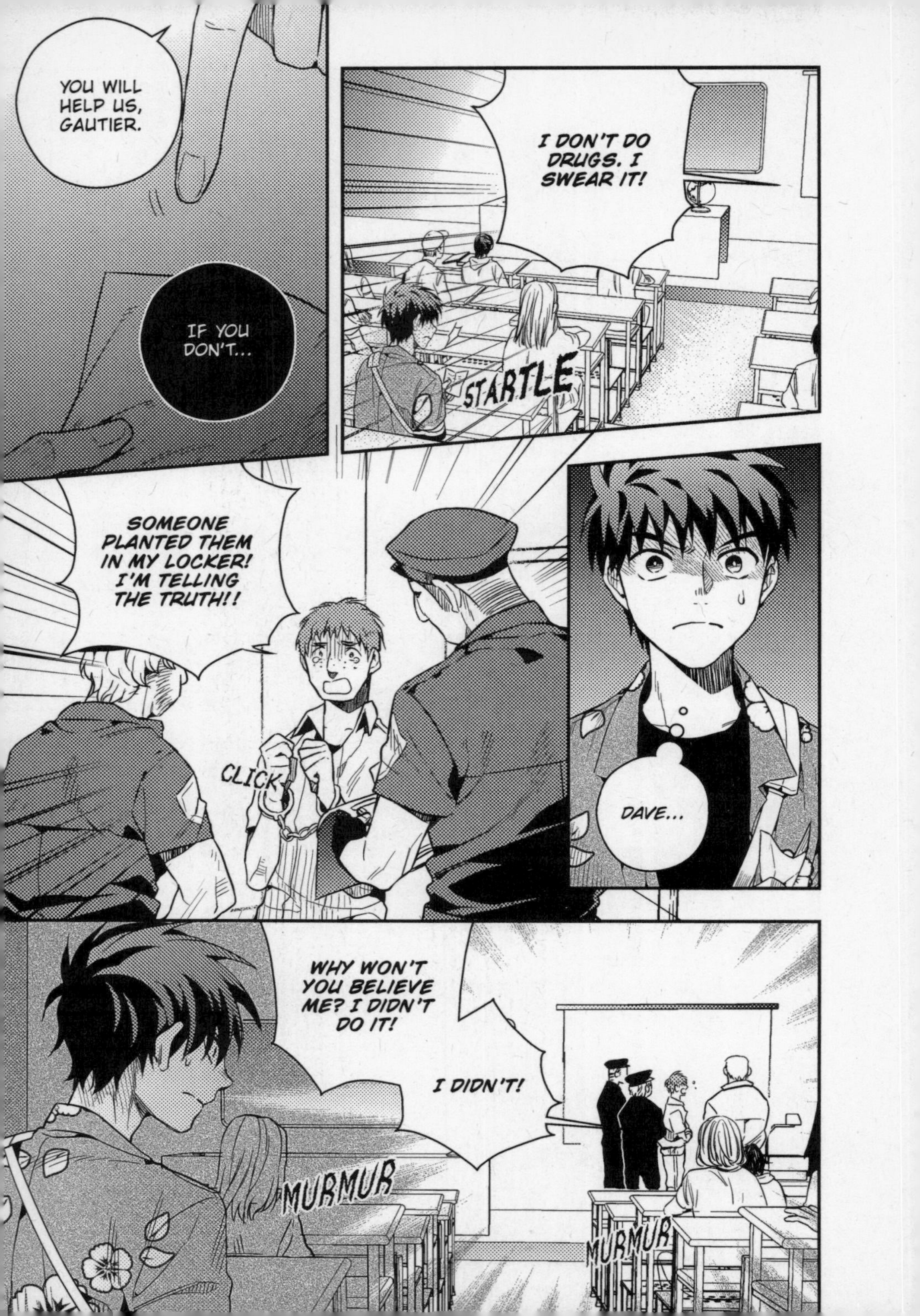
YOU WILL HELP US, GAUTIER.
I DON'T DO DRUGS. I SWEAR IT!
IF YOU DON'T...
STARTLE
SOMEONE PLANTED THEM IN MY LOCKER! I'M TELLING THE TRUTH!!
CLICK
DAVE...
WHY WON'T YOU BELIEVE ME? I DIDN'T DO IT!
I DIDN'T!
MURMUR
MURMUR

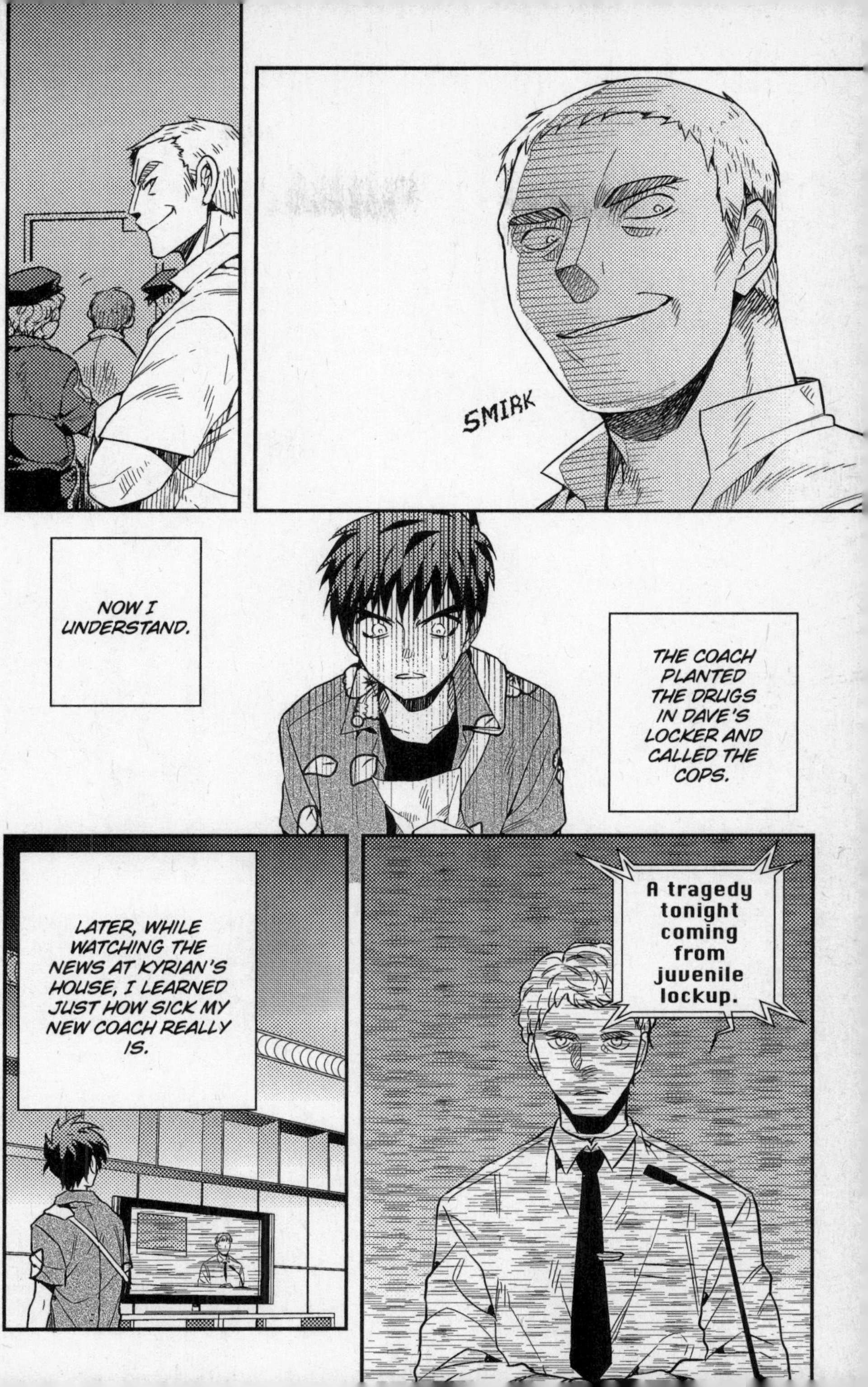
SMIRK
NOW I UNDERSTAND.
THE COACH PLANTED THE DRUGS IN DAVE'S LOCKER AND CALLED THE COPS.
LATER, WHILE WATCHING THE NEWS AT KYRIAN'S HOUSE, I LEARNED JUST HOW SICK MY NEW COACH REALLY IS.
A tragedy tonight coming from juvenile lockup.

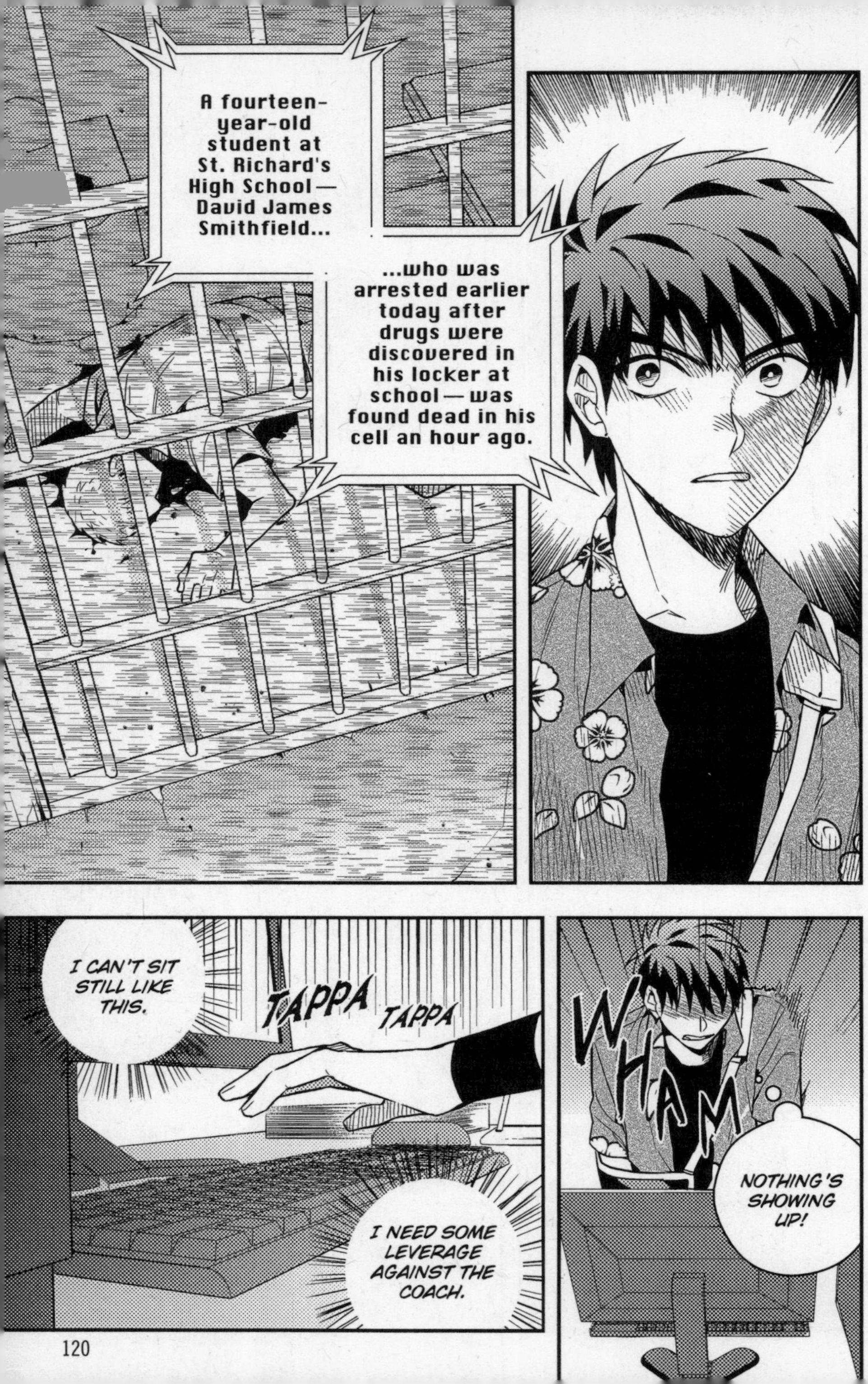
A fourteen-year-old student at St. Richard's High School—David James Smithfield...
...who was arrested earlier today after drugs were discovered in his locker at school—was found dead in his cell an hour ago.
I CAN'T SIT STILL LIKE THIS.
TAPPA TAPPA
I NEED SOME LEVERAGE AGAINST THE COACH.
WHAM
NOTHING'S SHOWING UP!

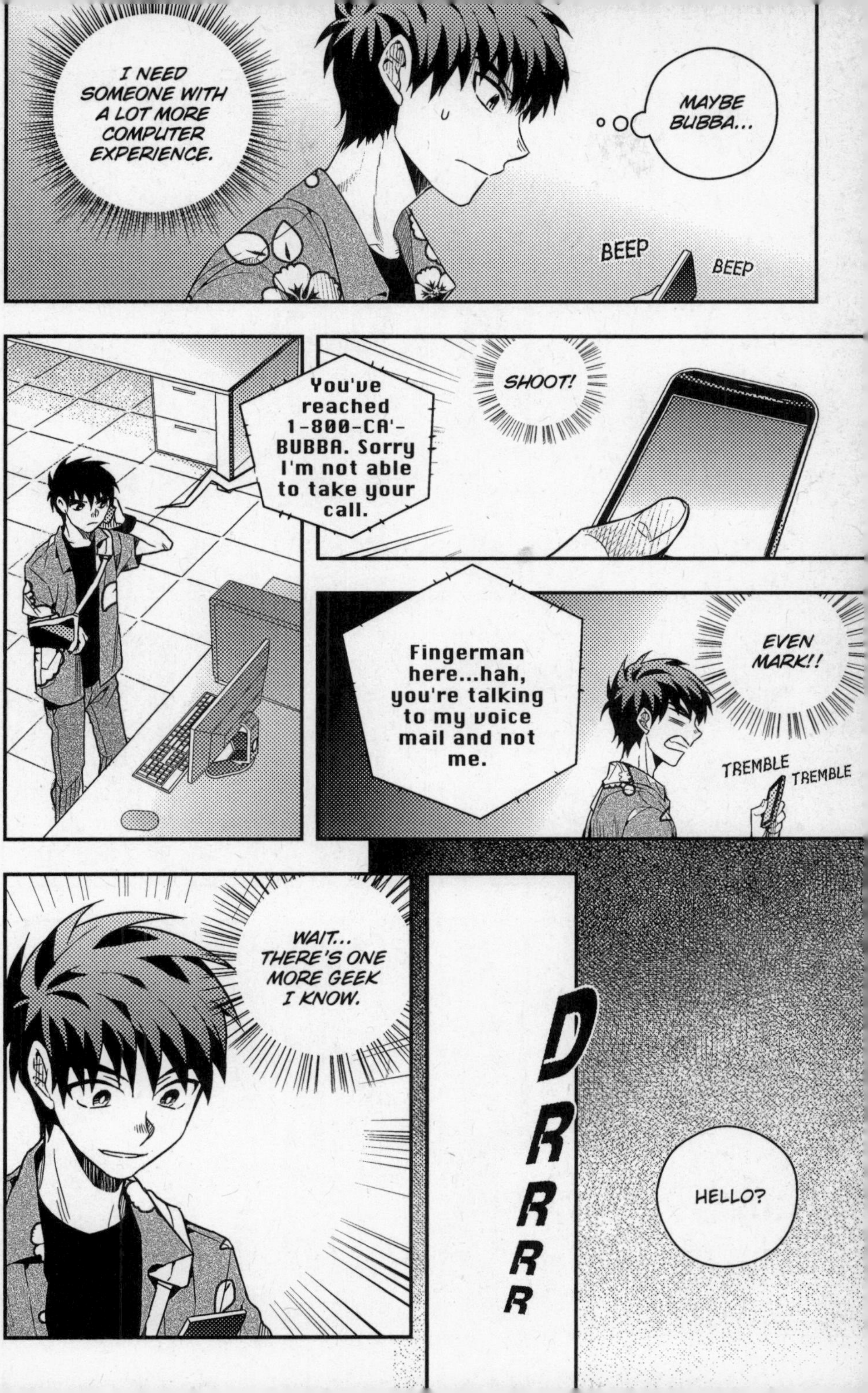
I NEED SOMEONE WITH A LOT MORE COMPUTER EXPERIENCE.
MAYBE BUBBA...
BEEP
BEEP
SHOOT!
You've reached 1-800-CA'-BUBBA. Sorry I'm not able to take your call.
EVEN MARK!!
Fingerman here...hah, you're talking to my voice mail and not me.
TREMBLE
TREMBLE
WAIT... THERE'S ONE MORE GEEK I KNOW.
DRRRR
HELLO?

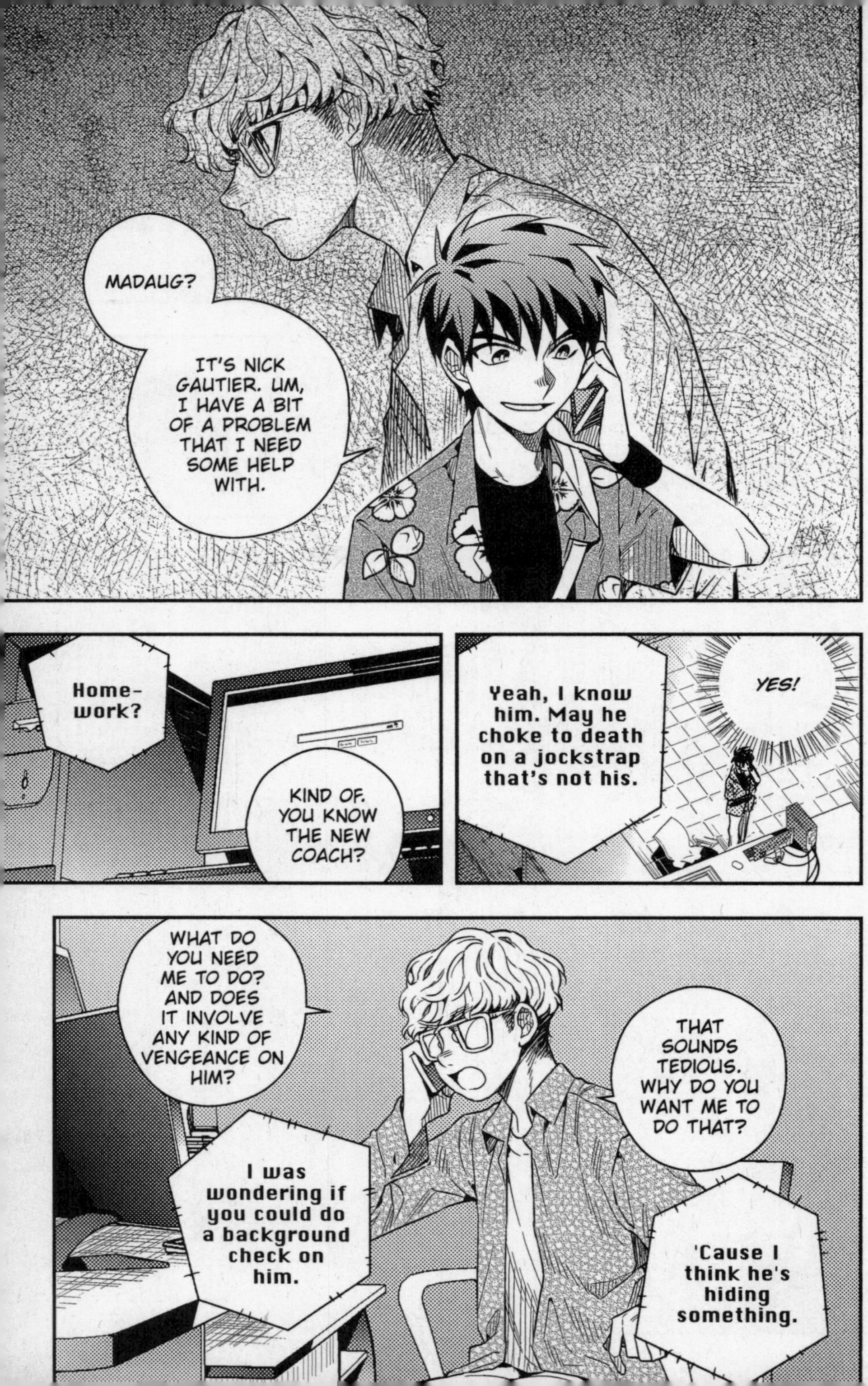
MADAUG?
IT'S NICK GAUTIER. UM, I HAVE A BIT OF A PROBLEM THAT I NEED SOME HELP WITH.
Home-work?
KIND OF. YOU KNOW THE NEW COACH?
Yeah, I know him. May he choke to death on a jockstrap that's not his.
YES!
WHAT DO YOU NEED ME TO DO? AND DOES IT INVOLVE ANY KIND OF VENGEANCE ON HIM?
I was wondering if you could do a background check on him.
THAT SOUNDS TEDIOUS. WHY DO YOU WANT ME TO DO THAT?
'Cause I think he's hiding something.

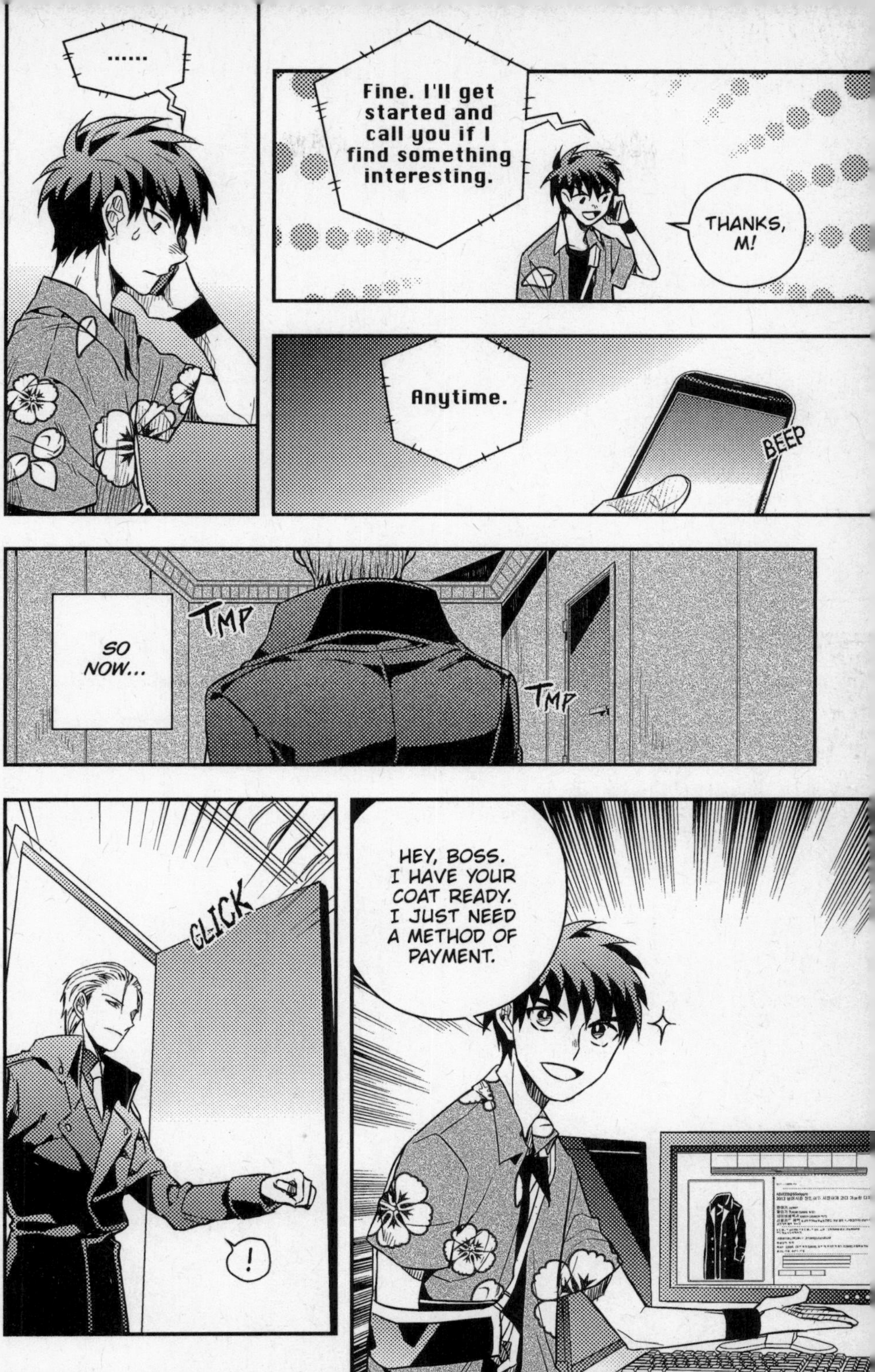
......
Fine. I'll get started and call you if I find something interesting.
THANKS, M!
Anytime.
BEEP
SO NOW...
TMP
TMP
GLICK
!
HEY, BOSS. I HAVE YOUR COAT READY. I JUST NEED A METHOD OF PAYMENT.

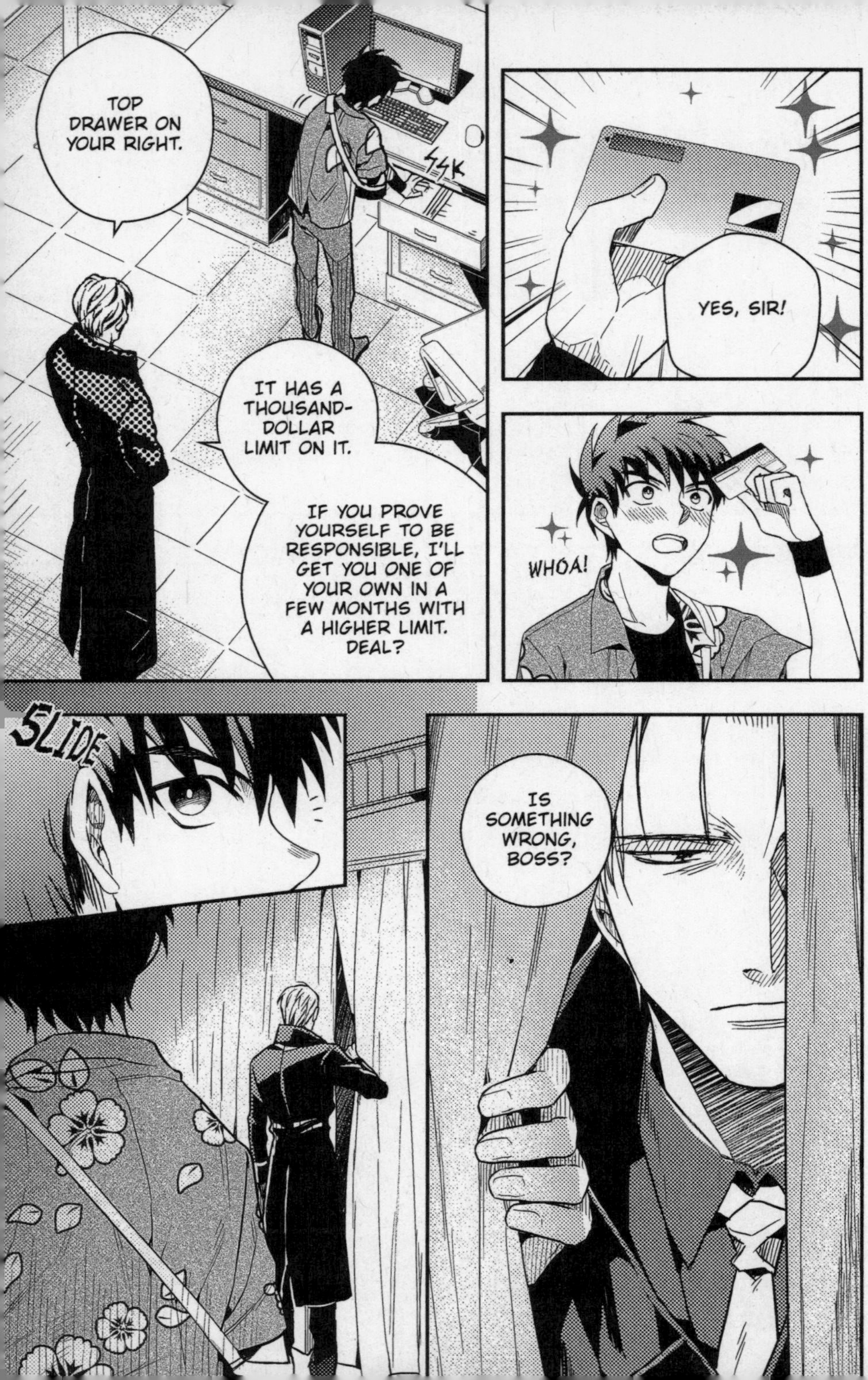
TOP DRAWER ON YOUR RIGHT.
SSK
YES, SIR!
IT HAS A THOUSAND-DOLLAR LIMIT ON IT.
IF YOU PROVE YOURSELF TO BE RESPONSIBLE, I'LL GET YOU ONE OF YOUR OWN IN A FEW MONTHS WITH A HIGHER LIMIT. DEAL?
WHOA!
IS SOMETHING WRONG, BOSS?
SLIDE

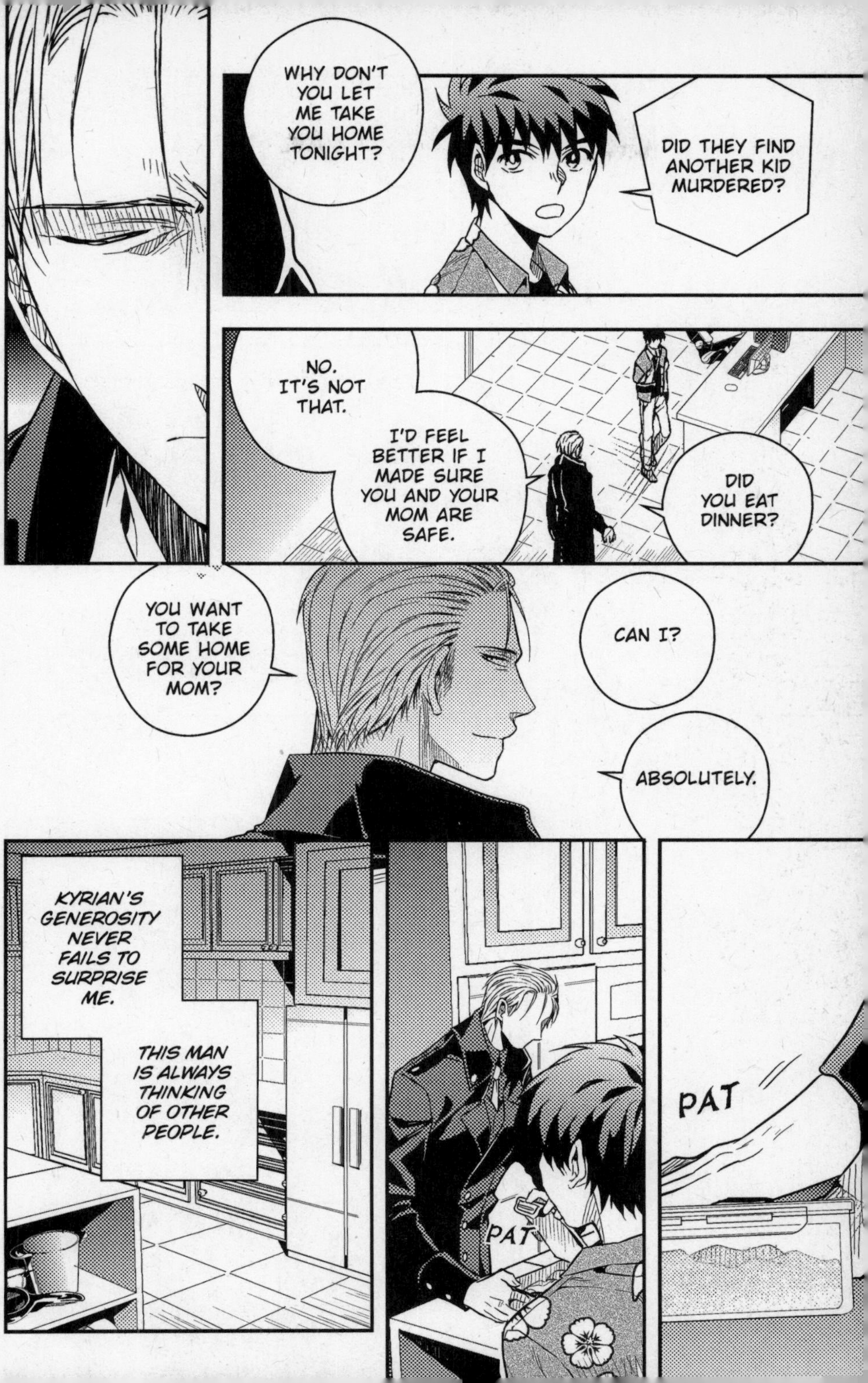
DID THEY FIND ANOTHER KID MURDERED?
WHY DON'T YOU LET ME TAKE YOU HOME TONIGHT?
NO. IT'S NOT THAT.
I'D FEEL BETTER IF I MADE SURE YOU AND YOUR MOM ARE SAFE.
DID YOU EAT DINNER?
YOU WANT TO TAKE SOME HOME FOR YOUR MOM?
CAN I?
ABSOLUTELY.
KYRIAN'S GENEROSITY NEVER FAILS TO SURPRISE ME.
THIS MAN IS ALWAYS THINKING OF OTHER PEOPLE.
PAT
PAT

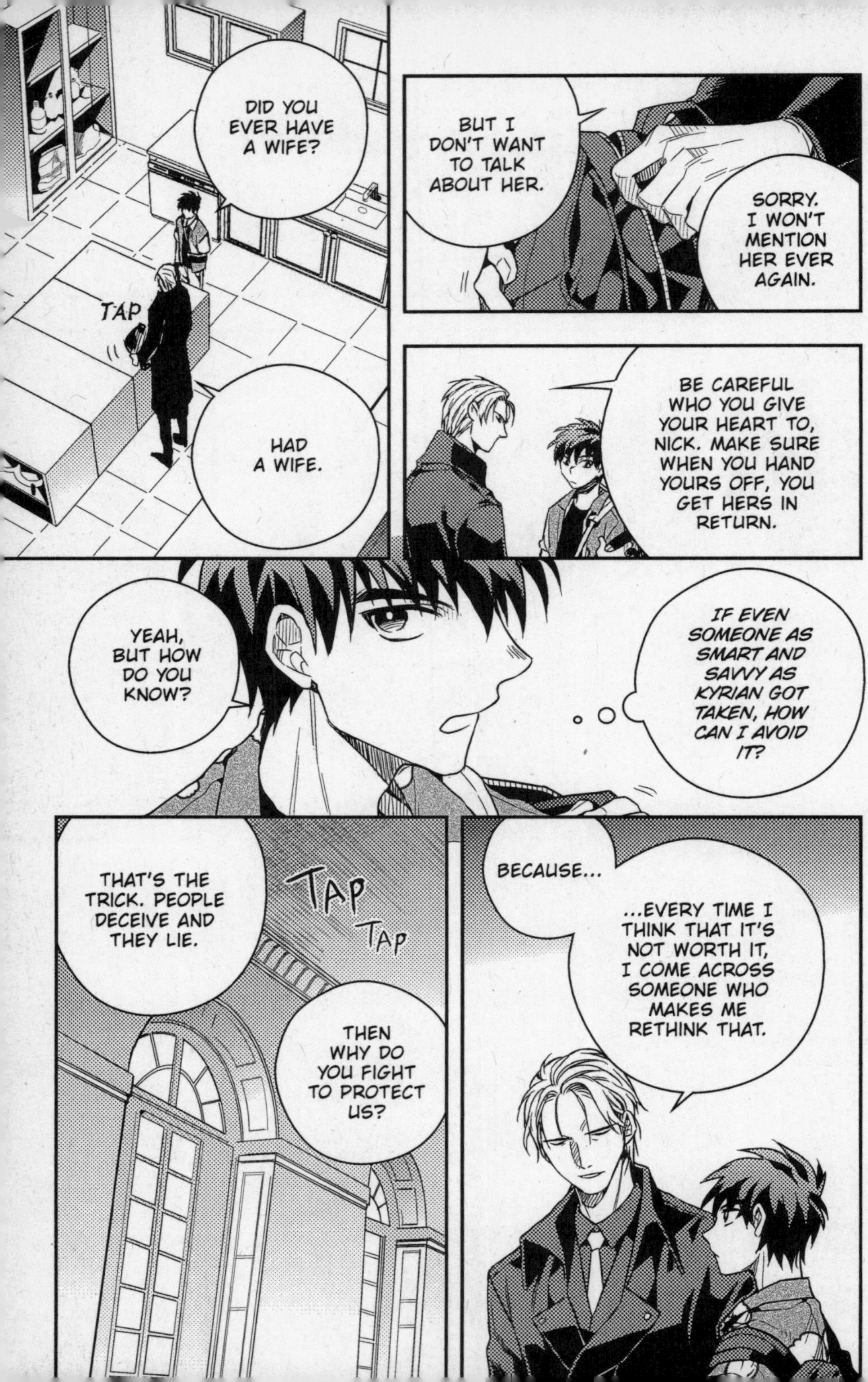
DID YOU EVER HAVE A WIFE?
TAP
HAD A WIFE.
BUT I DON'T WANT TO TALK ABOUT HER.
SORRY. I WON'T MENTION HER EVER AGAIN.
BE CAREFUL WHO YOU GIVE YOUR HEART TO, NICK. MAKE SURE WHEN YOU HAND YOURS OFF, YOU GET HERS IN RETURN.
YEAH, BUT HOW DO YOU KNOW?
IF EVEN SOMEONE AS SMART AND SAVVY AS KYRIAN GOT TAKEN, HOW CAN I AVOID IT?
THAT'S THE TRICK. PEOPLE DECEIVE AND THEY LIE.
TAP
TAP
THEN WHY DO YOU FIGHT TO PROTECT US?
BECAUSE...
...EVERY TIME I THINK THAT IT'S NOT WORTH IT, I COME ACROSS SOMEONE WHO MAKES ME RETHINK THAT.

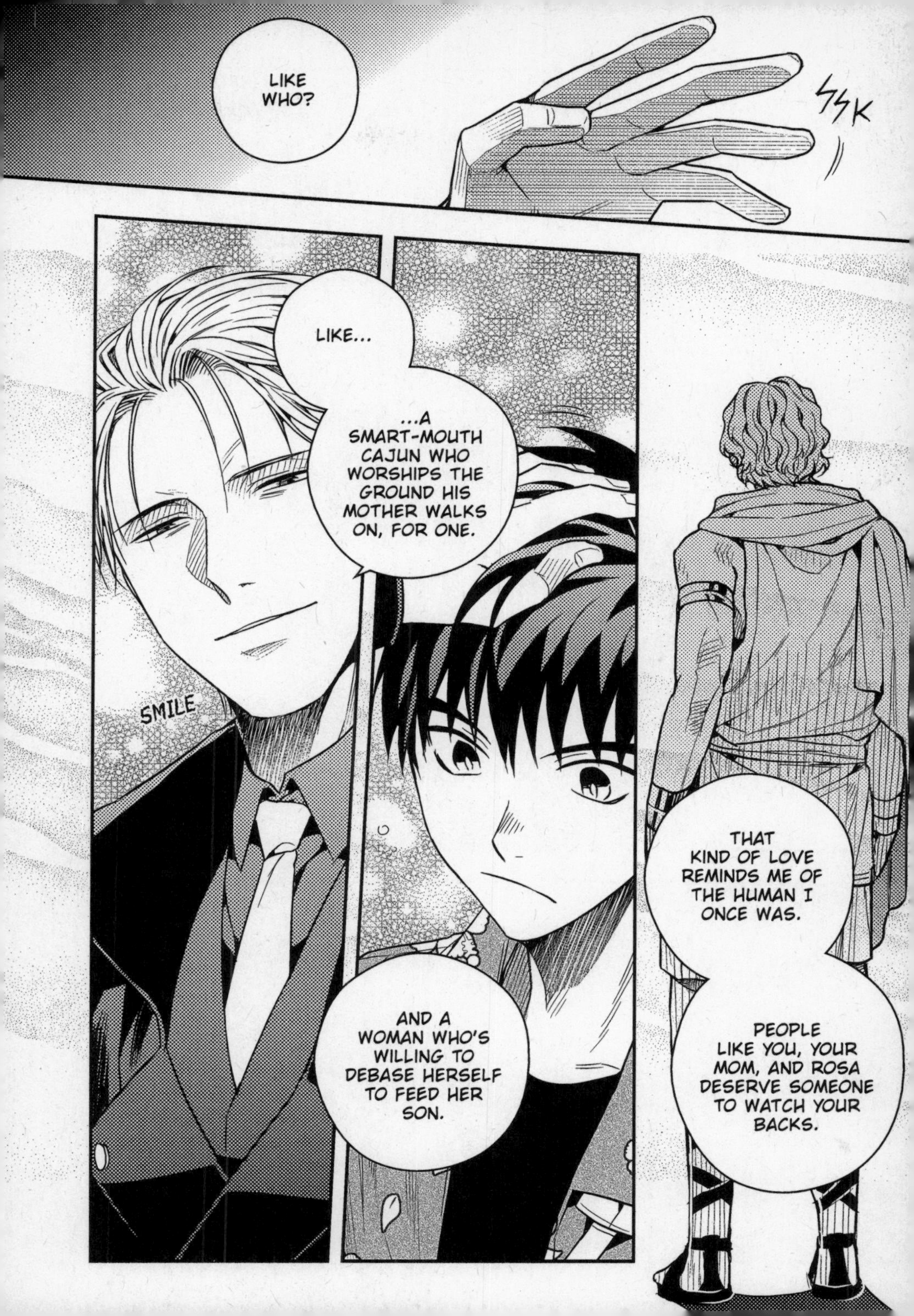
LIKE WHO?
SSK
LIKE...
...A SMART-MOUTH CAJUN WHO WORSHIPS THE GROUND HIS MOTHER WALKS ON, FOR ONE.
SMILE
AND A WOMAN WHO'S WILLING TO DEBASE HERSELF TO FEED HER SON.
THAT KIND OF LOVE REMINDS ME OF THE HUMAN I ONCE WAS.
PEOPLE LIKE YOU, YOUR MOM, AND ROSA DESERVE SOMEONE TO WATCH YOUR BACKS.

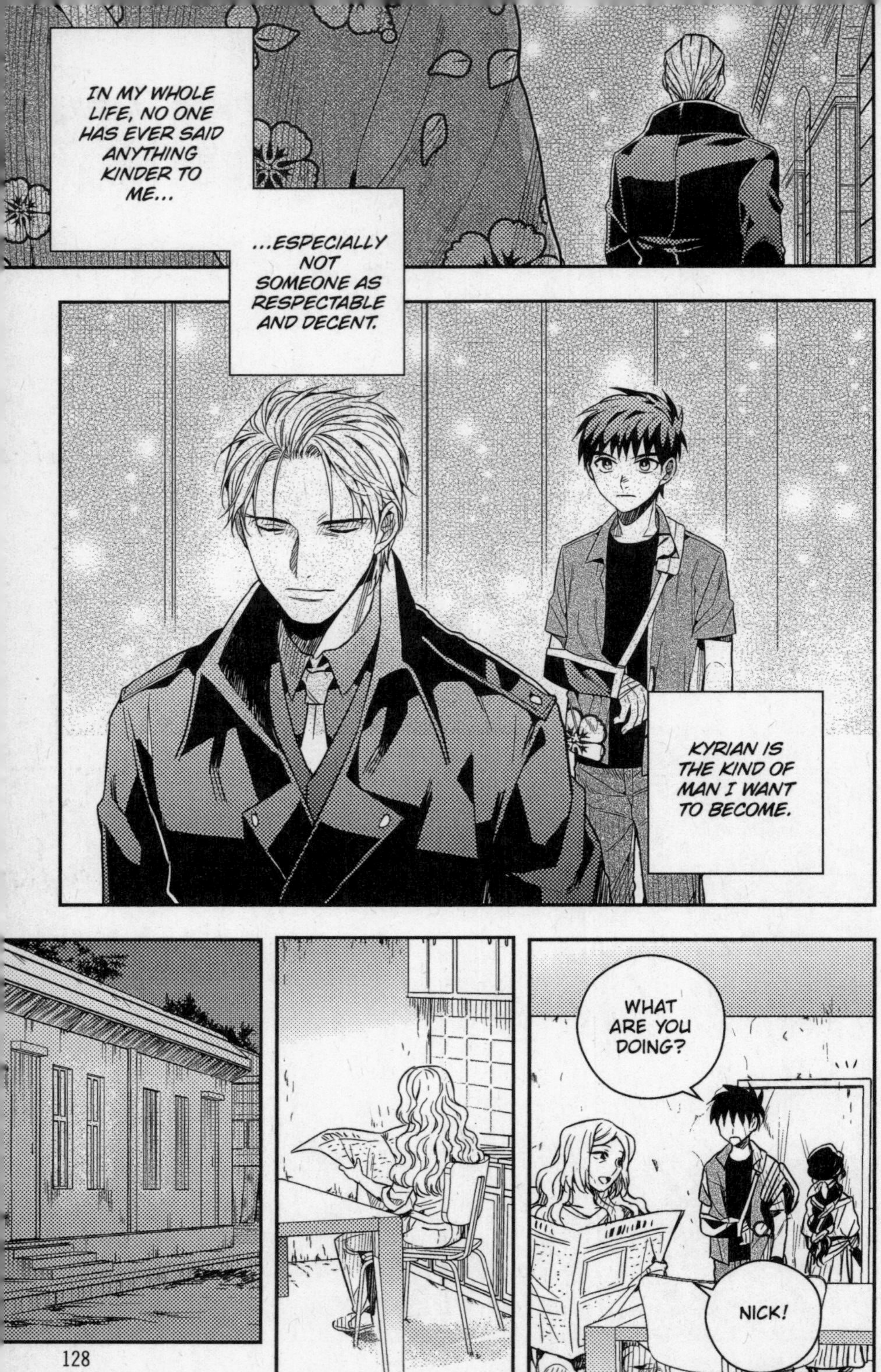
IN MY WHOLE LIFE, NO ONE HAS EVER SAID ANYTHING KINDER TO ME...
...ESPECIALLY NOT SOMEONE AS RESPECTABLE AND DECENT.
KYRIAN IS THE KIND OF MAN I WANT TO BECOME.
WHAT ARE YOU DOING?
NICK!

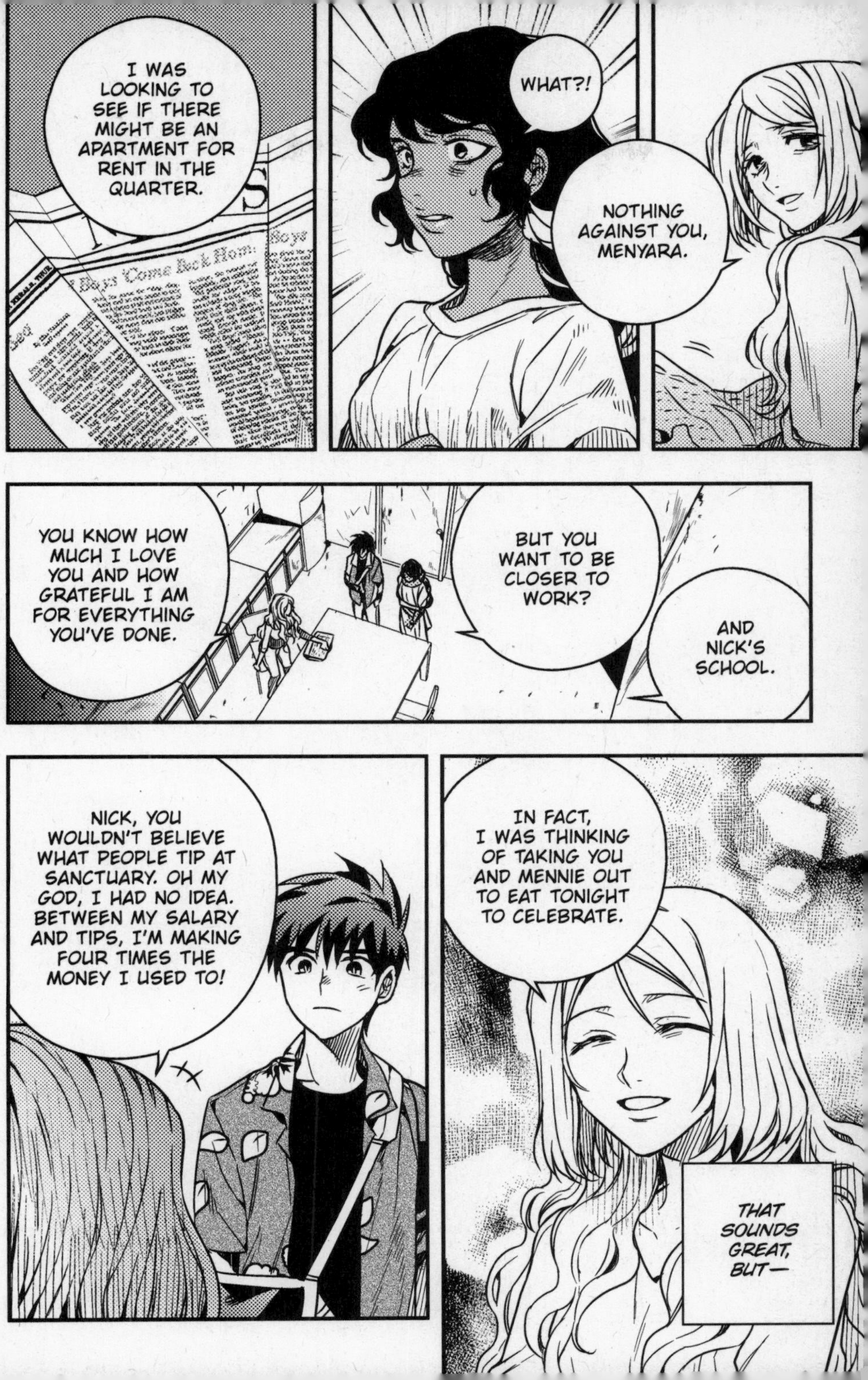
I WAS LOOKING TO SEE IF THERE MIGHT BE AN APARTMENT FOR RENT IN THE QUARTER.
WHAT?!
NOTHING AGAINST YOU, MENYARA.
YOU KNOW HOW MUCH I LOVE YOU AND HOW GRATEFUL I AM FOR EVERYTHING YOU'VE DONE.
BUT YOU WANT TO BE CLOSER TO WORK?
AND NICK'S SCHOOL.
NICK, YOU WOULDN'T BELIEVE WHAT PEOPLE TIP AT SANCTUARY. OH MY GOD, I HAD NO IDEA. BETWEEN MY SALARY AND TIPS, I'M MAKING FOUR TIMES THE MONEY I USED TO!
IN FACT, I WAS THINKING OF TAKING YOU AND MENNIE OUT TO EAT TONIGHT TO CELEBRATE.
THAT SOUNDS GREAT, BUT—

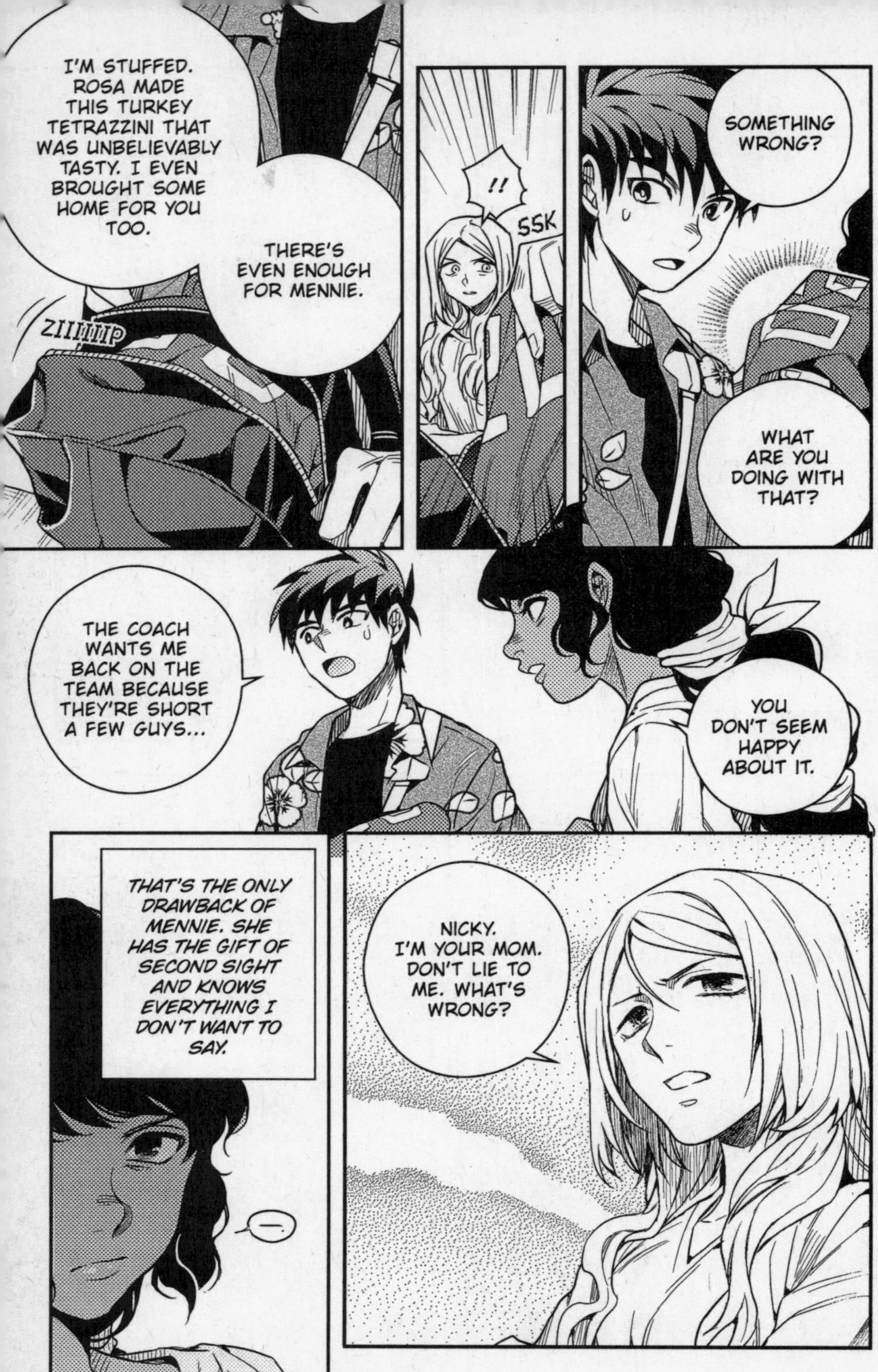
I'M STUFFED. ROSA MADE THIS TURKEY TETRAZZINI THAT WAS UNBELIEVABLY TASTY. I EVEN BROUGHT SOME HOME FOR YOU TOO.
THERE'S EVEN ENOUGH FOR MENNIE.
ZIIIIIIP
!!
SSK
SOMETHING WRONG?
WHAT ARE YOU DOING WITH THAT?
THE COACH WANTS ME BACK ON THE TEAM BECAUSE THEY'RE SHORT A FEW GUYS...
YOU DON'T SEEM HAPPY ABOUT IT.
THAT'S THE ONLY DRAWBACK OF MENNIE. SHE HAS THE GIFT OF SECOND SIGHT AND KNOWS EVERYTHING I DON'T WANT TO SAY.
NICKY. I'M YOUR MOM. DON'T LIE TO ME. WHAT'S WRONG?
—.

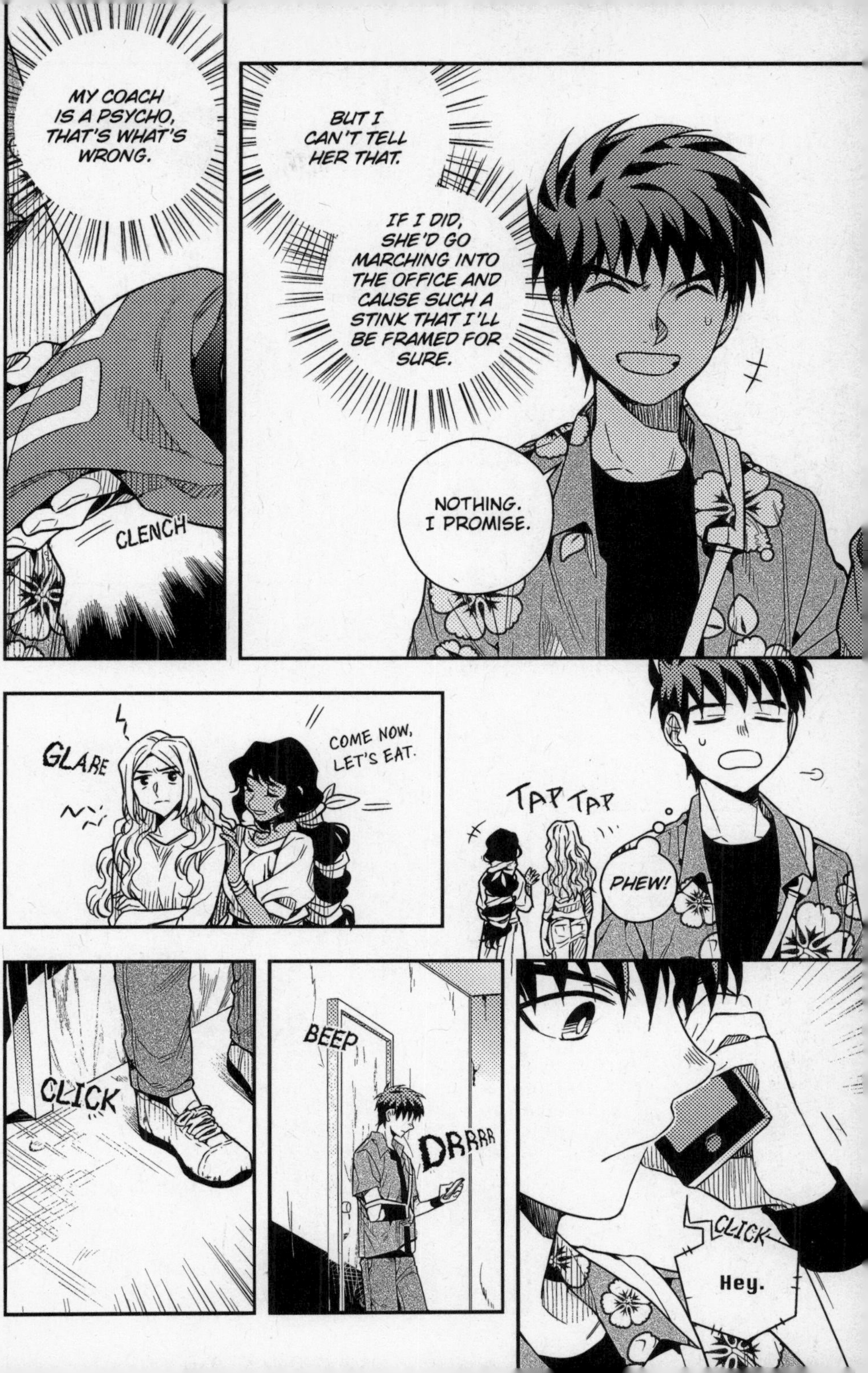
MY COACH IS A PSYCHO, THAT'S WHAT'S WRONG.
CLENCH
BUT I CAN'T TELL HER THAT.
IF I DID, SHE'D GO MARCHING INTO THE OFFICE AND CAUSE SUCH A STINK THAT I'LL BE FRAMED FOR SURE.
NOTHING. I PROMISE.
GLARE
COME NOW, LET'S EAT.
TAP TAP
PHEW!
CLICK
BEEP
DRRRR
CLICK
Hey.

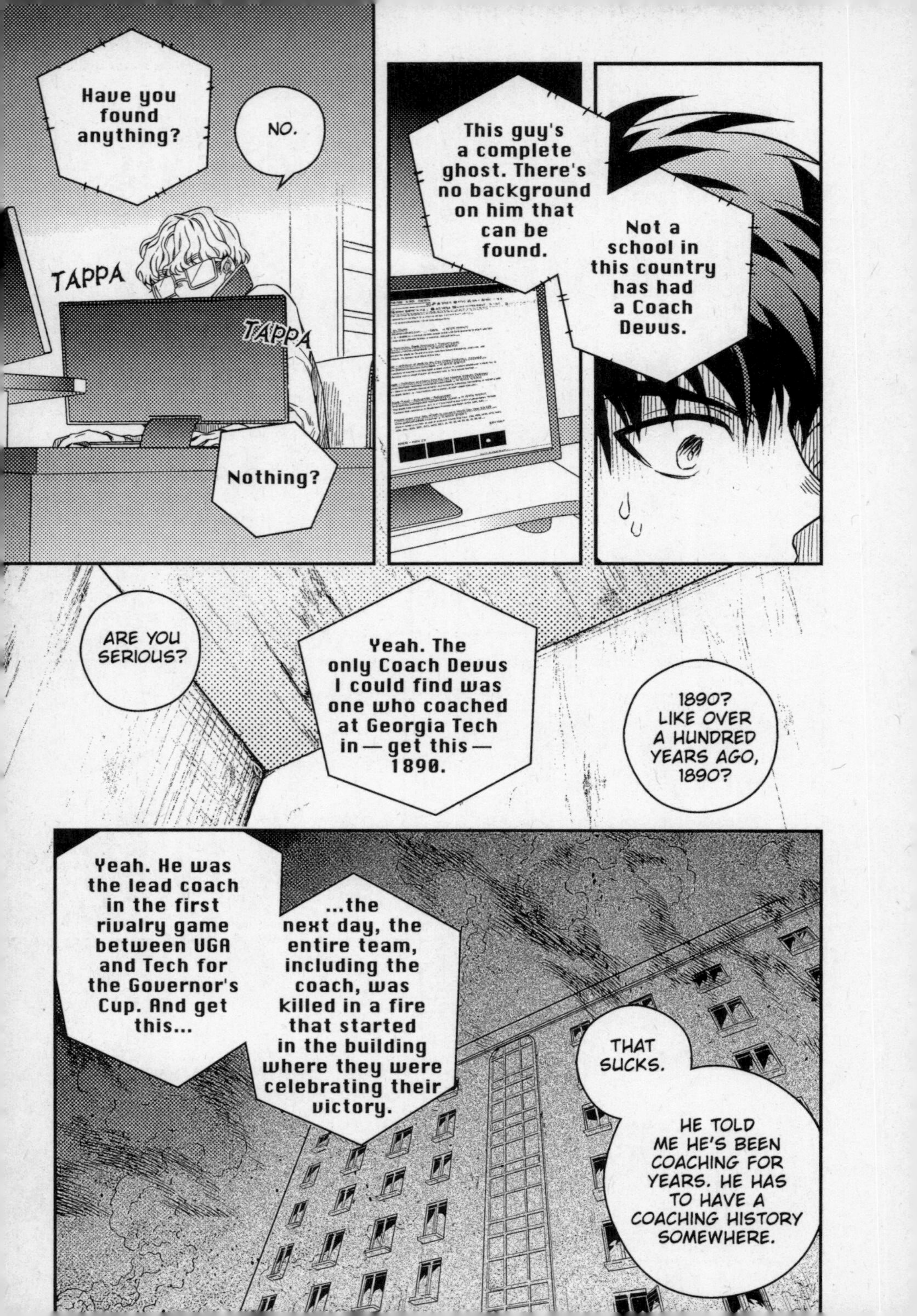
Have you found anything?
NO.
TAPPA
TAPPA
Nothing?
This guy's a complete ghost. There's no background on him that can be found.
Not a school in this country has had a Coach Devus.
ARE YOU SERIOUS?
Yeah. The only Coach Devus I could find was one who coached at Georgia Tech in — get this — 1890.
1890? LIKE OVER A HUNDRED YEARS AGO, 1890?
Yeah. He was the lead coach in the first rivalry game between UGA and Tech for the Governor's Cup. And get this...
...the next day, the entire team, including the coach, was killed in a fire that started in the building where they were celebrating their victory.
THAT SUCKS.
HE TOLD ME HE'S BEEN COACHING FOR YEARS. HE HAS TO HAVE A COACHING HISTORY SOMEWHERE.

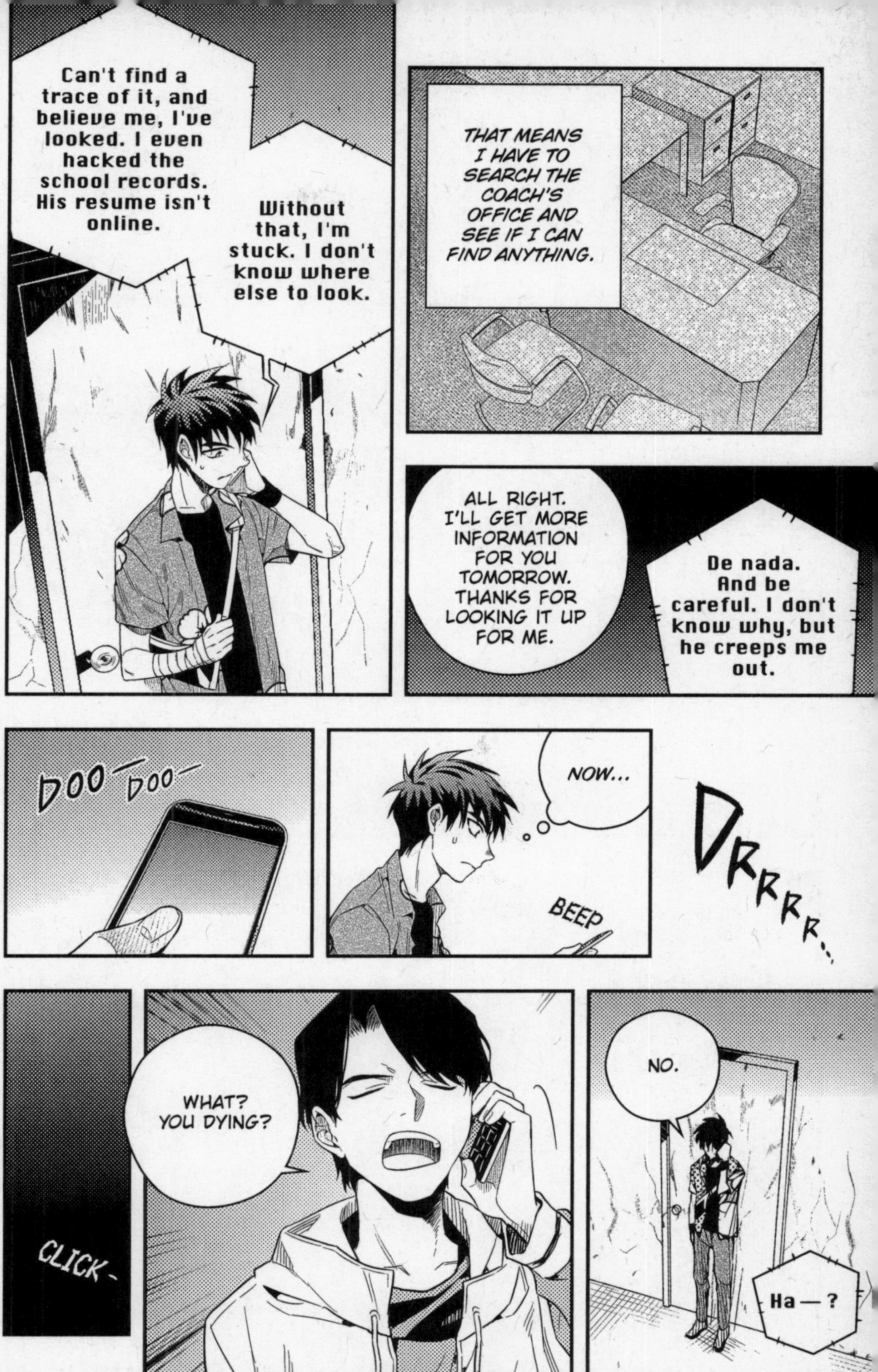
Can't find a trace of it, and believe me, I've looked. I even hacked the school records. His resume isn't online.
Without that, I'm stuck. I don't know where else to look.
THAT MEANS I HAVE TO SEARCH THE COACH'S OFFICE AND SEE IF I CAN FIND ANYTHING.
ALL RIGHT. I'LL GET MORE INFORMATION FOR YOU TOMORROW. THANKS FOR LOOKING IT UP FOR ME.
De nada. And be careful. I don't know why, but he creeps me out.
DOO DOO
NOW...
BEEP
DRRRRR...
CLICK-
WHAT? YOU DYING?
NO.
Ha—?

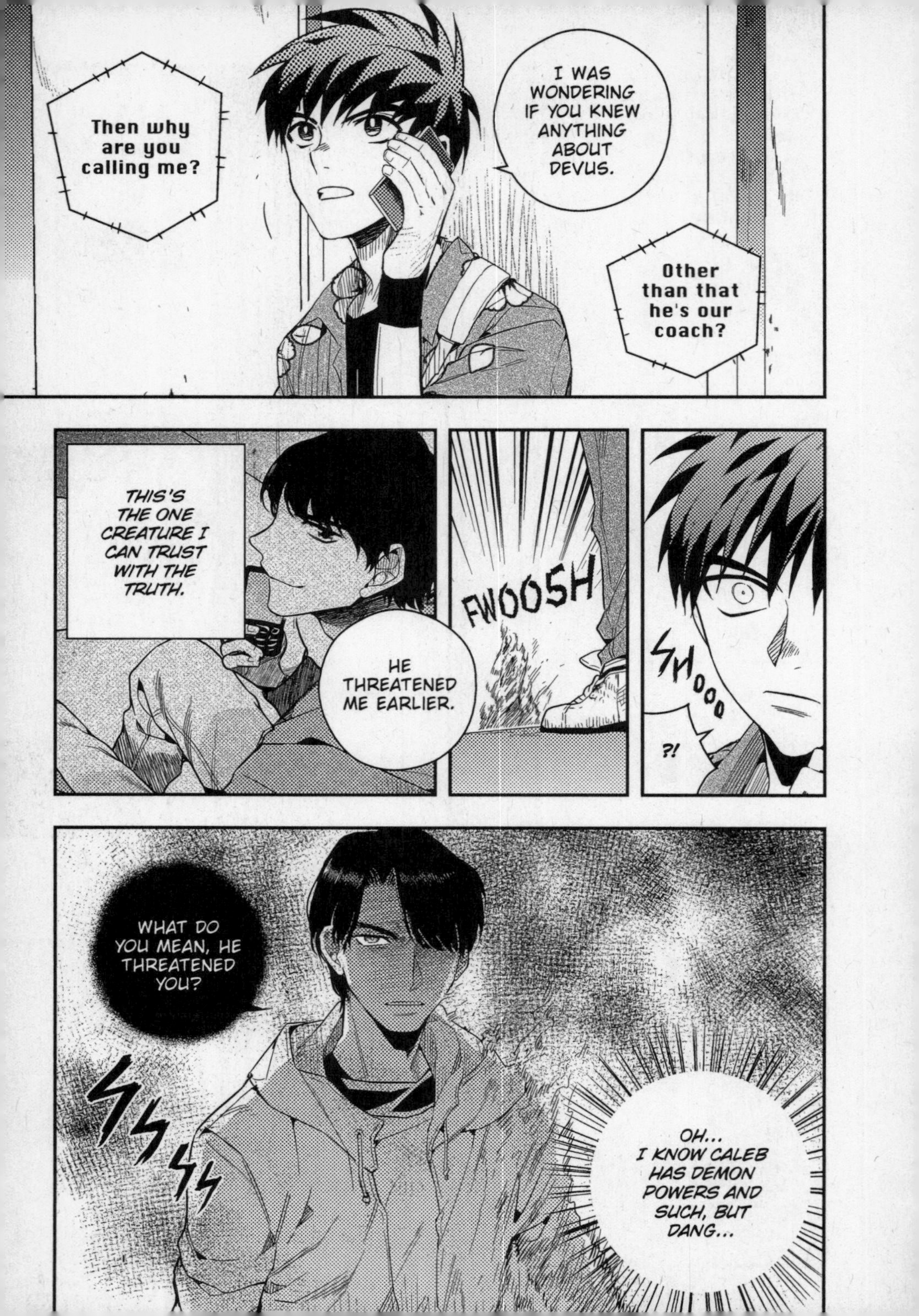
Then why are you calling me?
I WAS WONDERING IF YOU KNEW ANYTHING ABOUT DEVUS.
Other than that he's our coach?
THIS'S THE ONE CREATURE I CAN TRUST WITH THE TRUTH.
HE THREATENED ME EARLIER.
FWOOSH
SHOOO
?!
WHAT DO YOU MEAN, HE THREATENED YOU?
OH... I KNOW CALEB HAS DEMON POWERS AND SUCH, BUT DANG...

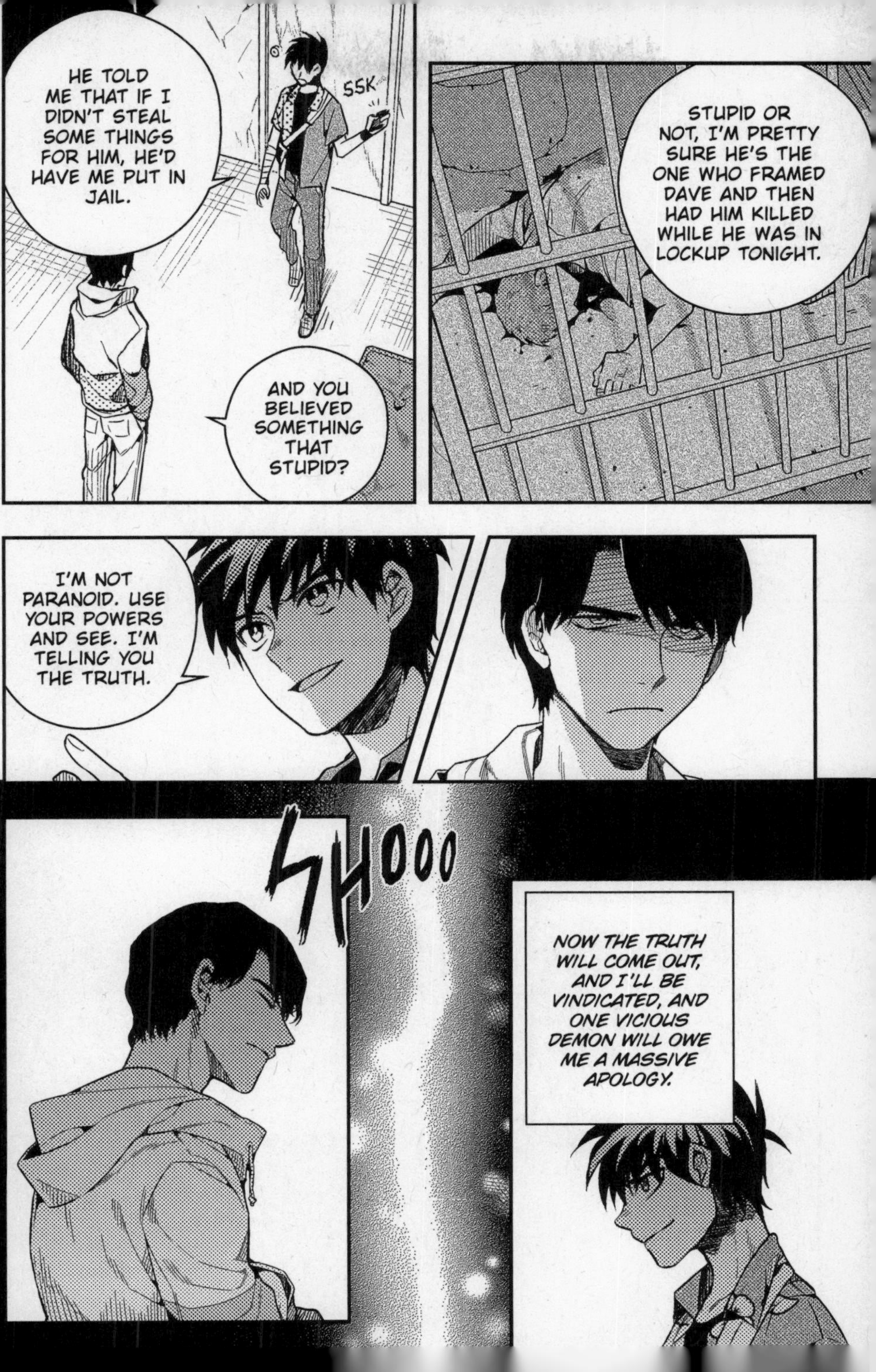
HE TOLD ME THAT IF I DIDN'T STEAL SOME THINGS FOR HIM, HE'D HAVE ME PUT IN JAIL.
SSK
AND YOU BELIEVED SOMETHING THAT STUPID?
STUPID OR NOT, I'M PRETTY SURE HE'S THE ONE WHO FRAMED DAVE AND THEN HAD HIM KILLED WHILE HE WAS IN LOCKUP TONIGHT.
I'M NOT PARANOID. USE YOUR POWERS AND SEE. I'M TELLING YOU THE TRUTH.
SHOOO
NOW THE TRUTH WILL COME OUT, AND I'LL BE VINDICATED, AND ONE VICIOUS DEMON WILL OWE ME A MASSIVE APOLOGY.

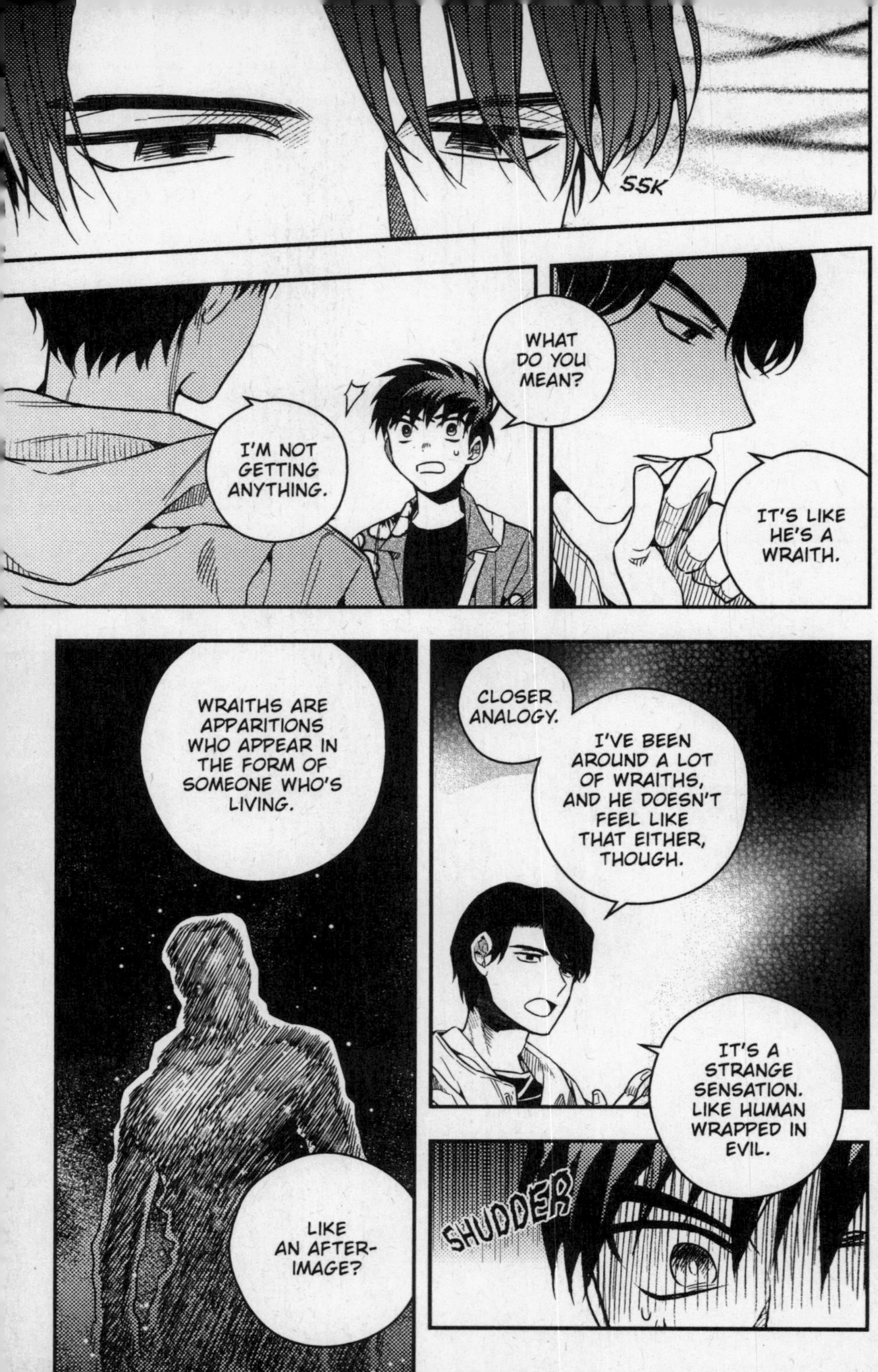
SSK
WHAT DO YOU MEAN?
I'M NOT GETTING ANYTHING.
IT'S LIKE HE'S A WRAITH.
CLOSER ANALOGY.
I'VE BEEN AROUND A LOT OF WRAITHS, AND HE DOESN'T FEEL LIKE THAT EITHER, THOUGH.
WRAITHS ARE APPARITIONS WHO APPEAR IN THE FORM OF SOMEONE WHO'S LIVING.
IT'S A STRANGE SENSATION. LIKE HUMAN WRAPPED IN EVIL.
SHUDDER
LIKE AN AFTER-IMAGE?

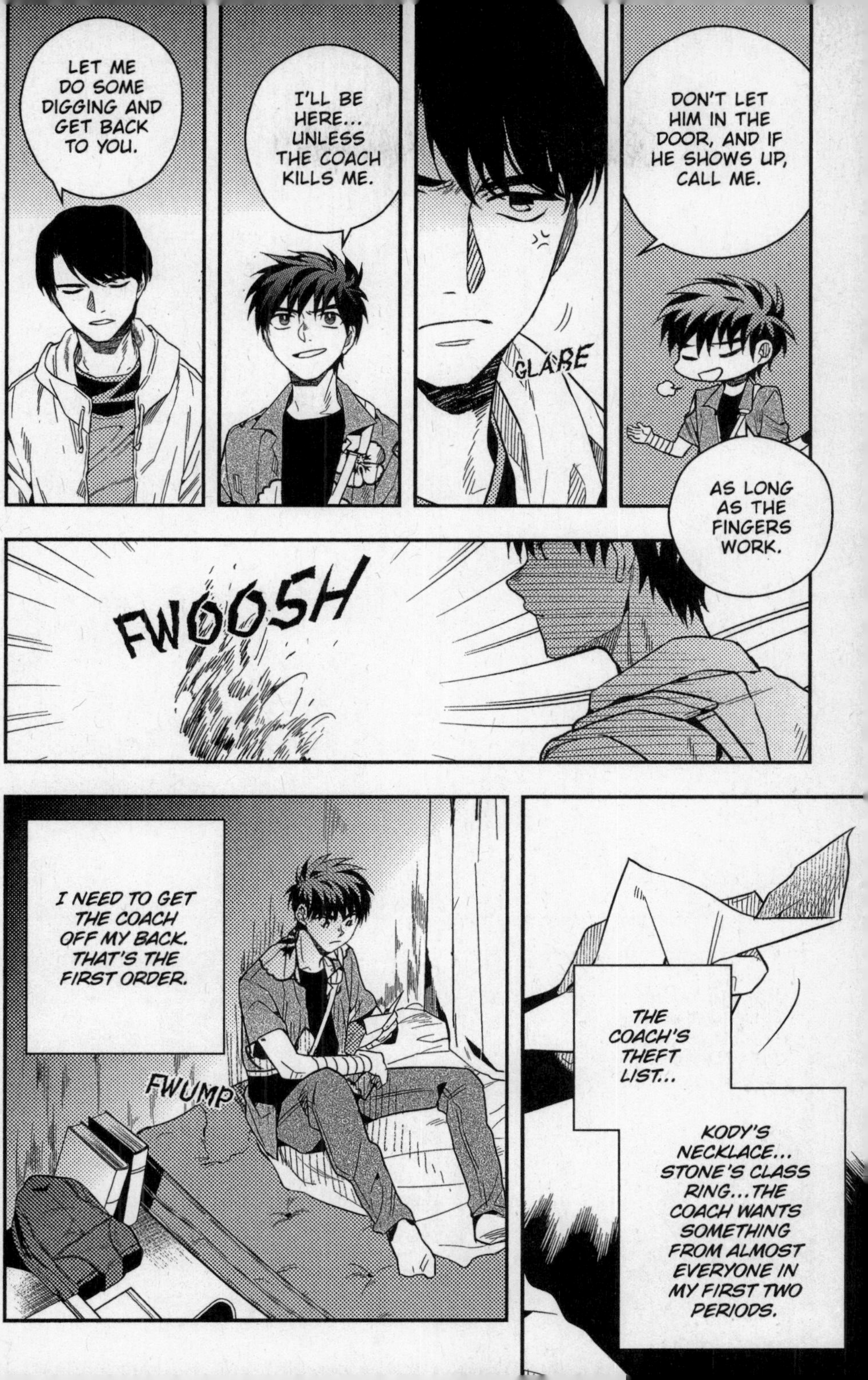
LET ME DO SOME DIGGING AND GET BACK TO YOU.
I'LL BE HERE... UNLESS THE COACH KILLS ME.
GLARE
DON'T LET HIM IN THE DOOR, AND IF HE SHOWS UP, CALL ME.
AS LONG AS THE FINGERS WORK.
FWOOSH
I NEED TO GET THE COACH OFF MY BACK. THAT'S THE FIRST ORDER.
FWUMP
THE COACH'S THEFT LIST...
KODY'S NECKLACE... STONE'S CLASS RING...THE COACH WANTS SOMETHING FROM ALMOST EVERYONE IN MY FIRST TWO PERIODS.

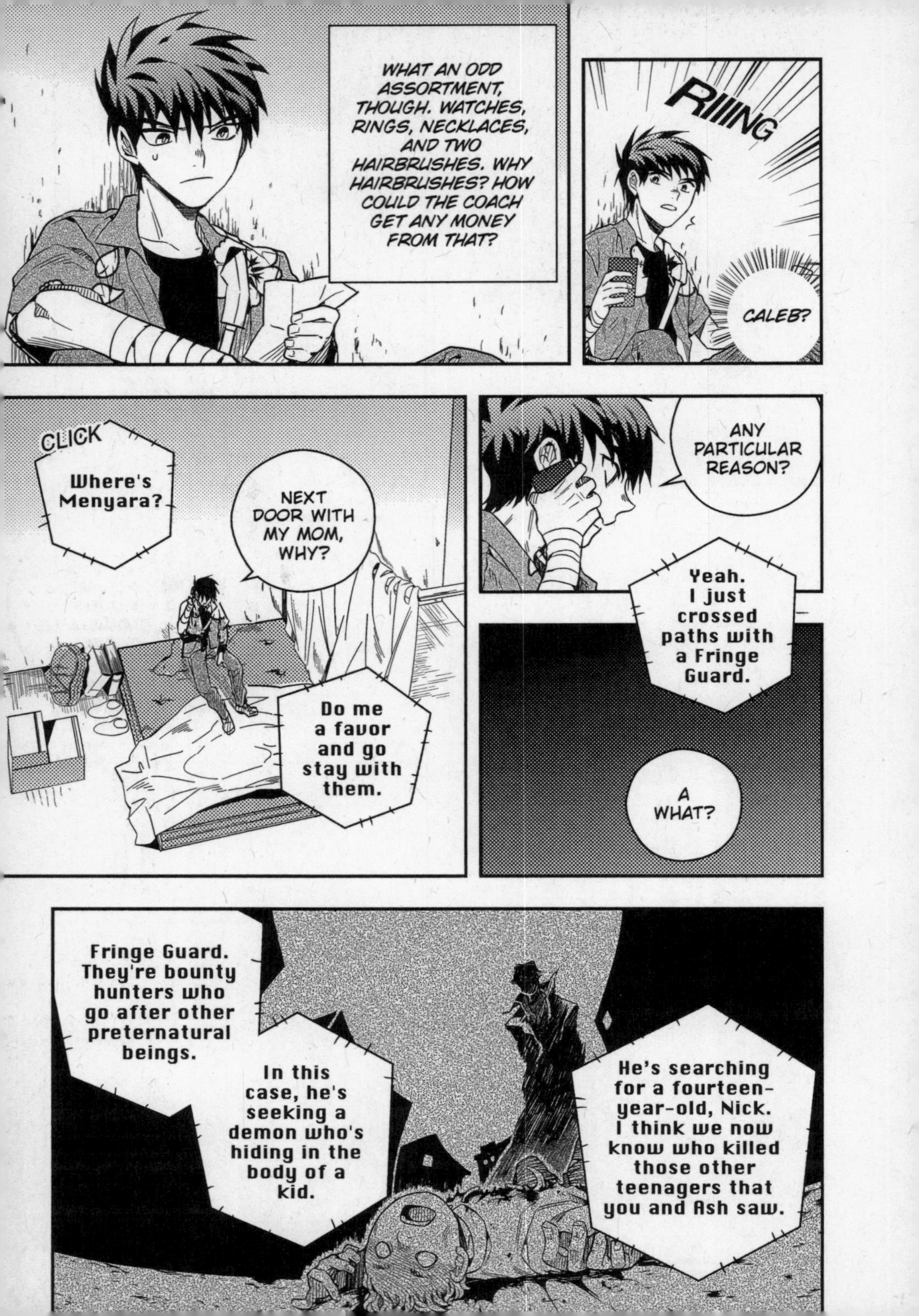
WHAT AN ODD ASSORTMENT, THOUGH. WATCHES, RINGS, NECKLACES, AND TWO HAIRBRUSHES. WHY HAIRBRUSHES? HOW COULD THE COACH GET ANY MONEY FROM THAT?
RIIING
CALEB?
CLICK
Where's Menyara?
NEXT DOOR WITH MY MOM, WHY?
Do me a favor and go stay with them.
ANY PARTICULAR REASON?
Yeah. I just crossed paths with a Fringe Guard.
A WHAT?
Fringe Guard. They're bounty hunters who go after other preternatural beings.
In this case, he's seeking a demon who's hiding in the body of a kid.
He's searching for a fourteen-year-old, Nick. I think we now know who killed those other teenagers that you and Ash saw.

THE DARK-HUNTERS: INFINITY

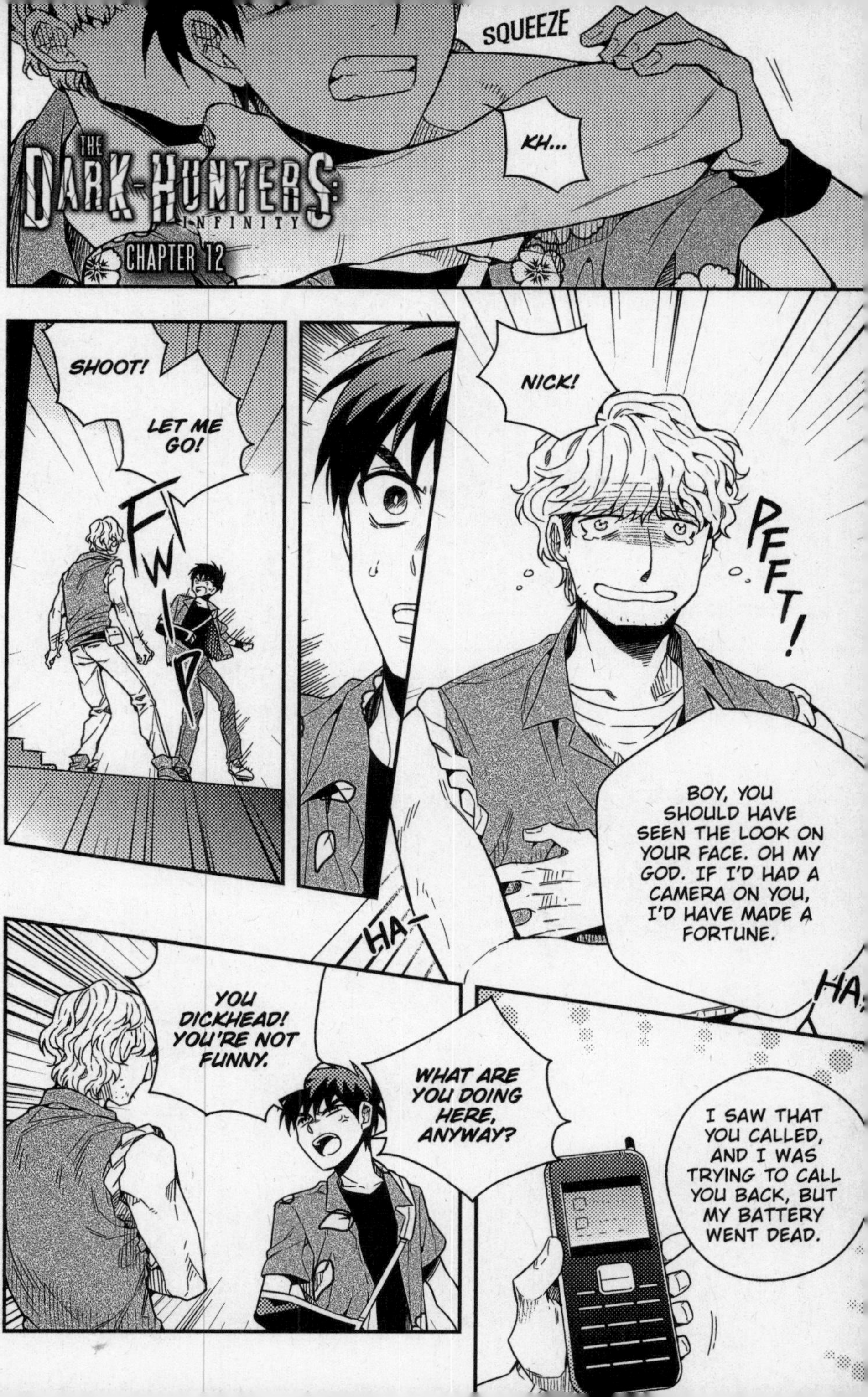
THE DARK-HUNTERS: INFINITY
CHAPTER 12
SQUEEZE
KH...
SHOOT!
LET ME GO!
FWIP
NICK!
PFFT!
BOY, YOU SHOULD HAVE SEEN THE LOOK ON YOUR FACE. OH MY GOD. IF I'D HAD A CAMERA ON YOU, I'D HAVE MADE A FORTUNE.
HA-
HA-
YOU DICKHEAD! YOU'RE NOT FUNNY.
WHAT ARE YOU DOING HERE, ANYWAY?
I SAW THAT YOU CALLED, AND I WAS TRYING TO CALL YOU BACK, BUT MY BATTERY WENT DEAD.

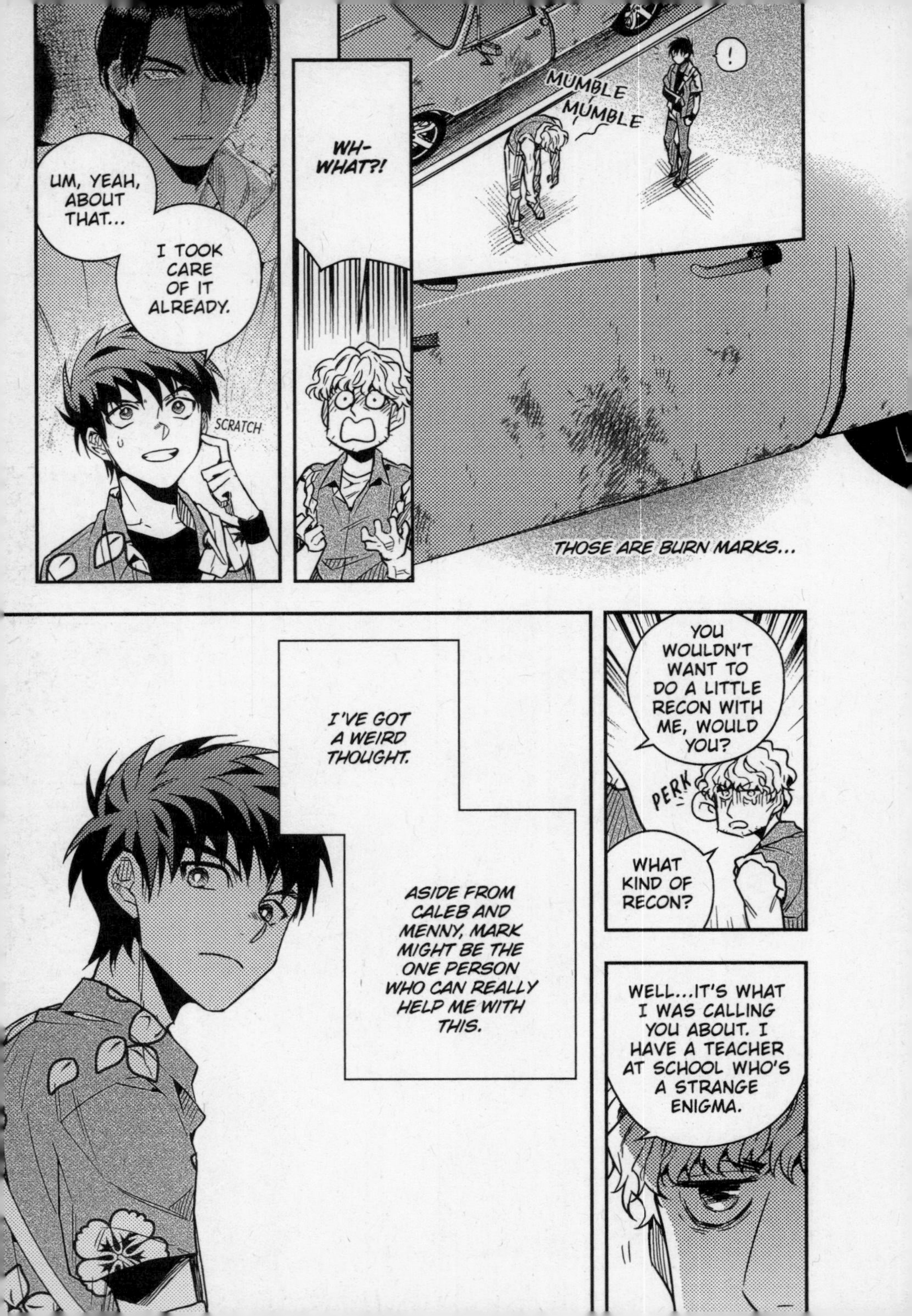
!
MUMBLE MUMBLE MUMBLE
UM, YEAH, ABOUT THAT...
I TOOK CARE OF IT ALREADY.
SCRATCH
WH- WHAT?!
THOSE ARE BURN MARKS...
YOU WOULDN'T WANT TO DO A LITTLE RECON WITH ME, WOULD YOU?
PERK
WHAT KIND OF RECON?
WELL...IT'S WHAT I WAS CALLING YOU ABOUT. I HAVE A TEACHER AT SCHOOL WHO'S A STRANGE ENIGMA.
I'VE GOT A WEIRD THOUGHT.
ASIDE FROM CALEB AND MENNY, MARK MIGHT BE THE ONE PERSON WHO CAN REALLY HELP ME WITH THIS.

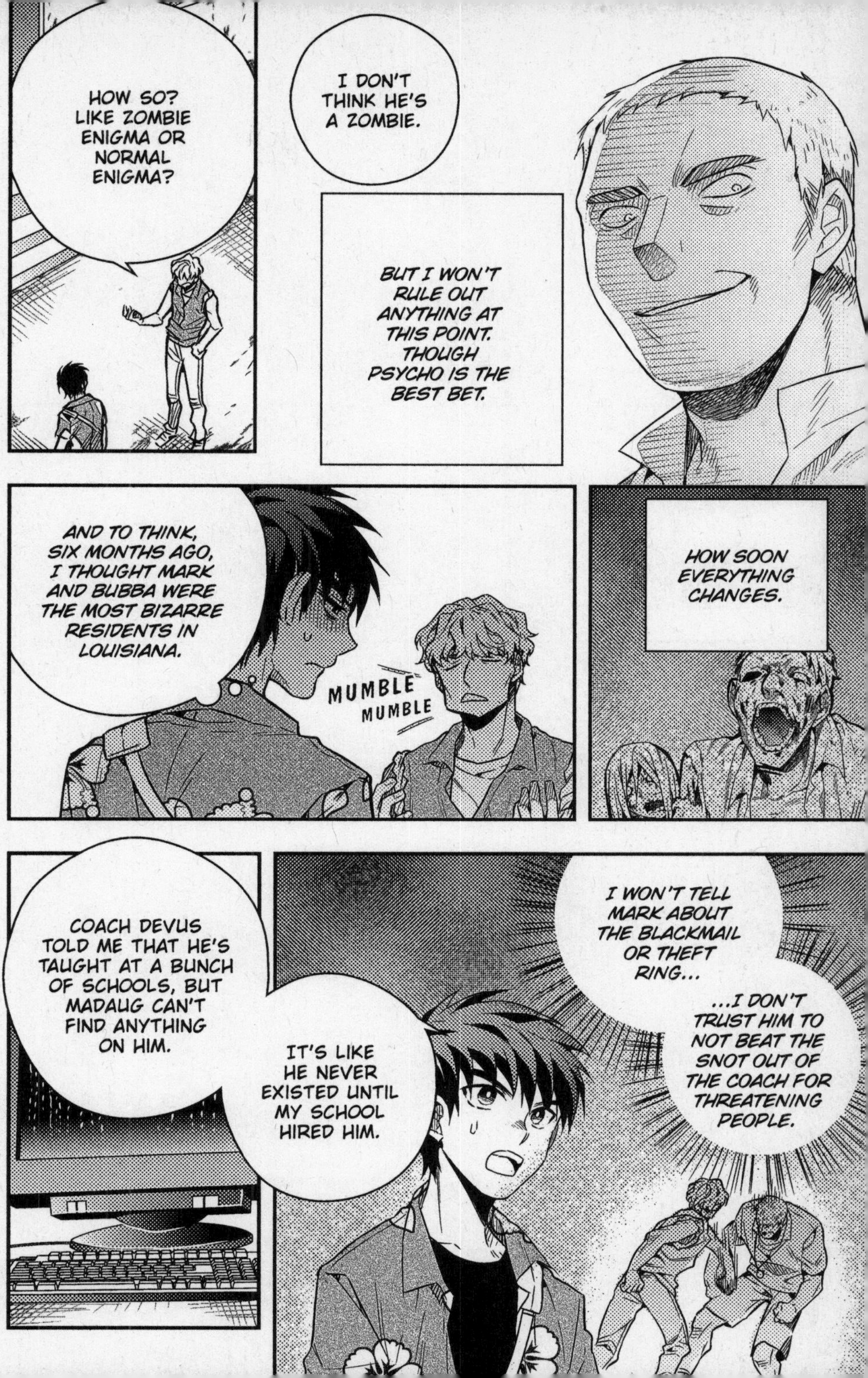
HOW SO? LIKE ZOMBIE ENIGMA OR NORMAL ENIGMA?
I DON'T THINK HE'S A ZOMBIE.
BUT I WON'T RULE OUT ANYTHING AT THIS POINT. THOUGH PSYCHO IS THE BEST BET.
AND TO THINK, SIX MONTHS AGO, I THOUGHT MARK AND BUBBA WERE THE MOST BIZARRE RESIDENTS IN LOUISIANA.
MUMBLE MUMBLE
HOW SOON EVERYTHING CHANGES.
COACH DEVUS TOLD ME THAT HE'S TAUGHT AT A BUNCH OF SCHOOLS, BUT MADAUG CAN'T FIND ANYTHING ON HIM.
IT'S LIKE HE NEVER EXISTED UNTIL MY SCHOOL HIRED HIM.
I WON'T TELL MARK ABOUT THE BLACKMAIL OR THEFT RING...
...I DON'T TRUST HIM TO NOT BEAT THE SNOT OUT OF THE COACH FOR THREATENING PEOPLE.

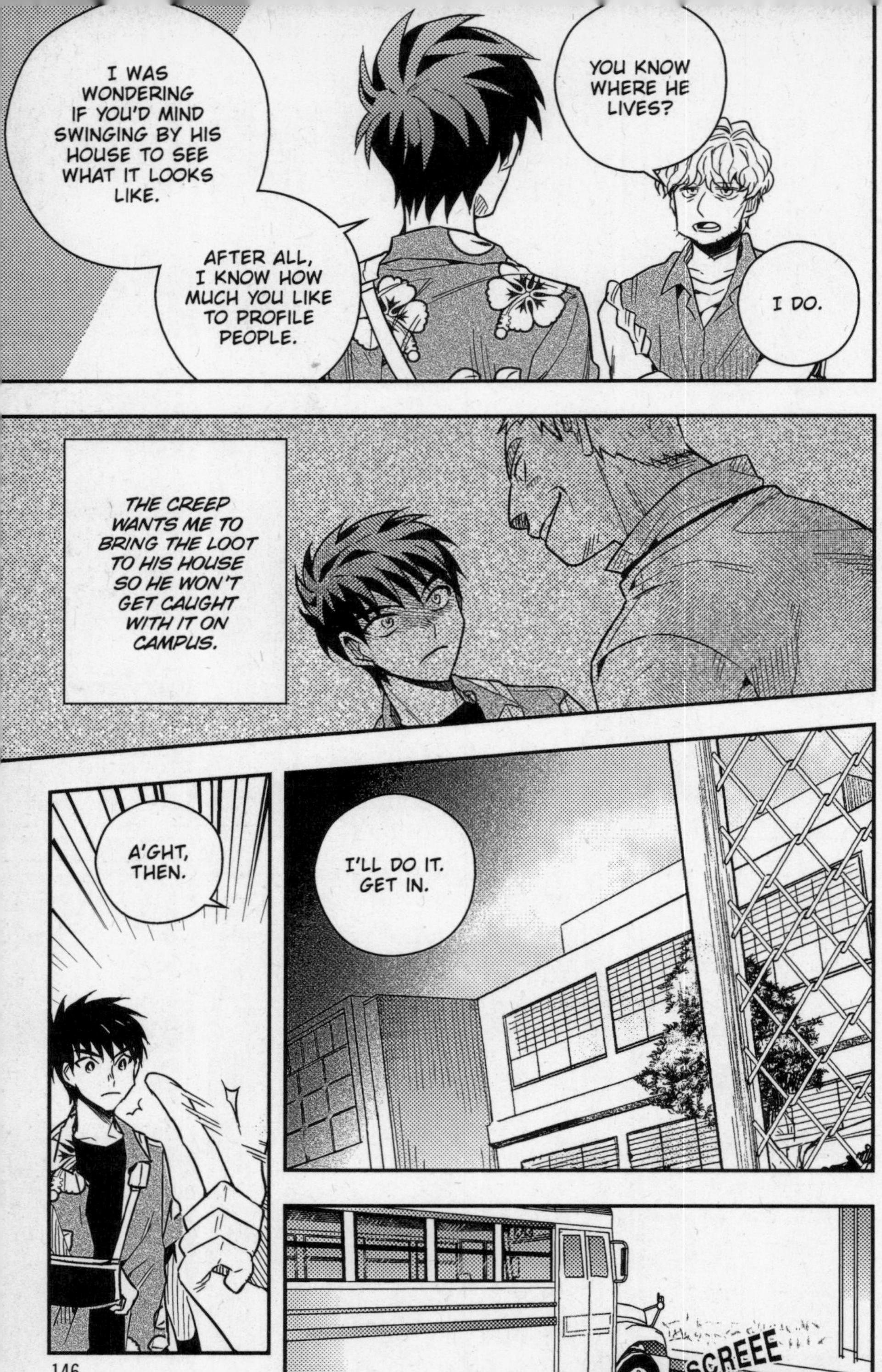
I WAS WONDERING IF YOU'D MIND SWINGING BY HIS HOUSE TO SEE WHAT IT LOOKS LIKE.
AFTER ALL, I KNOW HOW MUCH YOU LIKE TO PROFILE PEOPLE.
YOU KNOW WHERE HE LIVES?
I DO.
THE CREEP WANTS ME TO BRING THE LOOT TO HIS HOUSE SO HE WON'T GET CAUGHT WITH IT ON CAMPUS.
A'GHT, THEN.
I'LL DO IT. GET IN.
SCREEE

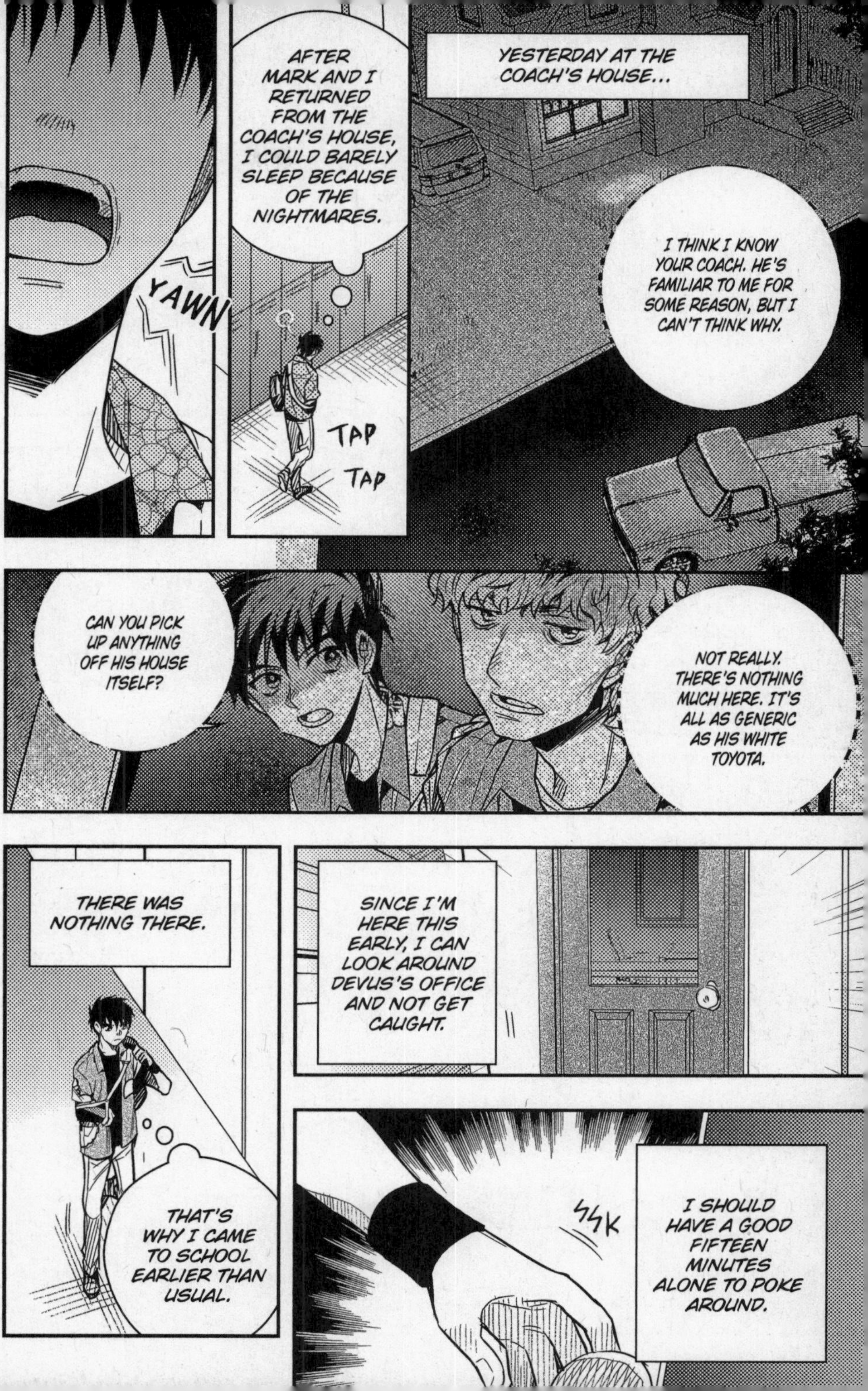
YAWN
AFTER MARK AND I RETURNED FROM THE COACH'S HOUSE, I COULD BARELY SLEEP BECAUSE OF THE NIGHTMARES.
TAP
TAP
YESTERDAY AT THE COACH'S HOUSE...
I THINK I KNOW YOUR COACH. HE'S FAMILIAR TO ME FOR SOME REASON, BUT I CAN'T THINK WHY.
CAN YOU PICK UP ANYTHING OFF HIS HOUSE ITSELF?
NOT REALLY. THERE'S NOTHING MUCH HERE. IT'S ALL AS GENERIC AS HIS WHITE TOYOTA.
THERE WAS NOTHING THERE.
THAT'S WHY I CAME TO SCHOOL EARLIER THAN USUAL.
SINCE I'M HERE THIS EARLY, I CAN LOOK AROUND DEVUS'S OFFICE AND NOT GET CAUGHT.
SSK
I SHOULD HAVE A GOOD FIFTEEN MINUTES ALONE TO POKE AROUND.

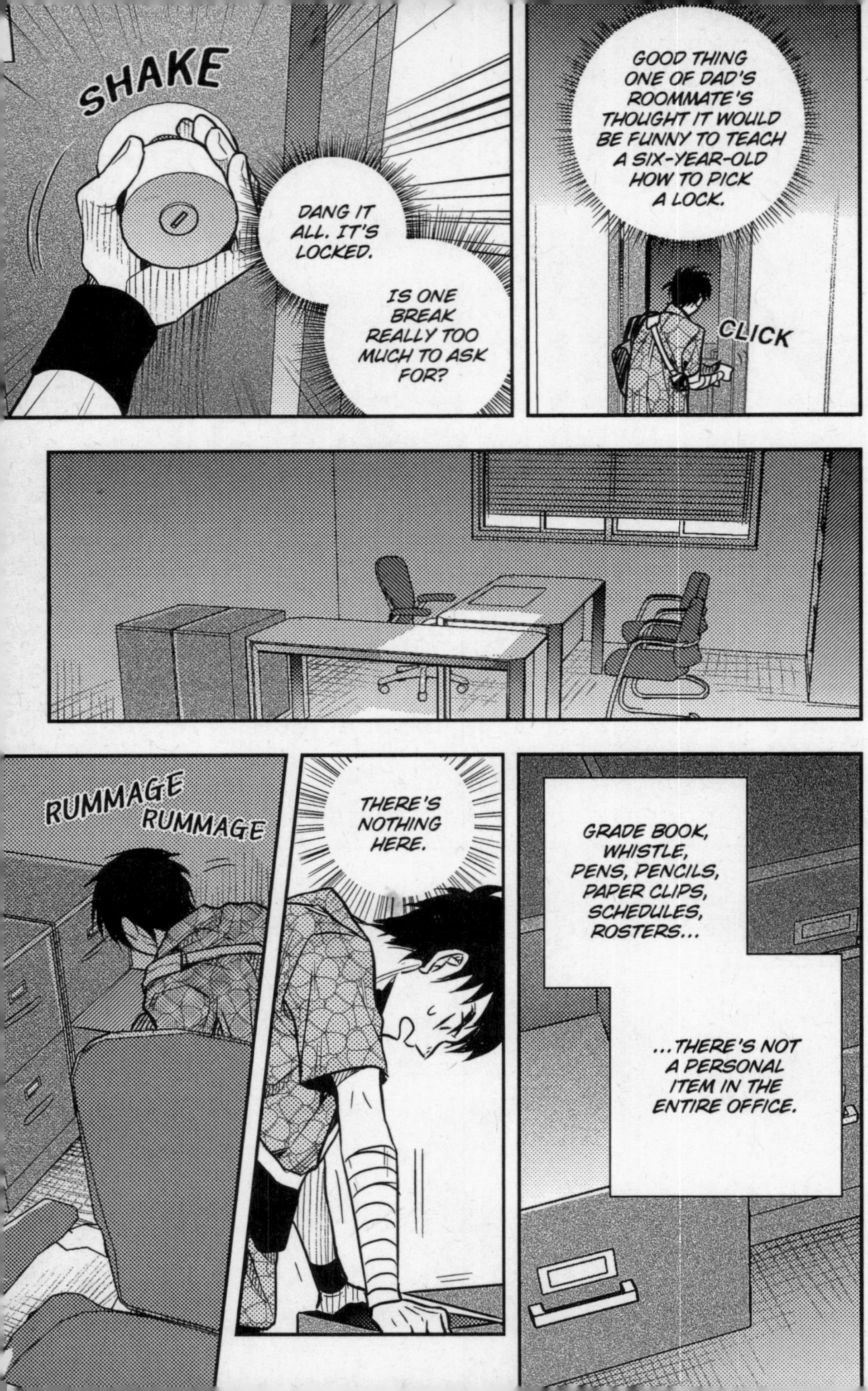
SHAKE
DANG IT ALL. IT'S LOCKED.
IS ONE BREAK REALLY TOO MUCH TO ASK FOR?
GOOD THING ONE OF DAD'S ROOMMATE'S THOUGHT IT WOULD BE FUNNY TO TEACH A SIX-YEAR-OLD HOW TO PICK A LOCK.
CLICK
RUMMAGE RUMMAGE
THERE'S NOTHING HERE.
GRADE BOOK, WHISTLE, PENS, PENCILS, PAPER CLIPS, SCHEDULES, ROSTERS...
...THERE'S NOT A PERSONAL ITEM IN THE ENTIRE OFFICE.

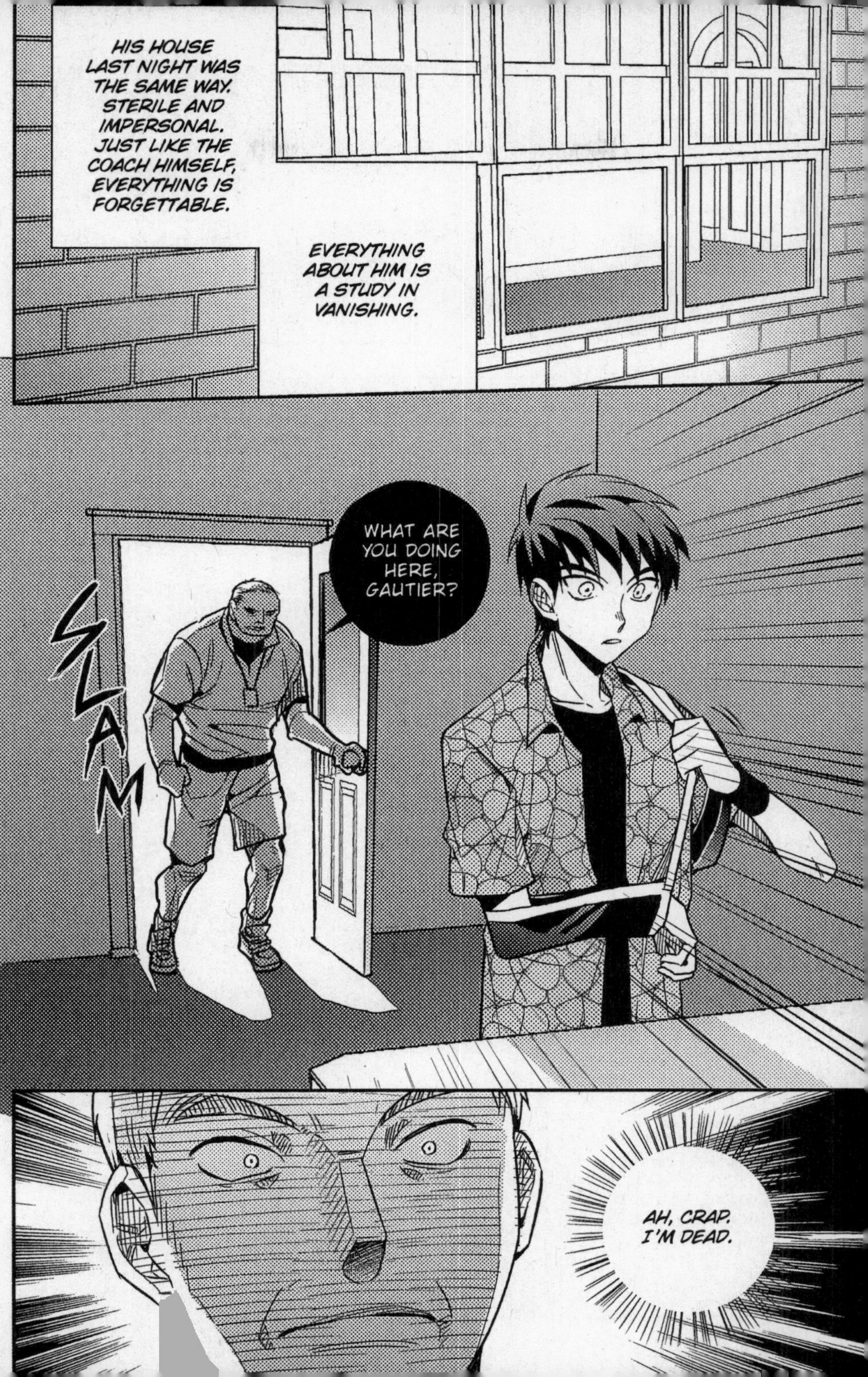
HIS HOUSE LAST NIGHT WAS THE SAME WAY. STERILE AND IMPERSONAL. JUST LIKE THE COACH HIMSELF, EVERYTHING IS FORGETTABLE.
EVERYTHING ABOUT HIM IS A STUDY IN VANISHING.
SLAM
WHAT ARE YOU DOING HERE, GAUTIER?
AH, CRAP. I'M DEAD.

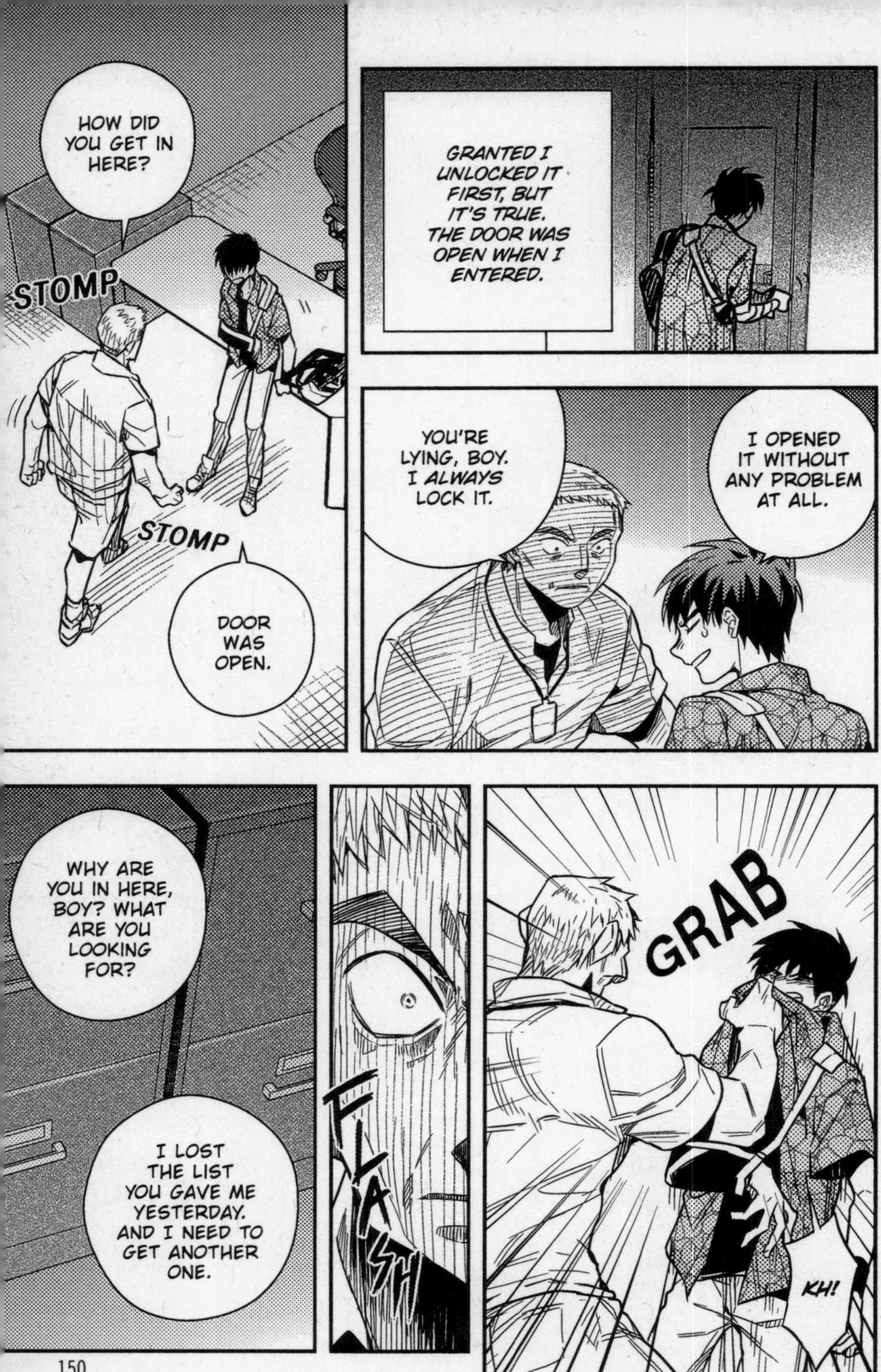
HOW DID YOU GET IN HERE?
STOMP
STOMP
DOOR WAS OPEN.
GRANTED I UNLOCKED IT FIRST, BUT IT'S TRUE. THE DOOR WAS OPEN WHEN I ENTERED.
YOU'RE LYING, BOY. I *ALWAYS* LOCK IT.
I OPENED IT WITHOUT ANY PROBLEM AT ALL.
WHY ARE YOU IN HERE, BOY? WHAT ARE YOU LOOKING FOR?
I LOST THE LIST YOU GAVE ME YESTERDAY. AND I NEED TO GET ANOTHER ONE.
FLASH
GRAB
KH!

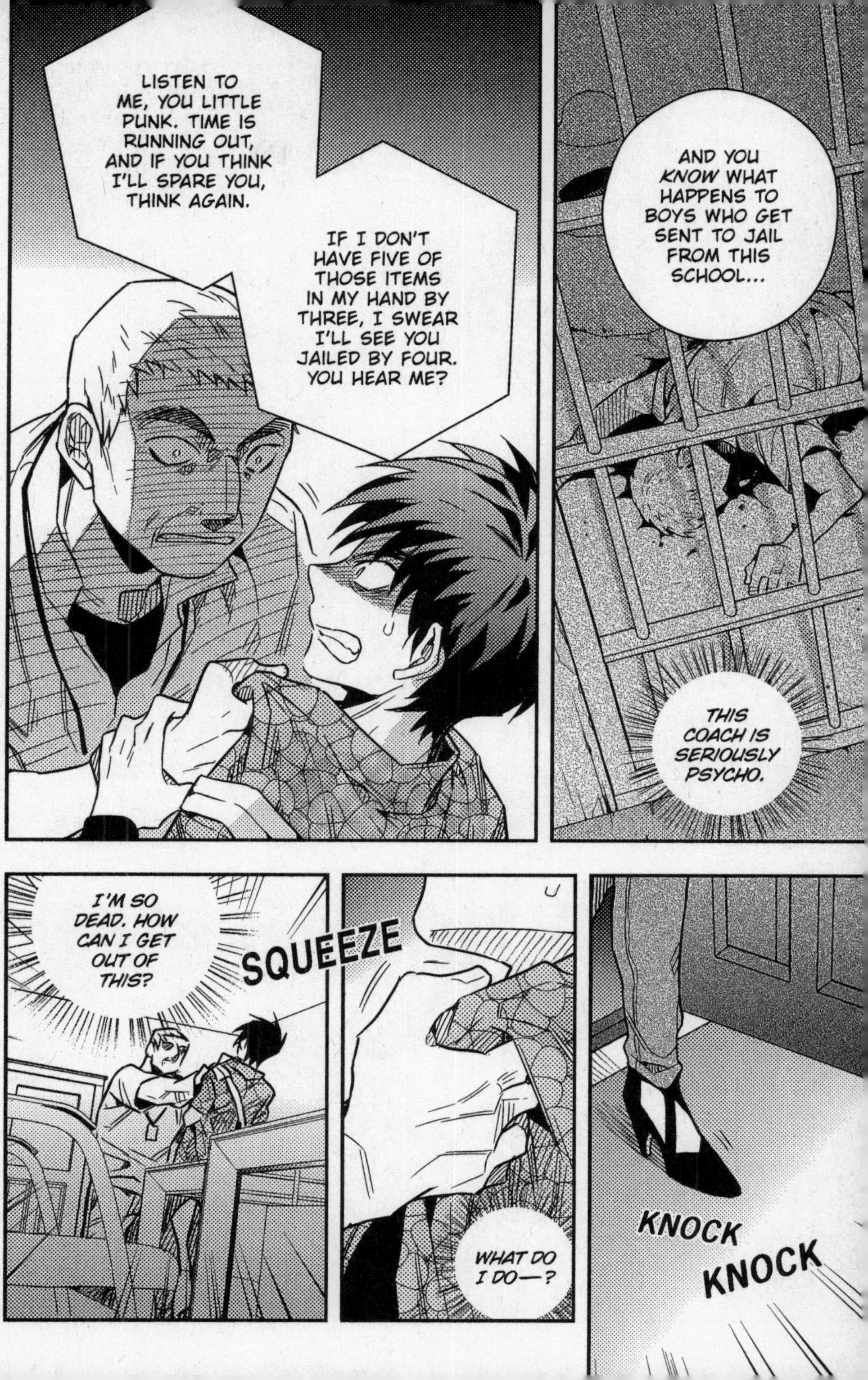
LISTEN TO ME, YOU LITTLE PUNK. TIME IS RUNNING OUT, AND IF YOU THINK I'LL SPARE YOU, THINK AGAIN.
IF I DON'T HAVE FIVE OF THOSE ITEMS IN MY HAND BY THREE, I SWEAR I'LL SEE YOU JAILED BY FOUR. YOU HEAR ME?
AND YOU *KNOW* WHAT HAPPENS TO BOYS WHO GET SENT TO JAIL FROM THIS SCHOOL...
THIS COACH IS SERIOUSLY PSYCHO.
I'M SO DEAD. HOW CAN I GET OUT OF THIS?
SQUEEZE
WHAT DO I DO—?
KNOCK
KNOCK

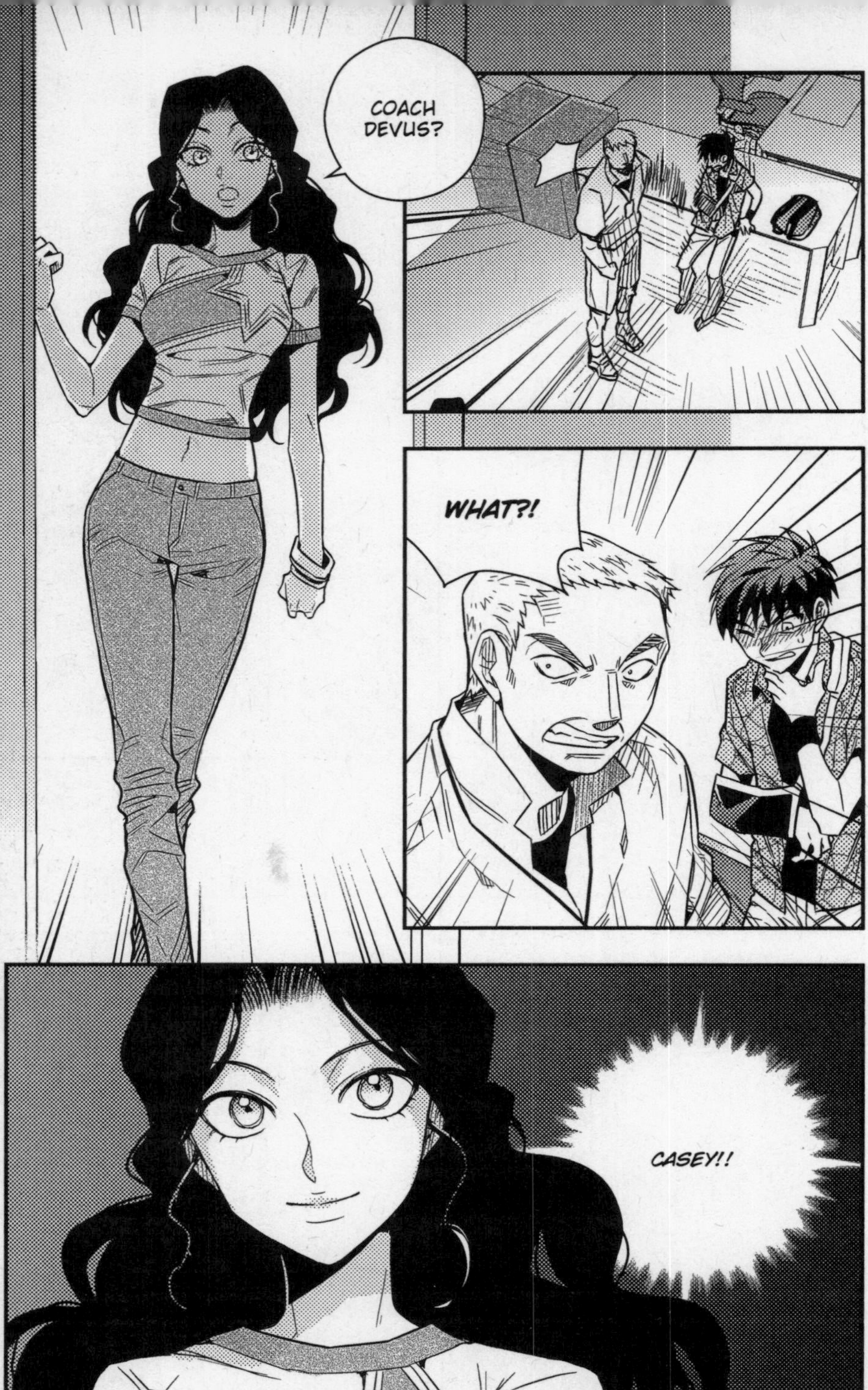
COACH DEVUS?
WHAT?!
CASEY!!

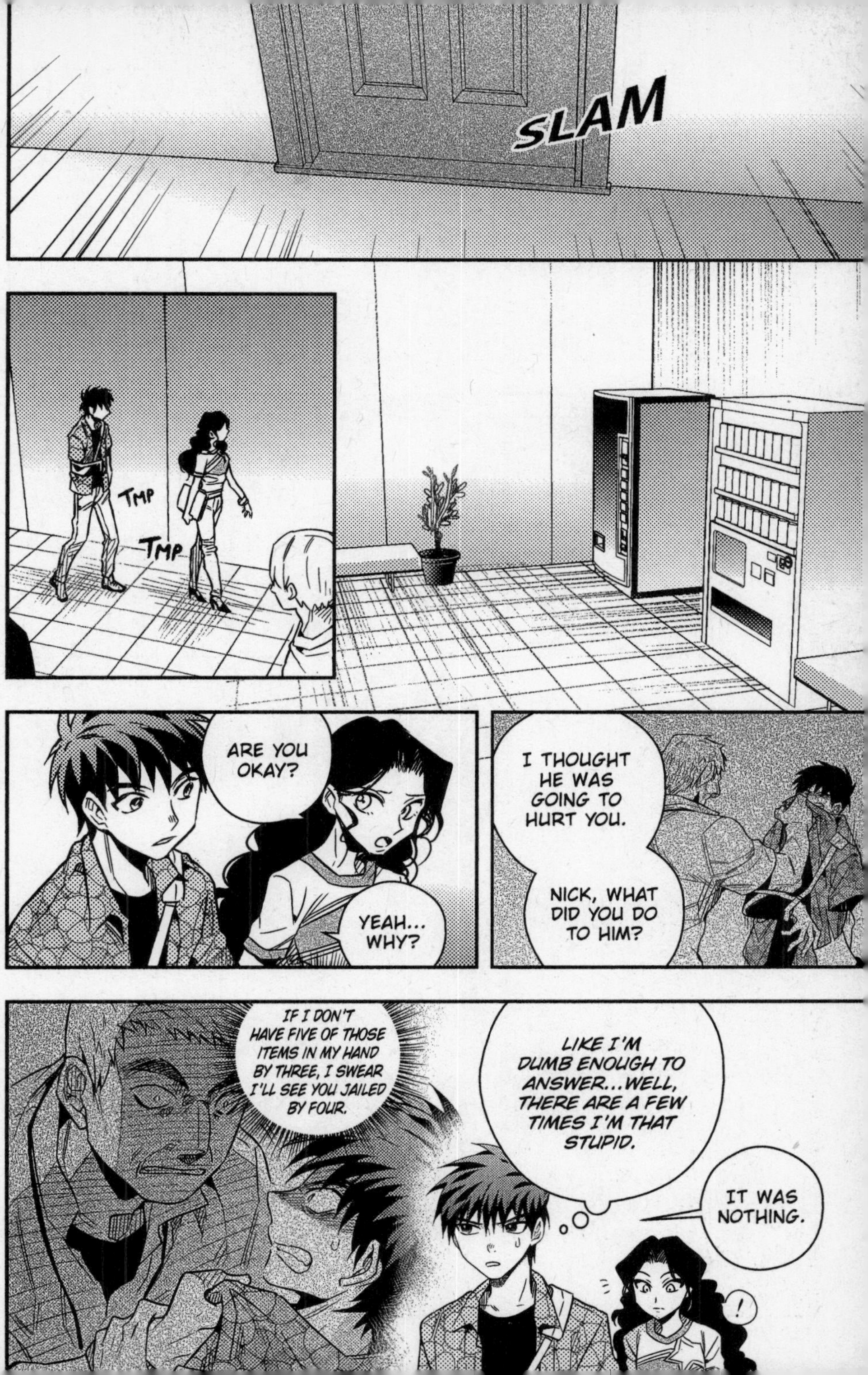
SLAM
TMP
TMP
ARE YOU OKAY?
YEAH... WHY?
I THOUGHT HE WAS GOING TO HURT YOU.
NICK, WHAT DID YOU DO TO HIM?
LIKE I'M DUMB ENOUGH TO ANSWER...WELL, THERE ARE A FEW TIMES I'M THAT STUPID.
IF I DON'T HAVE FIVE OF THOSE ITEMS IN MY HAND BY THREE, I SWEAR I'LL SEE YOU JAILED BY FOUR.
IT WAS NOTHING.
!

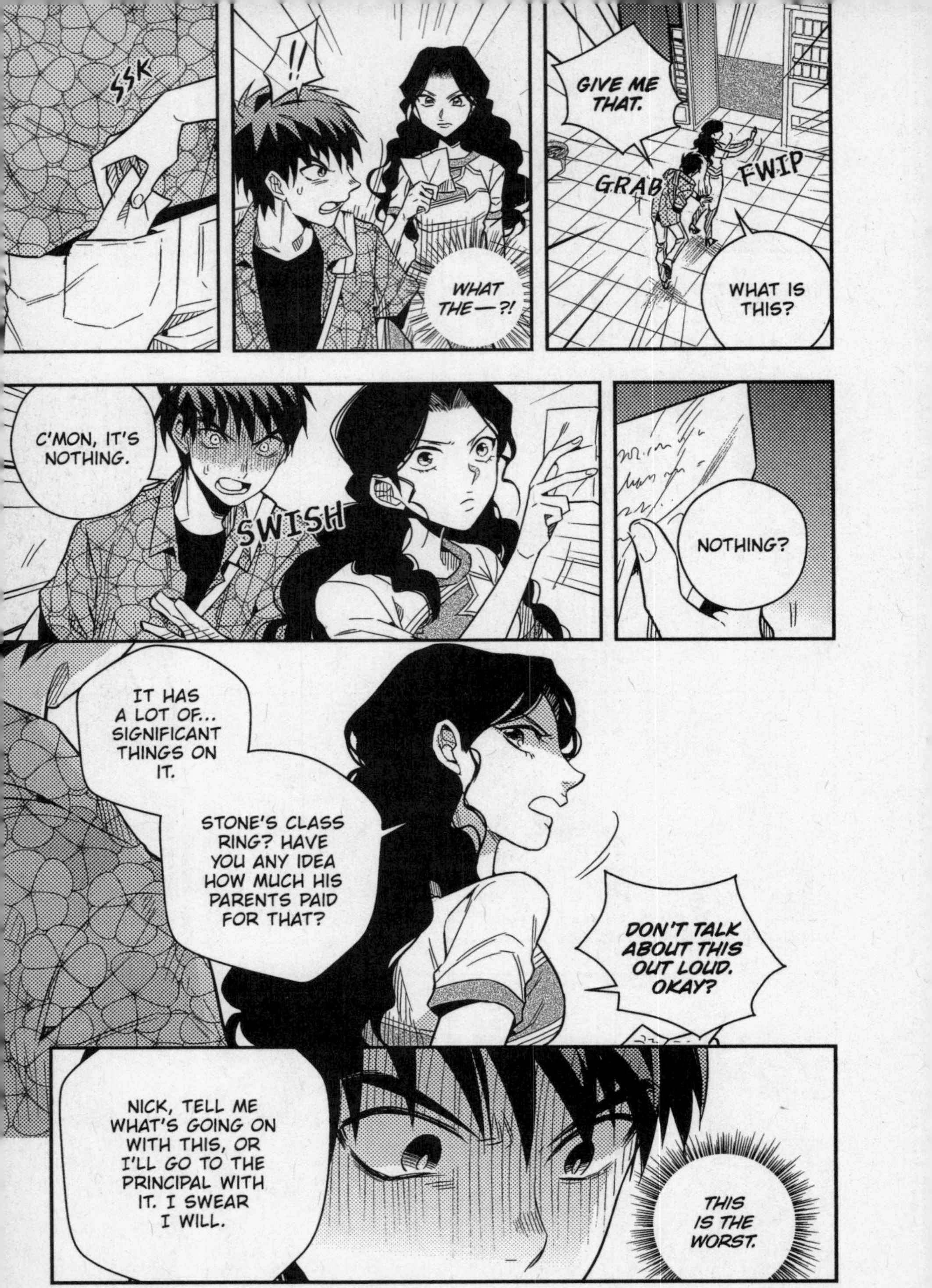
SSK
!!
WHAT THE—?!
GIVE ME THAT.
GRAB
FWIP
WHAT IS THIS?
C'MON, IT'S NOTHING.
SWISH
NOTHING?
IT HAS A LOT OF... SIGNIFICANT THINGS ON IT.
STONE'S CLASS RING? HAVE YOU ANY IDEA HOW MUCH HIS PARENTS PAID FOR THAT?
DON'T TALK ABOUT THIS OUT LOUD. OKAY?
NICK, TELL ME WHAT'S GOING ON WITH THIS, OR I'LL GO TO THE PRINCIPAL WITH IT. I SWEAR I WILL.
THIS IS THE WORST.

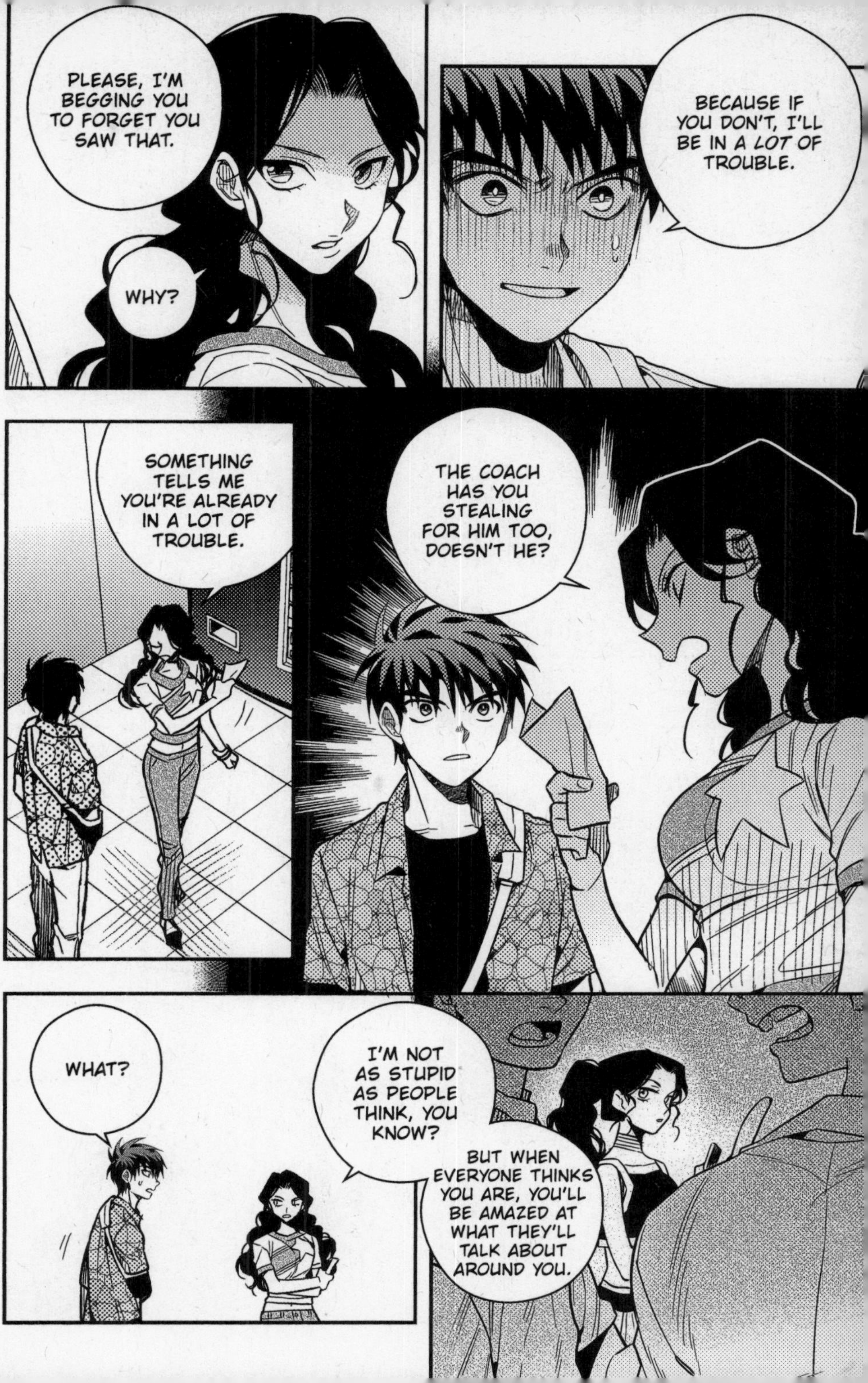
PLEASE, I'M BEGGING YOU TO FORGET YOU SAW THAT.
WHY?
BECAUSE IF YOU DON'T, I'LL BE IN A *LOT* OF TROUBLE.
SOMETHING TELLS ME YOU'RE ALREADY IN A LOT OF TROUBLE.
THE COACH HAS YOU STEALING FOR HIM TOO, DOESN'T HE?
WHAT?
I'M NOT AS STUPID AS PEOPLE THINK, YOU KNOW?
BUT WHEN EVERYONE THINKS YOU ARE, YOU'LL BE AMAZED AT WHAT THEY'LL TALK ABOUT AROUND YOU.

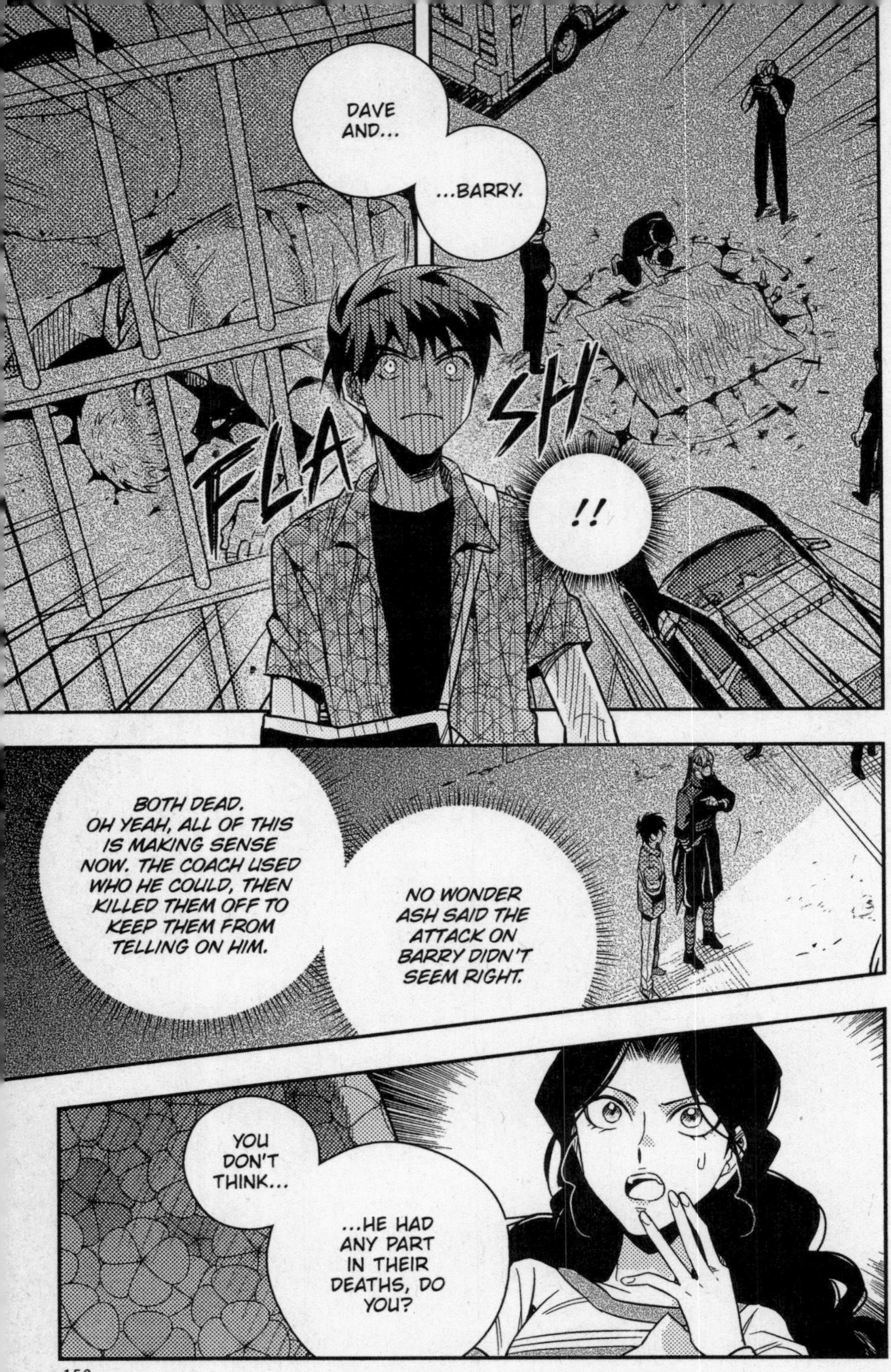

DAVE AND...
...BARRY.
FLASH
!!
BOTH DEAD. OH YEAH, ALL OF THIS IS MAKING SENSE NOW. THE COACH USED WHO HE COULD, THEN KILLED THEM OFF TO KEEP THEM FROM TELLING ON HIM.
NO WONDER ASH SAID THE ATTACK ON BARRY DIDN'T SEEM RIGHT.
YOU DON'T THINK...
...HE HAD ANY PART IN THEIR DEATHS, DO YOU?

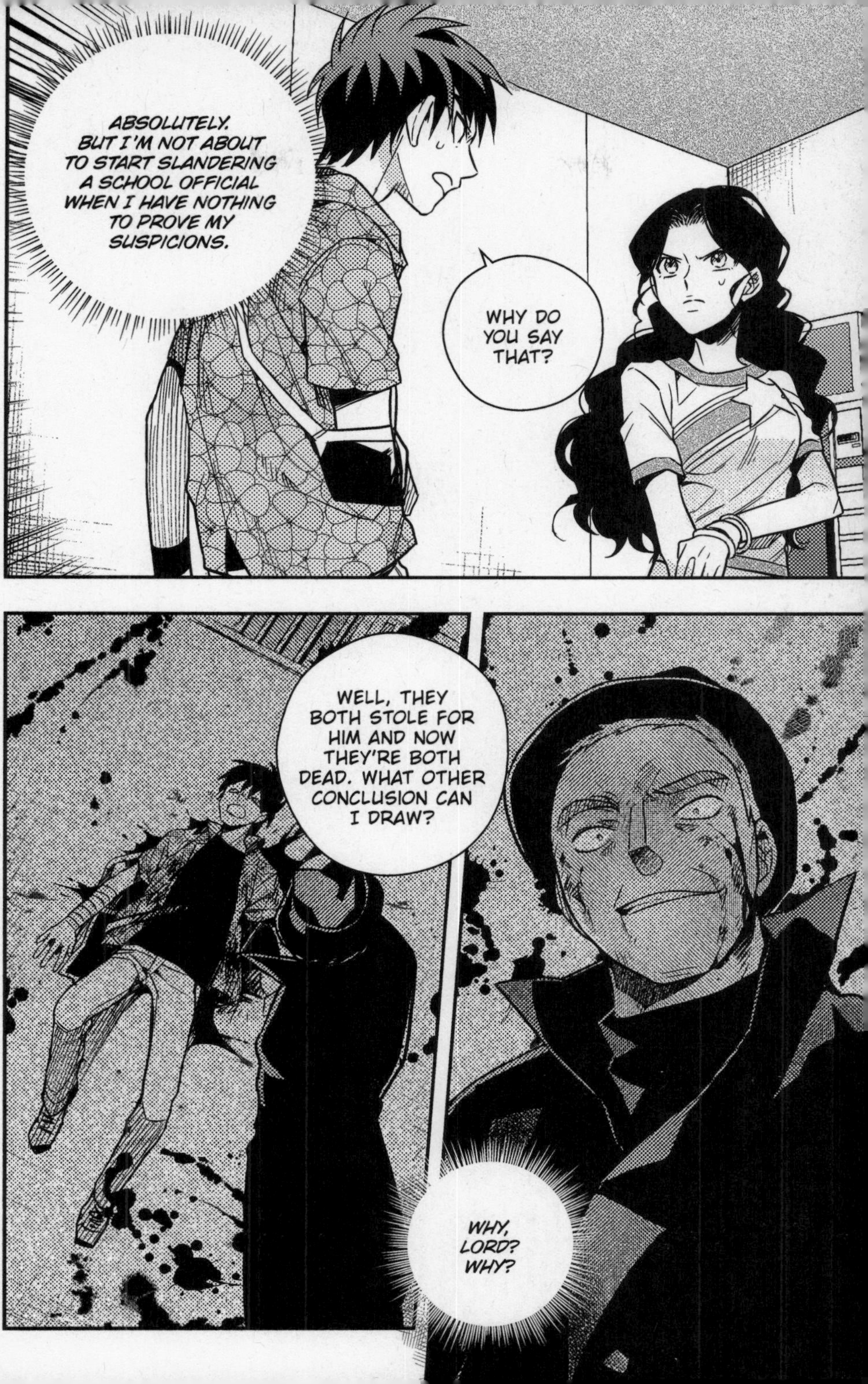
ABSOLUTELY. BUT I'M NOT ABOUT TO START SLANDERING A SCHOOL OFFICIAL WHEN I HAVE NOTHING TO PROVE MY SUSPICIONS.
WHY DO YOU SAY THAT?
WELL, THEY BOTH STOLE FOR HIM AND NOW THEY'RE BOTH DEAD. WHAT OTHER CONCLUSION CAN I DRAW?
WHY, LORD? WHY?

THE DARK-HUNTERS: INFINITY

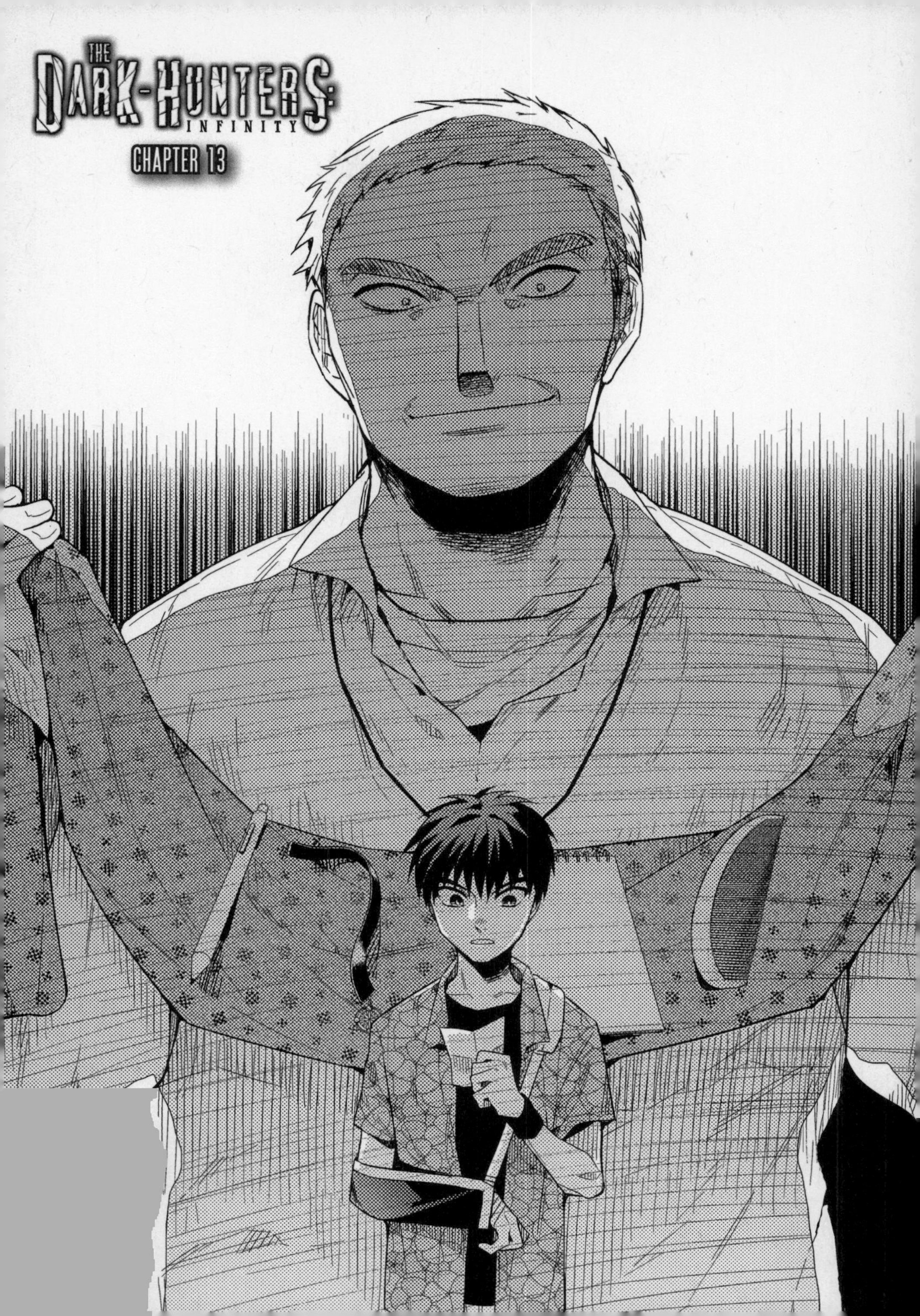
THE DARK-HUNTERS: INFINITY
CHAPTER 13

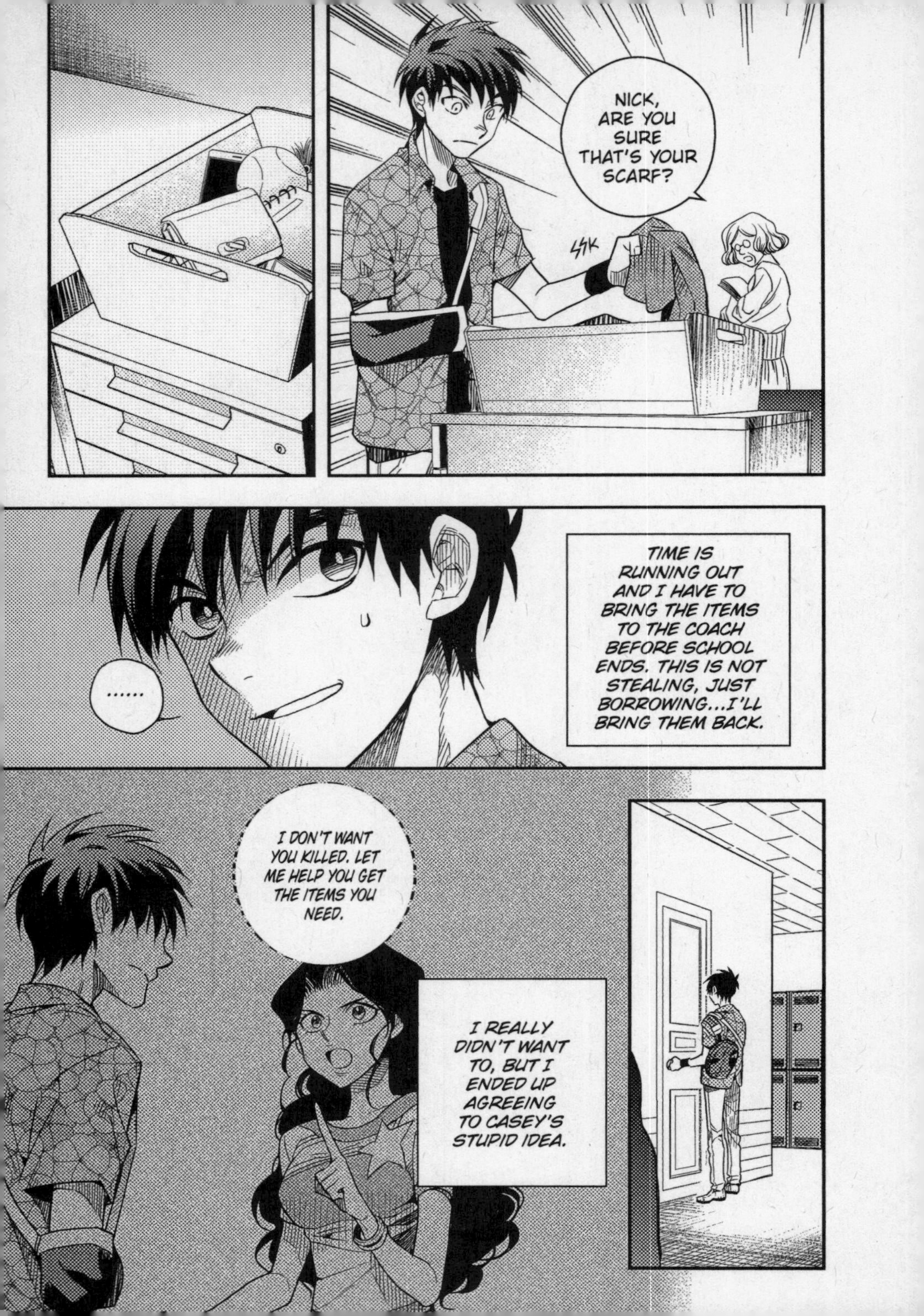
NICK, ARE YOU SURE THAT'S YOUR SCARF?
SSK
......
TIME IS RUNNING OUT AND I HAVE TO BRING THE ITEMS TO THE COACH BEFORE SCHOOL ENDS. THIS IS NOT STEALING, JUST BORROWING...I'LL BRING THEM BACK.
I DON'T WANT YOU KILLED. LET ME HELP YOU GET THE ITEMS YOU NEED.
I REALLY DIDN'T WANT TO, BUT I ENDED UP AGREEING TO CASEY'S STUPID IDEA.

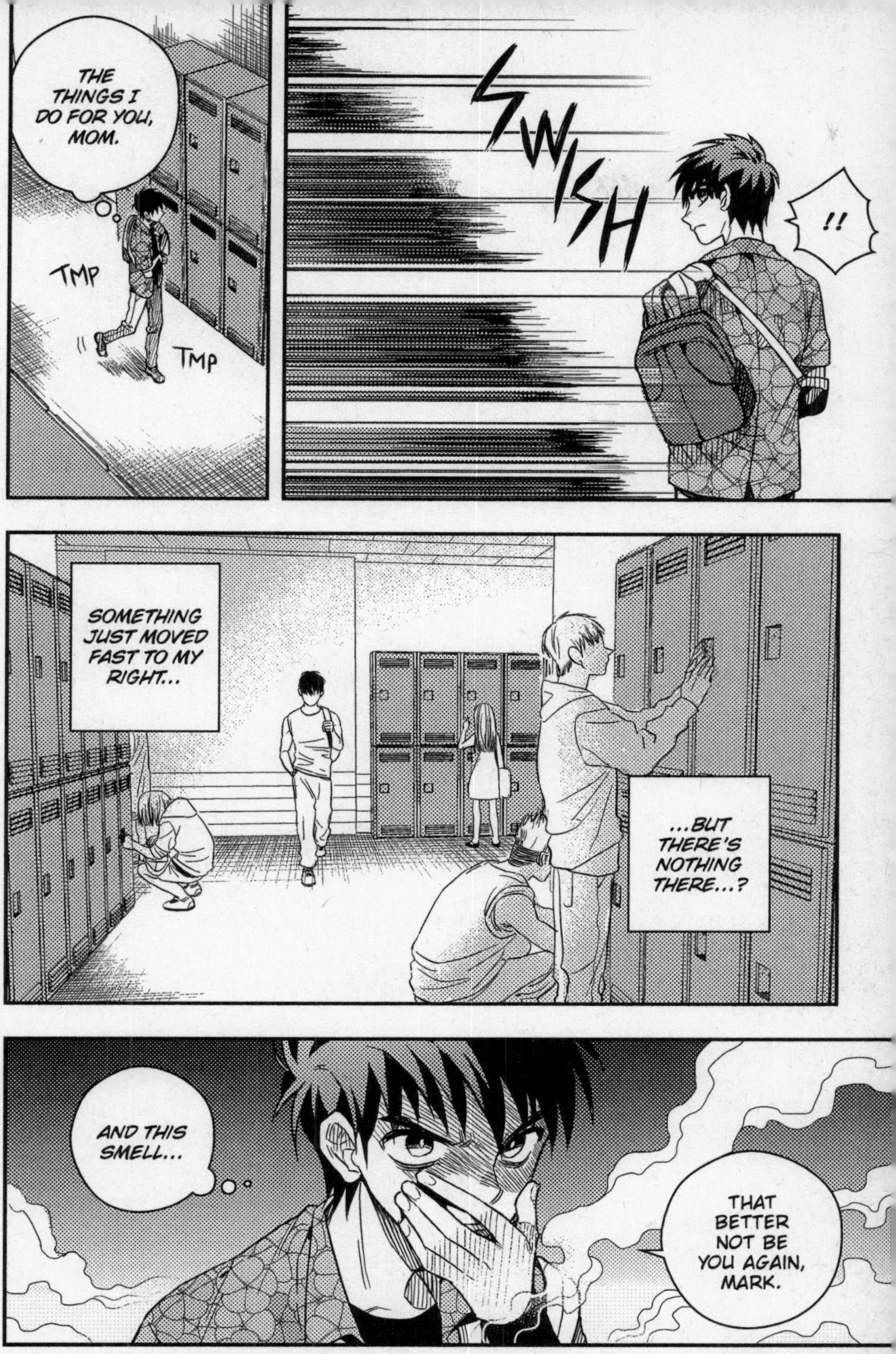
THE THINGS I DO FOR YOU, MOM.
TMP
TMP
SWISH
!!
SOMETHING JUST MOVED FAST TO MY RIGHT...
...BUT THERE'S NOTHING THERE...?
AND THIS SMELL...
THAT BETTER NOT BE YOU AGAIN, MARK.

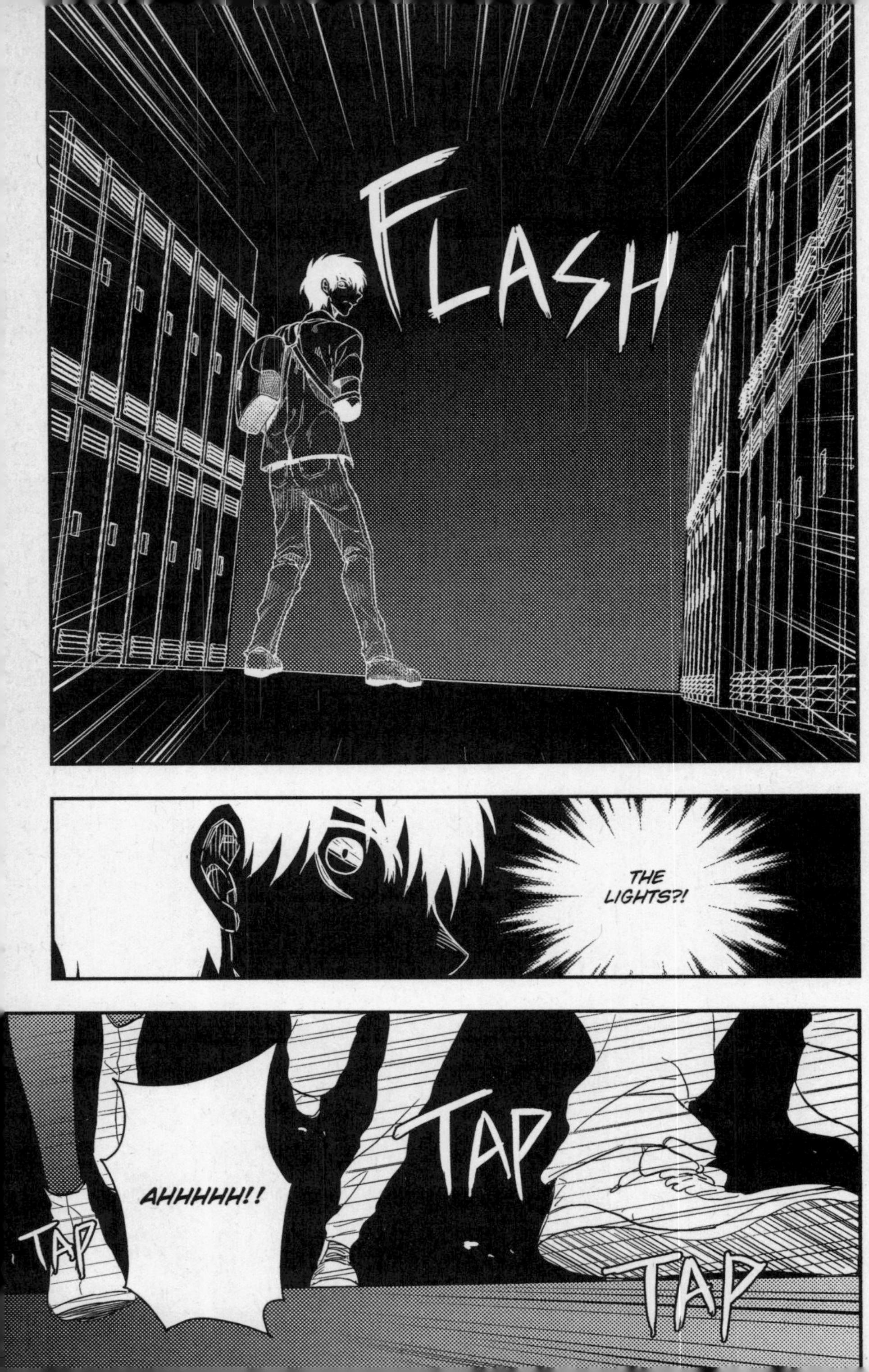
FLASH
THE LIGHTS?!
TAP
AHHHHH!!
TAP
TAP

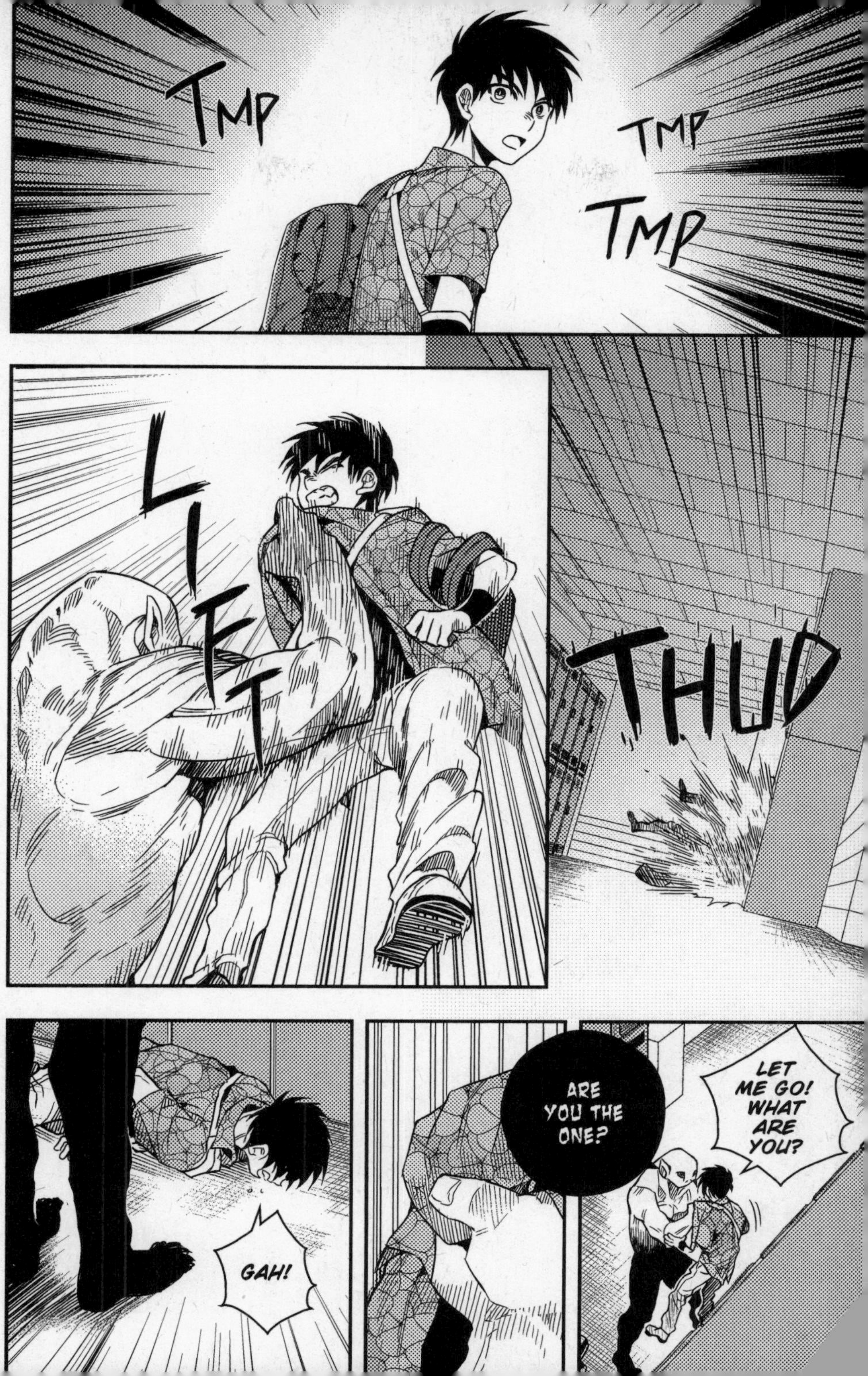
TMP
TMP
TMP
LIFT
THUD
GAH!
ARE YOU THE ONE?
LET ME GO! WHAT ARE YOU?

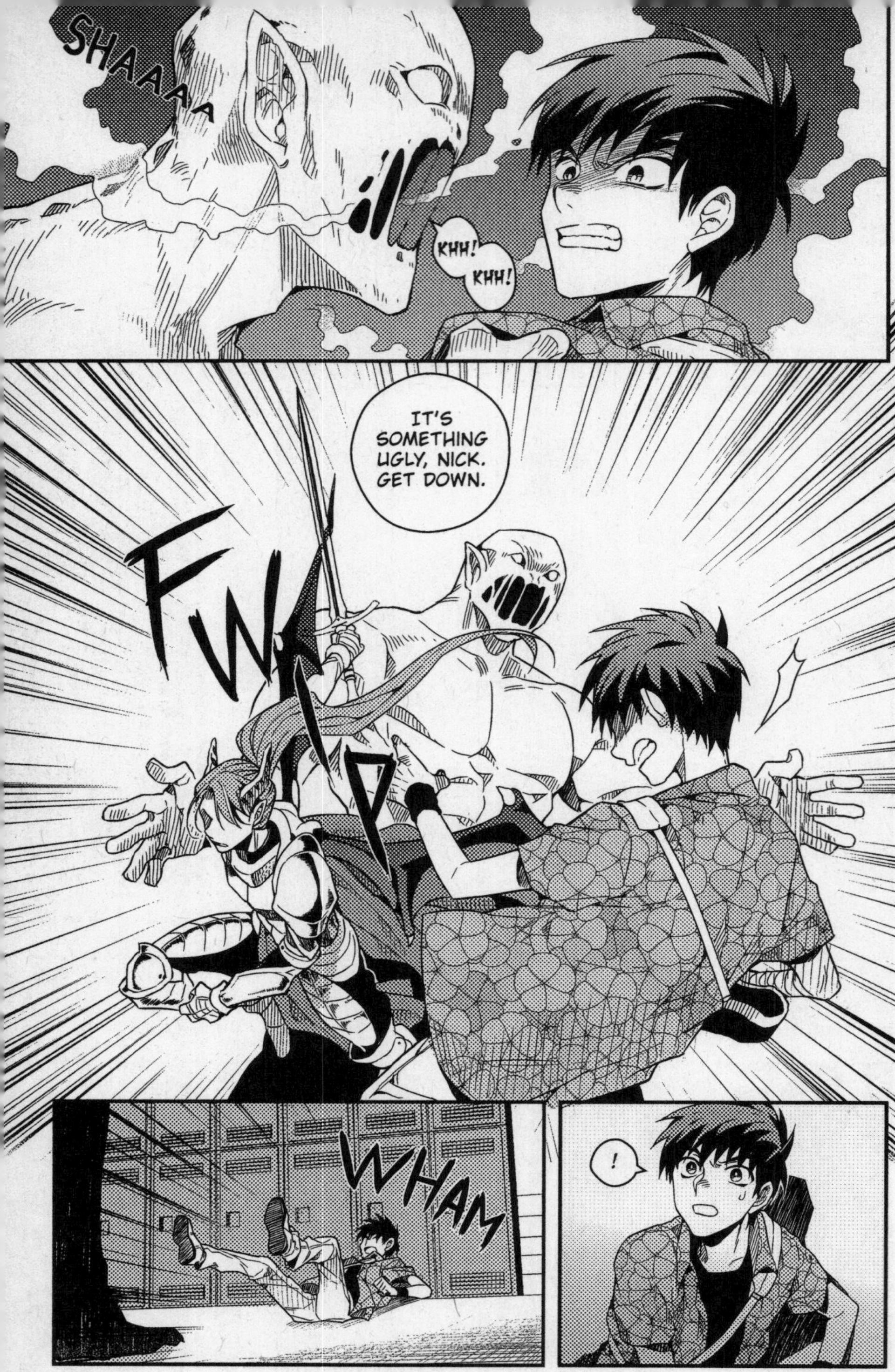
SHAAAAA
KHH!
KHH!
IT'S SOMETHING UGLY, NICK. GET DOWN.
FWHIP
WHAM
!

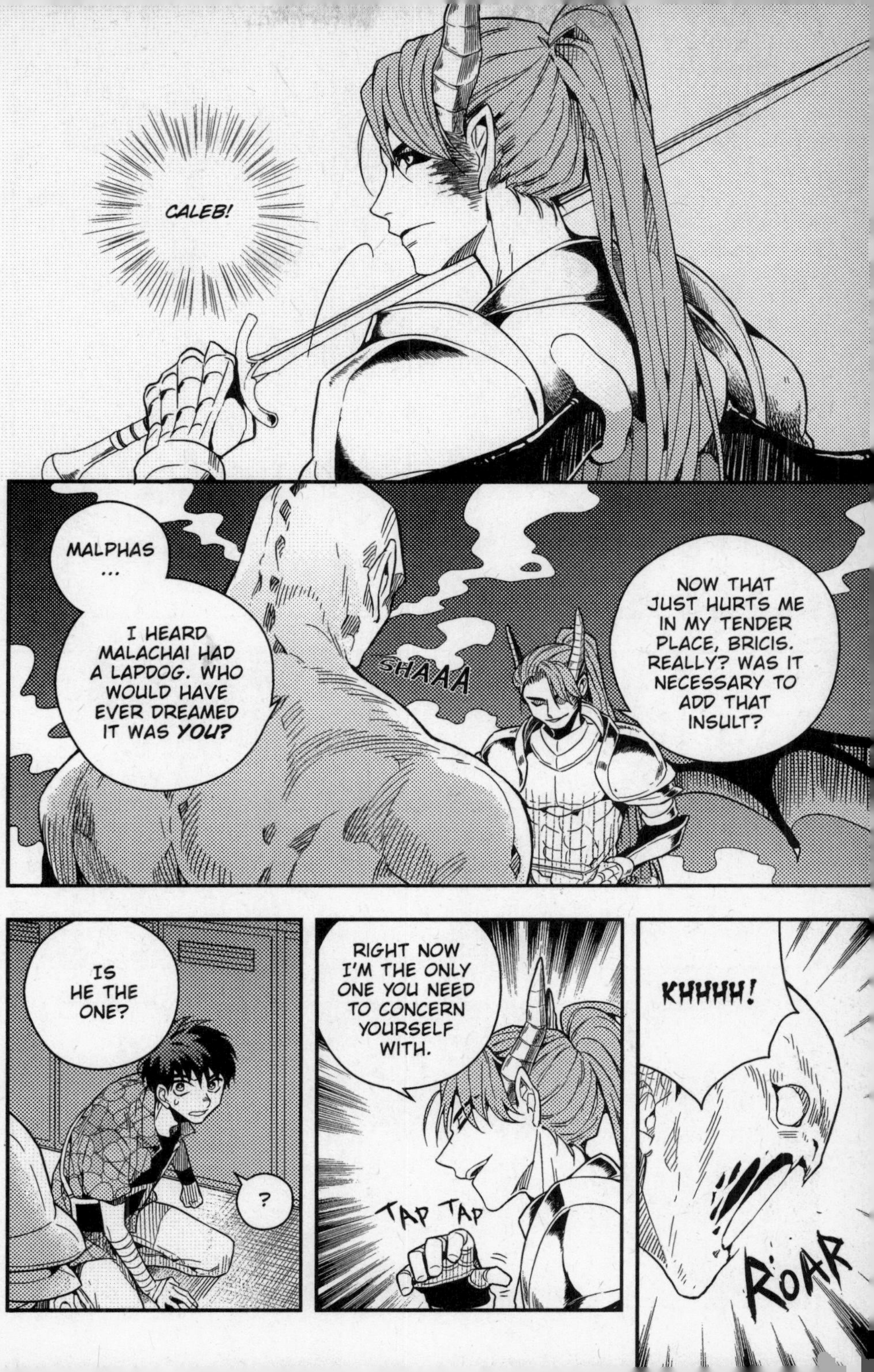
CALEB!
MALPHAS ...
I HEARD MALACHAI HAD A LAPDOG. WHO WOULD HAVE EVER DREAMED IT WAS YOU?
SHAAA
NOW THAT JUST HURTS ME IN MY TENDER PLACE, BRICIS. REALLY? WAS IT NECESSARY TO ADD THAT INSULT?
IS HE THE ONE?
?
RIGHT NOW I'M THE ONLY ONE YOU NEED TO CONCERN YOURSELF WITH.
TAP TAP
KHHHH!
ROAR

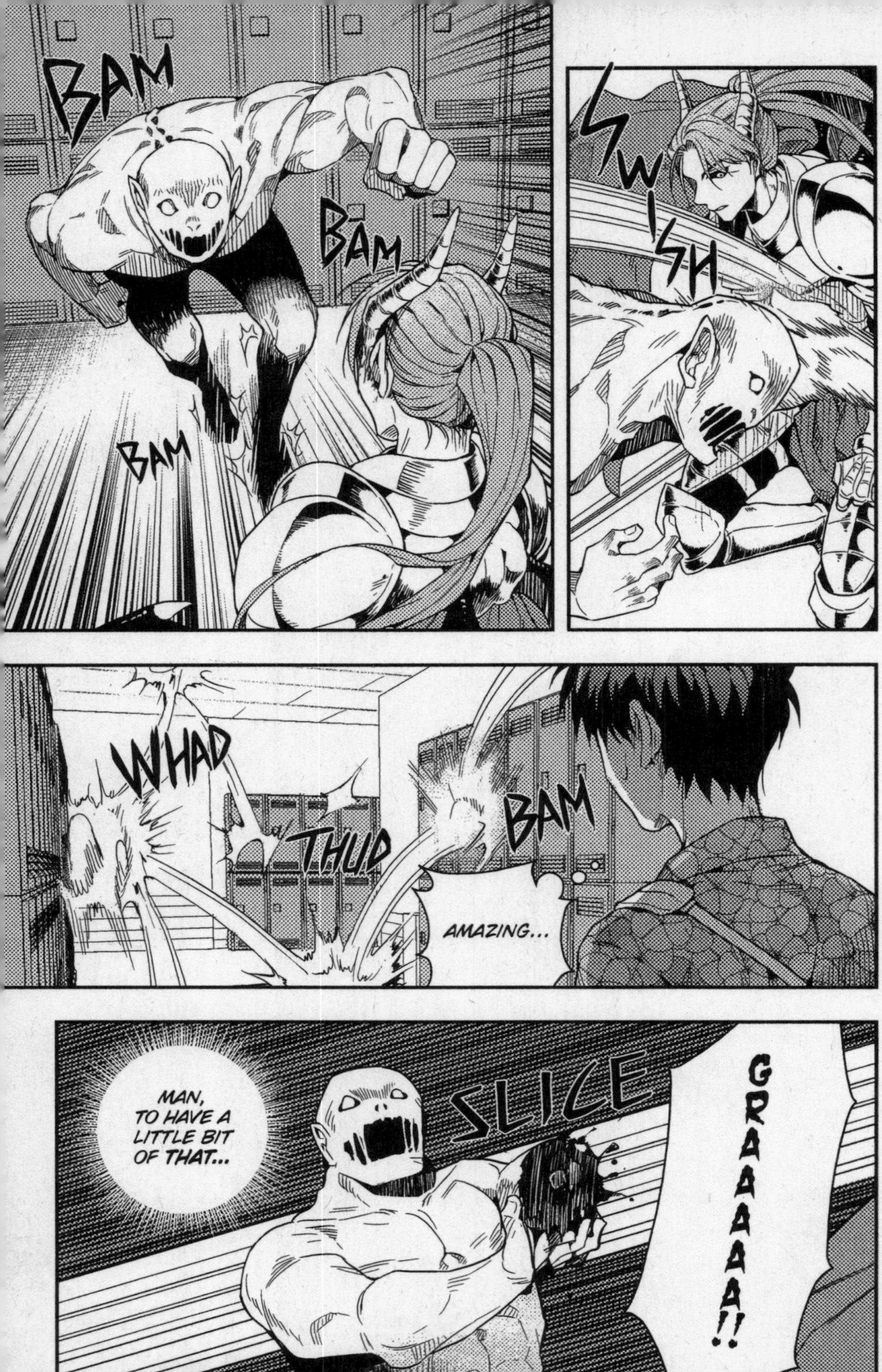
BAM
BAM
BAM
SWISH
WHAD
THUD
BAM
AMAZING...
MAN, TO HAVE A LITTLE BIT OF THAT...
SLICE
GRAAAAAA!!

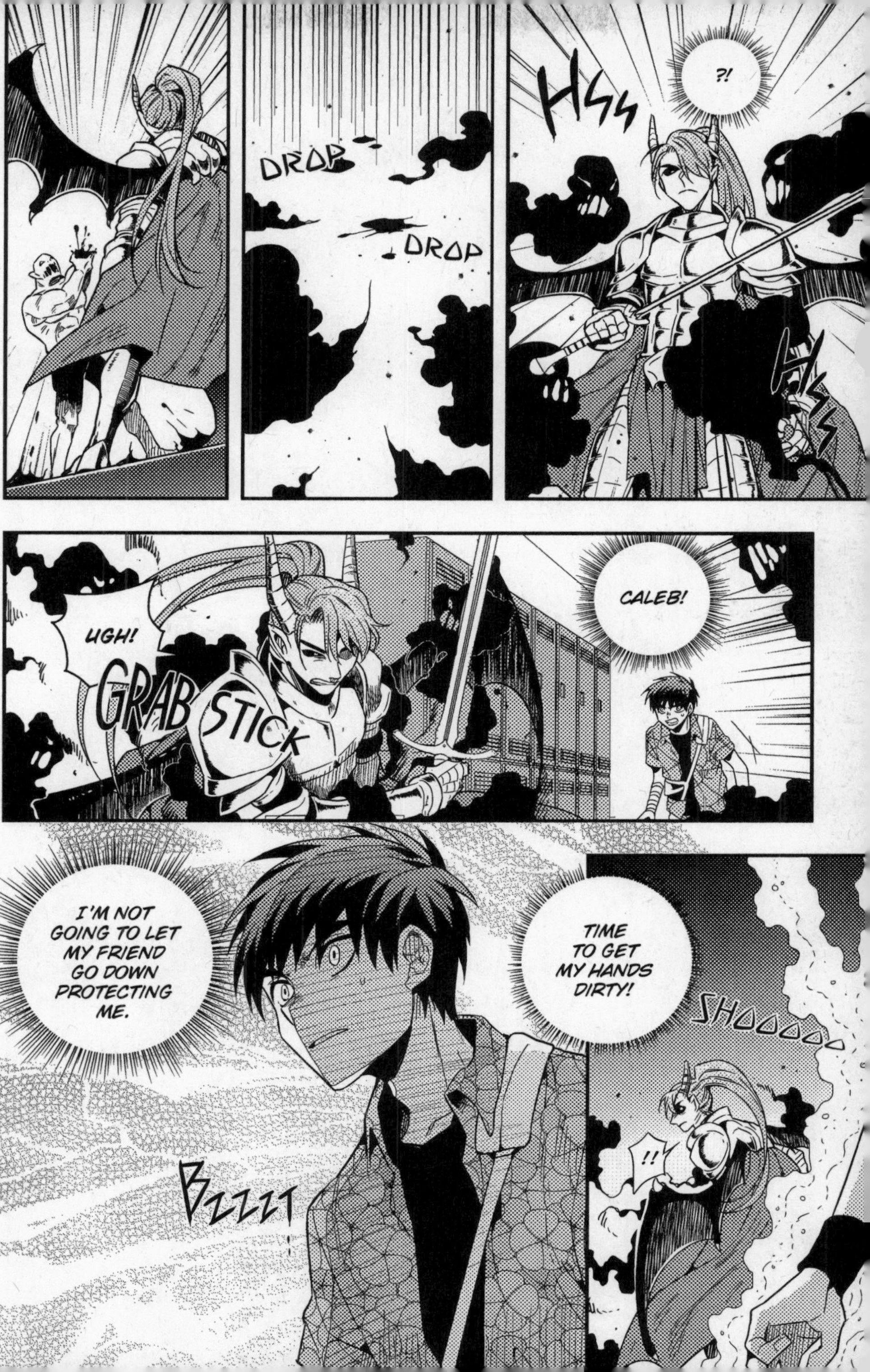
DROP
DROP
HSS
?!
HSS
UGH!
GRAB
STICK
CALEB!
I'M NOT GOING TO LET MY FRIEND GO DOWN PROTECTING ME.
TIME TO GET MY HANDS DIRTY!
SHOOOOO
!!
BZZZZ

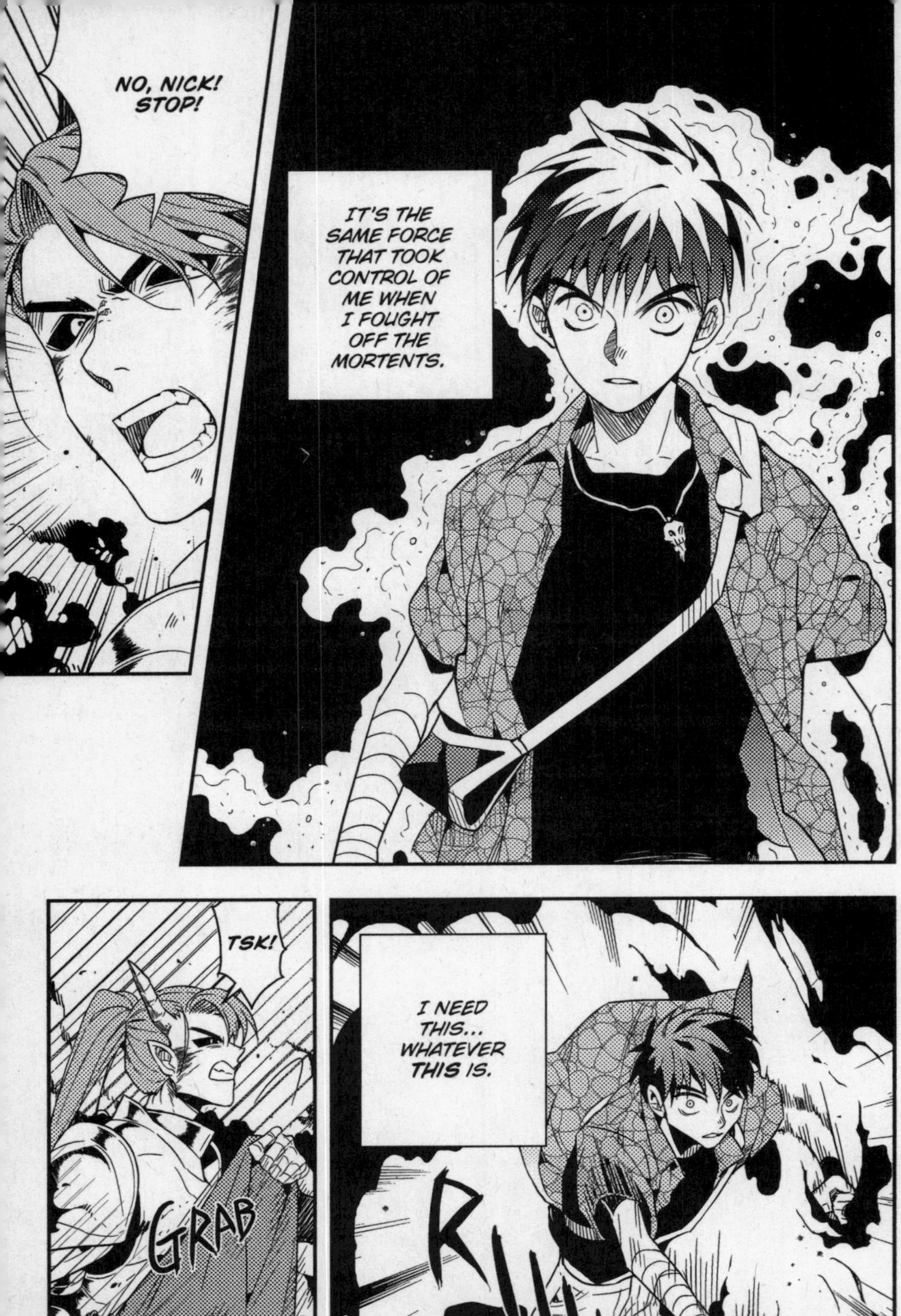
NO, NICK! STOP!
IT'S THE SAME FORCE THAT TOOK CONTROL OF ME WHEN I FOUGHT OFF THE MORTENTS.
TSK!
GRAB
I NEED THIS... WHATEVER THIS IS.
RIIIP

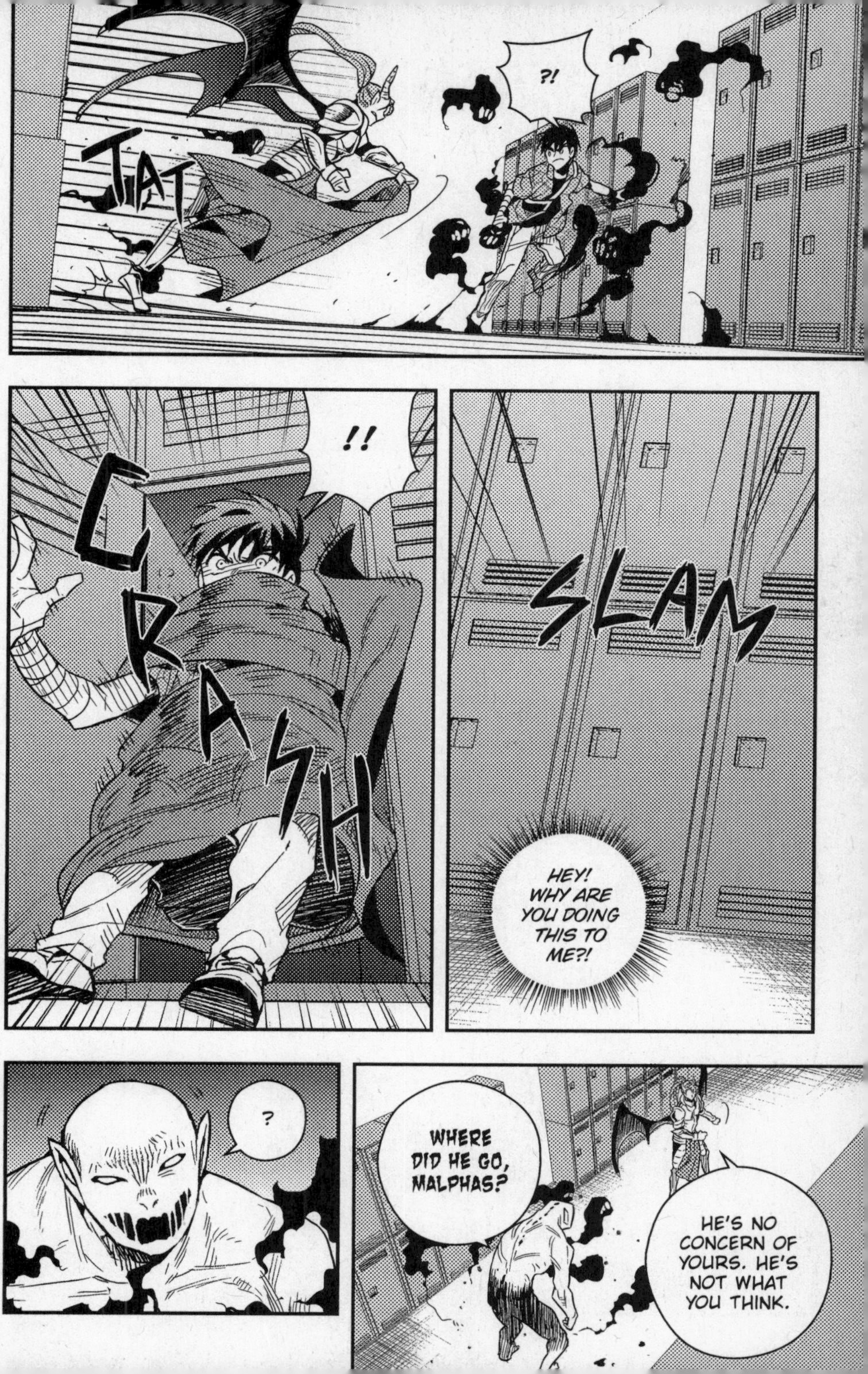

?!
TAT
!!
CRASH
SLAM
HEY! WHY ARE YOU DOING THIS TO ME?!
?
WHERE DID HE GO, MALPHAS?
HE'S NO CONCERN OF YOURS. HE'S NOT WHAT YOU THINK.

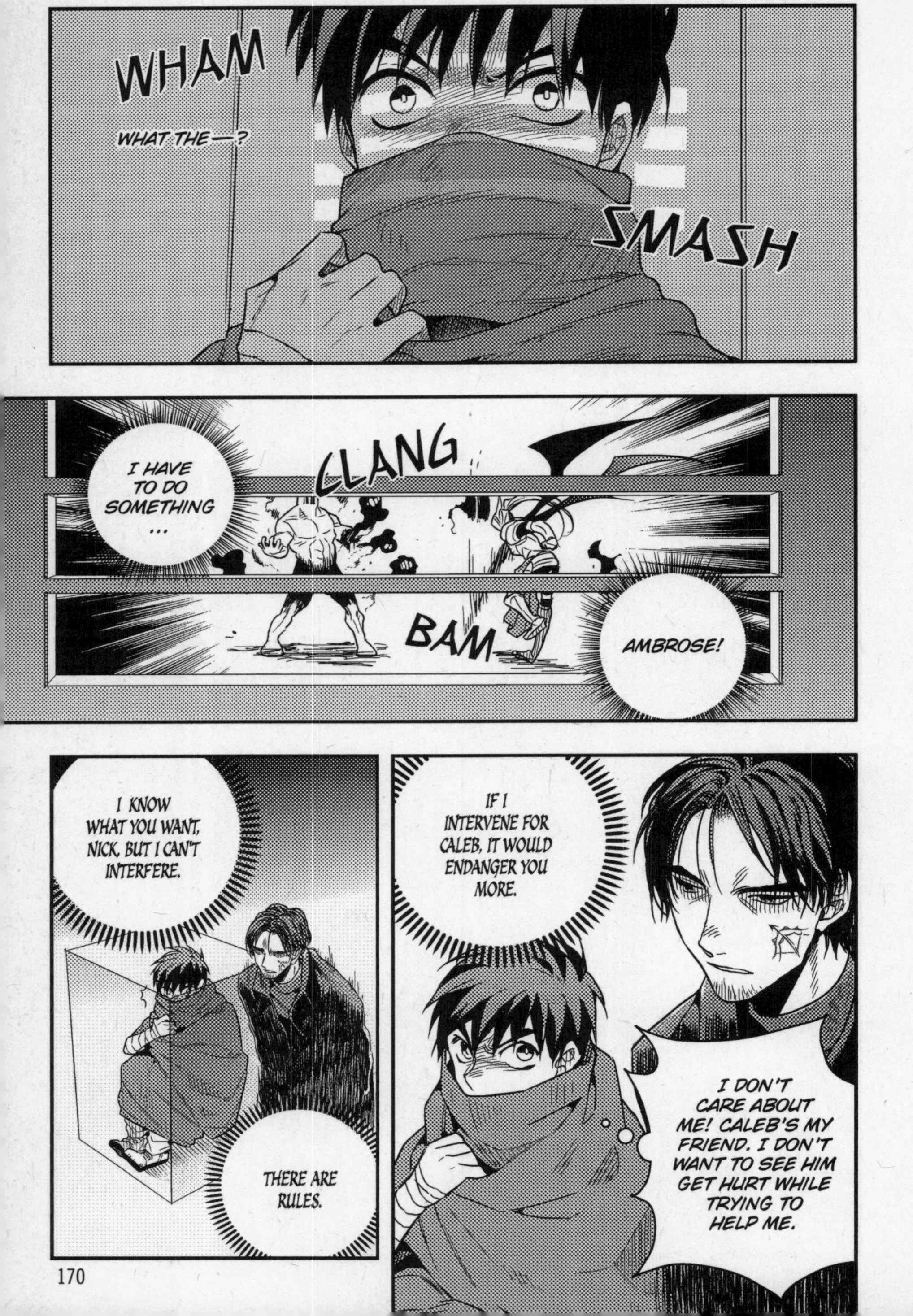
WHAM
WHAT THE—?
SMASH
I HAVE TO DO SOMETHING ...
CLANG
BAM
AMBROSE!
I KNOW WHAT YOU WANT, NICK, BUT I CAN'T INTERFERE.
THERE ARE RULES.
IF I INTERVENE FOR CALEB, IT WOULD ENDANGER YOU MORE.
I DON'T CARE ABOUT ME! CALEB'S MY FRIEND. I DON'T WANT TO SEE HIM GET HURT WHILE TRYING TO HELP ME.

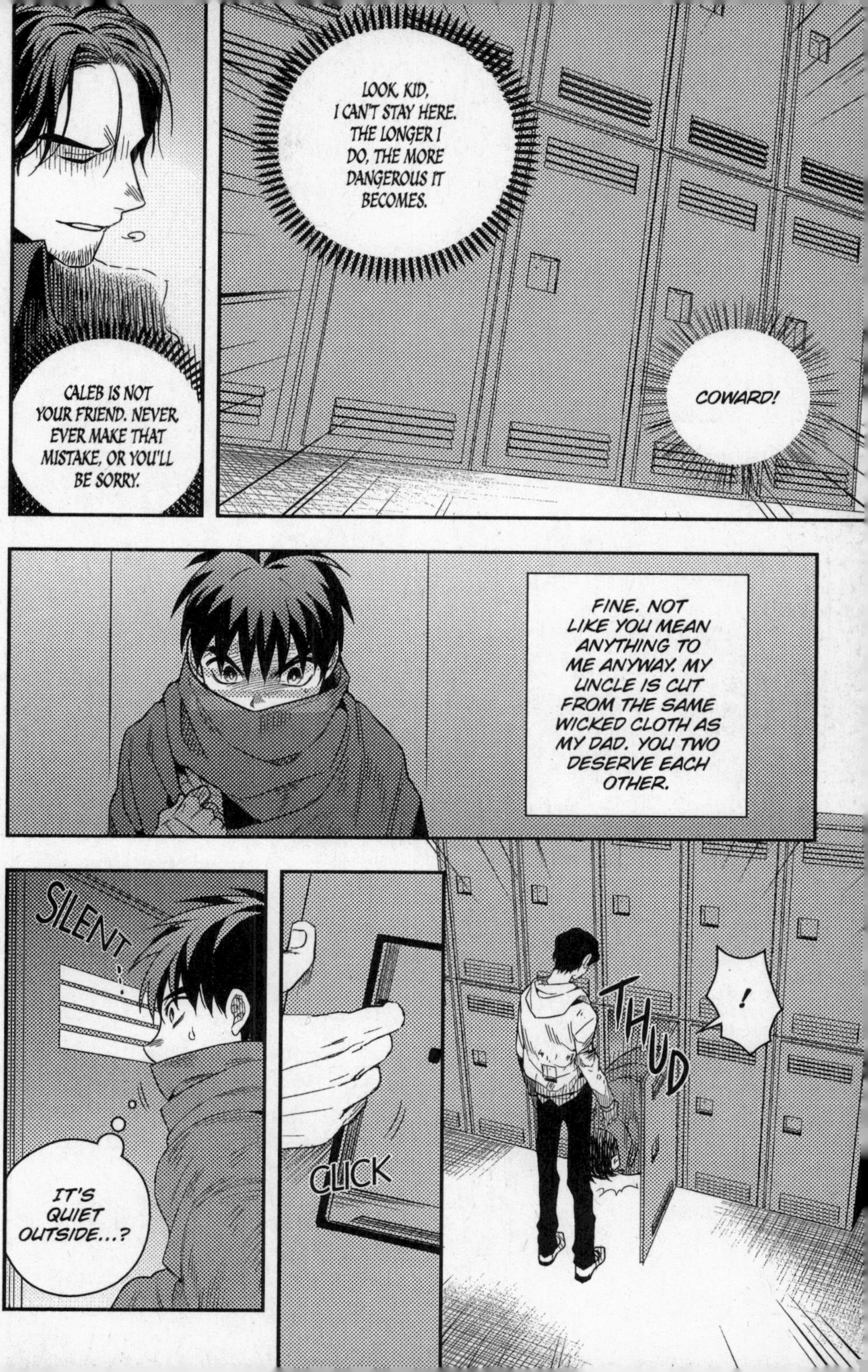
LOOK, KID, I CAN'T STAY HERE. THE LONGER I DO, THE MORE DANGEROUS IT BECOMES.
CALEB IS NOT YOUR FRIEND. NEVER, EVER MAKE THAT MISTAKE, OR YOU'LL BE SORRY.
COWARD!
FINE. NOT LIKE YOU MEAN ANYTHING TO ME ANYWAY. MY UNCLE IS CUT FROM THE SAME WICKED CLOTH AS MY DAD. YOU TWO DESERVE EACH OTHER.
!
THUD
CLICK
SILENT...
IT'S QUIET OUTSIDE...?

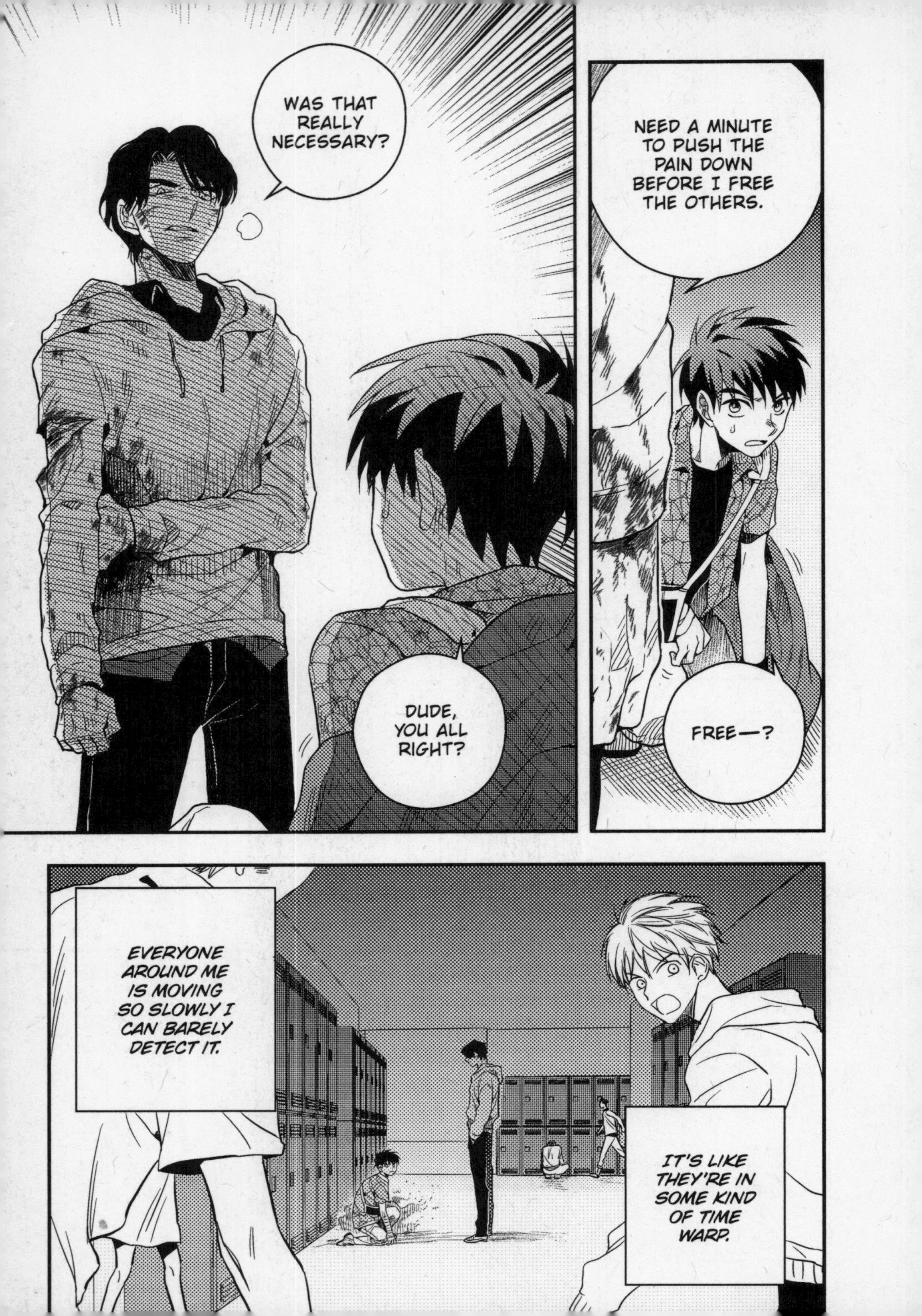
WAS THAT REALLY NECESSARY?
NEED A MINUTE TO PUSH THE PAIN DOWN BEFORE I FREE THE OTHERS.
DUDE, YOU ALL RIGHT?
FREE—?
EVERYONE AROUND ME IS MOVING SO SLOWLY I CAN BARELY DETECT IT.
IT'S LIKE THEY'RE IN SOME KIND OF TIME WARP.

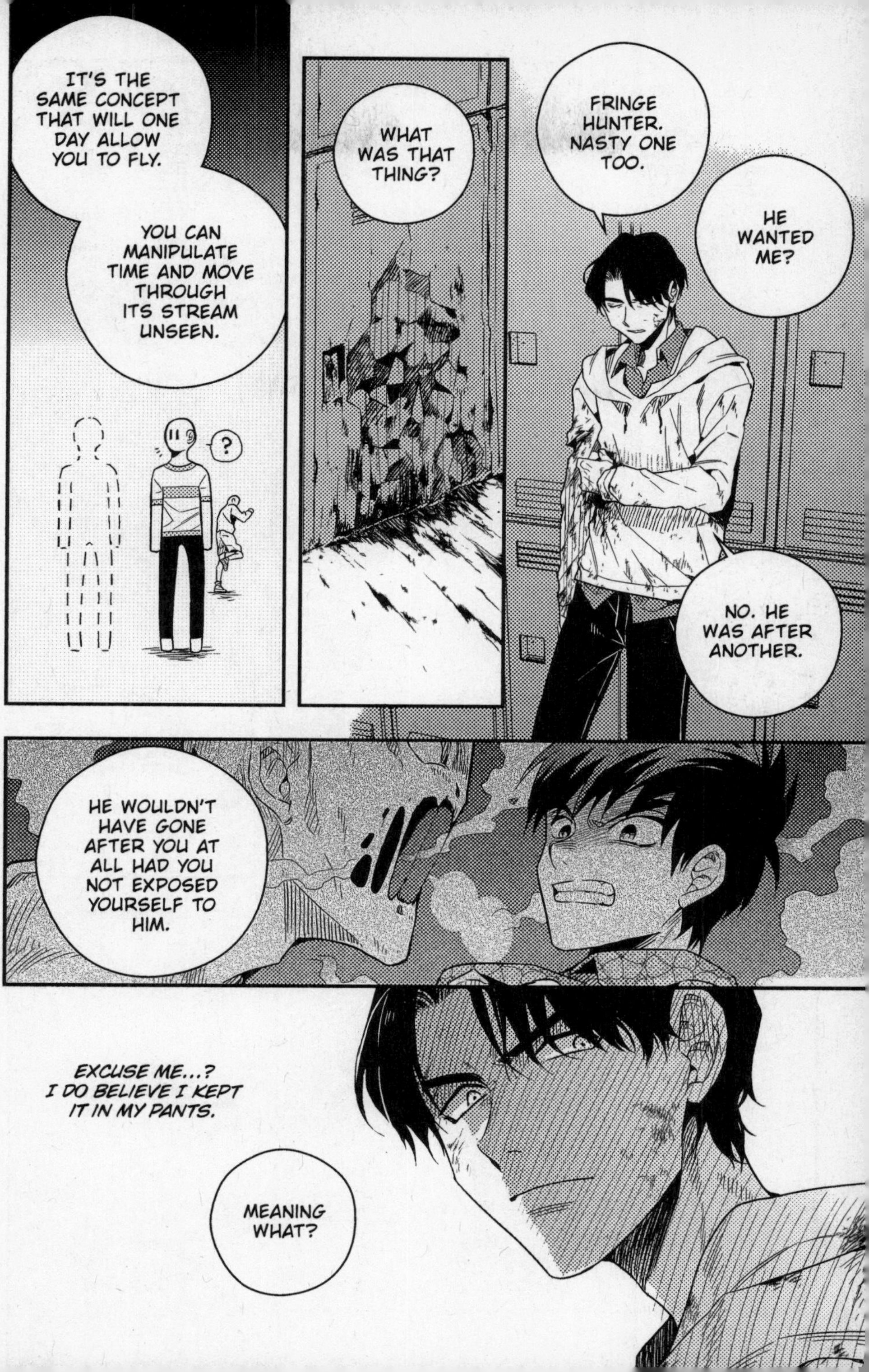
IT'S THE SAME CONCEPT THAT WILL ONE DAY ALLOW YOU TO FLY.
YOU CAN MANIPULATE TIME AND MOVE THROUGH ITS STREAM UNSEEN.
?
WHAT WAS THAT THING?
FRINGE HUNTER. NASTY ONE TOO.
HE WANTED ME?
NO. HE WAS AFTER ANOTHER.
HE WOULDN'T HAVE GONE AFTER YOU AT ALL HAD YOU NOT EXPOSED YOURSELF TO HIM.
EXCUSE ME...? I DO BELIEVE I KEPT IT IN MY PANTS.
MEANING WHAT?

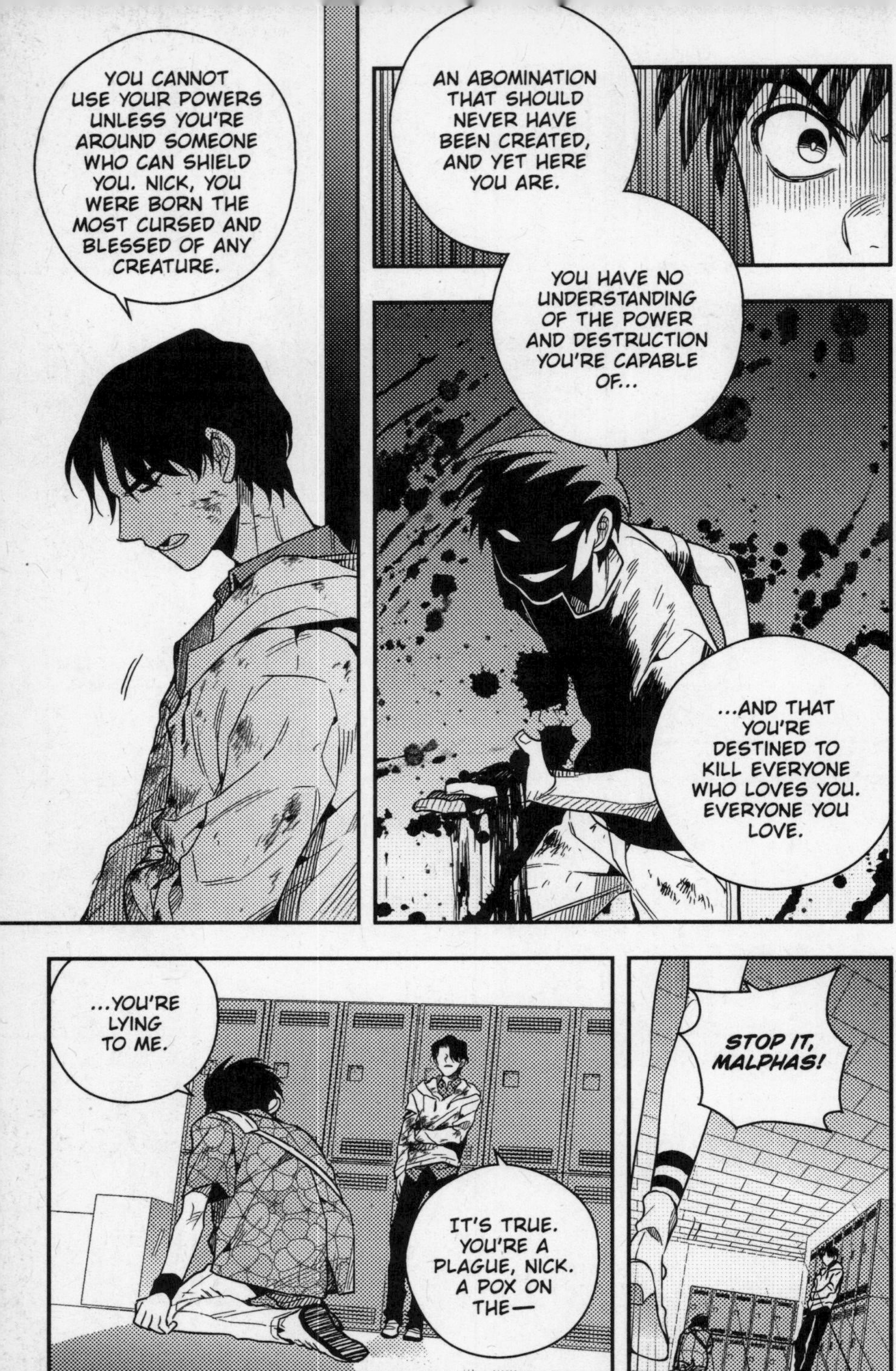
YOU CANNOT USE YOUR POWERS UNLESS YOU'RE AROUND SOMEONE WHO CAN SHIELD YOU. NICK, YOU WERE BORN THE MOST CURSED AND BLESSED OF ANY CREATURE.
AN ABOMINATION THAT SHOULD NEVER HAVE BEEN CREATED, AND YET HERE YOU ARE.
YOU HAVE NO UNDERSTANDING OF THE POWER AND DESTRUCTION YOU'RE CAPABLE OF...
...AND THAT YOU'RE DESTINED TO KILL EVERYONE WHO LOVES YOU. EVERYONE YOU LOVE.
...YOU'RE LYING TO ME.
IT'S TRUE. YOU'RE A PLAGUE, NICK. A POX ON THE—
STOP IT, MALPHAS!

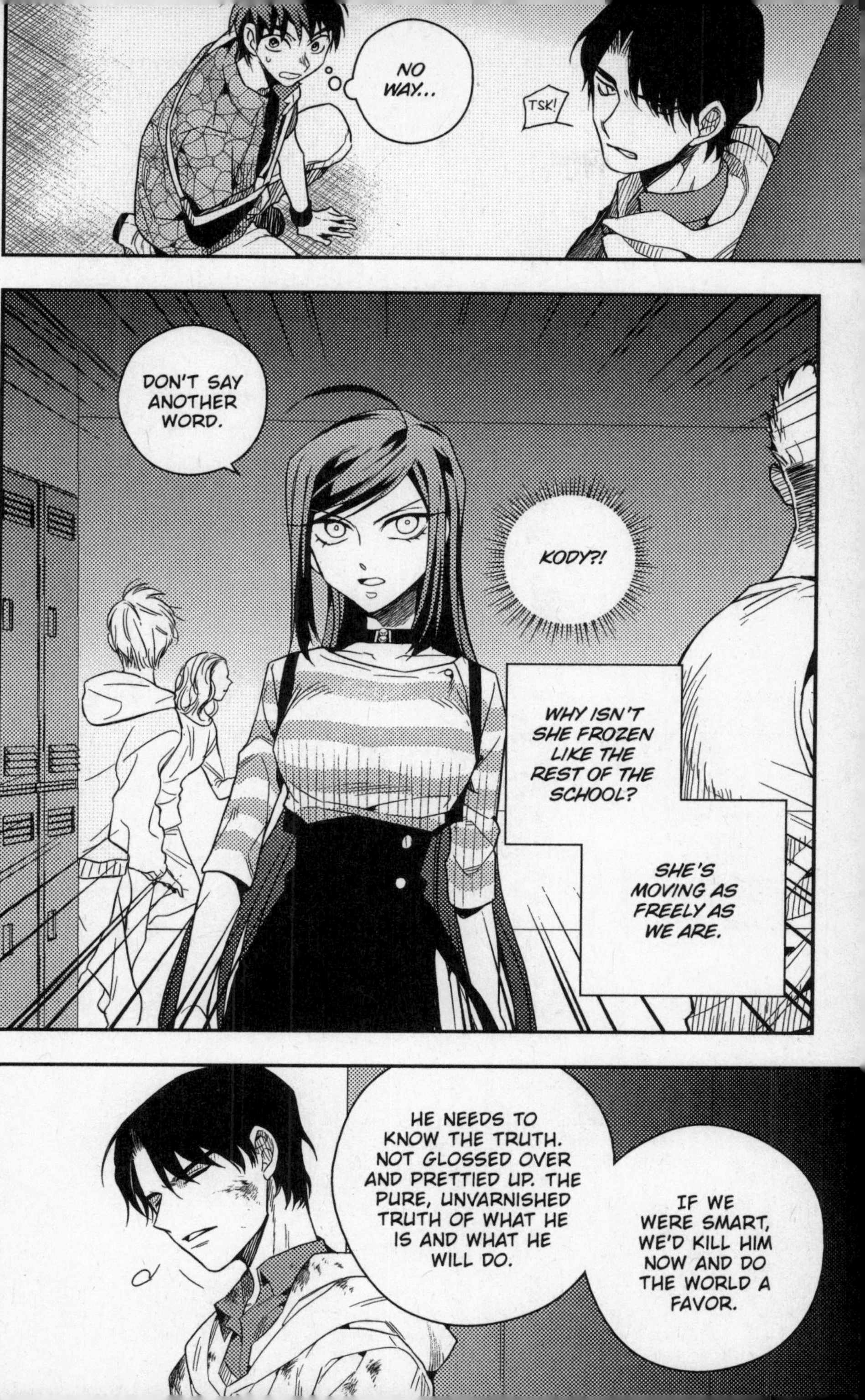
NO WAY...
TSK!
DON'T SAY ANOTHER WORD.
KODY?!
WHY ISN'T SHE FROZEN LIKE THE REST OF THE SCHOOL?
SHE'S MOVING AS FREELY AS WE ARE.
HE NEEDS TO KNOW THE TRUTH. NOT GLOSSED OVER AND PRETTIED UP. THE PURE, UNVARNISHED TRUTH OF WHAT HE IS AND WHAT HE WILL DO.
IF WE WERE SMART, WE'D KILL HIM NOW AND DO THE WORLD A FAVOR.

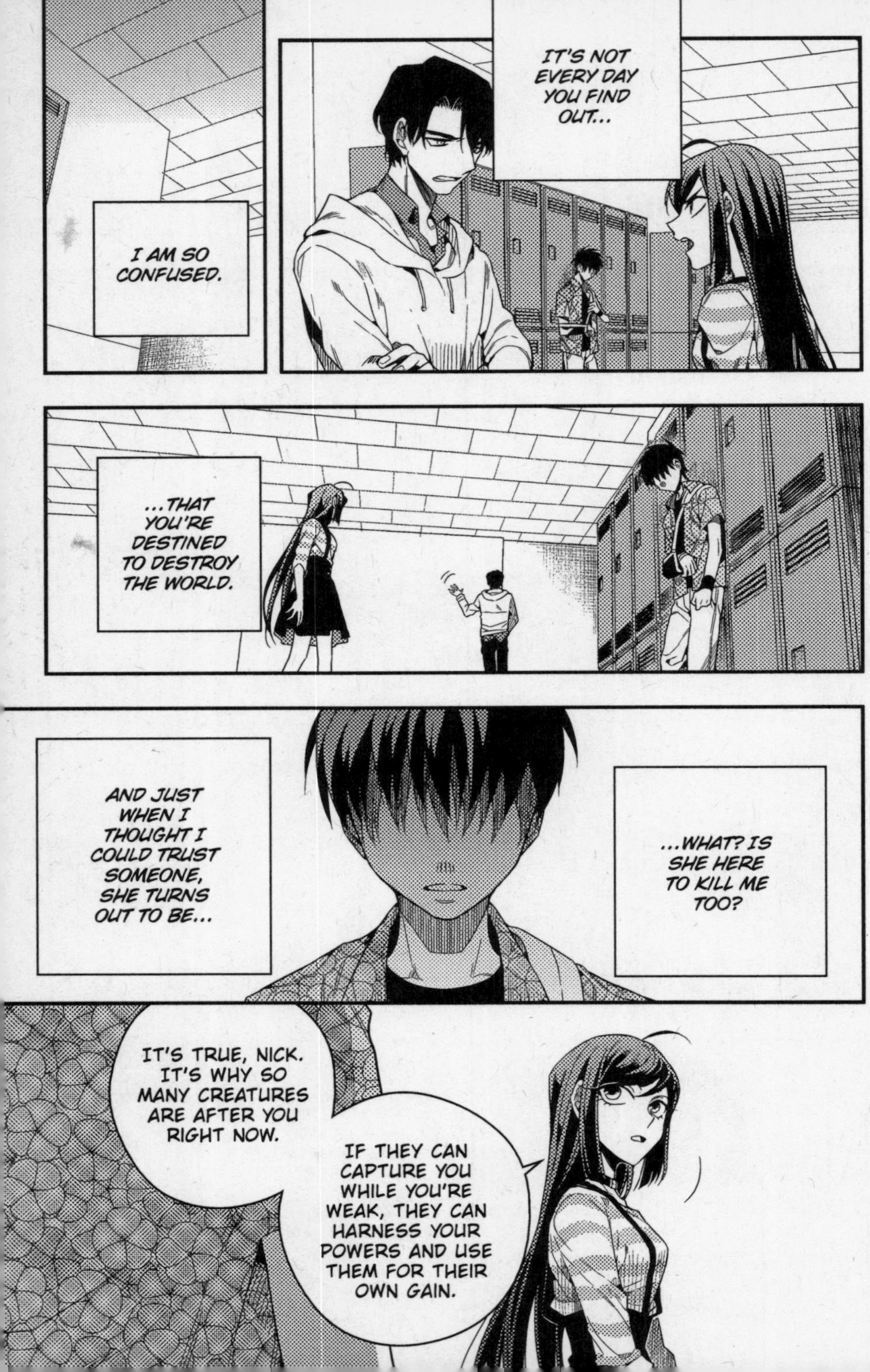
I AM SO CONFUSED.
IT'S NOT EVERY DAY YOU FIND OUT...
...THAT YOU'RE DESTINED TO DESTROY THE WORLD.
AND JUST WHEN I THOUGHT I COULD TRUST SOMEONE, SHE TURNS OUT TO BE...
...WHAT? IS SHE HERE TO KILL ME TOO?
IT'S TRUE, NICK. IT'S WHY SO MANY CREATURES ARE AFTER YOU RIGHT NOW.
IF THEY CAN CAPTURE YOU WHILE YOU'RE WEAK, THEY CAN HARNESS YOUR POWERS AND USE THEM FOR THEIR OWN GAIN.

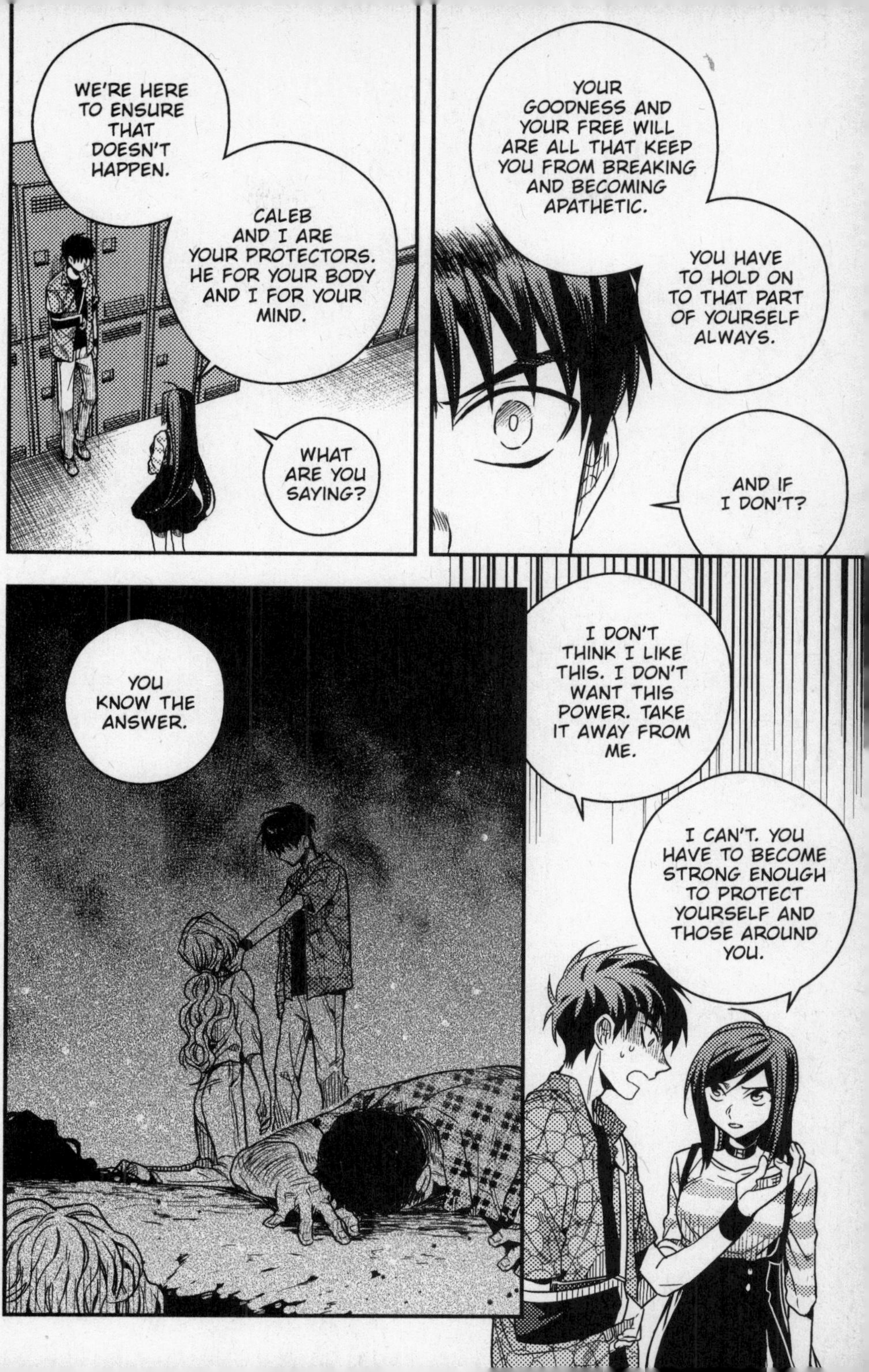
WE'RE HERE TO ENSURE THAT DOESN'T HAPPEN.
CALEB AND I ARE YOUR PROTECTORS. HE FOR YOUR BODY AND I FOR YOUR MIND.
WHAT ARE YOU SAYING?
YOUR GOODNESS AND YOUR FREE WILL ARE ALL THAT KEEP YOU FROM BREAKING AND BECOMING APATHETIC.
YOU HAVE TO HOLD ON TO THAT PART OF YOURSELF ALWAYS.
AND IF I DON'T?
YOU KNOW THE ANSWER.
I DON'T THINK I LIKE THIS. I DON'T WANT THIS POWER. TAKE IT AWAY FROM ME.
I CAN'T. YOU HAVE TO BECOME STRONG ENOUGH TO PROTECT YOURSELF AND THOSE AROUND YOU.

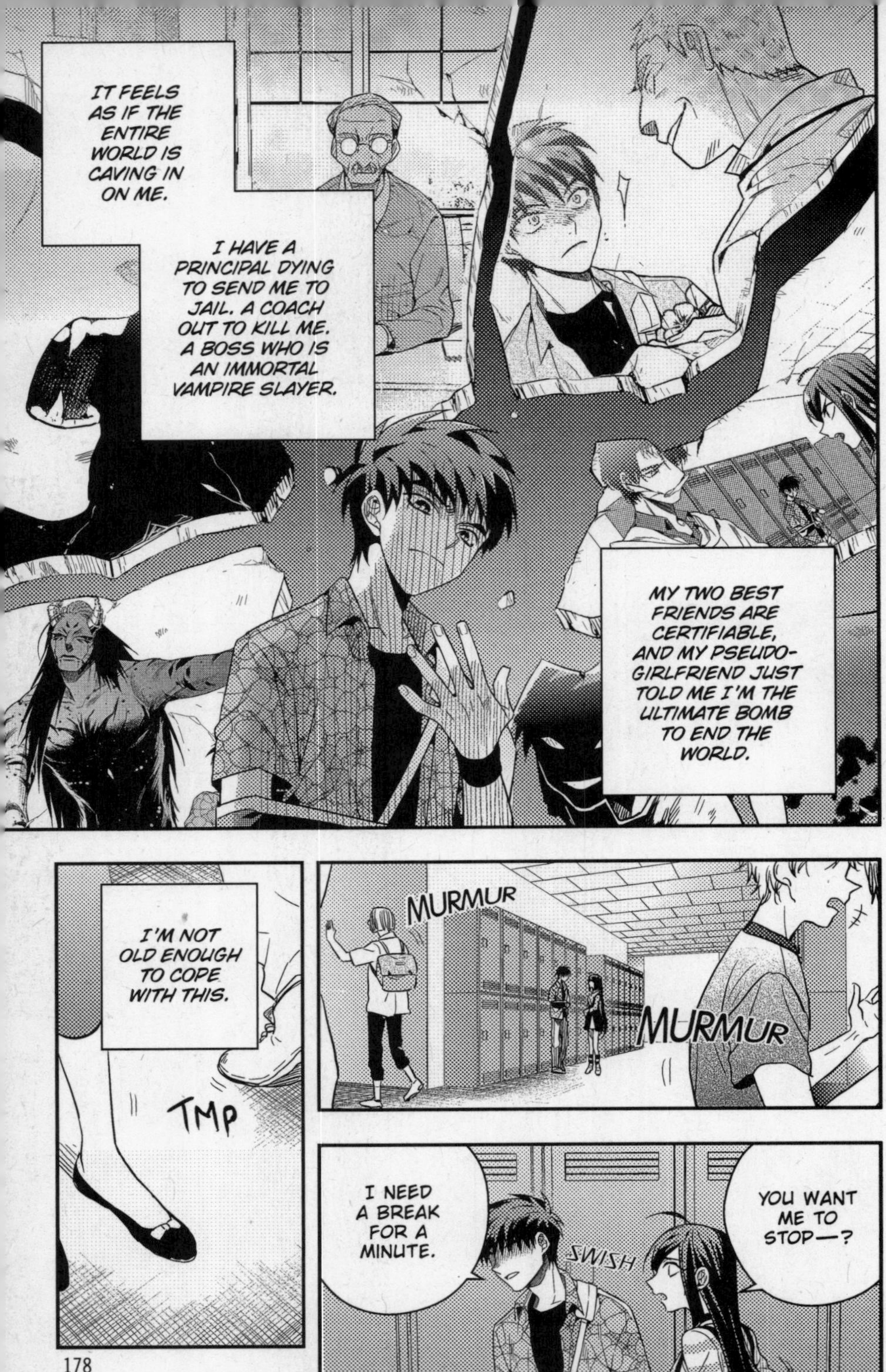
IT FEELS AS IF THE ENTIRE WORLD IS CAVING IN ON ME.
I HAVE A PRINCIPAL DYING TO SEND ME TO JAIL. A COACH OUT TO KILL ME. A BOSS WHO IS AN IMMORTAL VAMPIRE SLAYER.
MY TWO BEST FRIENDS ARE CERTIFIABLE, AND MY PSEUDO-GIRLFRIEND JUST TOLD ME I'M THE ULTIMATE BOMB TO END THE WORLD.
MURMUR
MURMUR
I'M NOT OLD ENOUGH TO COPE WITH THIS.
TMP
YOU WANT ME TO STOP—?
SWISH
I NEED A BREAK FOR A MINUTE.

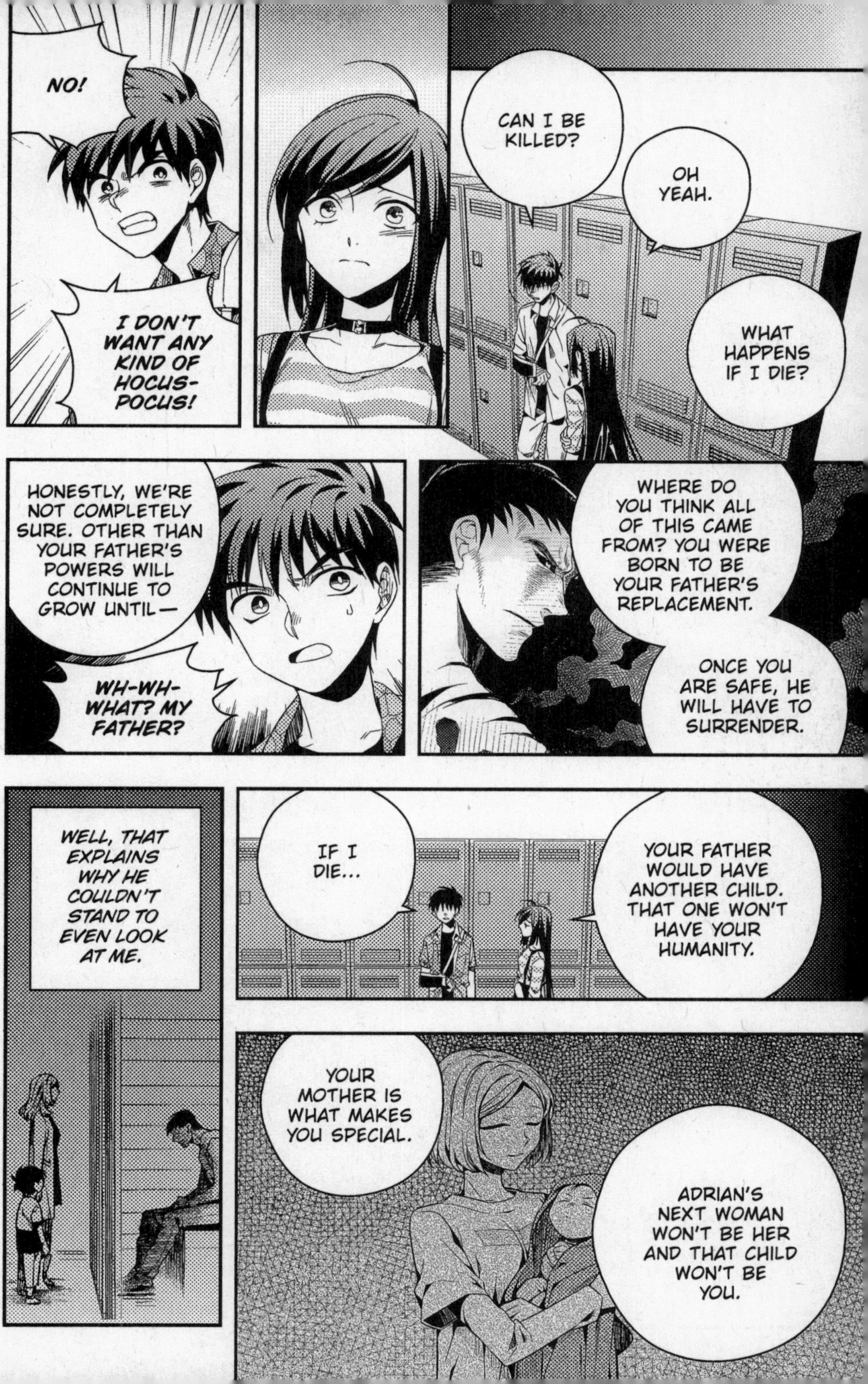
NO!
I DON'T WANT ANY KIND OF HOCUS-POCUS!
CAN I BE KILLED?
OH YEAH.
WHAT HAPPENS IF I DIE?
HONESTLY, WE'RE NOT COMPLETELY SURE. OTHER THAN YOUR FATHER'S POWERS WILL CONTINUE TO GROW UNTIL—
WH-WH-WHAT? MY FATHER?
WHERE DO YOU THINK ALL OF THIS CAME FROM? YOU WERE BORN TO BE YOUR FATHER'S REPLACEMENT.
ONCE YOU ARE SAFE, HE WILL HAVE TO SURRENDER.
WELL, THAT EXPLAINS WHY HE COULDN'T STAND TO EVEN LOOK AT ME.
IF I DIE...
YOUR FATHER WOULD HAVE ANOTHER CHILD. THAT ONE WON'T HAVE YOUR HUMANITY.
YOUR MOTHER IS WHAT MAKES YOU SPECIAL.
ADRIAN'S NEXT WOMAN WON'T BE HER AND THAT CHILD WON'T BE YOU.

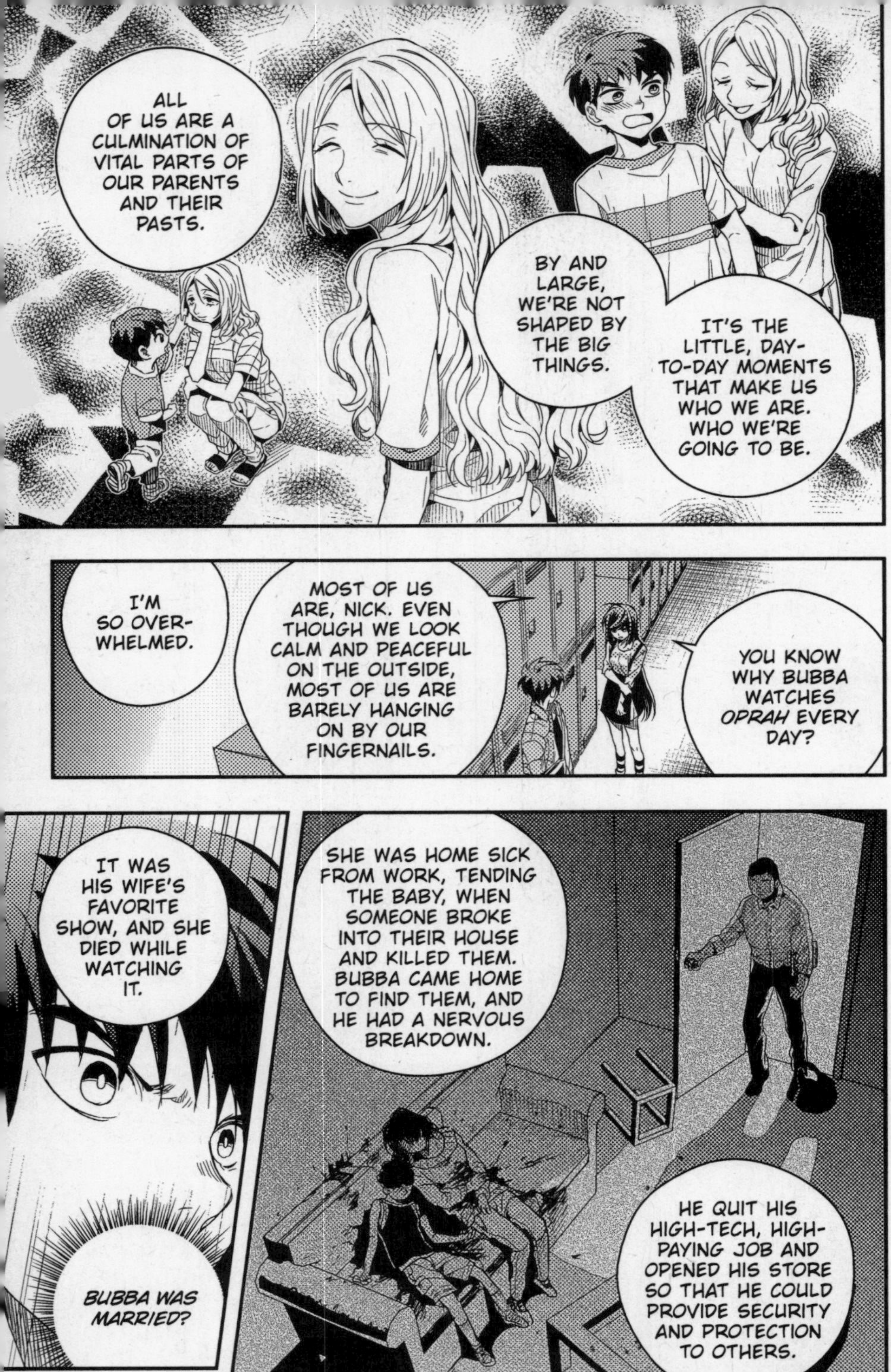
ALL OF US ARE A CULMINATION OF VITAL PARTS OF OUR PARENTS AND THEIR PASTS.
BY AND LARGE, WE'RE NOT SHAPED BY THE BIG THINGS.
IT'S THE LITTLE, DAY-TO-DAY MOMENTS THAT MAKE US WHO WE ARE. WHO WE'RE GOING TO BE.
I'M SO OVER-WHELMED.
MOST OF US ARE, NICK. EVEN THOUGH WE LOOK CALM AND PEACEFUL ON THE OUTSIDE, MOST OF US ARE BARELY HANGING ON BY OUR FINGERNAILS.
YOU KNOW WHY BUBBA WATCHES *OPRAH* EVERY DAY?
IT WAS HIS WIFE'S FAVORITE SHOW, AND SHE DIED WHILE WATCHING IT.
SHE WAS HOME SICK FROM WORK, TENDING THE BABY, WHEN SOMEONE BROKE INTO THEIR HOUSE AND KILLED THEM. BUBBA CAME HOME TO FIND THEM, AND HE HAD A NERVOUS BREAKDOWN.
BUBBA WAS MARRIED?
HE QUIT HIS HIGH-TECH, HIGH-PAYING JOB AND OPENED HIS STORE SO THAT HE COULD PROVIDE SECURITY AND PROTECTION TO OTHERS.

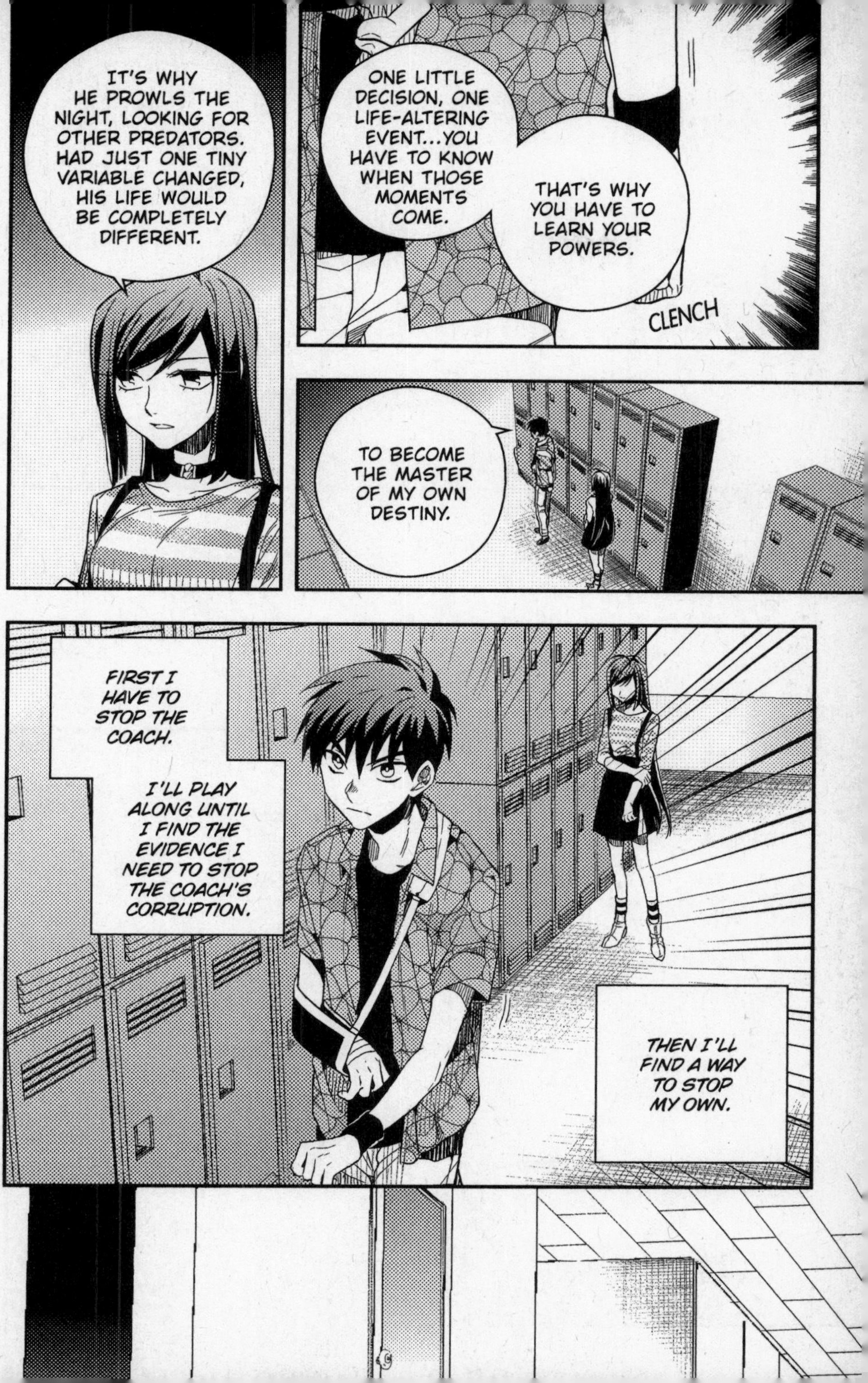
IT'S WHY HE PROWLS THE NIGHT, LOOKING FOR OTHER PREDATORS. HAD JUST ONE TINY VARIABLE CHANGED, HIS LIFE WOULD BE COMPLETELY DIFFERENT.
ONE LITTLE DECISION, ONE LIFE-ALTERING EVENT...YOU HAVE TO KNOW WHEN THOSE MOMENTS COME.
THAT'S WHY YOU HAVE TO LEARN YOUR POWERS.
CLENCH
TO BECOME THE MASTER OF MY OWN DESTINY.
FIRST I HAVE TO STOP THE COACH.
I'LL PLAY ALONG UNTIL I FIND THE EVIDENCE I NEED TO STOP THE COACH'S CORRUPTION.
THEN I'LL FIND A WAY TO STOP MY OWN.

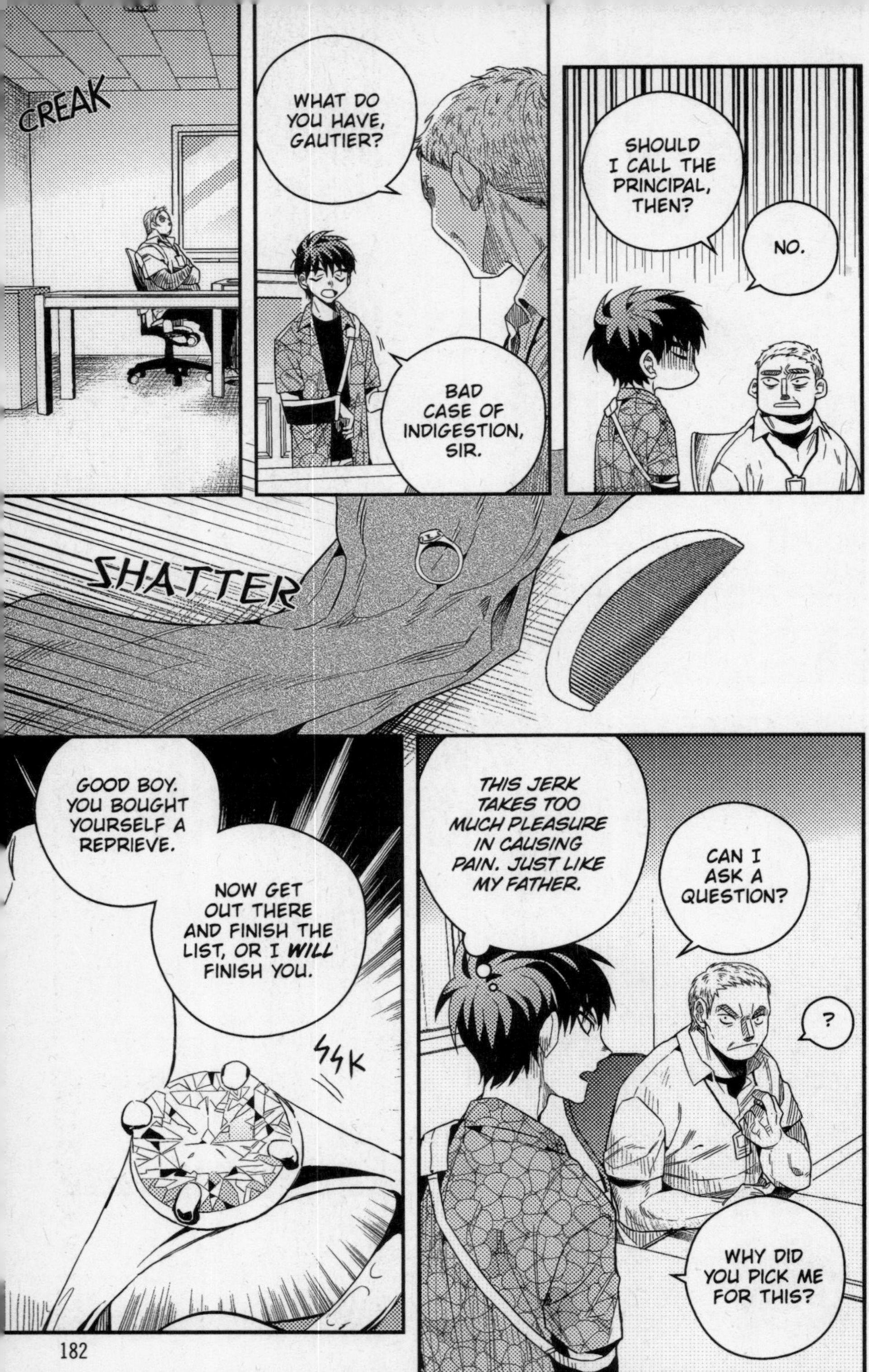
CREAK
WHAT DO YOU HAVE, GAUTIER?
BAD CASE OF INDIGESTION, SIR.
SHOULD I CALL THE PRINCIPAL, THEN?
NO.
SHATTER
GOOD BOY. YOU BOUGHT YOURSELF A REPRIEVE.
NOW GET OUT THERE AND FINISH THE LIST, OR I WILL FINISH YOU.
SSK
THIS JERK TAKES TOO MUCH PLEASURE IN CAUSING PAIN. JUST LIKE MY FATHER.
CAN I ASK A QUESTION?
?
WHY DID YOU PICK ME FOR THIS?

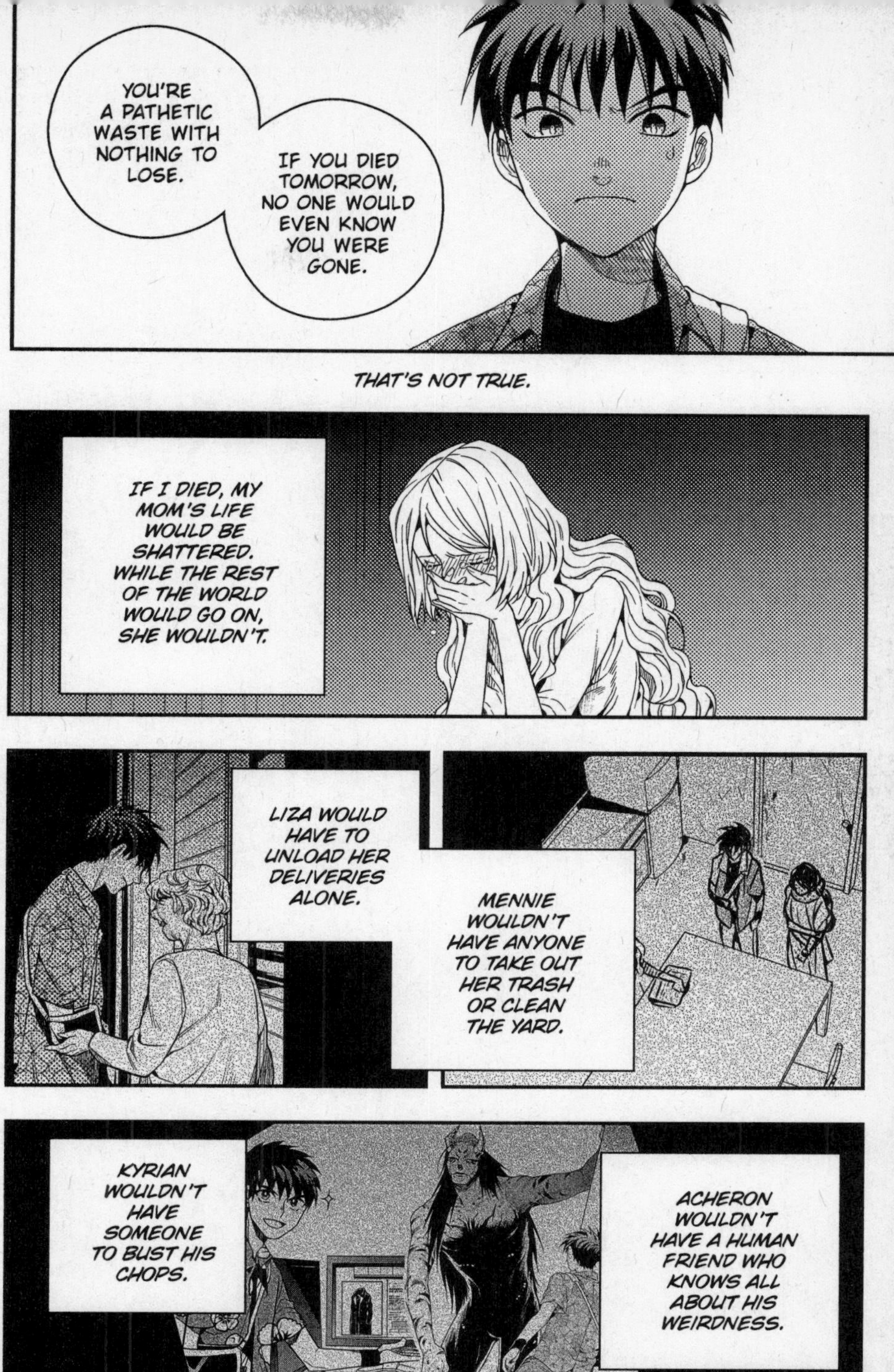
YOU'RE A PATHETIC WASTE WITH NOTHING TO LOSE.
IF YOU DIED TOMORROW, NO ONE WOULD EVEN KNOW YOU WERE GONE.
THAT'S NOT TRUE.
IF I DIED, MY MOM'S LIFE WOULD BE SHATTERED. WHILE THE REST OF THE WORLD WOULD GO ON, SHE WOULDN'T.
LIZA WOULD HAVE TO UNLOAD HER DELIVERIES ALONE.
MENNIE WOULDN'T HAVE ANYONE TO TAKE OUT HER TRASH OR CLEAN THE YARD.
KYRIAN WOULDN'T HAVE SOMEONE TO BUST HIS CHOPS.
ACHERON WOULDN'T HAVE A HUMAN FRIEND WHO KNOWS ALL ABOUT HIS WEIRDNESS.

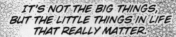

IT'S NOT THE BIG THINGS, BUT THE LITTLE THINGS IN LIFE THAT REALLY MATTER.

YOU'RE WRONG THERE, COACH.

HOW SO?

NO LIFE, NO MATTER WHAT YOU THINK, IS INSIGNIFICANT.

CLICK

EVERYONE HAS A PURPOSE. EVEN YOU.

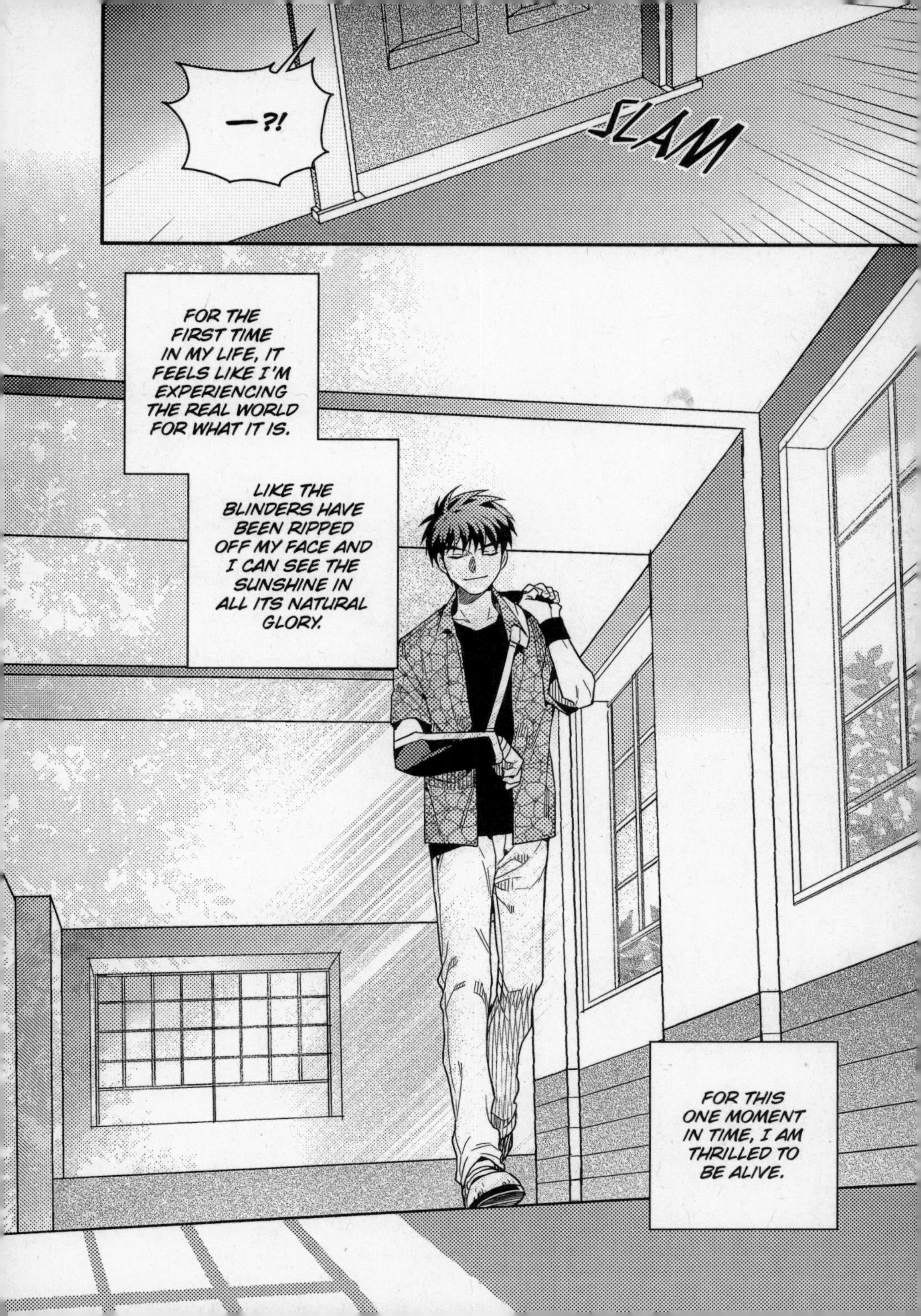
—?!
SLAM
FOR THE FIRST TIME IN MY LIFE, IT FEELS LIKE I'M EXPERIENCING THE REAL WORLD FOR WHAT IT IS.
LIKE THE BLINDERS HAVE BEEN RIPPED OFF MY FACE AND I CAN SEE THE SUNSHINE IN ALL ITS NATURAL GLORY.
FOR THIS ONE MOMENT IN TIME, I AM THRILLED TO BE ALIVE.

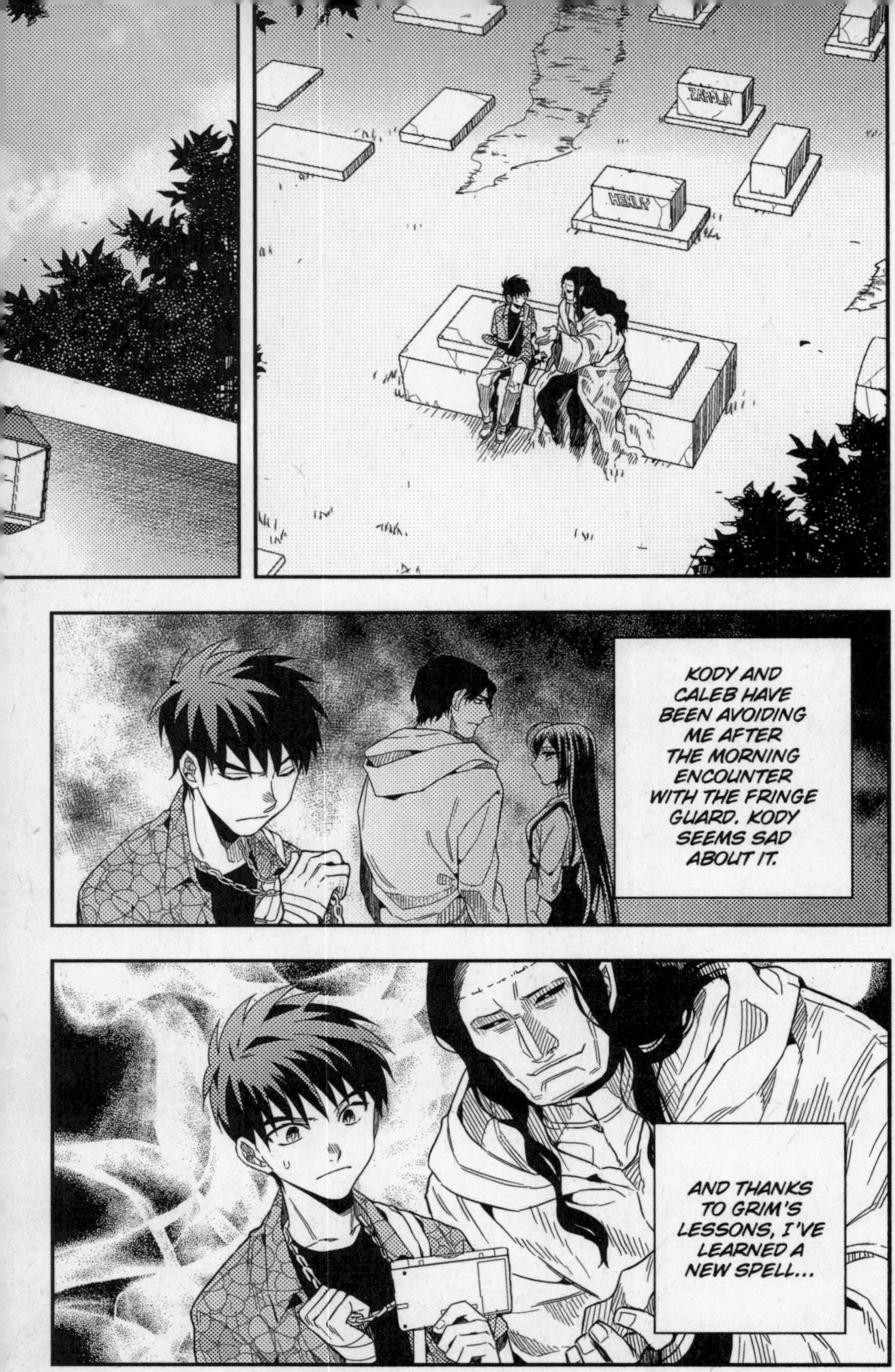

KODY AND CALEB HAVE BEEN AVOIDING ME AFTER THE MORNING ENCOUNTER WITH THE FRINGE GUARD. KODY SEEMS SAD ABOUT IT.
AND THANKS TO GRIM'S LESSONS, I'VE LEARNED A NEW SPELL...

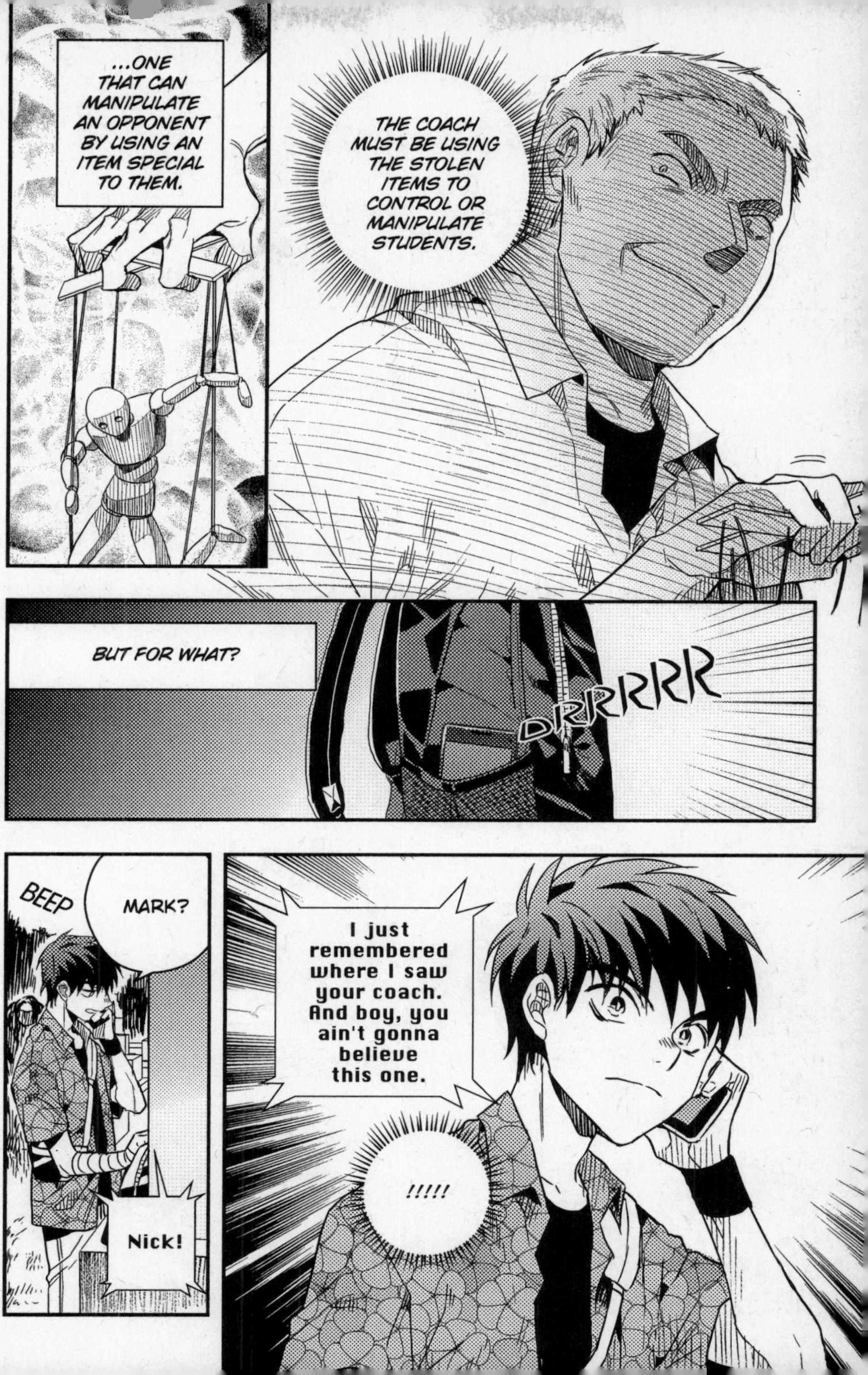
...ONE THAT CAN MANIPULATE AN OPPONENT BY USING AN ITEM SPECIAL TO THEM.
THE COACH MUST BE USING THE STOLEN ITEMS TO CONTROL OR MANIPULATE STUDENTS.
BUT FOR WHAT?
DRRRRR
BEEP
MARK?
Nick!
I just remembered where I saw your coach. And boy, you ain't gonna believe this one.
!!!!!

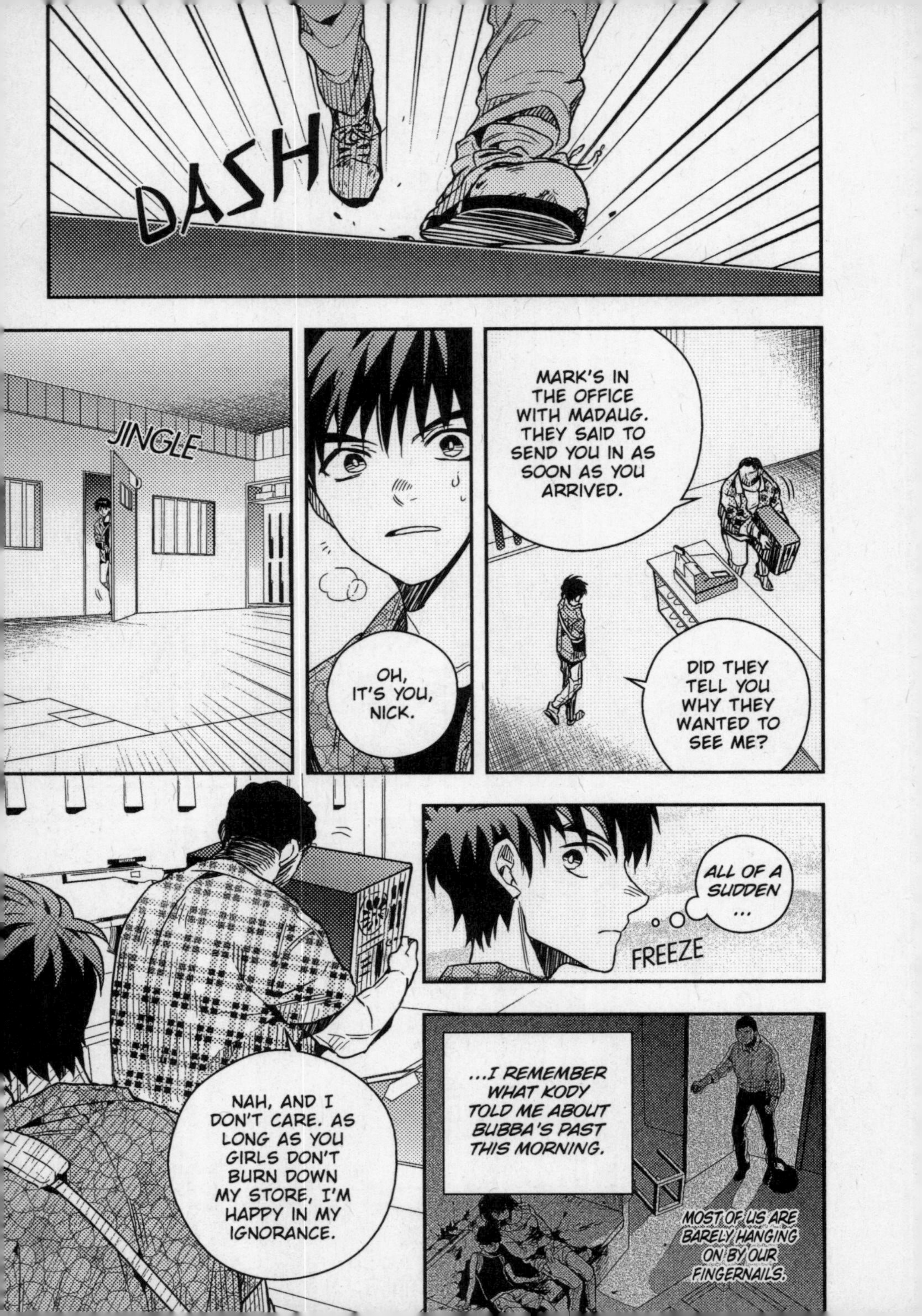
DASH
JINGLE
OH, IT'S YOU, NICK.
MARK'S IN THE OFFICE WITH MADAUG. THEY SAID TO SEND YOU IN AS SOON AS YOU ARRIVED.
DID THEY TELL YOU WHY THEY WANTED TO SEE ME?
ALL OF A SUDDEN ...
FREEZE
NAH, AND I DON'T CARE. AS LONG AS YOU GIRLS DON'T BURN DOWN MY STORE, I'M HAPPY IN MY IGNORANCE.
...I REMEMBER WHAT KODY TOLD ME ABOUT BUBBA'S PAST THIS MORNING.
MOST OF US ARE BARELY HANGING ON BY OUR FINGERNAILS.

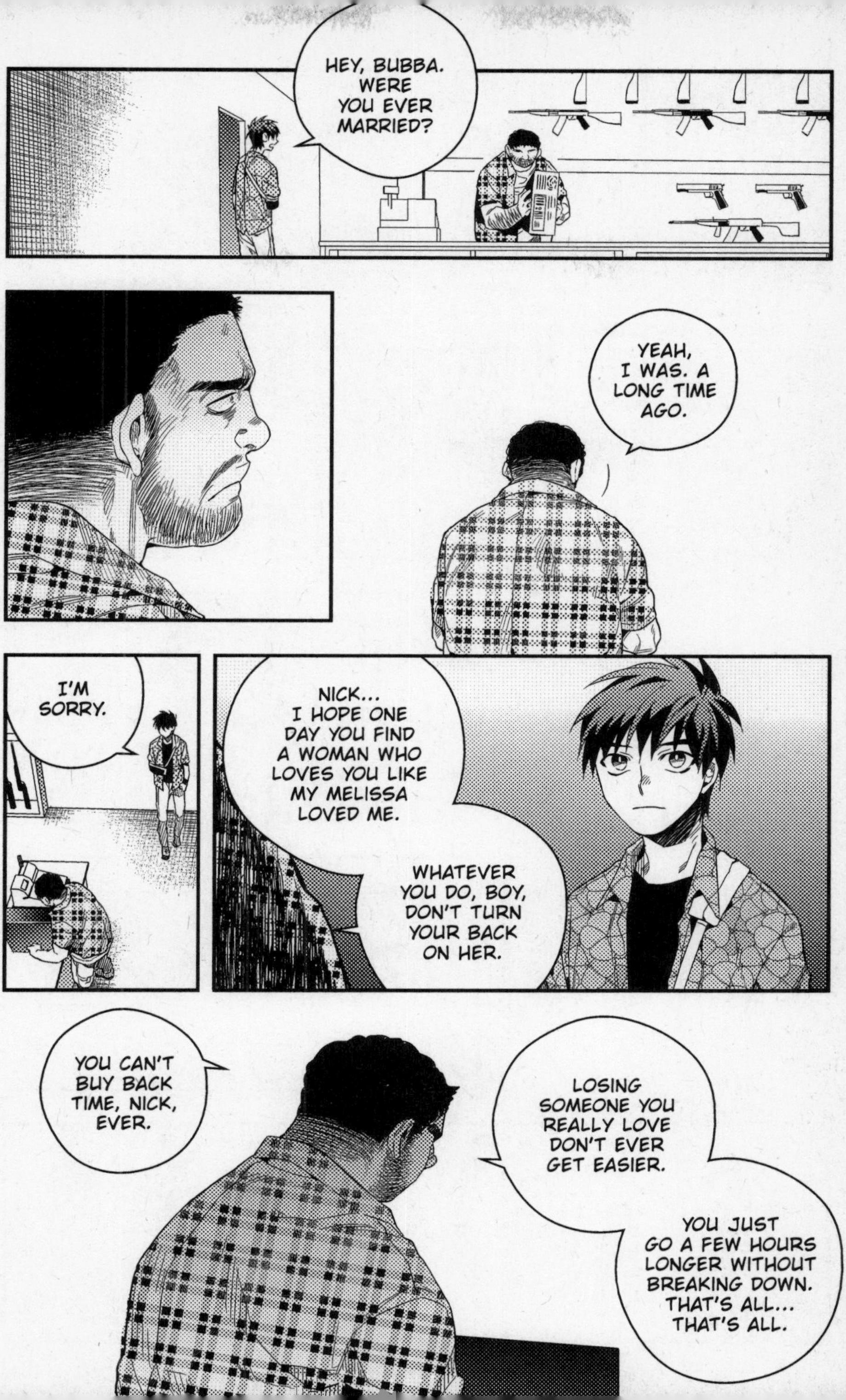
HEY, BUBBA. WERE YOU EVER MARRIED?
YEAH, I WAS. A LONG TIME AGO.
I'M SORRY.
NICK... I HOPE ONE DAY YOU FIND A WOMAN WHO LOVES YOU LIKE MY MELISSA LOVED ME.
WHATEVER YOU DO, BOY, DON'T TURN YOUR BACK ON HER.
YOU CAN'T BUY BACK TIME, NICK, EVER.
LOSING SOMEONE YOU REALLY LOVE DON'T EVER GET EASIER.
YOU JUST GO A FEW HOURS LONGER WITHOUT BREAKING DOWN. THAT'S ALL... THAT'S ALL.

BIG BUBBA BURDETTE IS A GROWLING BEAR OF A MAN. HUGE. TOUGH AS NAILS. NEVER LETS ANYTHING BOTHER HIM.

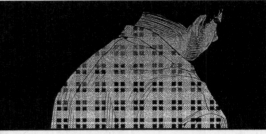

BUT WHO EVER WOULD HAVE THOUGHT THAT SUCH A FEARSOME, LARGER-THAN-LIFE BEAST COULD BE HAUNTED BY SOMETHING SO HUMAN AS THE LOSS OF HIS WIFE AND CHILD?

HUG

BOY, WHAT ARE YOU DOING? HAVE YOU LOST YOUR EVER-LOVING MIND?

YOU LOOKED LIKE YOU COULD USE A HUG.

THEN CALL UP TYRA BANKS AND SEND HER OVER!

DON'T WANT NO STRAGGLY TEENAGER RUBBING UP AGAINST ME. GEEZ.

YEAH, YEAH. I HEAR YOU, YOU OLD GRUMP.

TMP

HEY, NICK?

190

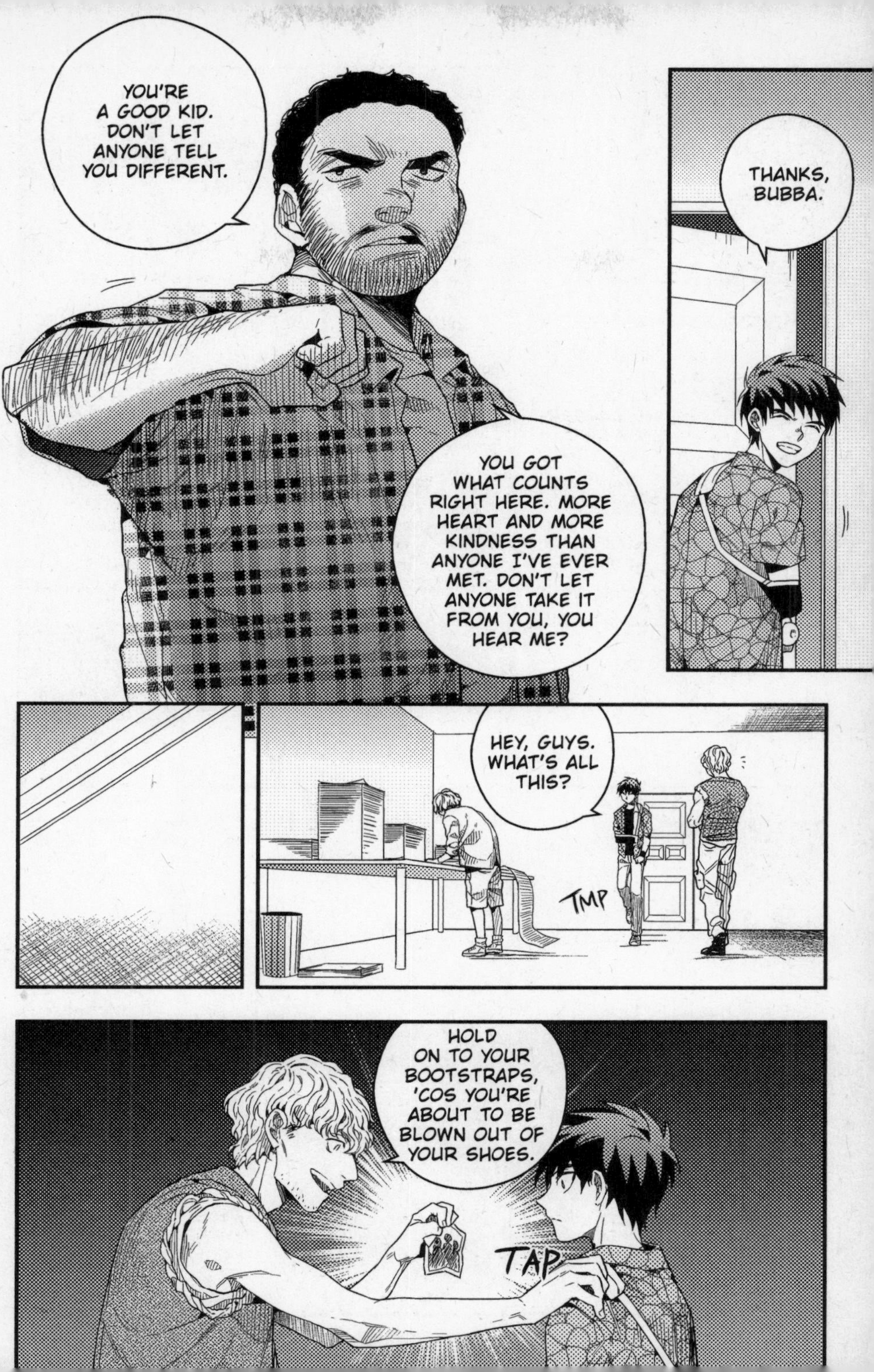
YOU'RE A GOOD KID. DON'T LET ANYONE TELL YOU DIFFERENT.
THANKS, BUBBA.
YOU GOT WHAT COUNTS RIGHT HERE. MORE HEART AND MORE KINDNESS THAN ANYONE I'VE EVER MET. DON'T LET ANYONE TAKE IT FROM YOU, YOU HEAR ME?
HEY, GUYS. WHAT'S ALL THIS?
TMP
HOLD ON TO YOUR BOOTSTRAPS, 'COS YOU'RE ABOUT TO BE BLOWN OUT OF YOUR SHOES.
TAP

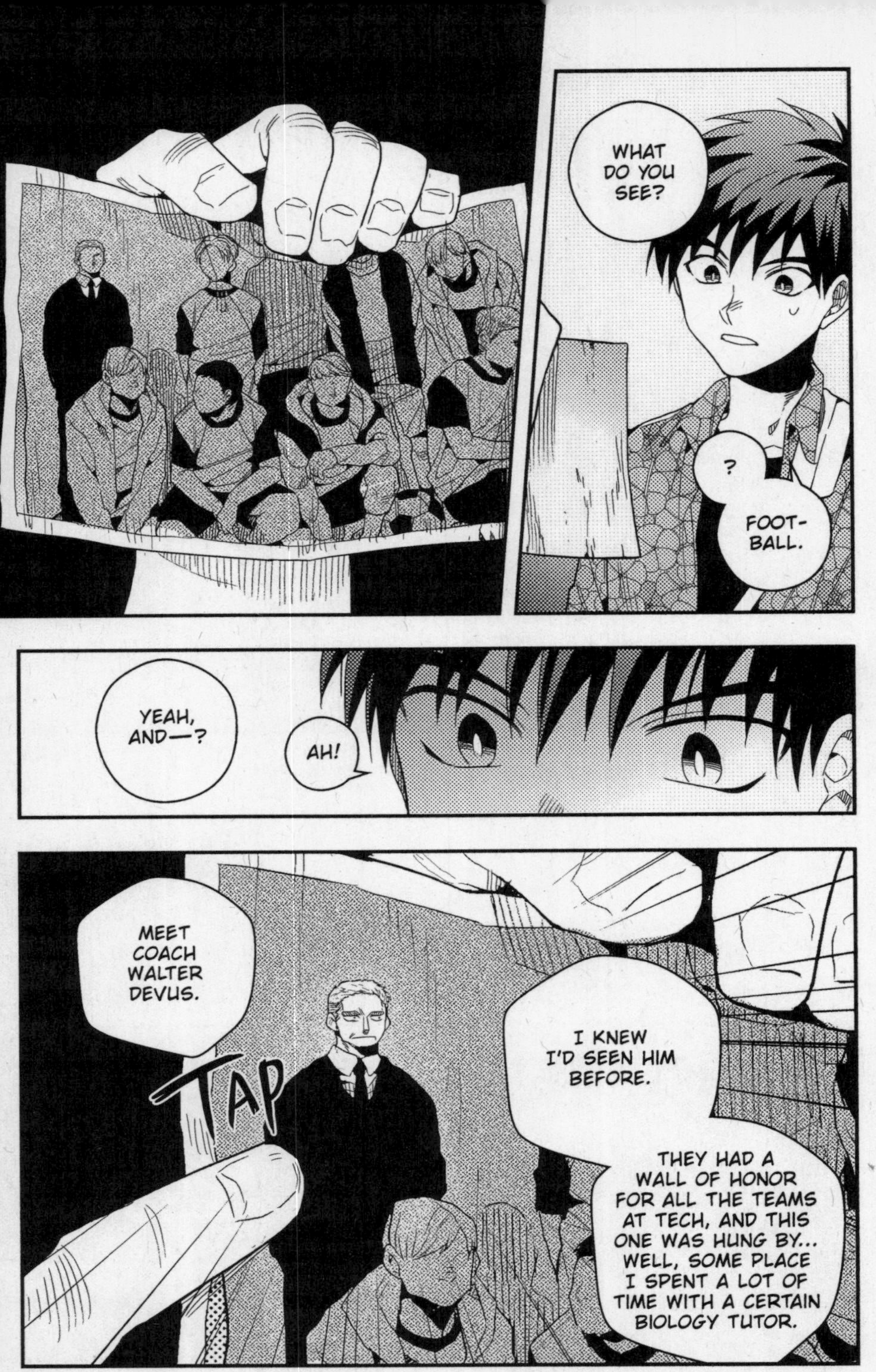
WHAT DO YOU SEE?
?
FOOT-BALL.
YEAH, AND—?
AH!
MEET COACH WALTER DEVUS.
TAP
I KNEW I'D SEEN HIM BEFORE.
THEY HAD A WALL OF HONOR FOR ALL THE TEAMS AT TECH, AND THIS ONE WAS HUNG BY... WELL, SOME PLACE I SPENT A LOT OF TIME WITH A CERTAIN BIOLOGY TUTOR.

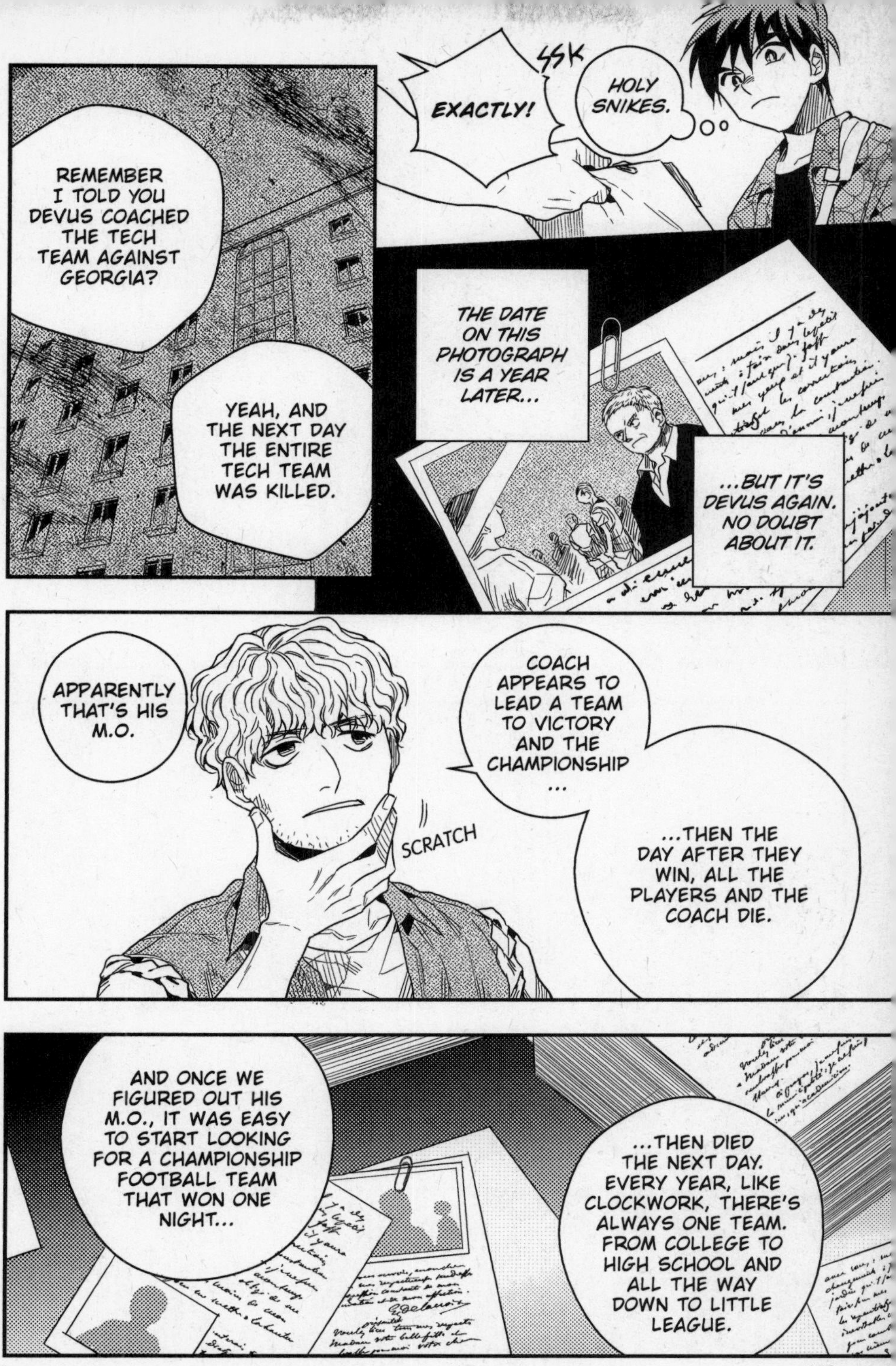
REMEMBER I TOLD YOU DEVUS COACHED THE TECH TEAM AGAINST GEORGIA?
EXACTLY!
SSK
HOLY SNIKES.
YEAH, AND THE NEXT DAY THE ENTIRE TECH TEAM WAS KILLED.
THE DATE ON THIS PHOTOGRAPH IS A YEAR LATER...
...BUT IT'S DEVUS AGAIN. NO DOUBT ABOUT IT.
APPARENTLY THAT'S HIS M.O.
COACH APPEARS TO LEAD A TEAM TO VICTORY AND THE CHAMPIONSHIP ...
SCRATCH
...THEN THE DAY AFTER THEY WIN, ALL THE PLAYERS AND THE COACH DIE.
AND ONCE WE FIGURED OUT HIS M.O., IT WAS EASY TO START LOOKING FOR A CHAMPIONSHIP FOOTBALL TEAM THAT WON ONE NIGHT...
...THEN DIED THE NEXT DAY. EVERY YEAR, LIKE CLOCKWORK, THERE'S ALWAYS ONE TEAM. FROM COLLEGE TO HIGH SCHOOL AND ALL THE WAY DOWN TO LITTLE LEAGUE.

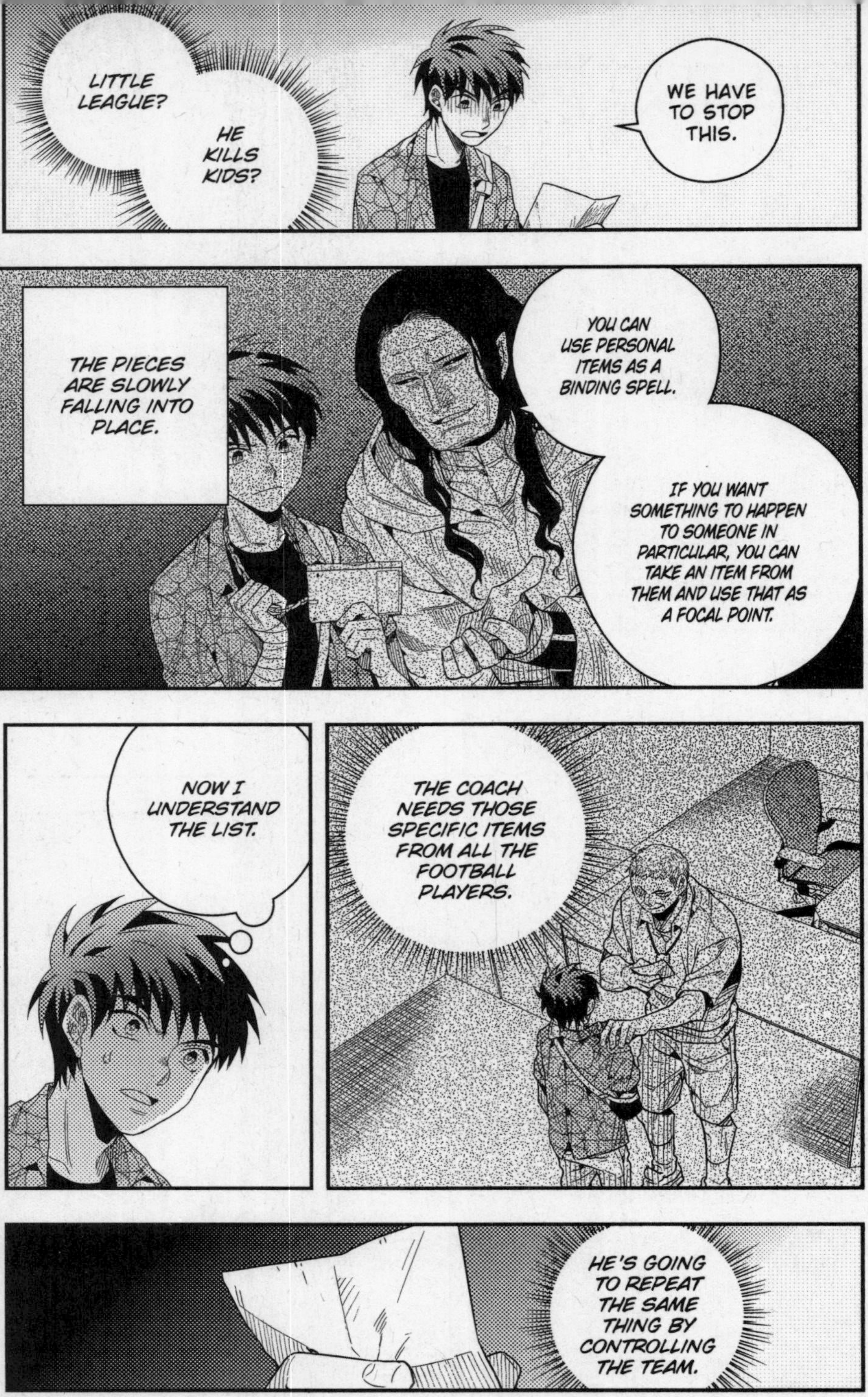
LITTLE LEAGUE?
HE KILLS KIDS?
WE HAVE TO STOP THIS.
THE PIECES ARE SLOWLY FALLING INTO PLACE.
YOU CAN USE PERSONAL ITEMS AS A BINDING SPELL.
IF YOU WANT SOMETHING TO HAPPEN TO SOMEONE IN PARTICULAR, YOU CAN TAKE AN ITEM FROM THEM AND USE THAT AS A FOCAL POINT.
NOW I UNDERSTAND THE LIST.
THE COACH NEEDS THOSE SPECIFIC ITEMS FROM ALL THE FOOTBALL PLAYERS.
HE'S GOING TO REPEAT THE SAME THING BY CONTROLLING THE TEAM.

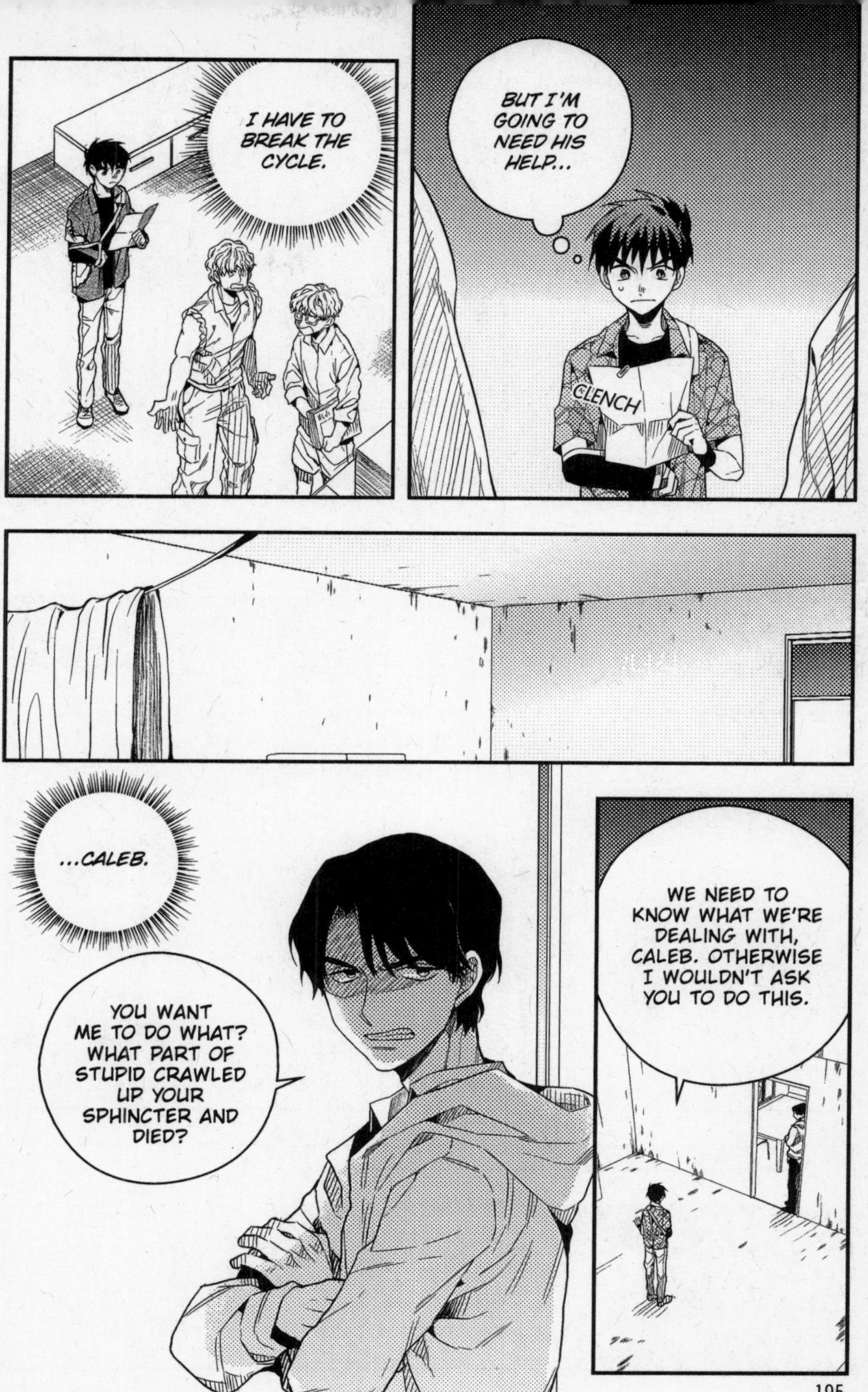
I HAVE TO BREAK THE CYCLE.
BUT I'M GOING TO NEED HIS HELP...
CLENCH
...CALEB.
YOU WANT ME TO DO WHAT? WHAT PART OF STUPID CRAWLED UP YOUR SPHINCTER AND DIED?
WE NEED TO KNOW WHAT WE'RE DEALING WITH, CALEB. OTHERWISE I WOULDN'T ASK YOU TO DO THIS.

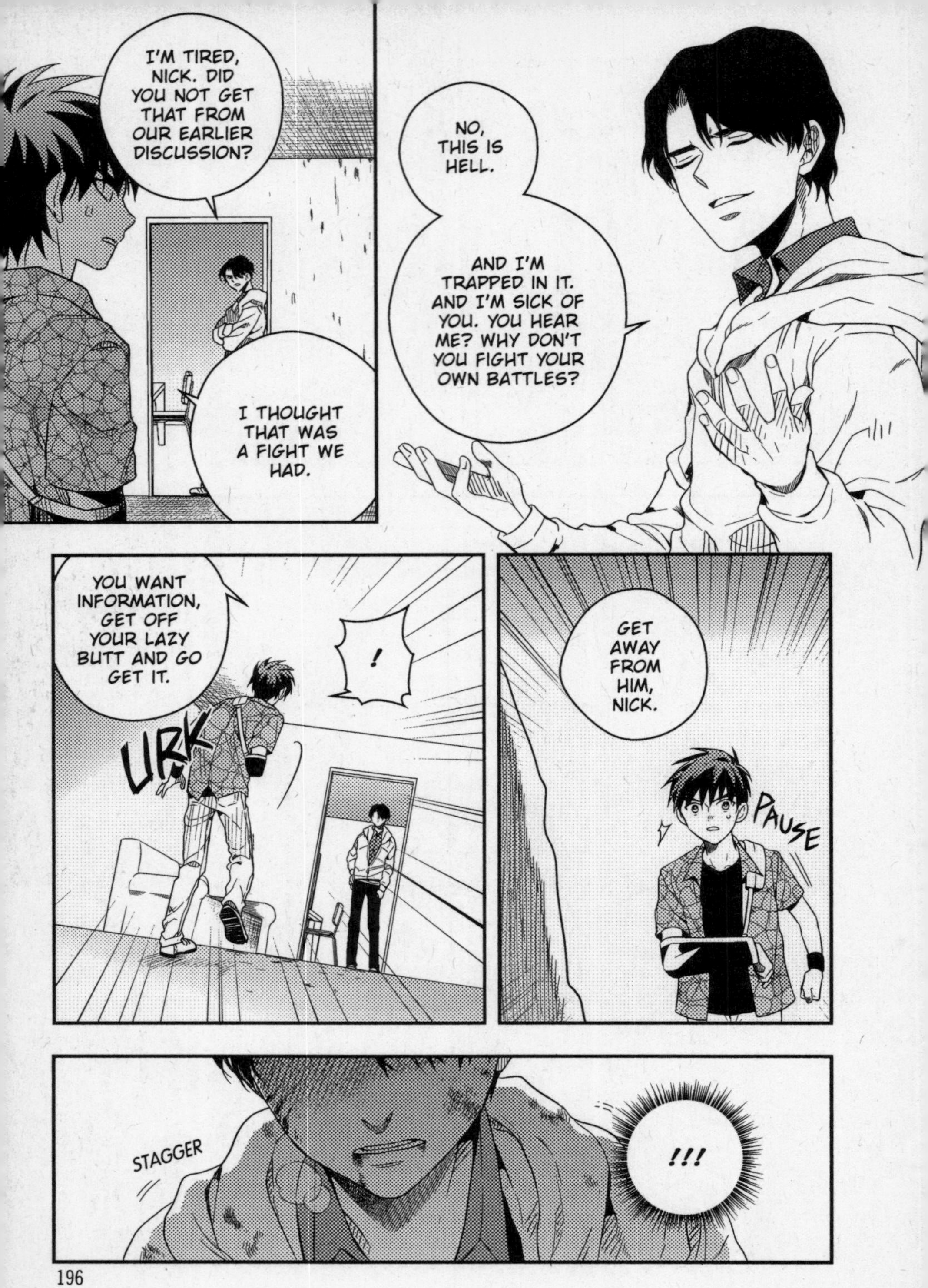

I'M TIRED, NICK. DID YOU NOT GET THAT FROM OUR EARLIER DISCUSSION?
I THOUGHT THAT WAS A FIGHT WE HAD.
NO, THIS IS HELL.
AND I'M TRAPPED IN IT. AND I'M SICK OF YOU. YOU HEAR ME? WHY DON'T YOU FIGHT YOUR OWN BATTLES?
YOU WANT INFORMATION, GET OFF YOUR LAZY BUTT AND GO GET IT.
URK
!
GET AWAY FROM HIM, NICK.
PAUSE
STAGGER
!!!

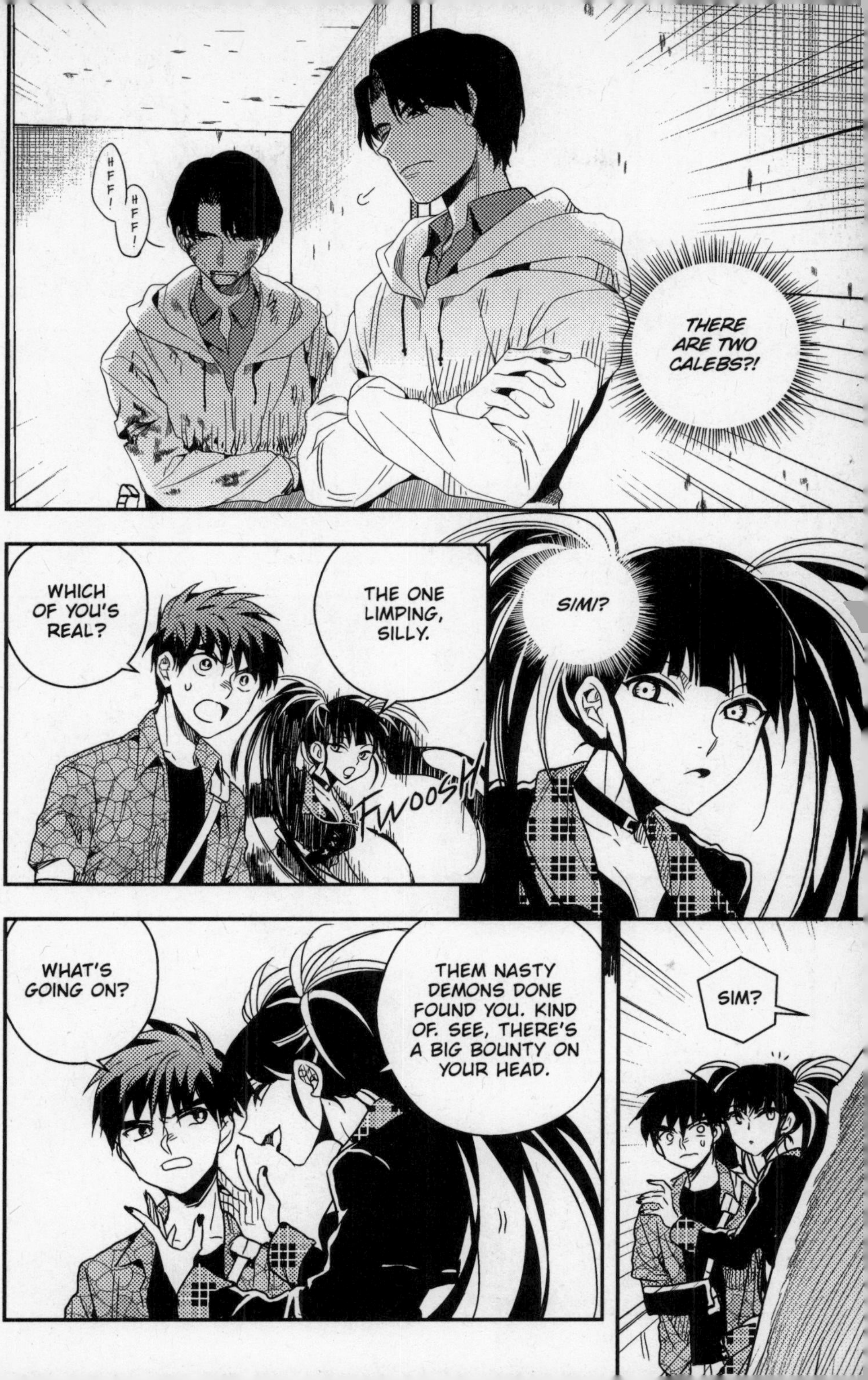
HFF! HFF!
THERE ARE TWO CALEBS?!
WHICH OF YOU'S REAL?
THE ONE LIMPING, SILLY.
FWOOSH
SIMI?
WHAT'S GOING ON?
THEM NASTY DEMONS DONE FOUND YOU. KIND OF. SEE, THERE'S A BIG BOUNTY ON YOUR HEAD.
SIM?

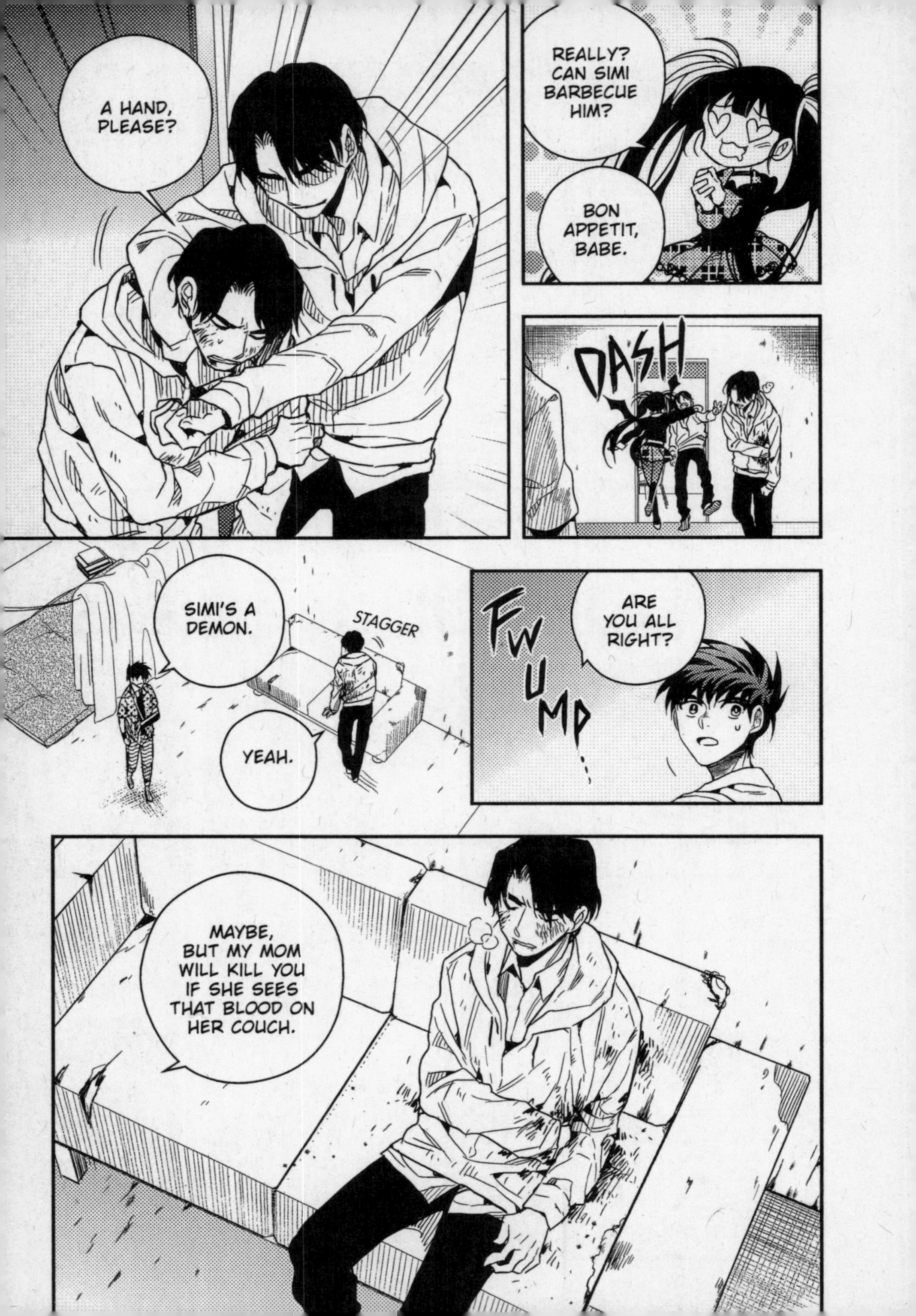
A HAND, PLEASE?
REALLY? CAN SIMI BARBECUE HIM?
BON APPETIT, BABE.
DASH
SIMI'S A DEMON.
STAGGER
YEAH.
FWUMP
ARE YOU ALL RIGHT?
MAYBE, BUT MY MOM WILL KILL YOU IF SHE SEES THAT BLOOD ON HER COUCH.

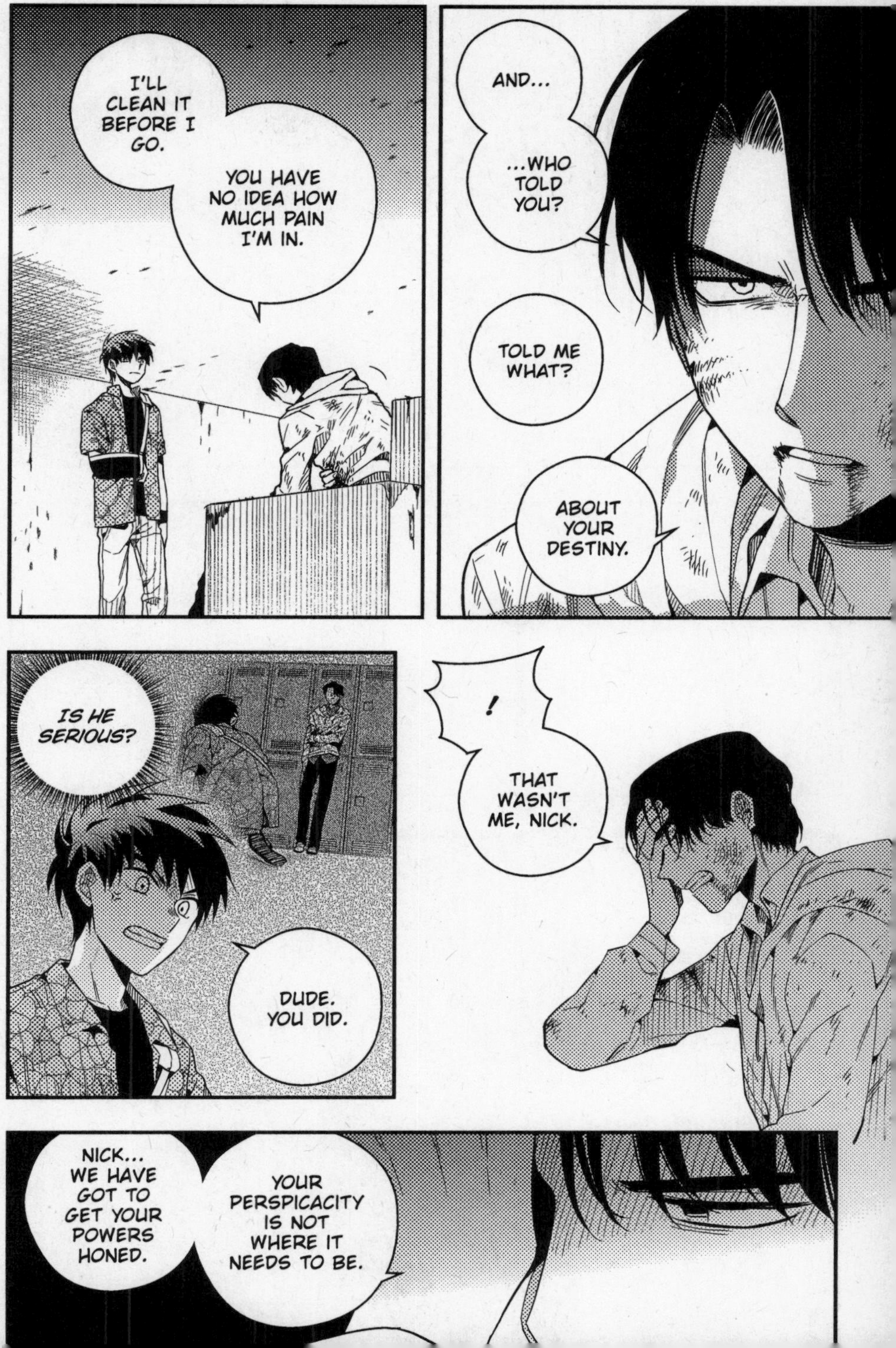
I'LL CLEAN IT BEFORE I GO.
YOU HAVE NO IDEA HOW MUCH PAIN I'M IN.
AND...
...WHO TOLD YOU?
TOLD ME WHAT?
ABOUT YOUR DESTINY.
IS HE SERIOUS?
DUDE. YOU DID.
!
THAT WASN'T ME, NICK.
NICK... WE HAVE GOT TO GET YOUR POWERS HONED.
YOUR PERSPICACITY IS NOT WHERE IT NEEDS TO BE.

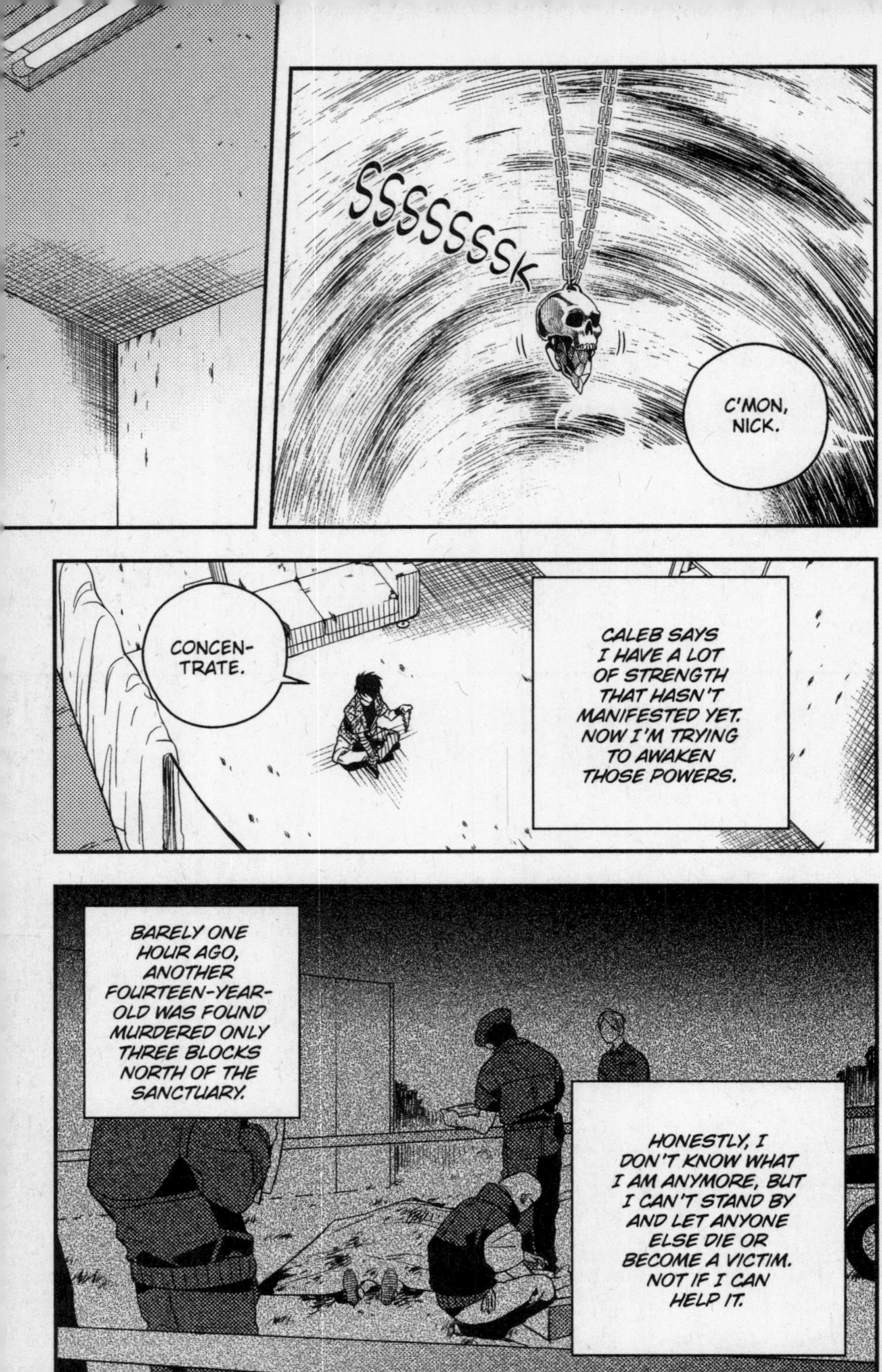
SSSSSSSSK
C'MON, NICK.
CONCEN-TRATE.
CALEB SAYS I HAVE A LOT OF STRENGTH THAT HASN'T MANIFESTED YET. NOW I'M TRYING TO AWAKEN THOSE POWERS.
BARELY ONE HOUR AGO, ANOTHER FOURTEEN-YEAR-OLD WAS FOUND MURDERED ONLY THREE BLOCKS NORTH OF THE SANCTUARY.
HONESTLY, I DON'T KNOW WHAT I AM ANYMORE, BUT I CAN'T STAND BY AND LET ANYONE ELSE DIE OR BECOME A VICTIM. NOT IF I CAN HELP IT.

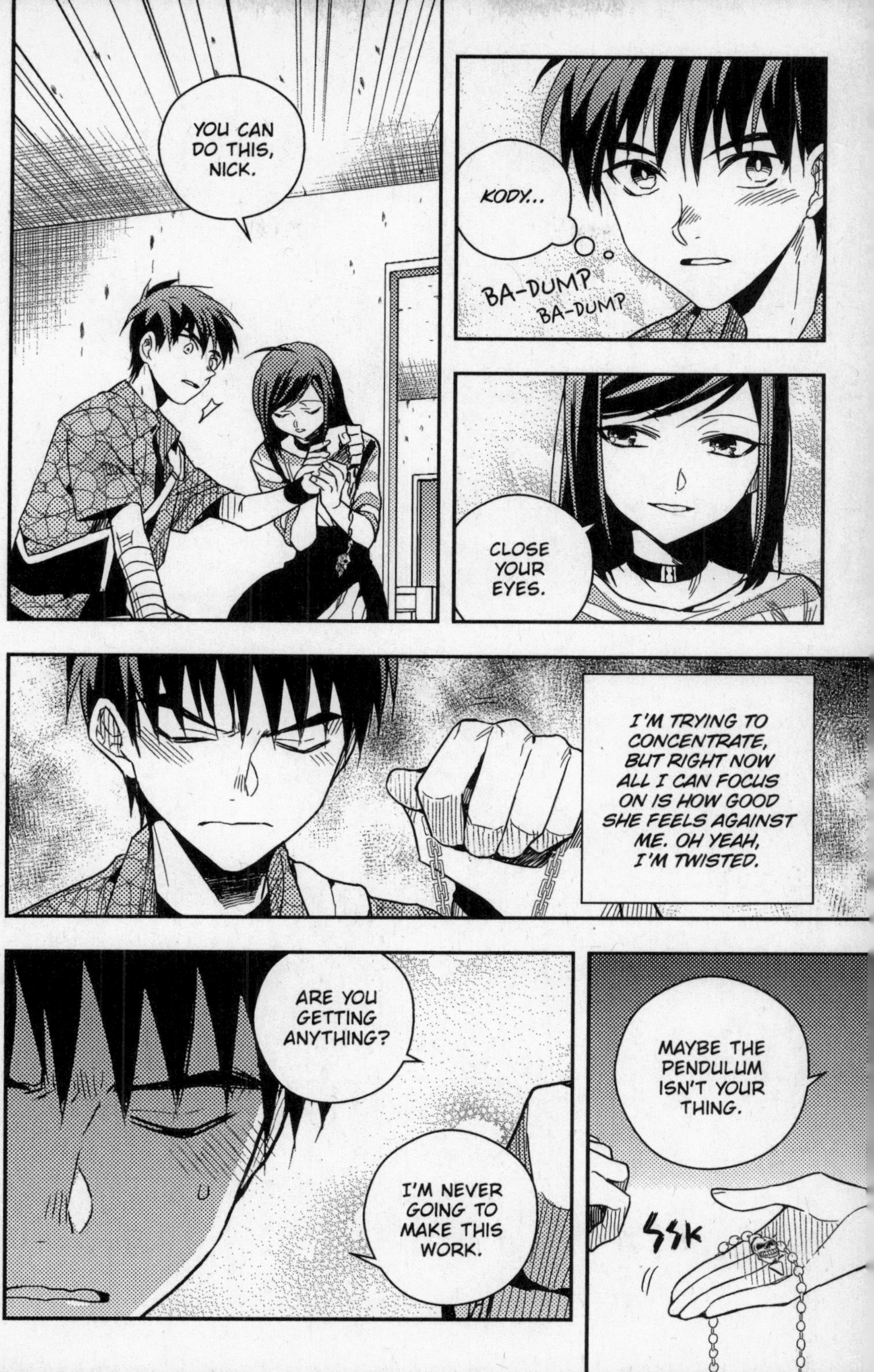
YOU CAN DO THIS, NICK.
KODY...
BA-DUMP
BA-DUMP
CLOSE YOUR EYES.
I'M TRYING TO CONCENTRATE, BUT RIGHT NOW ALL I CAN FOCUS ON IS HOW GOOD SHE FEELS AGAINST ME. OH YEAH, I'M TWISTED.
ARE YOU GETTING ANYTHING?
I'M NEVER GOING TO MAKE THIS WORK.
MAYBE THE PENDULUM ISN'T YOUR THING.
SSK

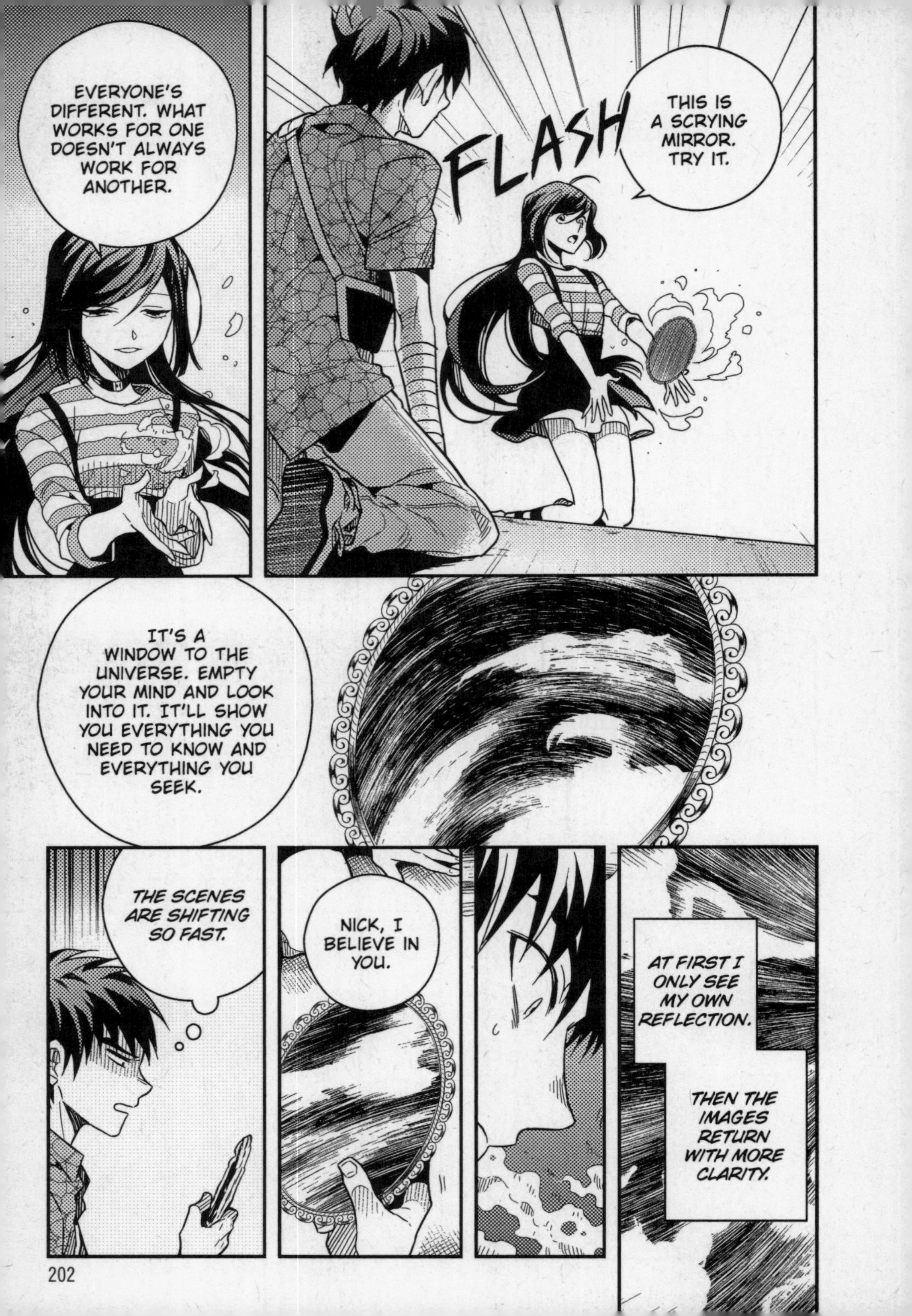
EVERYONE'S DIFFERENT. WHAT WORKS FOR ONE DOESN'T ALWAYS WORK FOR ANOTHER.
FLASH
THIS IS A SCRYING MIRROR. TRY IT.
IT'S A WINDOW TO THE UNIVERSE. EMPTY YOUR MIND AND LOOK INTO IT. IT'LL SHOW YOU EVERYTHING YOU NEED TO KNOW AND EVERYTHING YOU SEEK.
THE SCENES ARE SHIFTING SO FAST.
NICK, I BELIEVE IN YOU.
AT FIRST I ONLY SEE MY OWN REFLECTION.
THEN THE IMAGES RETURN WITH MORE CLARITY.

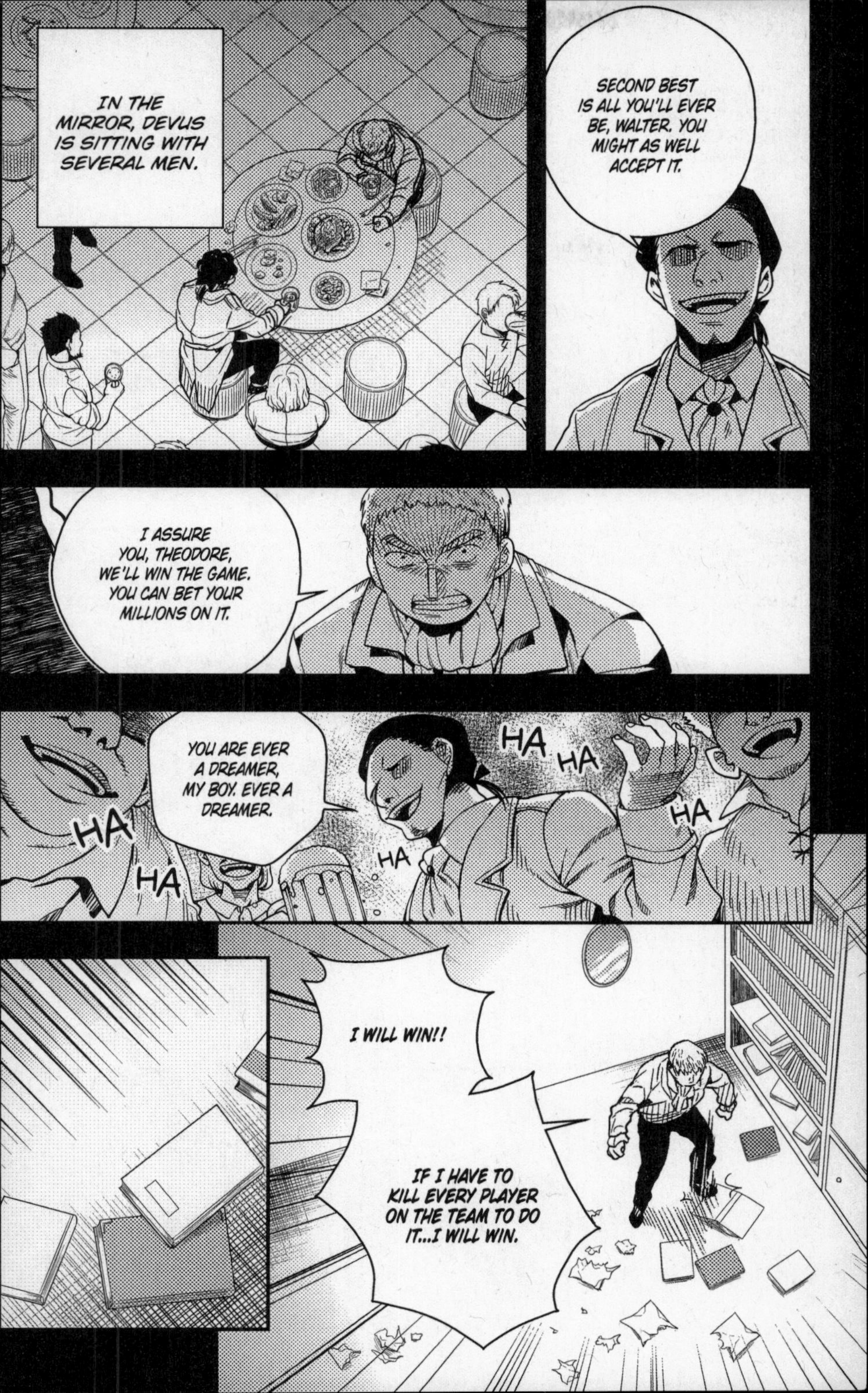
IN THE MIRROR, DEVUS IS SITTING WITH SEVERAL MEN.
SECOND BEST IS ALL YOU'LL EVER BE, WALTER. YOU MIGHT AS WELL ACCEPT IT.
I ASSURE YOU, THEODORE, WE'LL WIN THE GAME. YOU CAN BET YOUR MILLIONS ON IT.
YOU ARE EVER A DREAMER, MY BOY. EVER A DREAMER.
HA HA HA HA HA HA HA
I WILL WIN!!
IF I HAVE TO KILL EVERY PLAYER ON THE TEAM TO DO IT...I WILL WIN.

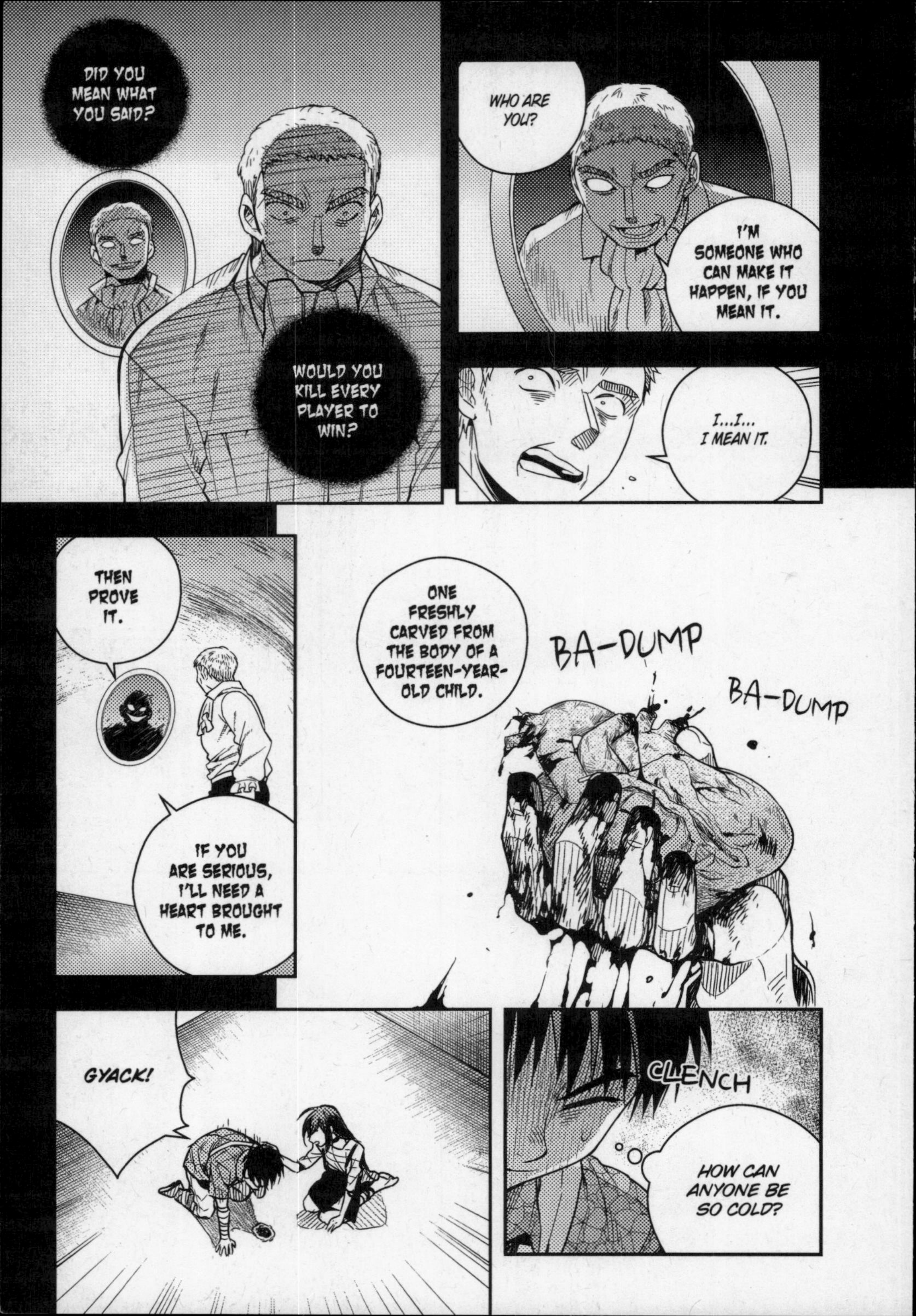
DID YOU MEAN WHAT YOU SAID?
WOULD YOU KILL EVERY PLAYER TO WIN?
WHO ARE YOU?
I'M SOMEONE WHO CAN MAKE IT HAPPEN, IF YOU MEAN IT.
I...I... I MEAN IT.
THEN PROVE IT.
IF YOU ARE SERIOUS, I'LL NEED A HEART BROUGHT TO ME.
ONE FRESHLY CARVED FROM THE BODY OF A FOURTEEN-YEAR-OLD CHILD.
BA-DUMP
BA-DUMP
GYACK!
CLENCH
HOW CAN ANYONE BE SO COLD?

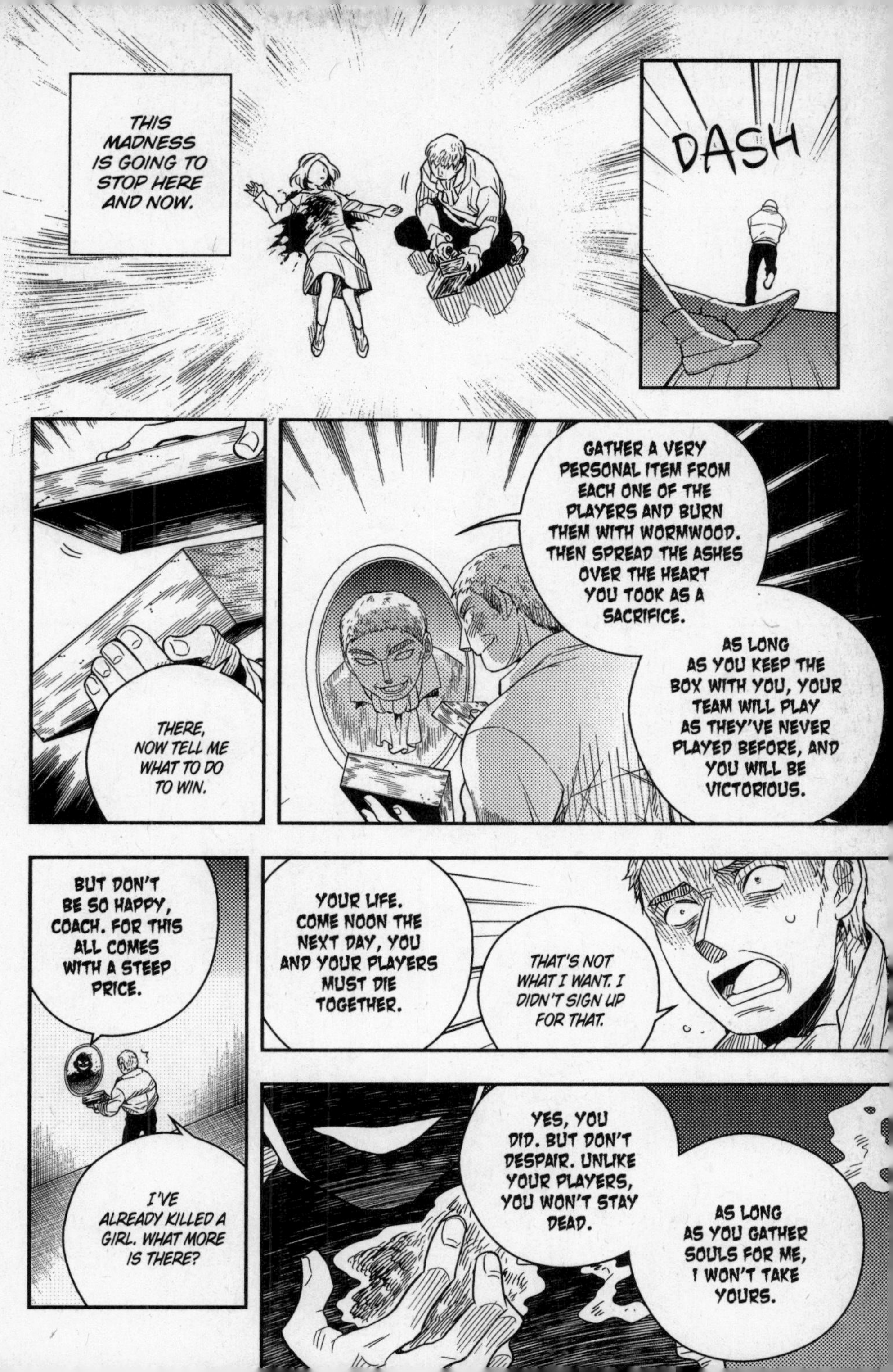
THIS MADNESS IS GOING TO STOP HERE AND NOW.
DASH
THERE, NOW TELL ME WHAT TO DO TO WIN.
GATHER A VERY PERSONAL ITEM FROM EACH ONE OF THE PLAYERS AND BURN THEM WITH WORMWOOD. THEN SPREAD THE ASHES OVER THE HEART YOU TOOK AS A SACRIFICE.
AS LONG AS YOU KEEP THE BOX WITH YOU, YOUR TEAM WILL PLAY AS THEY'VE NEVER PLAYED BEFORE, AND YOU WILL BE VICTORIOUS.
BUT DON'T BE SO HAPPY, COACH. FOR THIS ALL COMES WITH A STEEP PRICE.
I'VE ALREADY KILLED A GIRL. WHAT MORE IS THERE?
YOUR LIFE. COME NOON THE NEXT DAY, YOU AND YOUR PLAYERS MUST DIE TOGETHER.
THAT'S NOT WHAT I WANT. I DIDN'T SIGN UP FOR THAT.
YES, YOU DID. BUT DON'T DESPAIR. UNLIKE YOUR PLAYERS, YOU WON'T STAY DEAD.
AS LONG AS YOU GATHER SOULS FOR ME, I WON'T TAKE YOURS.

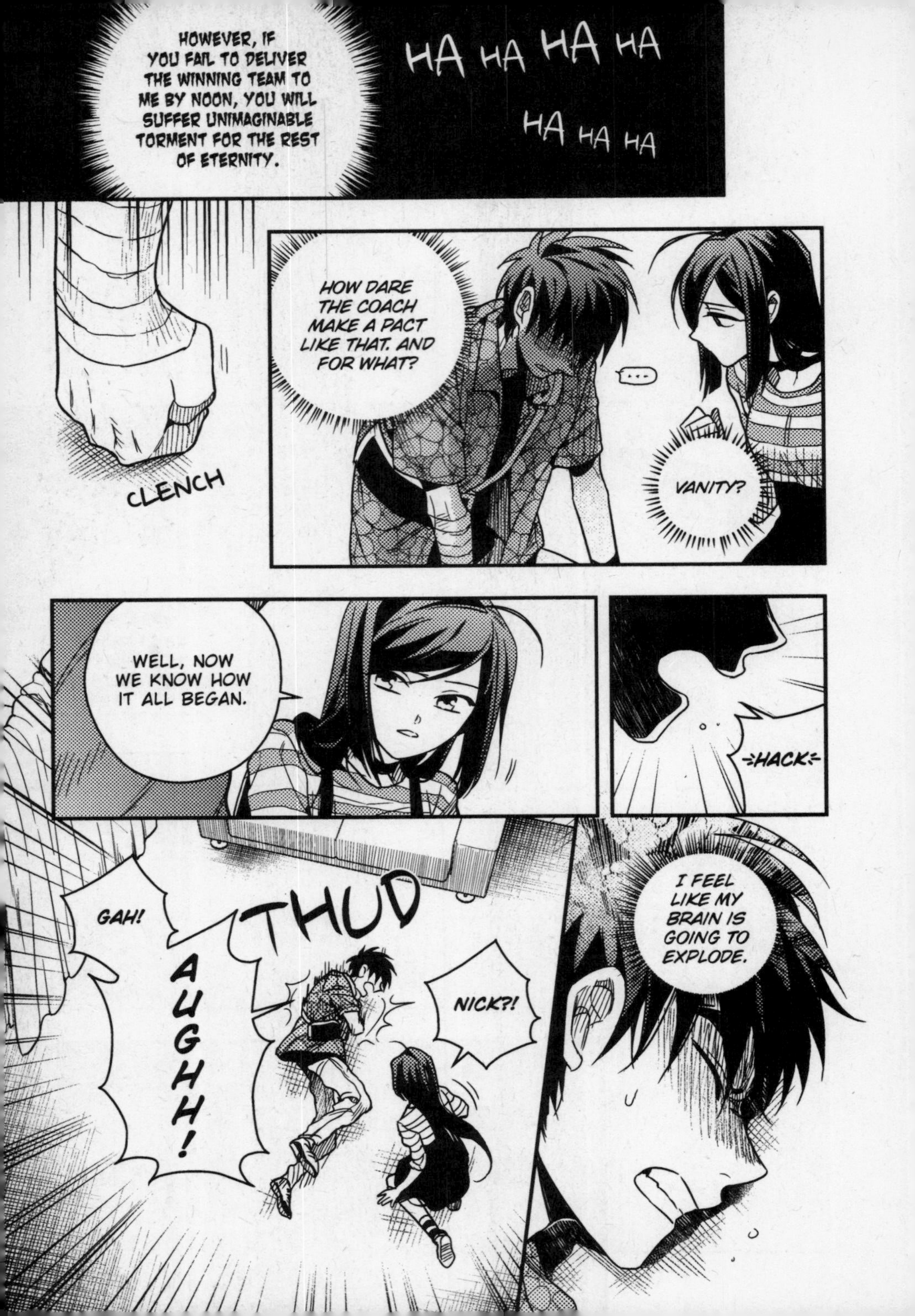
HOWEVER, IF YOU FAIL TO DELIVER THE WINNING TEAM TO ME BY NOON, YOU WILL SUFFER UNIMAGINABLE TORMENT FOR THE REST OF ETERNITY.
HA HA HA HA
HA HA HA
CLENCH
HOW DARE THE COACH MAKE A PACT LIKE THAT. AND FOR WHAT?
...
VANITY?
WELL, NOW WE KNOW HOW IT ALL BEGAN.
HACK
I FEEL LIKE MY BRAIN IS GOING TO EXPLODE.
GAH!
THUD
AUGHH!
NICK?!

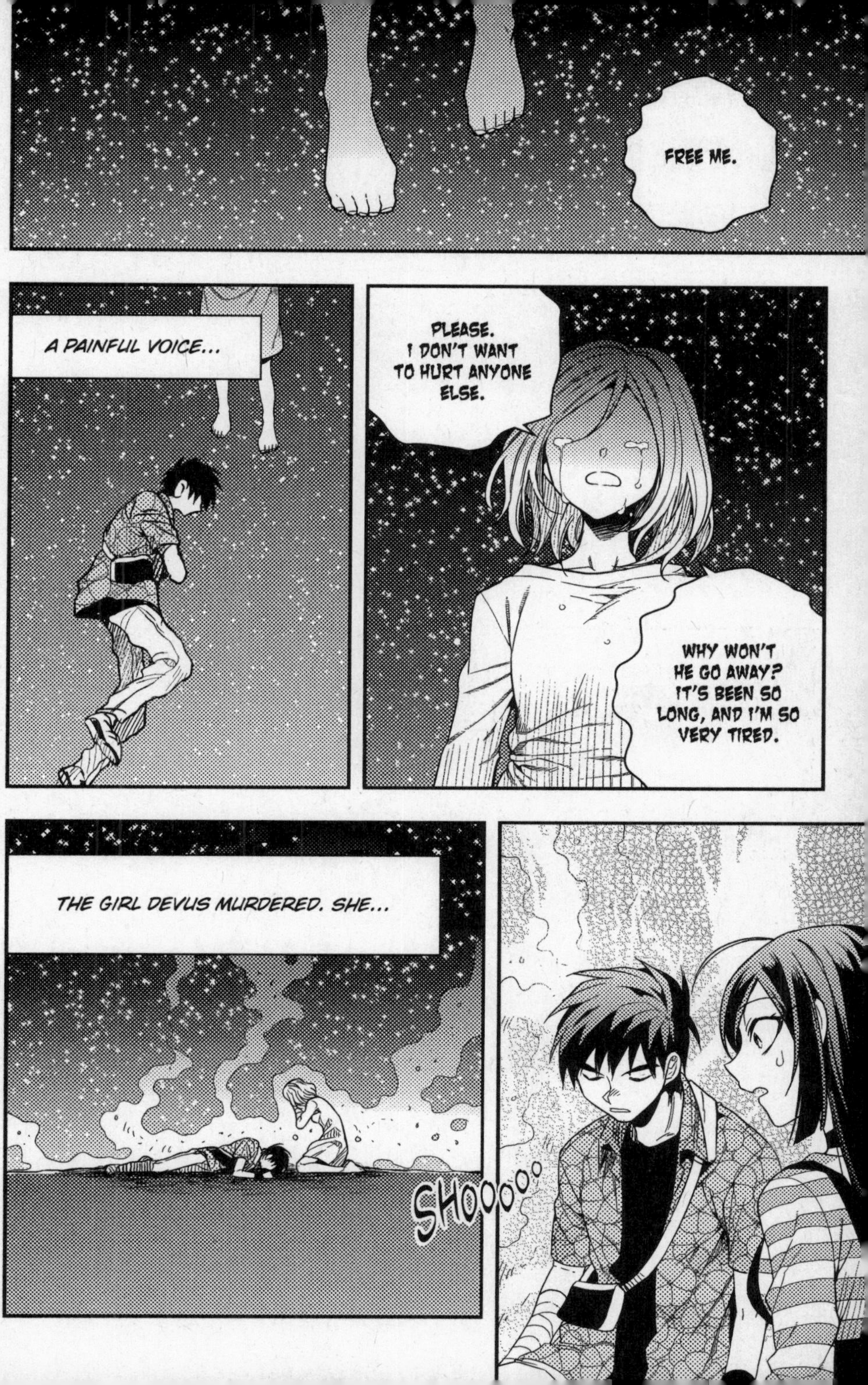
FREE ME.
A PAINFUL VOICE...
PLEASE. I DON'T WANT TO HURT ANYONE ELSE.
WHY WON'T HE GO AWAY? IT'S BEEN SO LONG, AND I'M SO VERY TIRED.
THE GIRL DEVUS MURDERED. SHE...
SHOOOOO

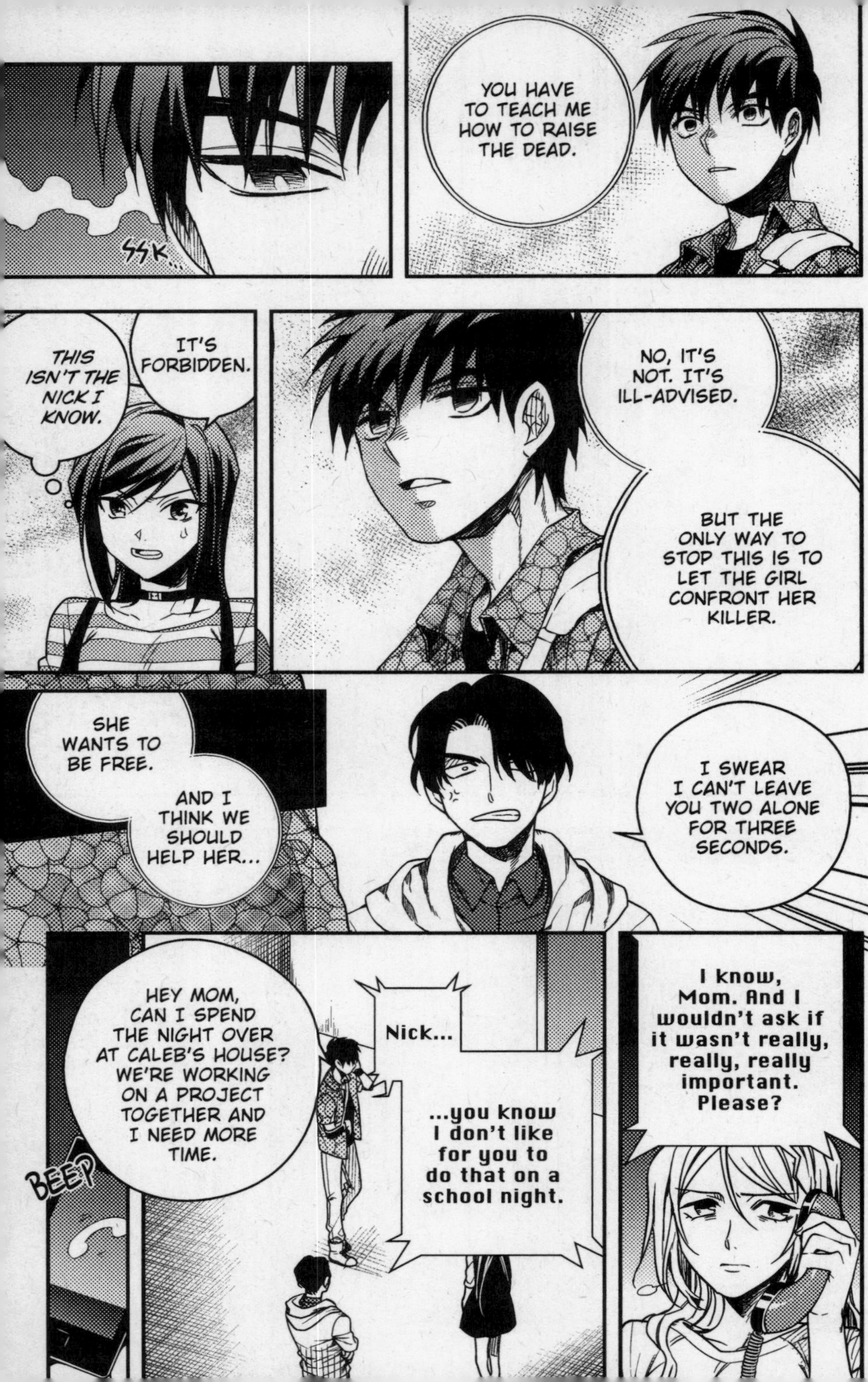

SSK...
YOU HAVE TO TEACH ME HOW TO RAISE THE DEAD.
IT'S FORBIDDEN.
THIS ISN'T THE NICK I KNOW.
NO, IT'S NOT. IT'S ILL-ADVISED.
BUT THE ONLY WAY TO STOP THIS IS TO LET THE GIRL CONFRONT HER KILLER.
SHE WANTS TO BE FREE.
AND I THINK WE SHOULD HELP HER...
I SWEAR I CAN'T LEAVE YOU TWO ALONE FOR THREE SECONDS.
HEY MOM, CAN I SPEND THE NIGHT OVER AT CALEB'S HOUSE? WE'RE WORKING ON A PROJECT TOGETHER AND I NEED MORE TIME.
BEEP
Nick...
...you know I don't like for you to do that on a school night.
I know, Mom. And I wouldn't ask if it wasn't really, really, really important. Please?

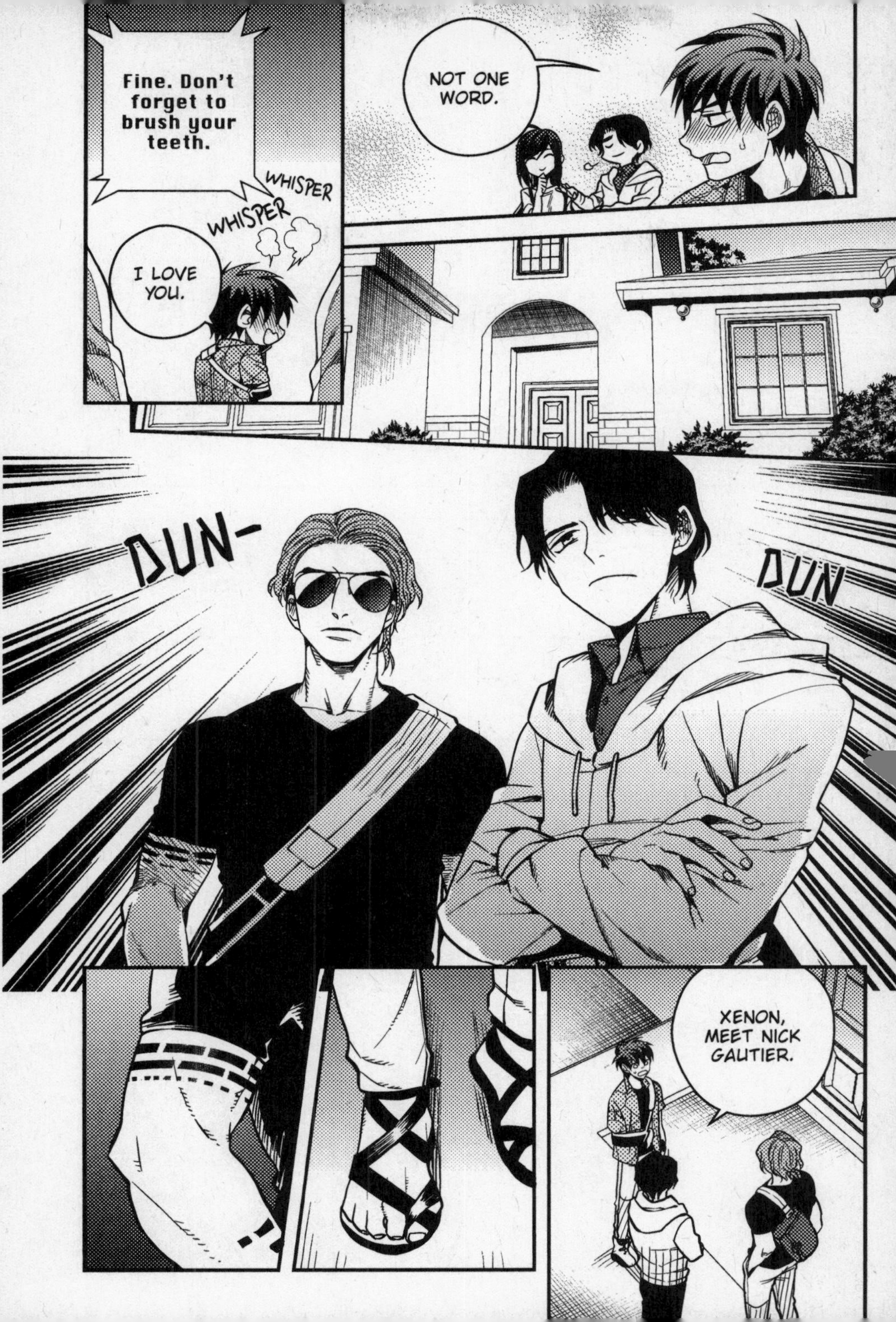
Fine. Don't forget to brush your teeth.
WHISPER
WHISPER
I LOVE YOU.
NOT ONE WORD.
DUN-
DUN
XENON, MEET NICK GAUTIER.

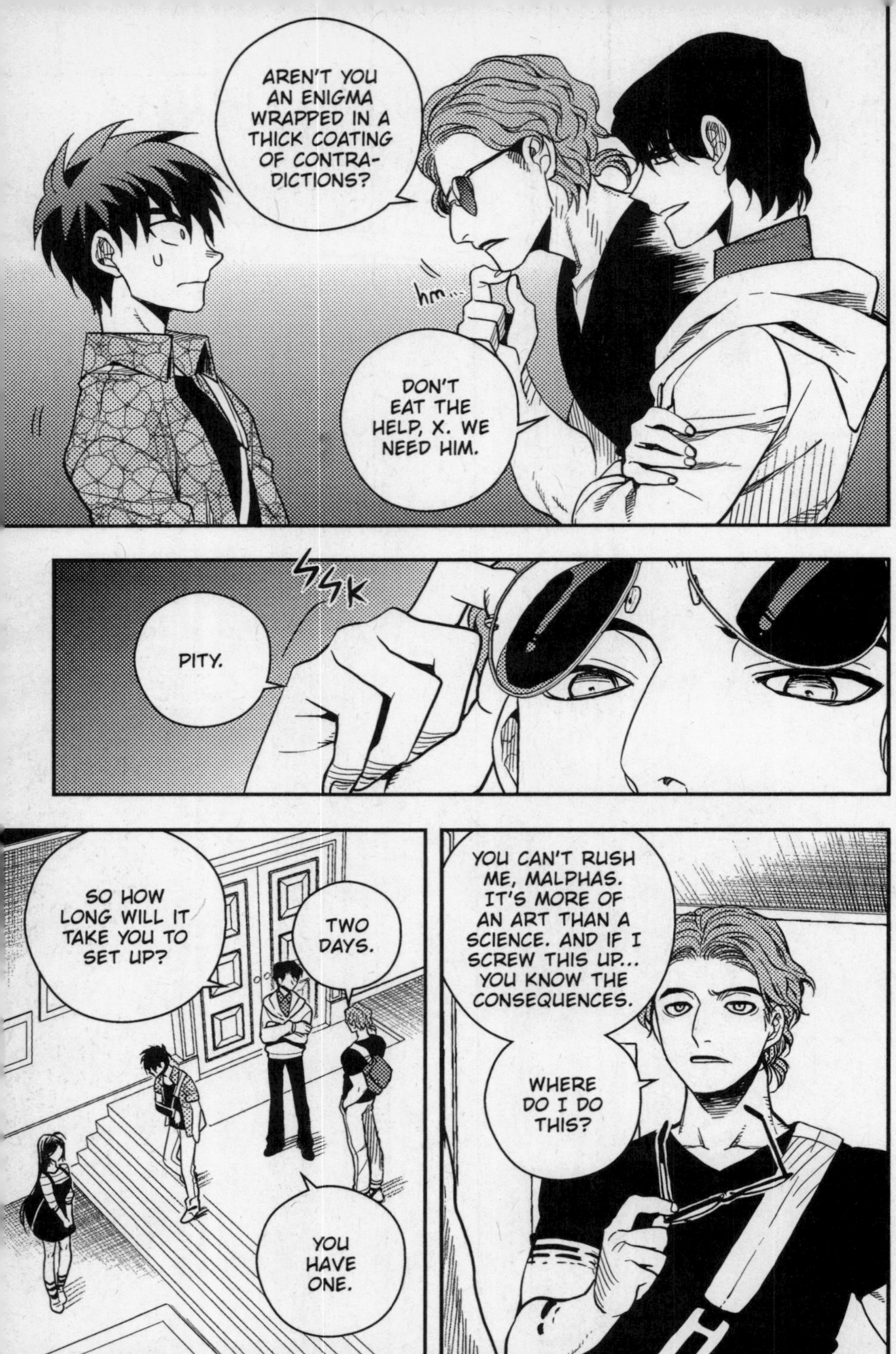
AREN'T YOU AN ENIGMA WRAPPED IN A THICK COATING OF CONTRA-DICTIONS?
hm...
DON'T EAT THE HELP, X. WE NEED HIM.
SSK
PITY.
SO HOW LONG WILL IT TAKE YOU TO SET UP?
TWO DAYS.
YOU HAVE ONE.
YOU CAN'T RUSH ME, MALPHAS. IT'S MORE OF AN ART THAN A SCIENCE. AND IF I SCREW THIS UP... YOU KNOW THE CONSEQUENCES.
WHERE DO I DO THIS?

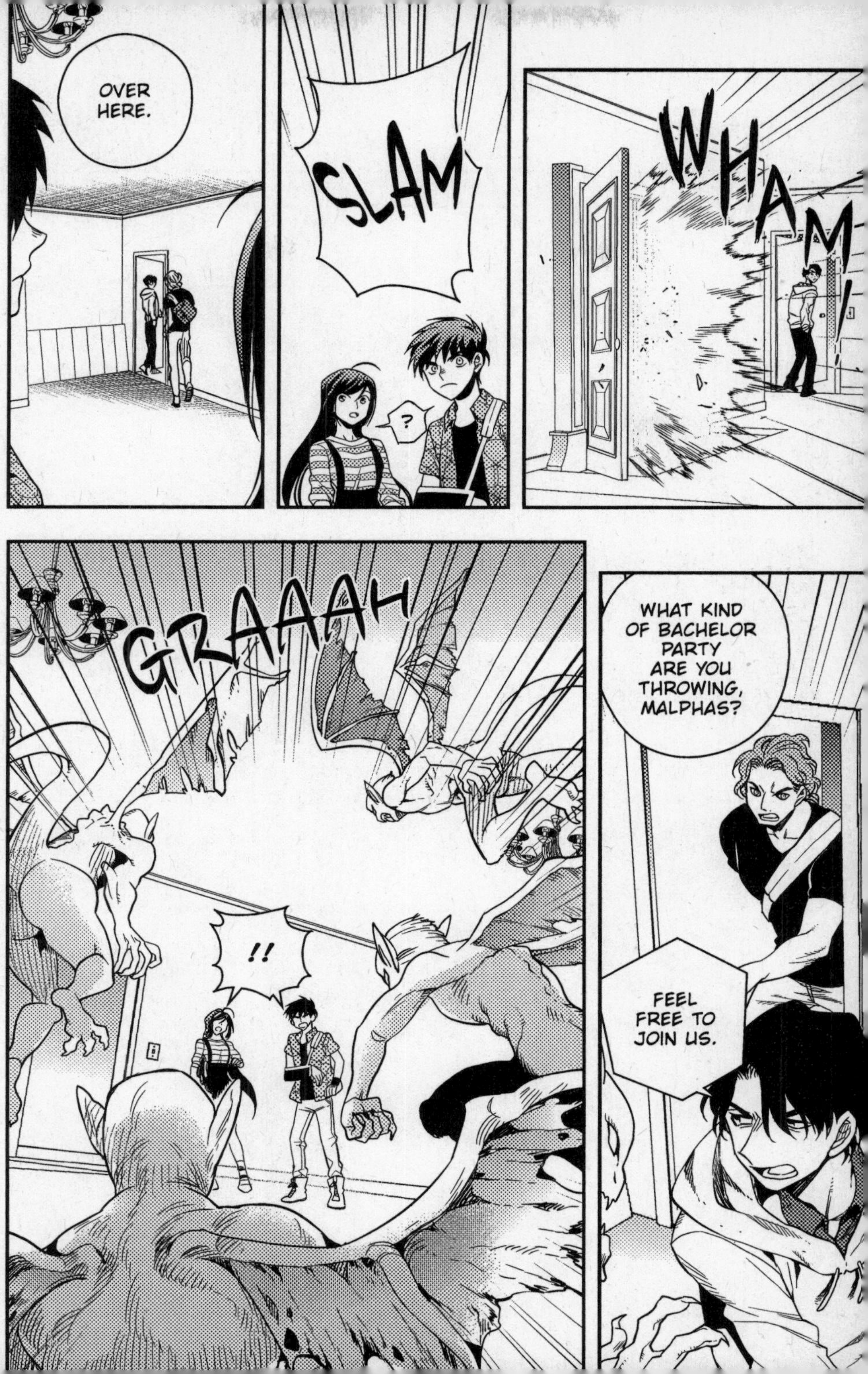
OVER HERE.
SLAM
?
WHAM!
GRAAAAH
!!
WHAT KIND OF BACHELOR PARTY ARE YOU THROWING, MALPHAS?
FEEL FREE TO JOIN US.

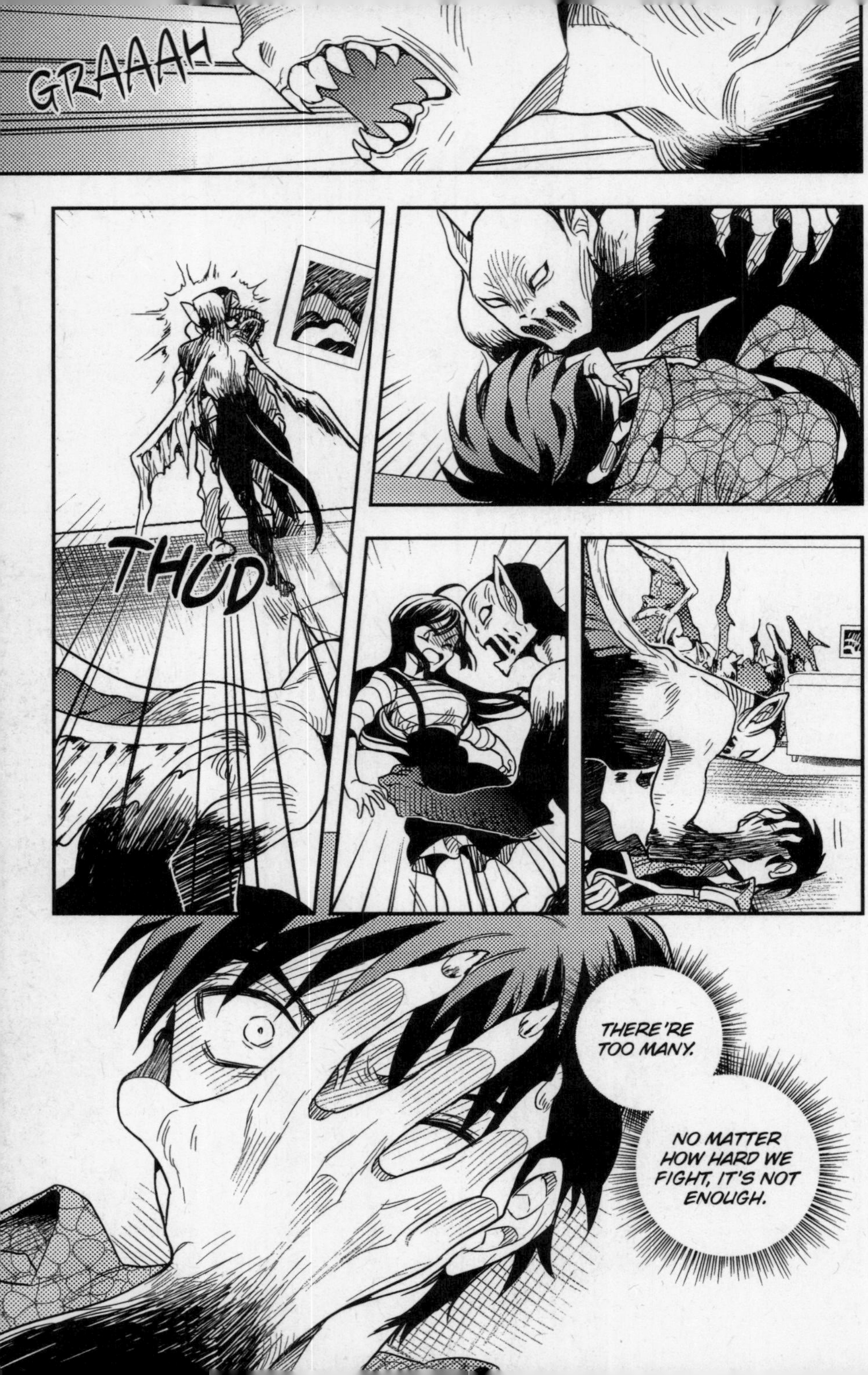
GRAAAH
THUD
THERE'RE TOO MANY.
NO MATTER HOW HARD WE FIGHT, IT'S NOT ENOUGH.

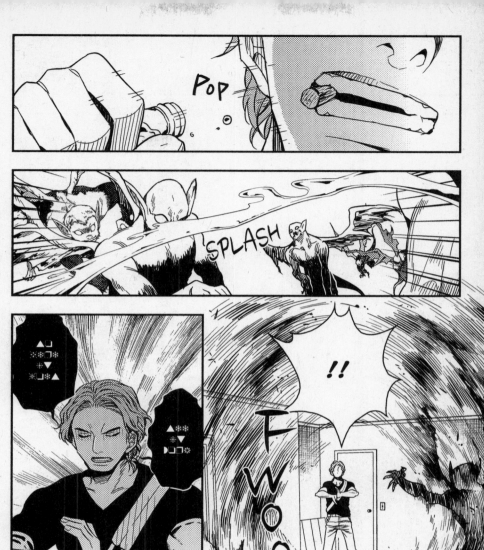

POP

SPLASH

!!

FWOOOSH

TAP

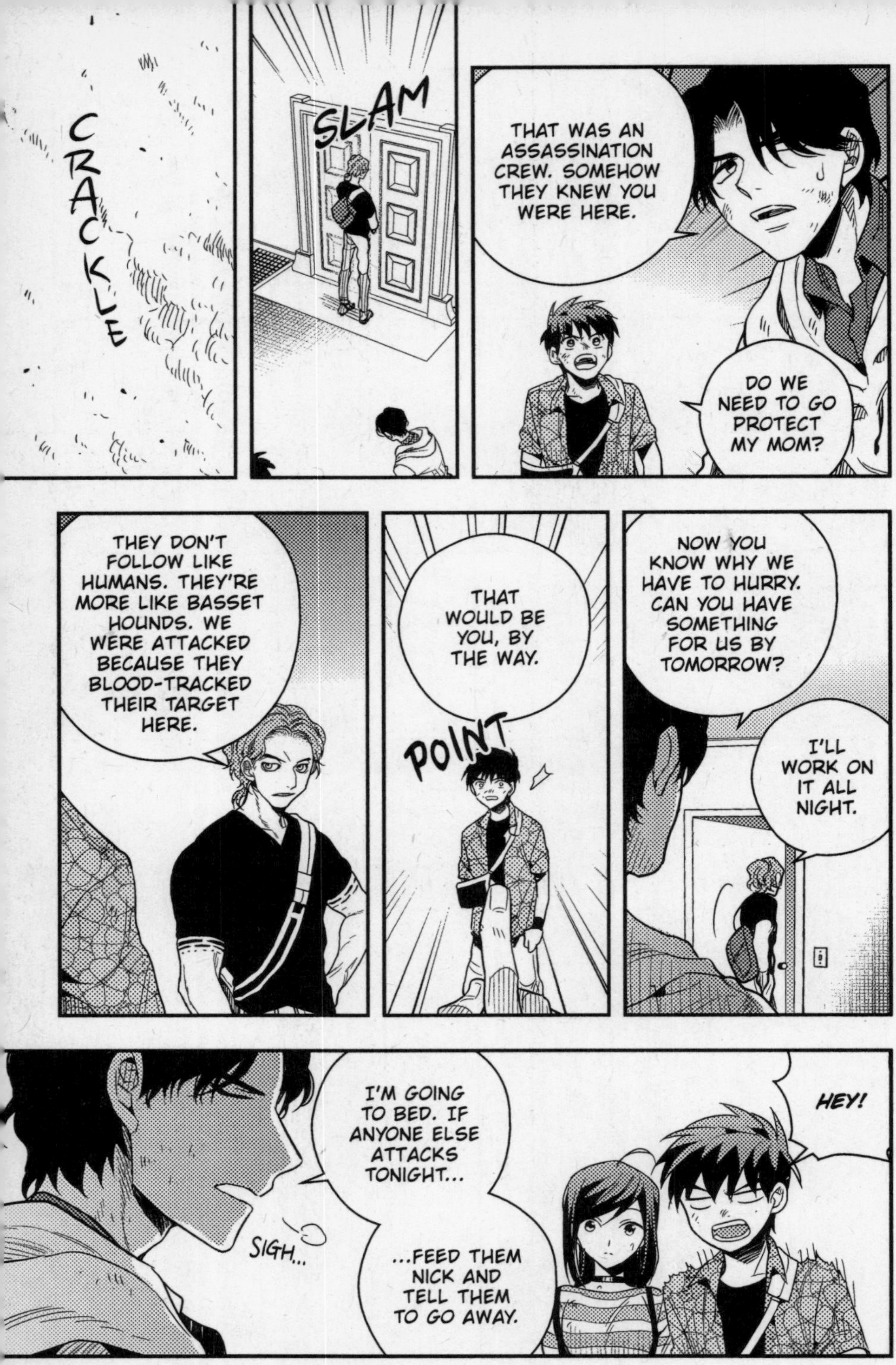
CRACKLE
SLAM
THAT WAS AN ASSASSINATION CREW. SOMEHOW THEY KNEW YOU WERE HERE.
DO WE NEED TO GO PROTECT MY MOM?
THEY DON'T FOLLOW LIKE HUMANS. THEY'RE MORE LIKE BASSET HOUNDS. WE WERE ATTACKED BECAUSE THEY BLOOD-TRACKED THEIR TARGET HERE.
THAT WOULD BE YOU, BY THE WAY.
POINT
NOW YOU KNOW WHY WE HAVE TO HURRY. CAN YOU HAVE SOMETHING FOR US BY TOMORROW?
I'LL WORK ON IT ALL NIGHT.
I'M GOING TO BED. IF ANYONE ELSE ATTACKS TONIGHT...
SIGH...
...FEED THEM NICK AND TELL THEM TO GO AWAY.
HEY!

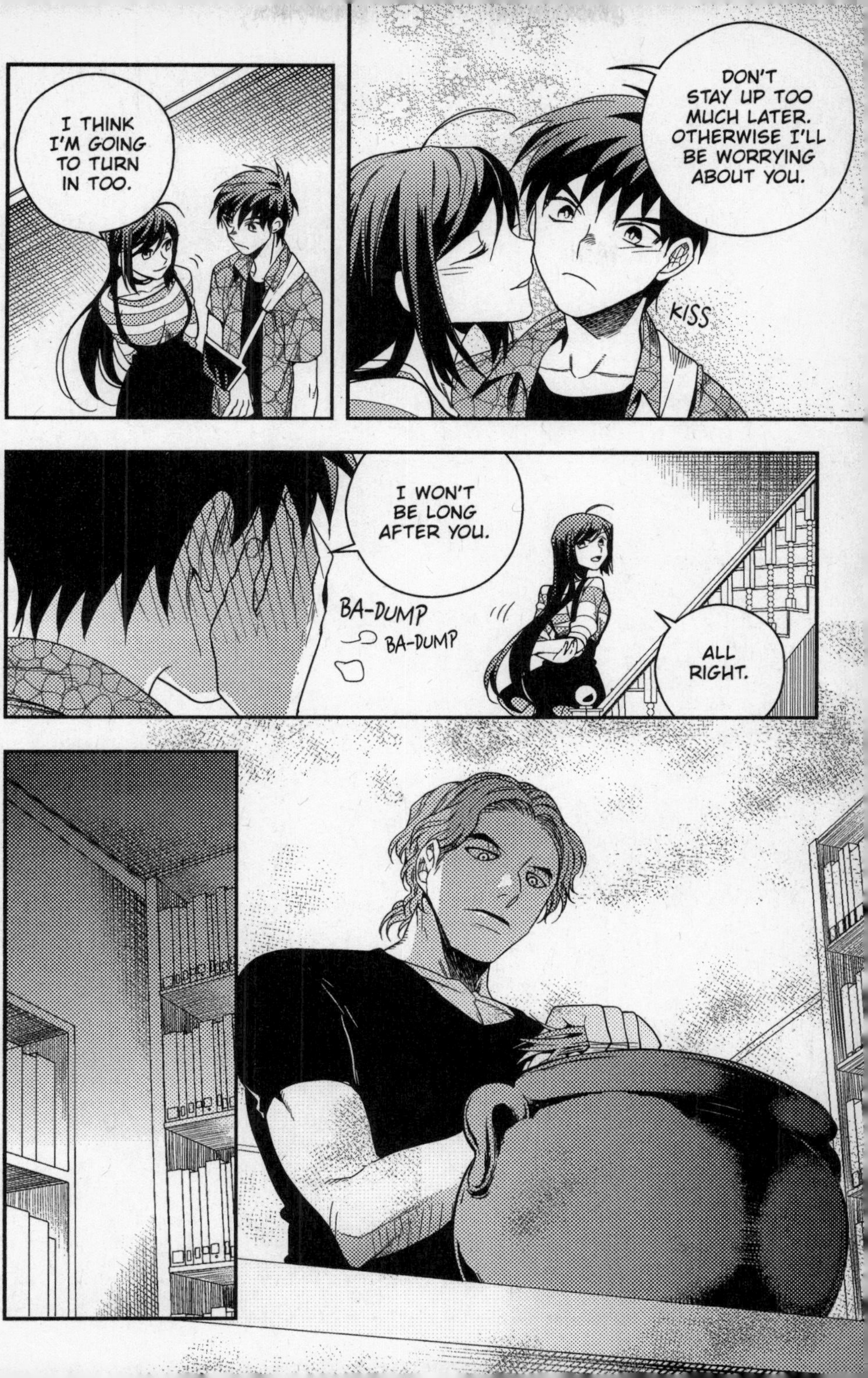
I THINK I'M GOING TO TURN IN TOO.
DON'T STAY UP TOO MUCH LATER. OTHERWISE I'LL BE WORRYING ABOUT YOU.
KISS
I WON'T BE LONG AFTER YOU.
BA-DUMP
BA-DUMP
ALL RIGHT.

YOU MIGHT AS WELL COME IN, NICK.

I CAN'T STAND SOMEONE AT MY BACK.

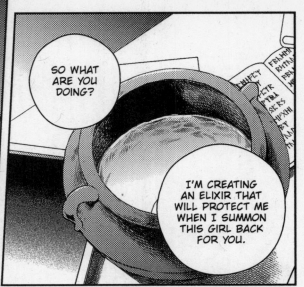

SO WHAT ARE YOU DOING?

I'M CREATING AN ELIXIR THAT WILL PROTECT ME WHEN I SUMMON THIS GIRL BACK FOR YOU.

ACTUALLY, KID, I NEED YOU FOR A SECOND.

WHY?

I NEED AN INGREDIENT FROM YOU.

I DON'T LIKE THE SOUND OF THAT AT ALL.

SLASH

AHH!

DON'T PULL AWAY.

THAT'S NOT SANITARY. EW!

"EW" IS RIGHT, BUT TRUST ME.

DROP DROP

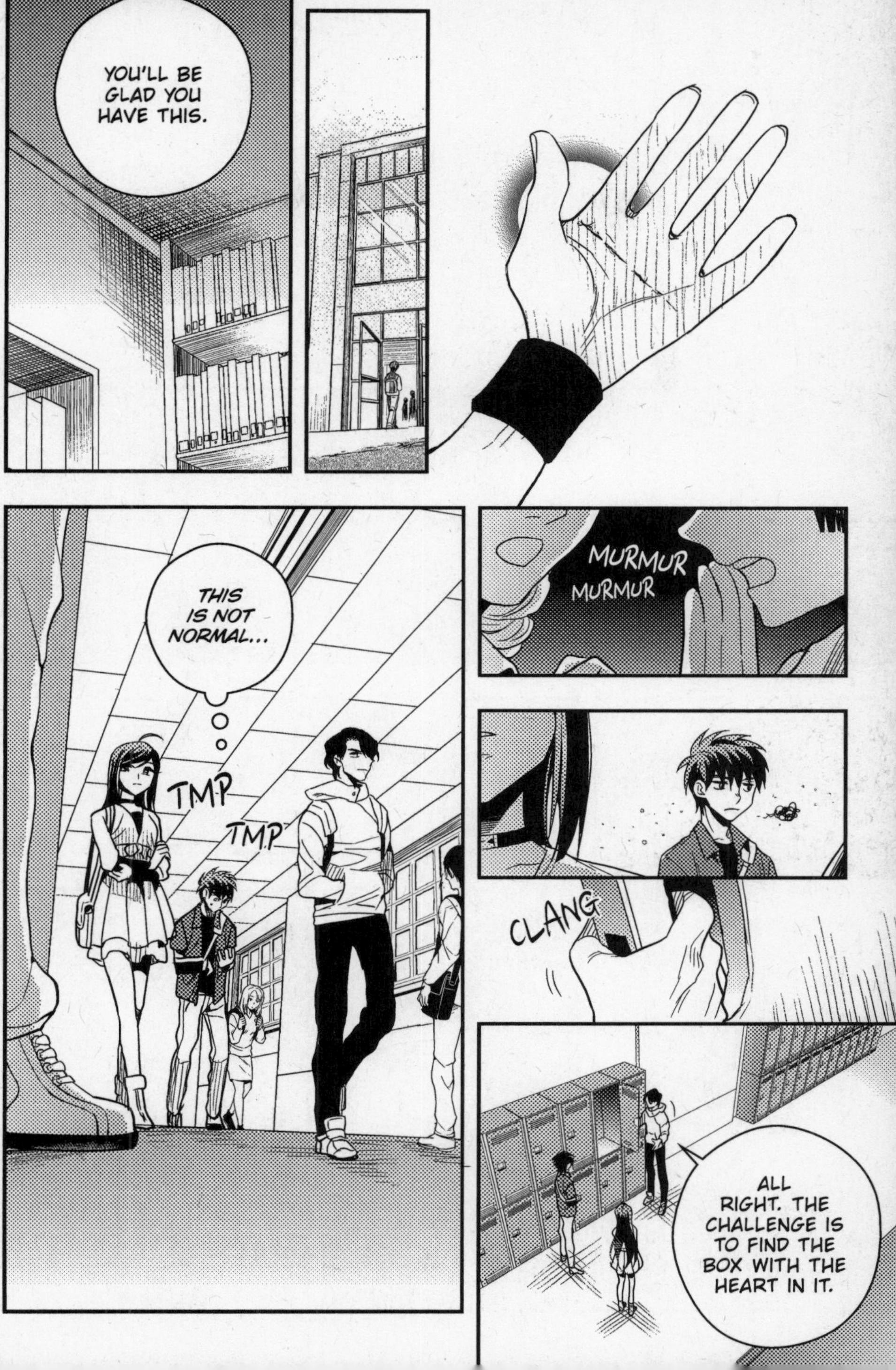
YOU'LL BE GLAD YOU HAVE THIS.
THIS IS NOT NORMAL...
TMP
TMP
MURMUR
MURMUR
CLANG
ALL RIGHT. THE CHALLENGE IS TO FIND THE BOX WITH THE HEART IN IT.

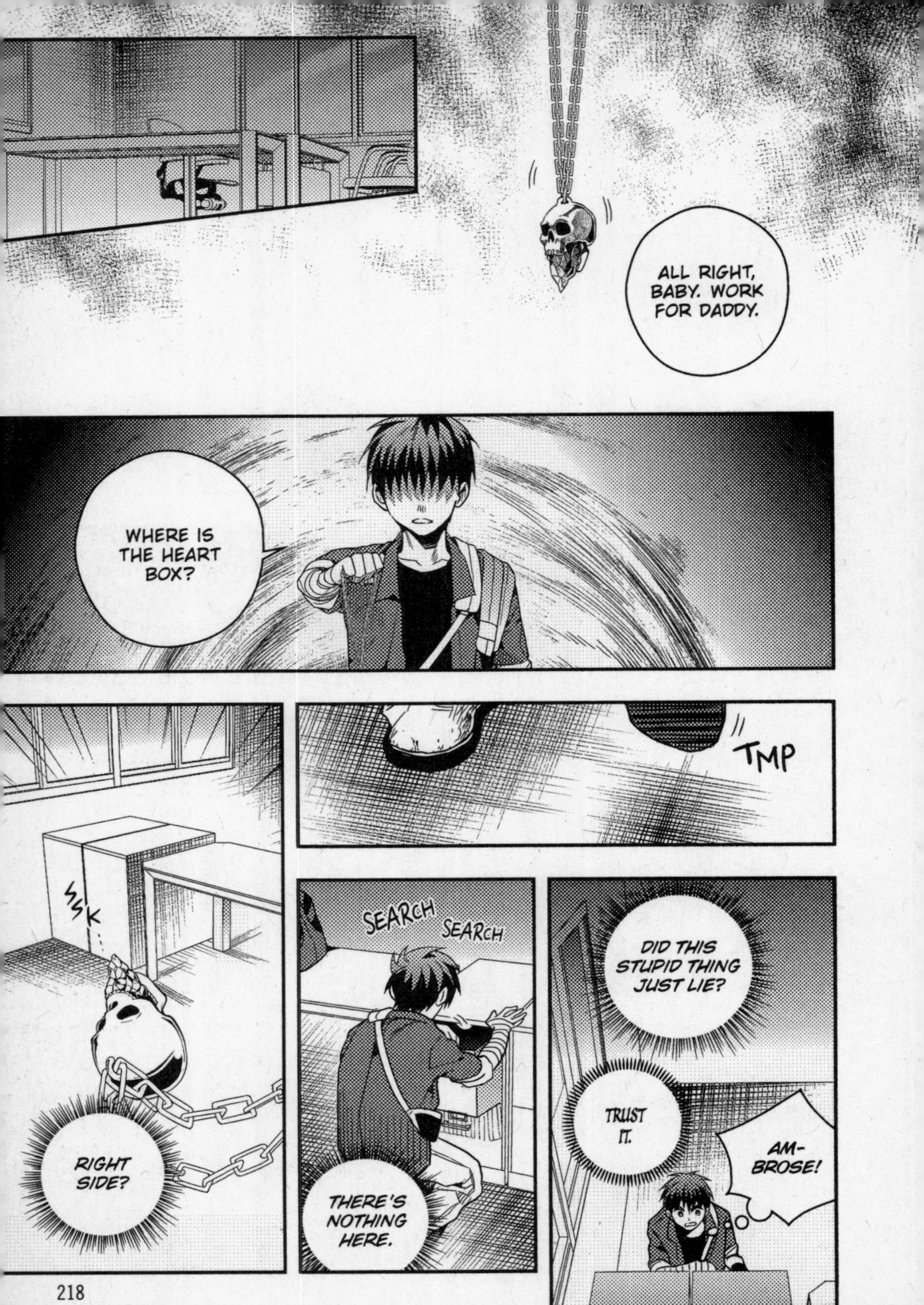
ALL RIGHT, BABY. WORK FOR DADDY.
WHERE IS THE HEART BOX?
TMP
SSK...
RIGHT SIDE?
SEARCH
SEARCH
THERE'S NOTHING HERE.
DID THIS STUPID THING JUST LIE?
TRUST IT.
AM-BROSE!

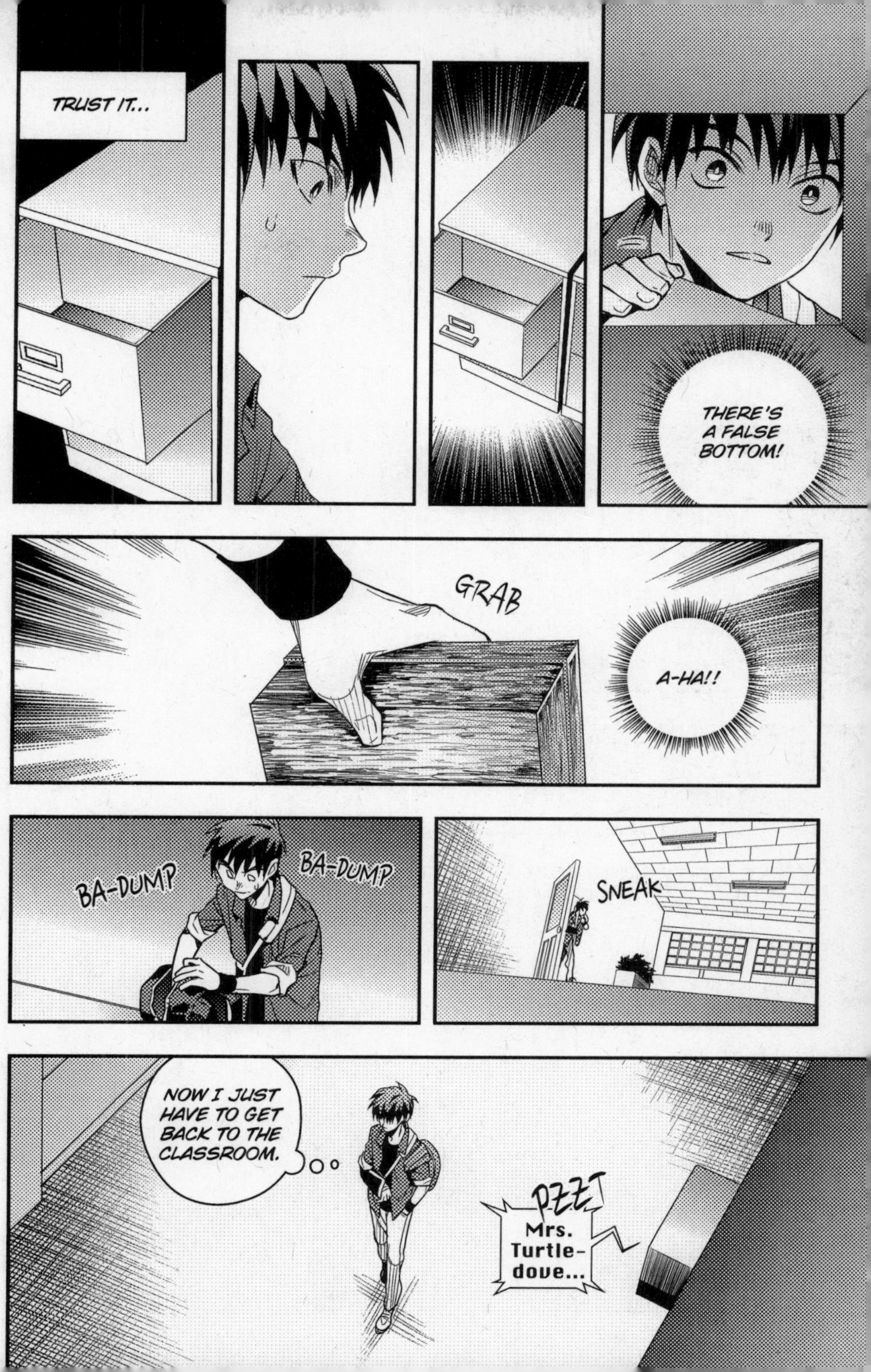

TRUST IT...
THERE'S A FALSE BOTTOM!
GRAB
A-HA!!
BA-DUMP
BA-DUMP
SNEAK
NOW I JUST HAVE TO GET BACK TO THE CLASSROOM.
PZZT
Mrs. Turtle-dove...

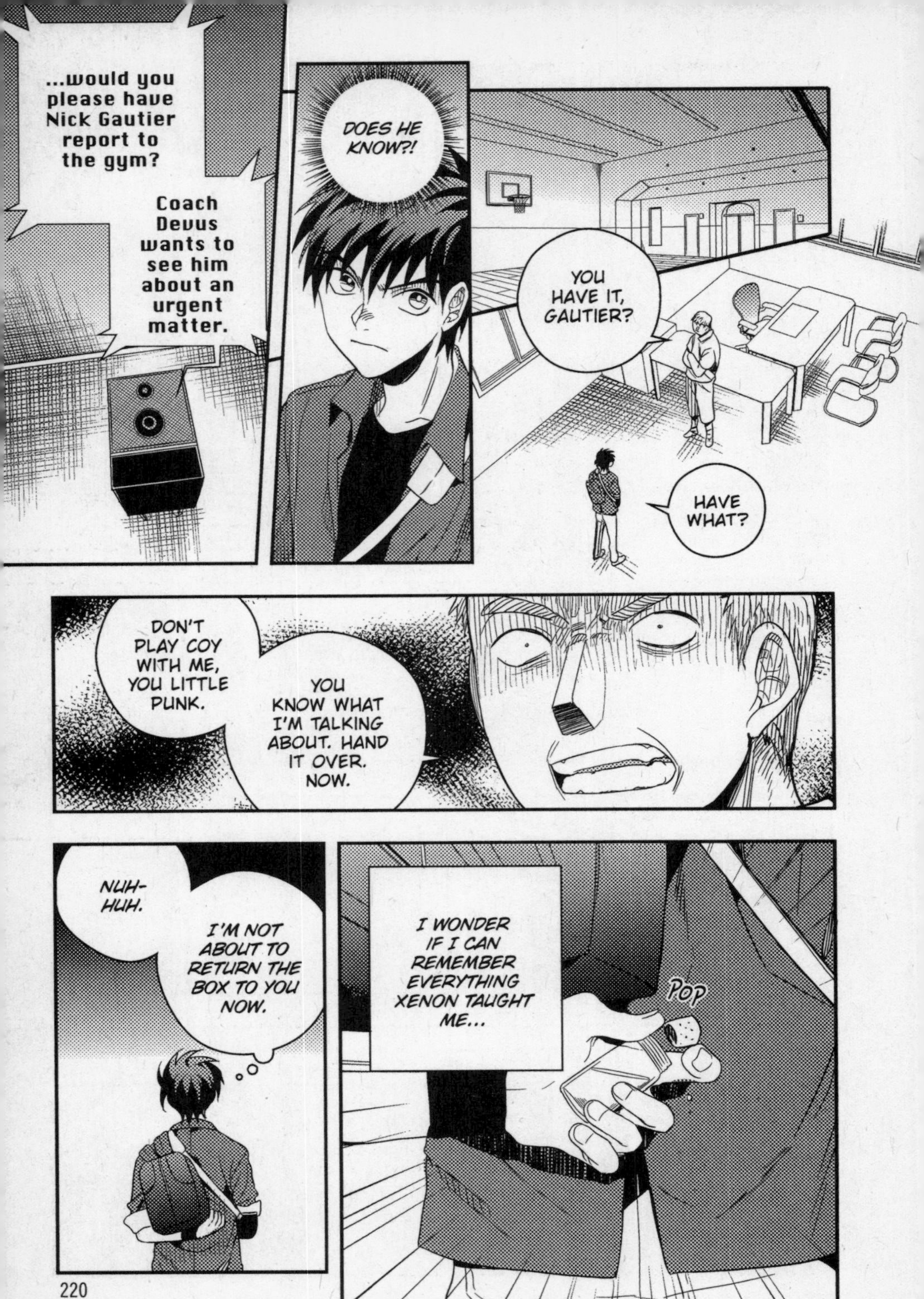
...would you please have Nick Gautier report to the gym?
Coach Devus wants to see him about an urgent matter.
DOES HE KNOW?!
YOU HAVE IT, GAUTIER?
HAVE WHAT?
DON'T PLAY COY WITH ME, YOU LITTLE PUNK.
YOU KNOW WHAT I'M TALKING ABOUT. HAND IT OVER. NOW.
NUH-HUH.
I'M NOT ABOUT TO RETURN THE BOX TO YOU NOW.
I WONDER IF I CAN REMEMBER EVERYTHING XENON TAUGHT ME...
POP

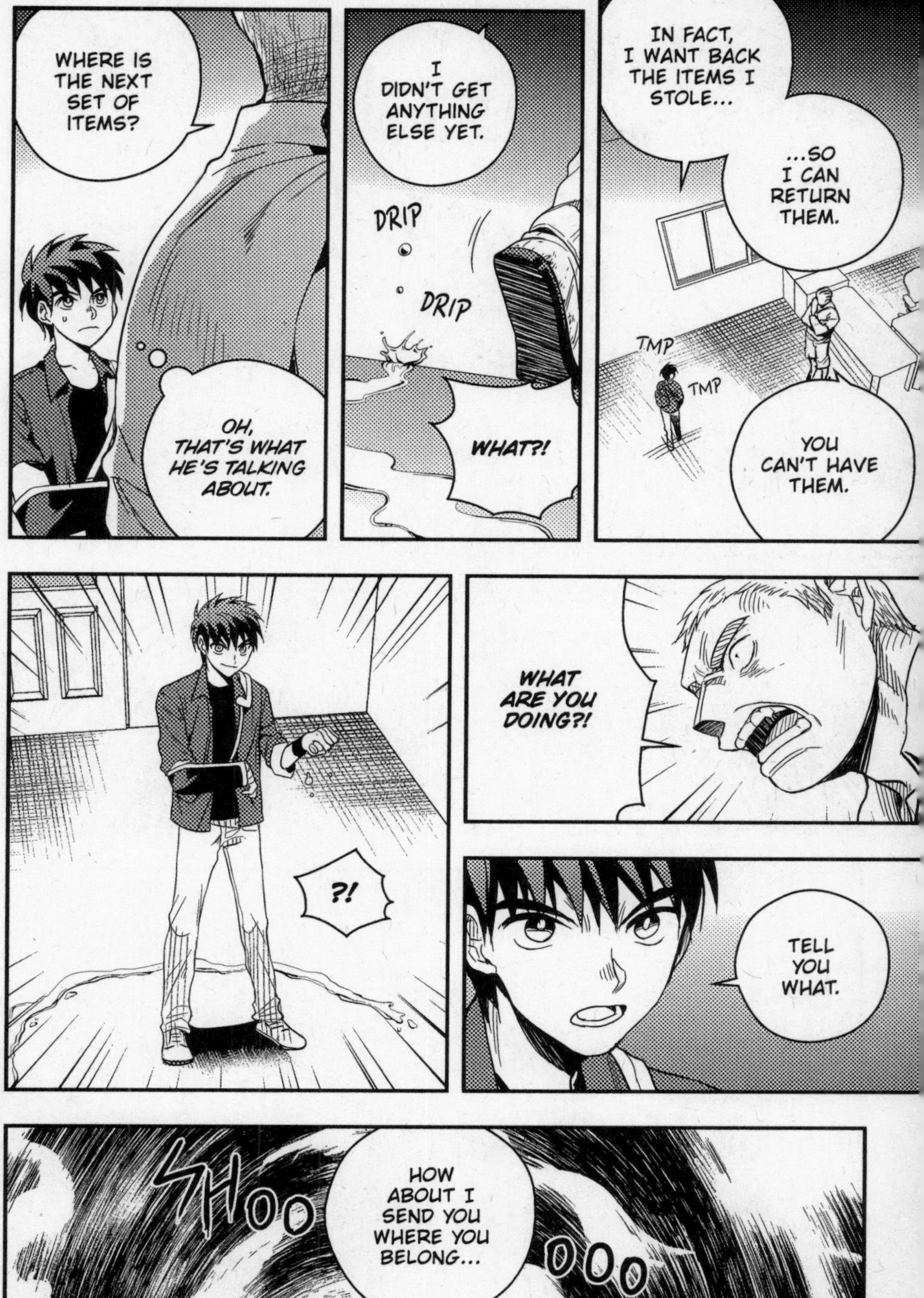
WHERE IS THE NEXT SET OF ITEMS?
OH, THAT'S WHAT HE'S TALKING ABOUT.
I DIDN'T GET ANYTHING ELSE YET.
DRIP
DRIP
WHAT?!
IN FACT, I WANT BACK THE ITEMS I STOLE...
...SO I CAN RETURN THEM.
TMP
TMP
YOU CAN'T HAVE THEM.
?!
WHAT ARE YOU DOING?!
TELL YOU WHAT.
SHOOOOO
HOW ABOUT I SEND YOU WHERE YOU BELONG...

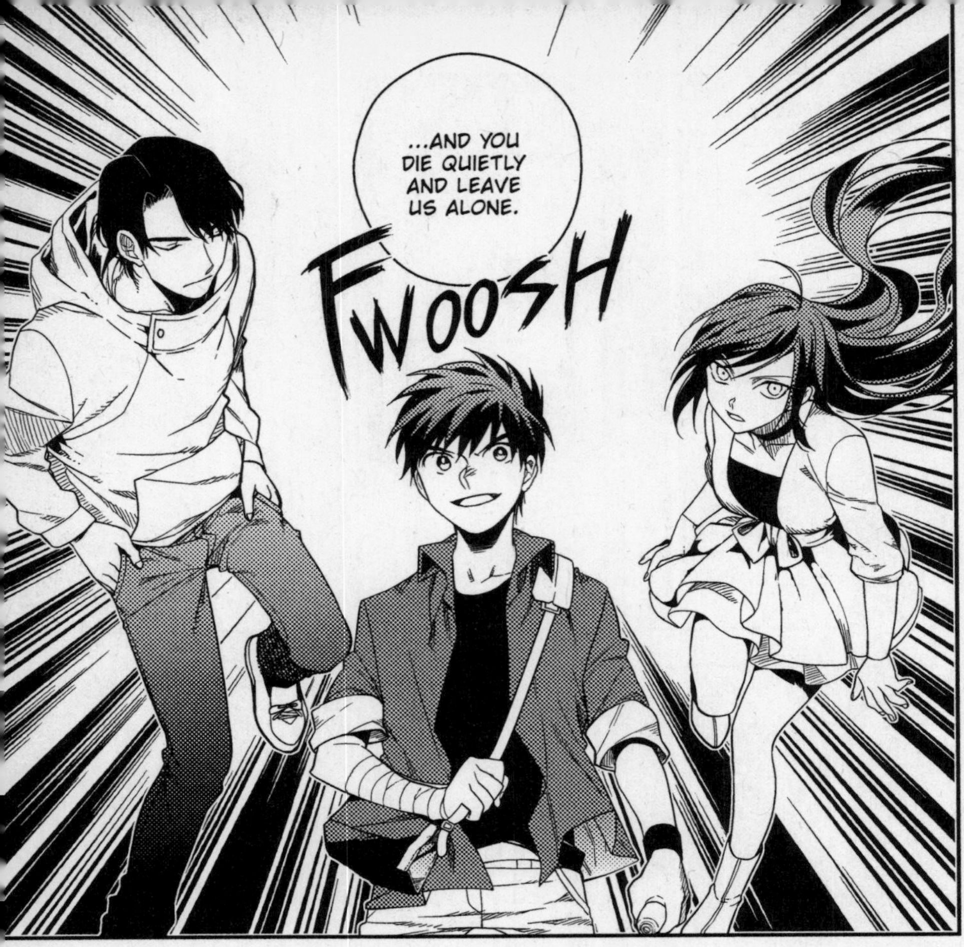
...AND YOU DIE QUIETLY AND LEAVE US ALONE.
FWOOSH

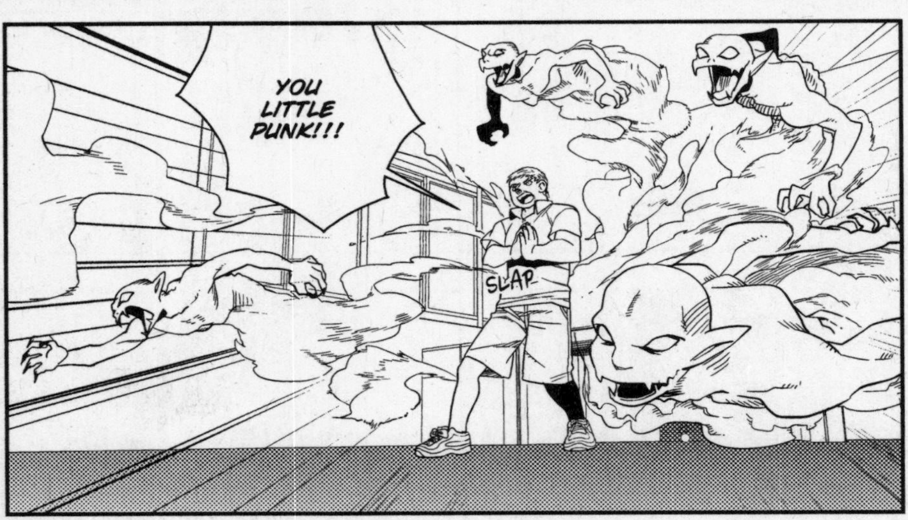
YOU LITTLE PUNK!!!
SLAP

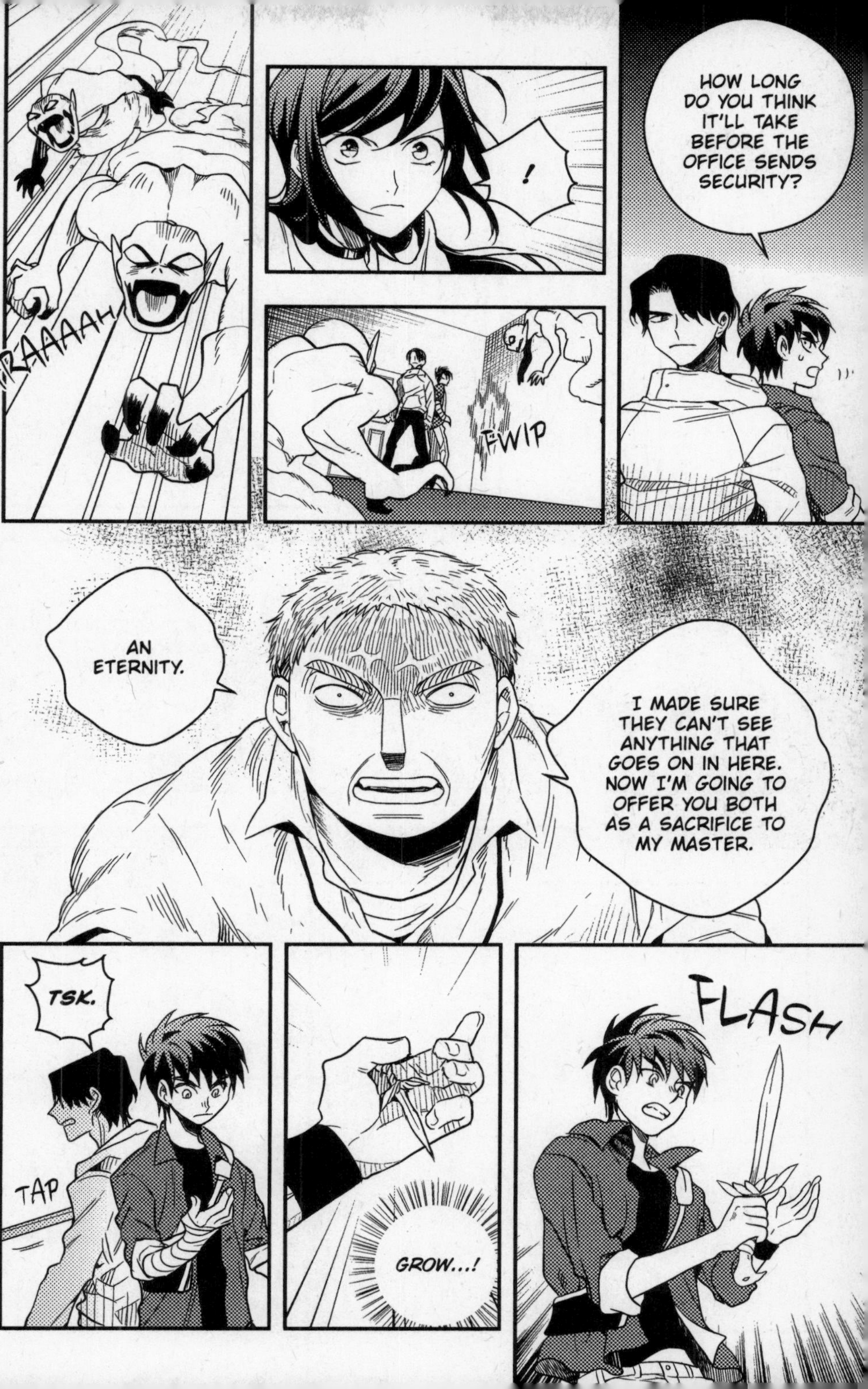
GRAAAAH
!
FWIP
HOW LONG DO YOU THINK IT'LL TAKE BEFORE THE OFFICE SENDS SECURITY?
AN ETERNITY.
I MADE SURE THEY CAN'T SEE ANYTHING THAT GOES ON IN HERE. NOW I'M GOING TO OFFER YOU BOTH AS A SACRIFICE TO MY MASTER.
TSK.
TAP
GROW...!
FLASH

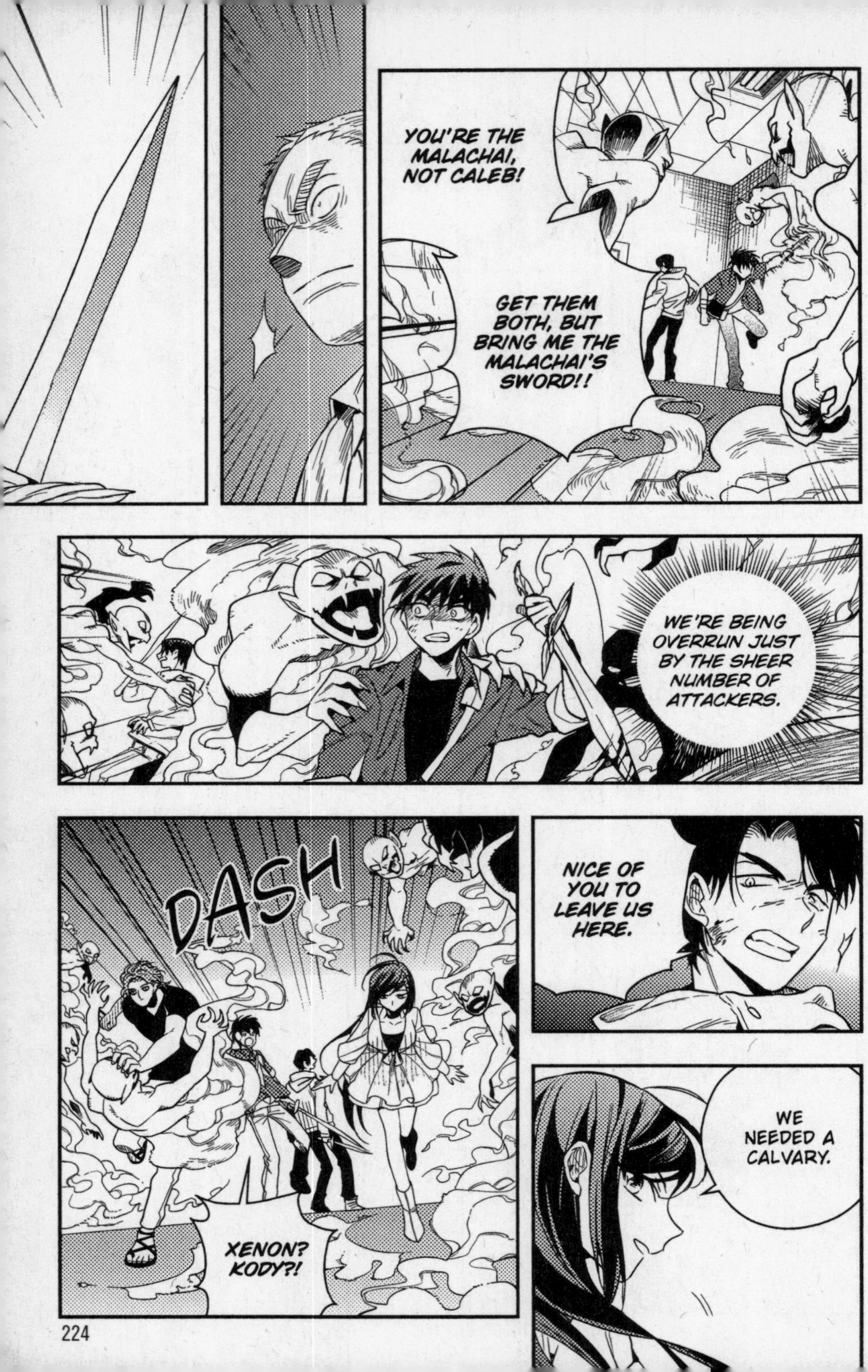
YOU'RE THE MALACHAI, NOT CALEB!
GET THEM BOTH, BUT BRING ME THE MALACHAI'S SWORD!!
WE'RE BEING OVERRUN JUST BY THE SHEER NUMBER OF ATTACKERS.
DASH
XENON? KODY?!
NICE OF YOU TO LEAVE US HERE.
WE NEEDED A CALVARY.

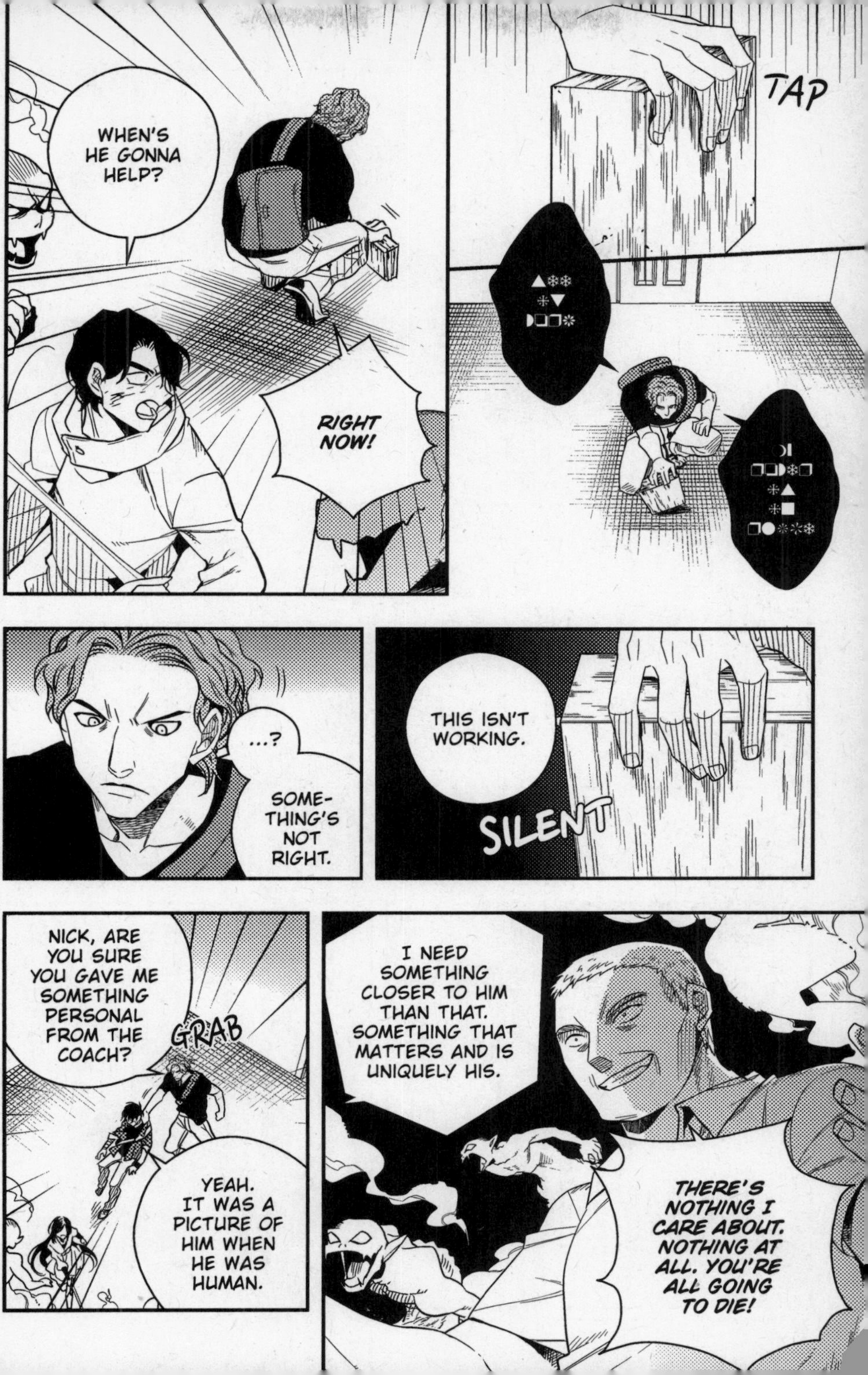
WHEN'S HE GONNA HELP?
RIGHT NOW!
TAP
...?
SOME-THING'S NOT RIGHT.
THIS ISN'T WORKING.
SILENT
NICK, ARE YOU SURE YOU GAVE ME SOMETHING PERSONAL FROM THE COACH?
GRAB
YEAH. IT WAS A PICTURE OF HIM WHEN HE WAS HUMAN.
I NEED SOMETHING CLOSER TO HIM THAN THAT. SOMETHING THAT MATTERS AND IS UNIQUELY HIS.
THERE'S NOTHING I CARE ABOUT. NOTHING AT ALL. YOU'RE ALL GOING TO DIE!

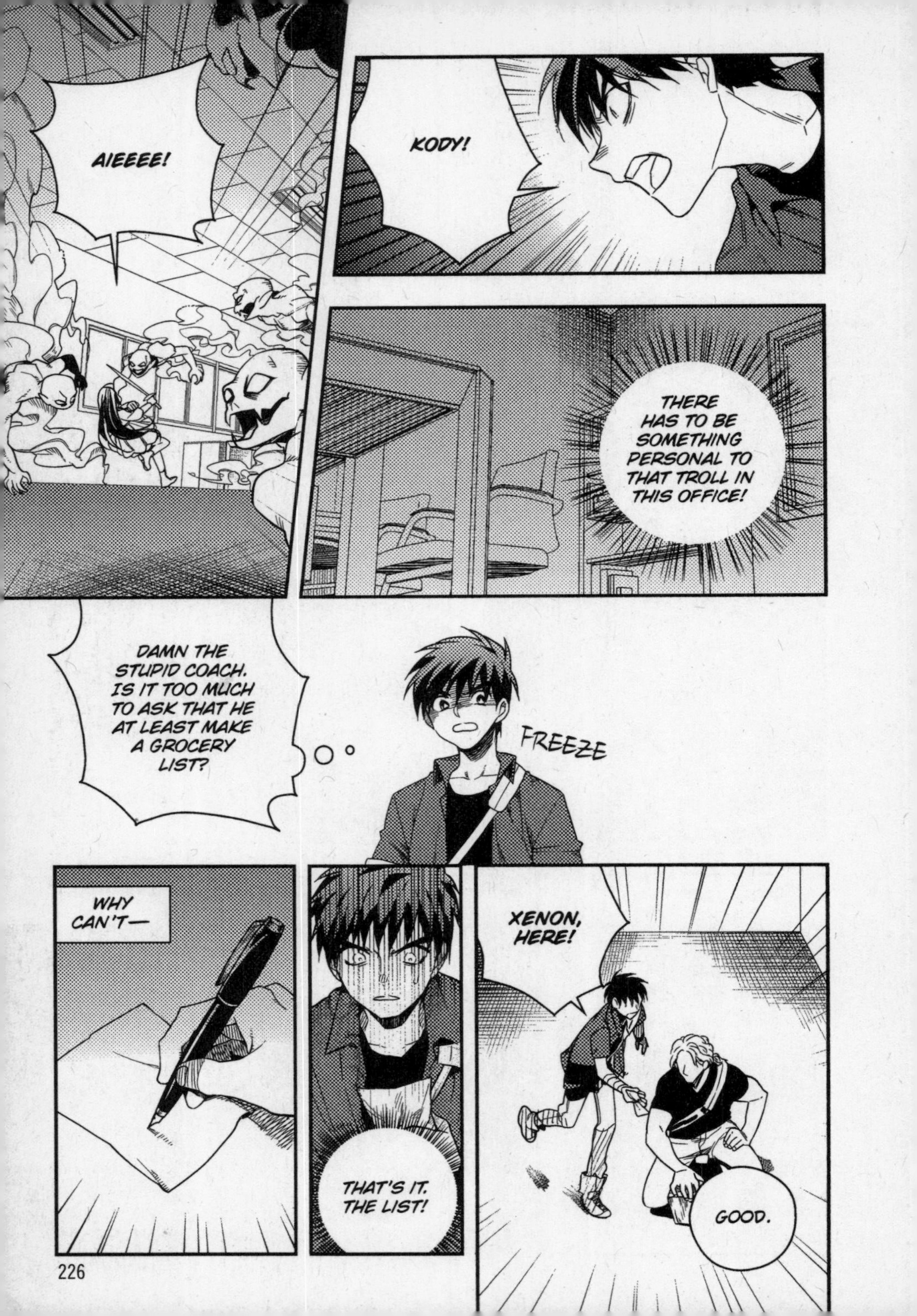

AIEEEE!
KODY!
THERE HAS TO BE SOMETHING PERSONAL TO THAT TROLL IN THIS OFFICE!
DAMN THE STUPID COACH. IS IT TOO MUCH TO ASK THAT HE AT LEAST MAKE A GROCERY LIST?
FREEZE
WHY CAN'T—
THAT'S IT. THE LIST!
XENON, HERE!
GOOD.

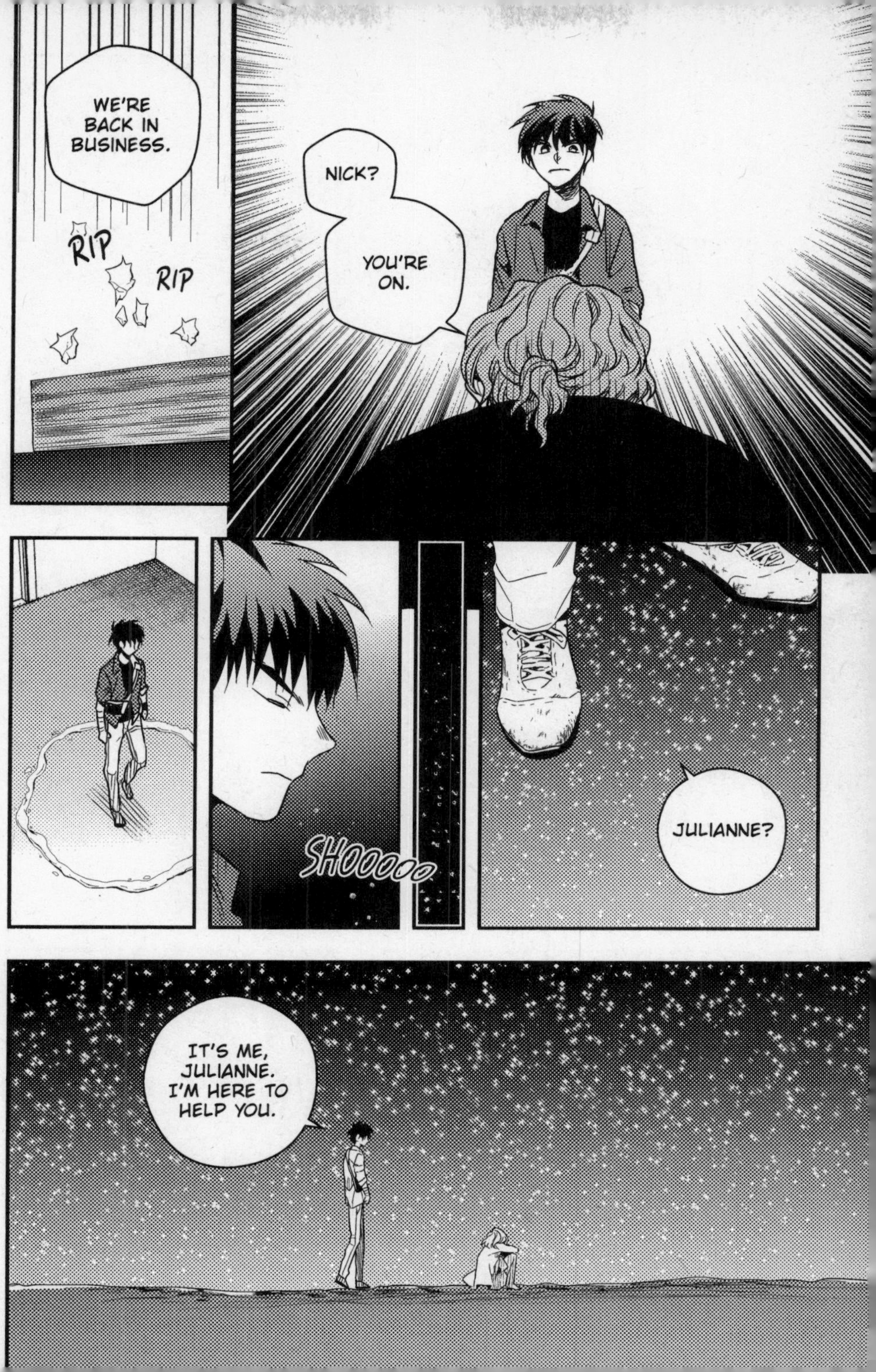

WE'RE BACK IN BUSINESS.
RIP
RIP
NICK?
YOU'RE ON.
SHOOOooo
JULIANNE?
IT'S ME, JULIANNE. I'M HERE TO HELP YOU.

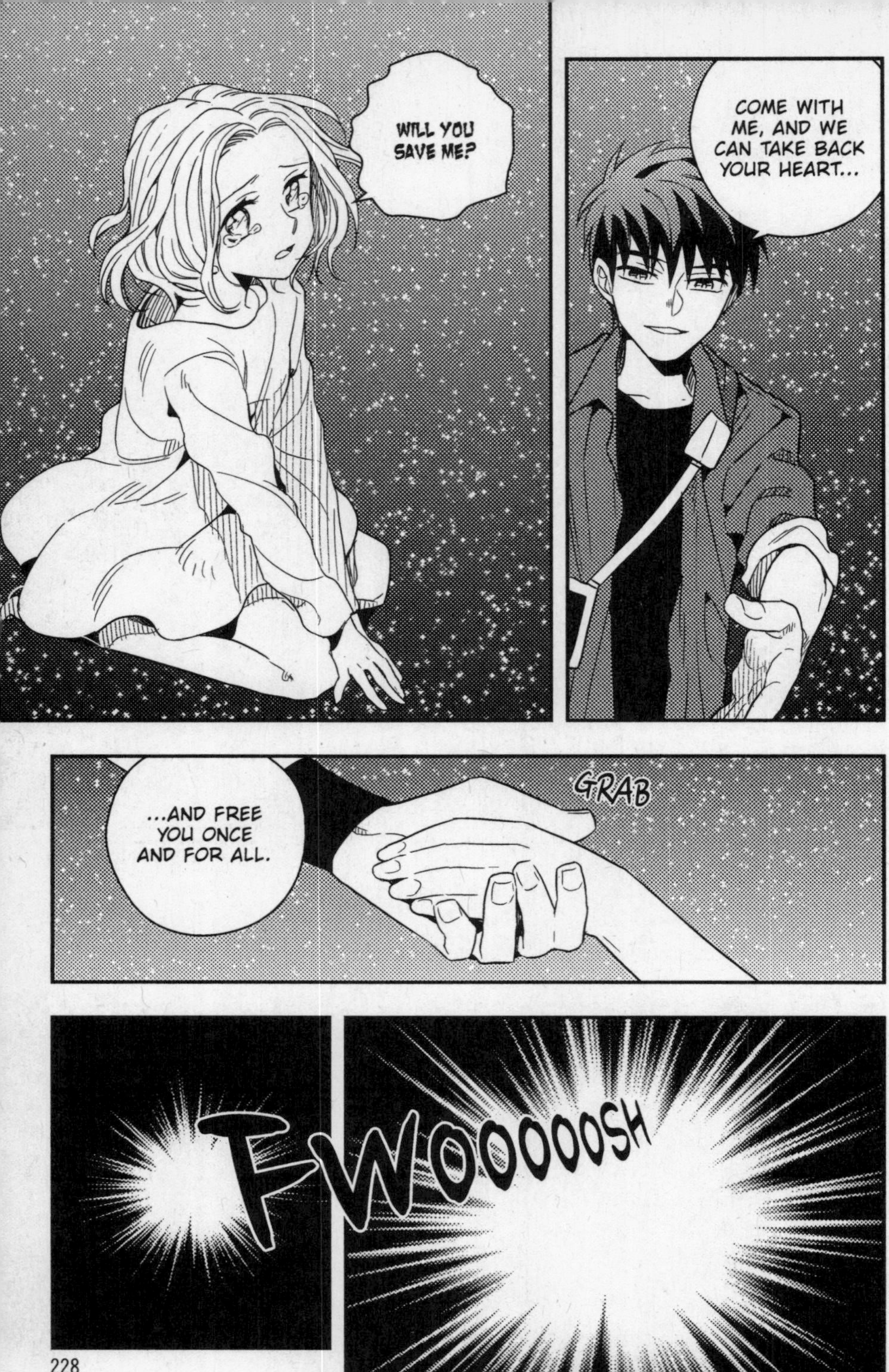
WILL YOU SAVE ME?
COME WITH ME, AND WE CAN TAKE BACK YOUR HEART...
GRAB
...AND FREE YOU ONCE AND FOR ALL.
FWOOOOSH

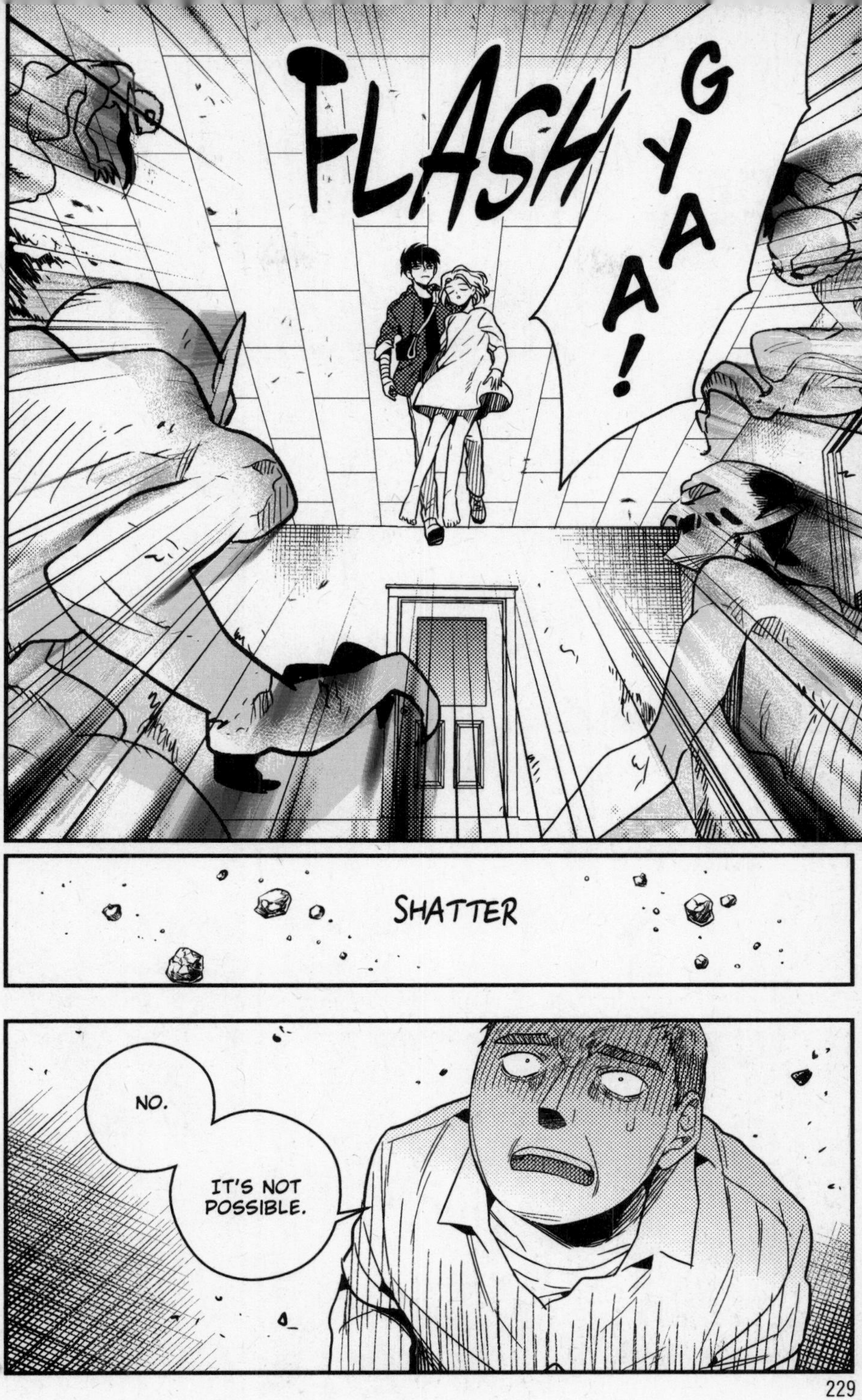
FLASH
GYAA!
SHATTER
NO.
IT'S NOT POSSIBLE.

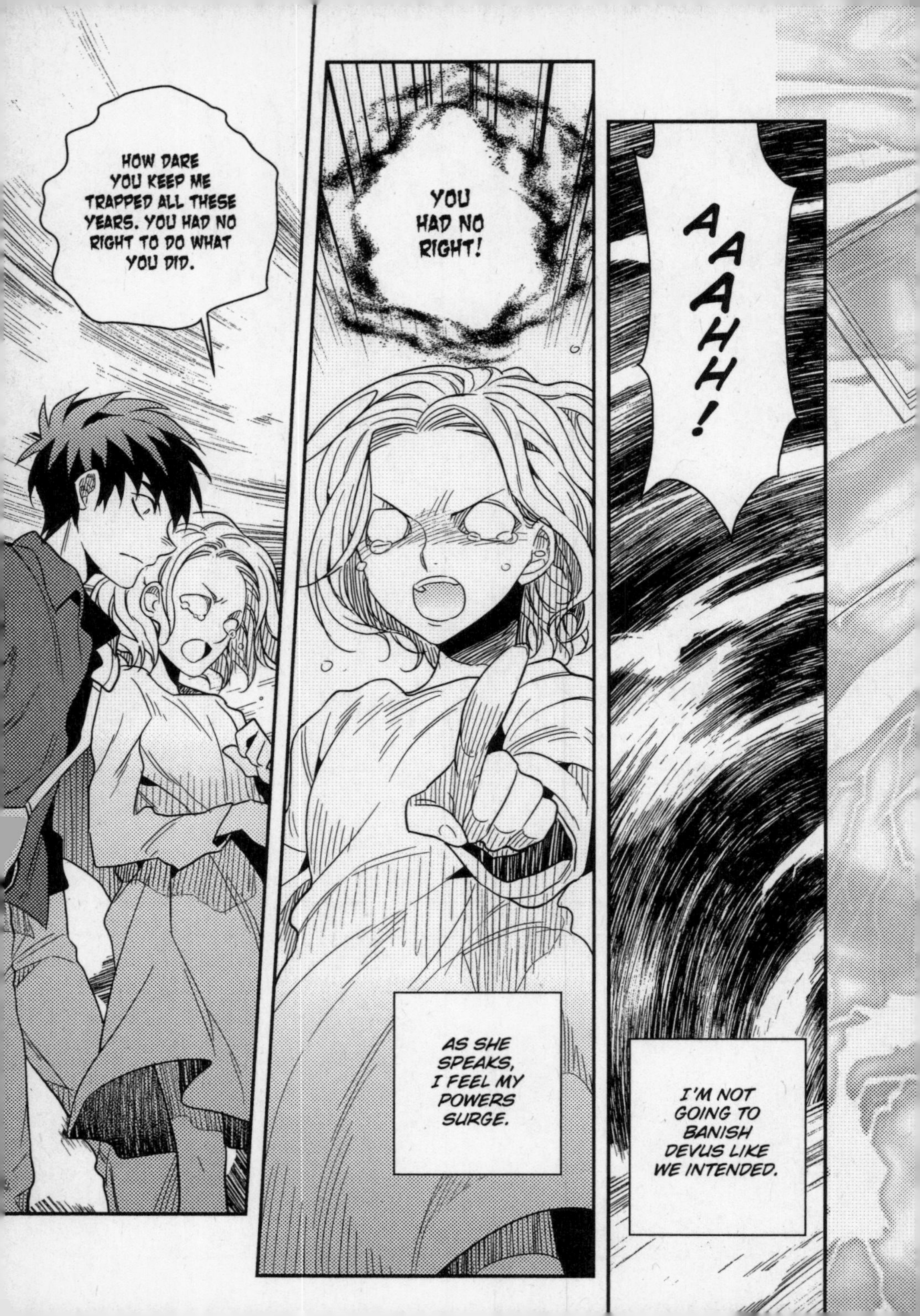
HOW DARE YOU KEEP ME TRAPPED ALL THESE YEARS. YOU HAD NO RIGHT TO DO WHAT YOU DID.
YOU HAD NO RIGHT!
AS SHE SPEAKS, I FEEL MY POWERS SURGE.
AAAHH!
I'M NOT GOING TO BANISH DEVUS LIKE WE INTENDED.

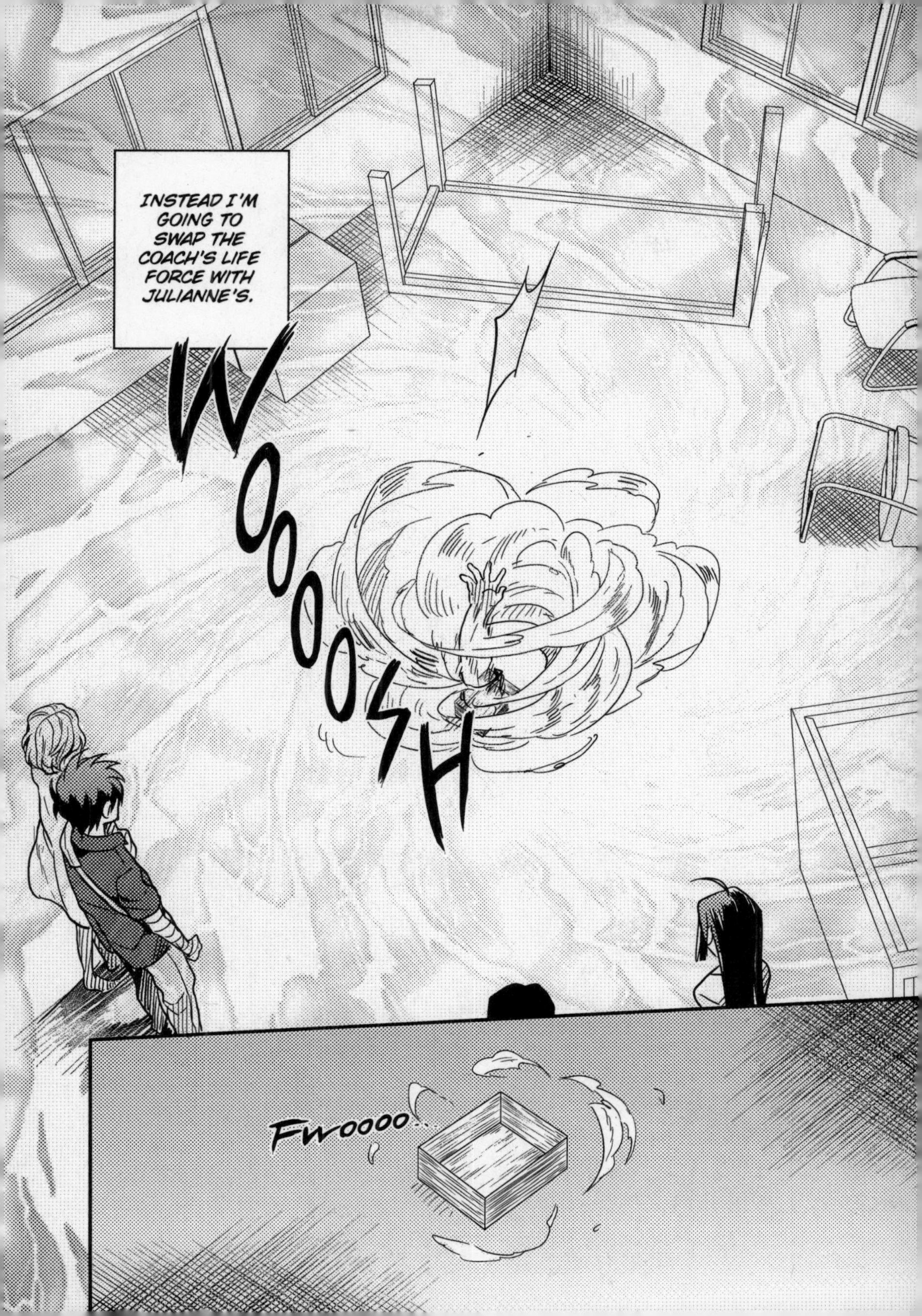
INSTEAD I'M GOING TO SWAP THE COACH'S LIFE FORCE WITH JULIANNE'S.
WOOOOOSH
Fwoooo...

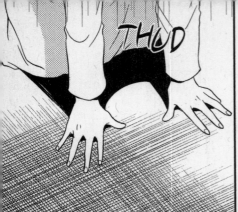

THUD

FLEX

FLEX

HOW DID YOU DO IT?

NO IDEA WHATSO-EVER.

YOU ARE MY HERO. THANK YOU!

A THOUSAND THANK-YOUS!

FLASH

232

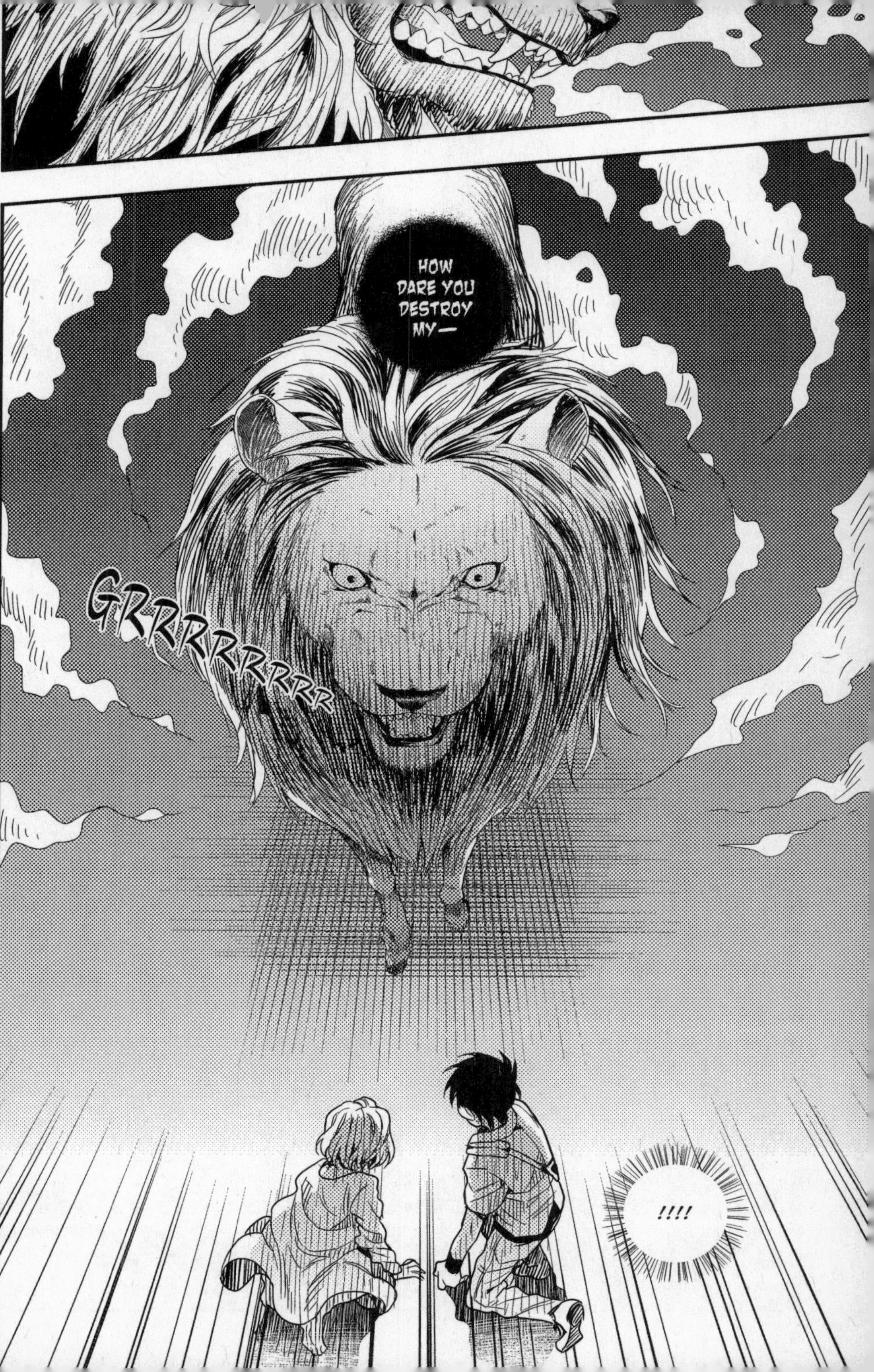
HOW DARE YOU DESTROY MY—
GRRRRRRRRRR
!!!!

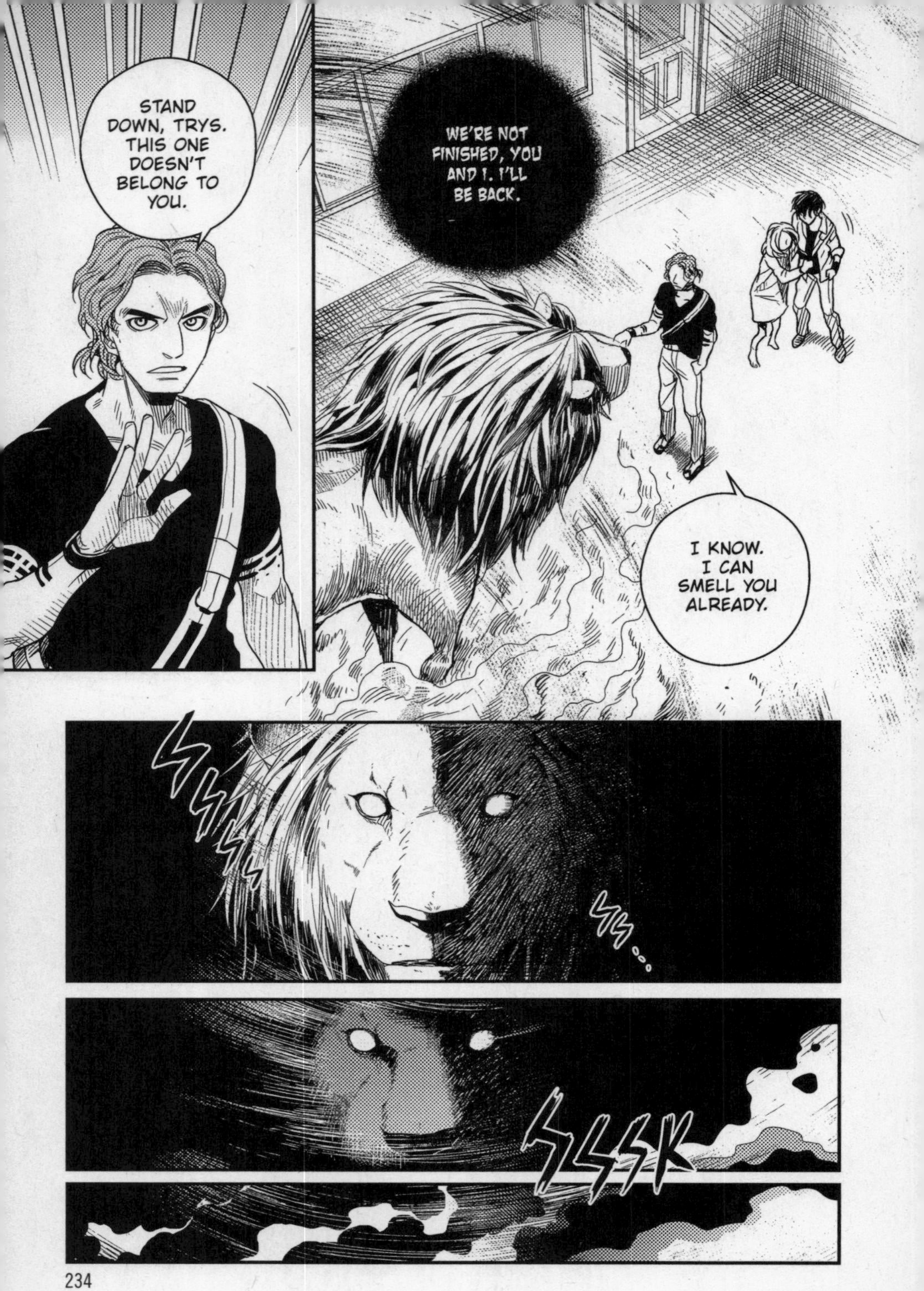
STAND DOWN, TRYS. THIS ONE DOESN'T BELONG TO YOU.
WE'RE NOT FINISHED, YOU AND I. I'LL BE BACK.
I KNOW. I CAN SMELL YOU ALREADY.
SSSSS
SS...
SSSK

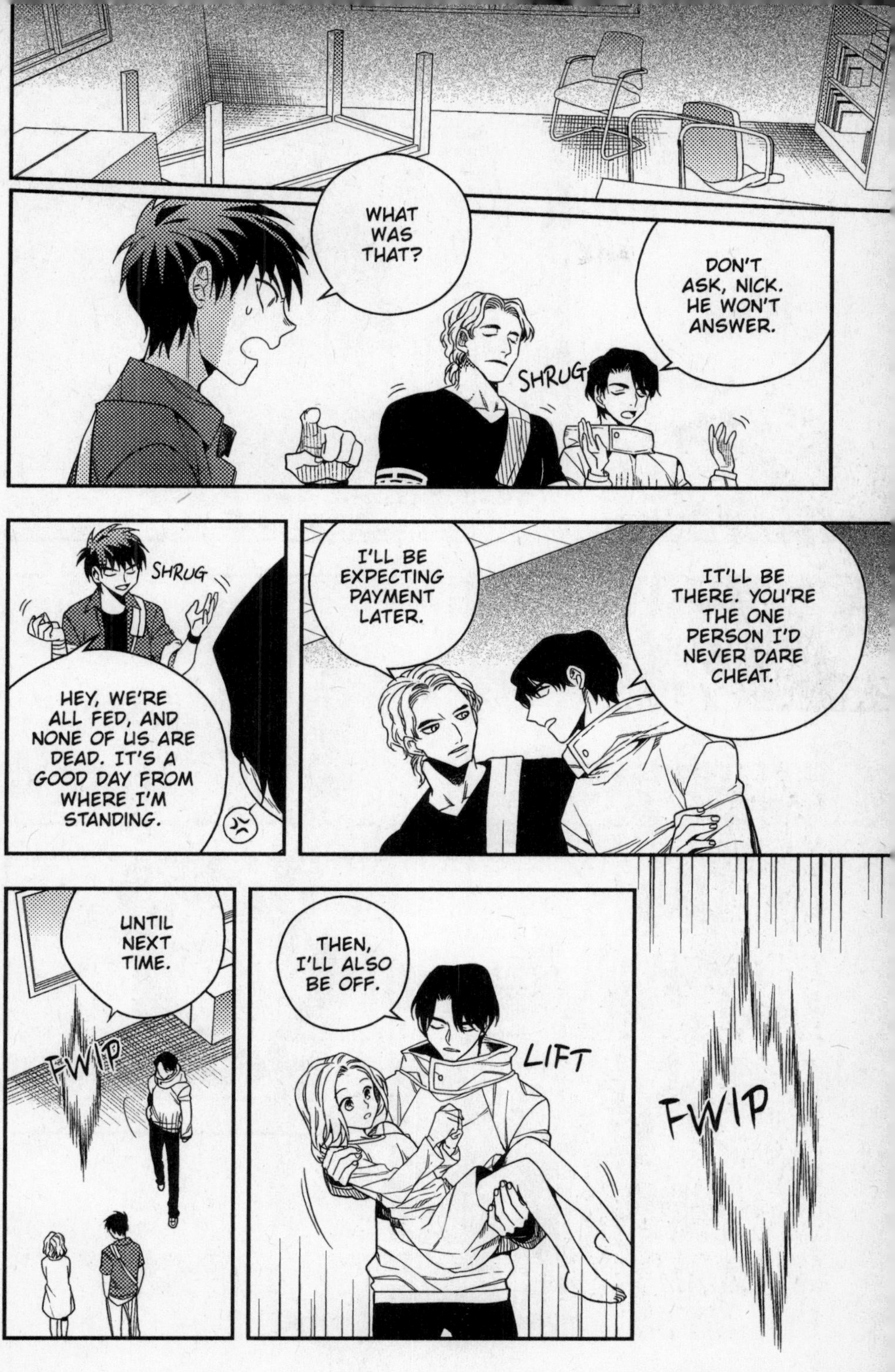
WHAT WAS THAT?
DON'T ASK, NICK. HE WON'T ANSWER.
SHRUG
SHRUG
HEY, WE'RE ALL FED, AND NONE OF US ARE DEAD. IT'S A GOOD DAY FROM WHERE I'M STANDING.
I'LL BE EXPECTING PAYMENT LATER.
IT'LL BE THERE. YOU'RE THE ONE PERSON I'D NEVER DARE CHEAT.
UNTIL NEXT TIME.
FWIP
THEN, I'LL ALSO BE OFF.
LIFT
FWIP

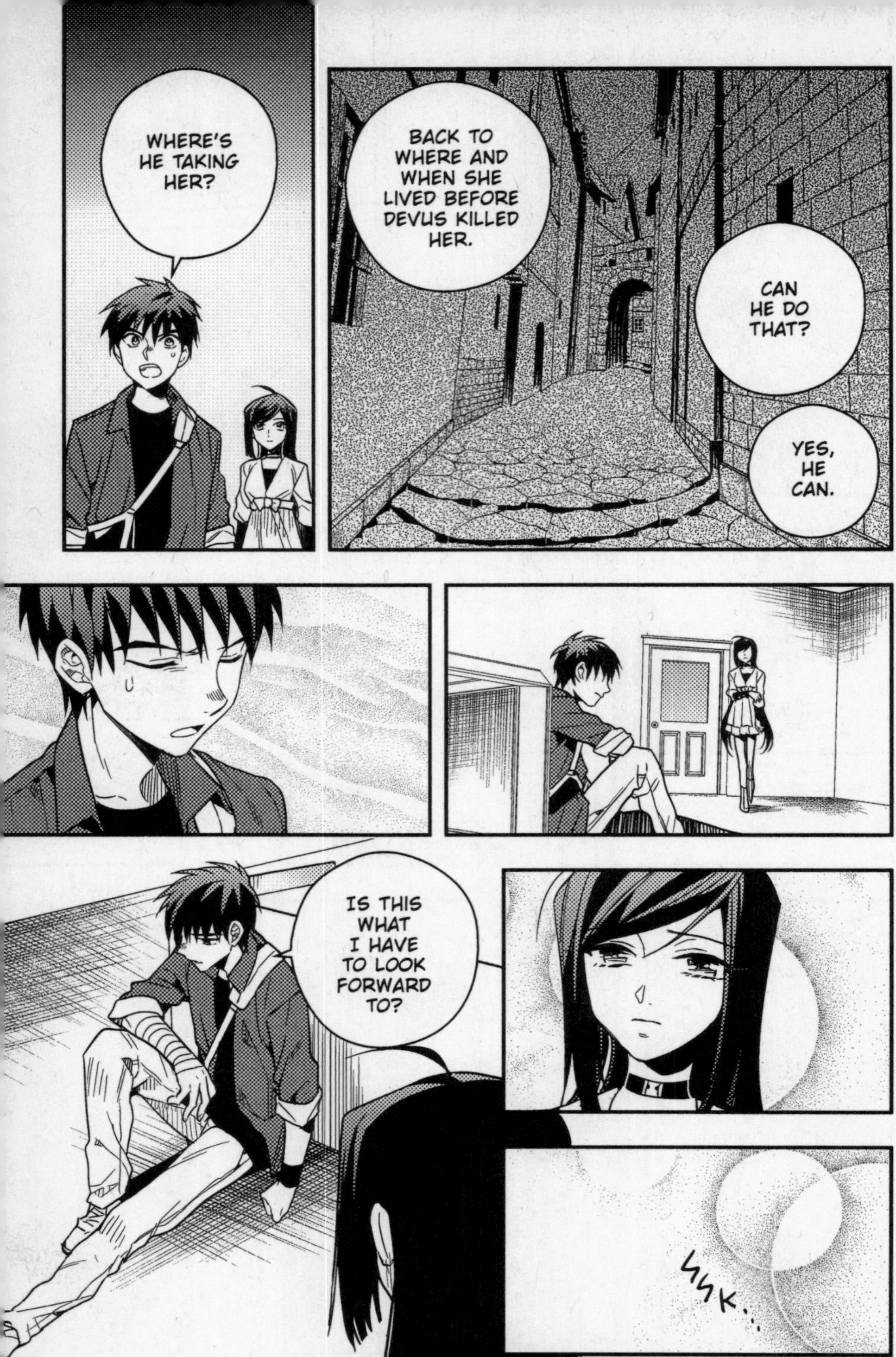
WHERE'S HE TAKING HER?
BACK TO WHERE AND WHEN SHE LIVED BEFORE DEVUS KILLED HER.
CAN HE DO THAT?
YES, HE CAN.
IS THIS WHAT I HAVE TO LOOK FORWARD TO?
UNK...

DON'T LOOK SO GLUM.

CHU

BA-DUMP
BA-DUMP
?

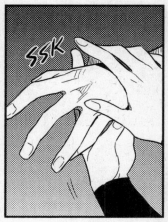

SSK

WHAT'S THIS?

TAP

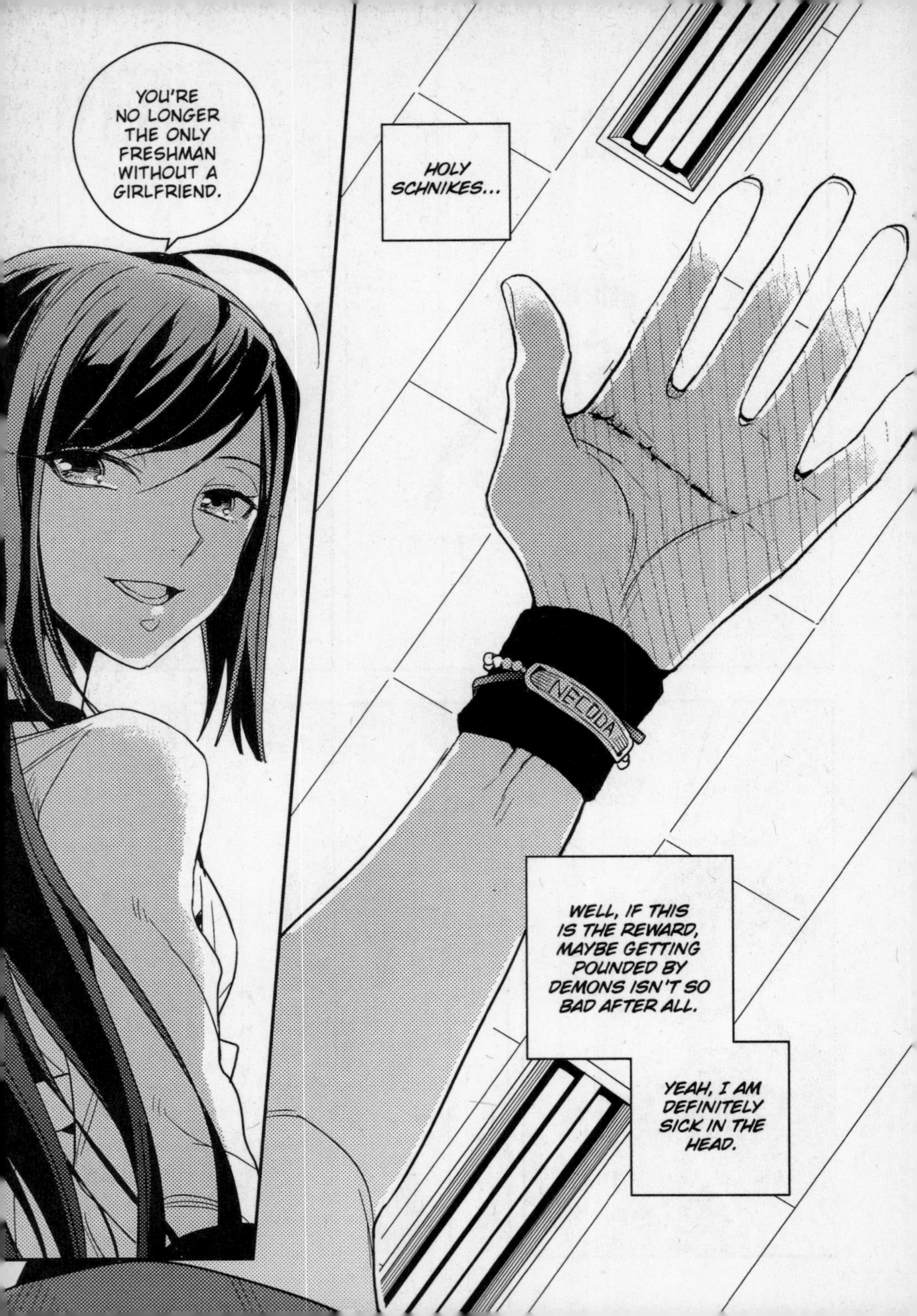
YOU'RE NO LONGER THE ONLY FRESHMAN WITHOUT A GIRLFRIEND.
HOLY SCHNIKES...
WELL, IF THIS IS THE REWARD, MAYBE GETTING POUNDED BY DEMONS ISN'T SO BAD AFTER ALL.
YEAH, I AM DEFINITELY SICK IN THE HEAD.

CLENCH

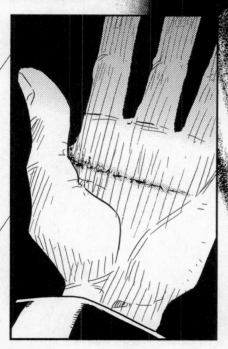

WELL? WHAT NEWS DO YOU HAVE?

OUR CORRUPTER IS IN PLACE AND IS ONE THE YOUNG MALACHAI NOW TRUSTS.

ARE YOU SURE?

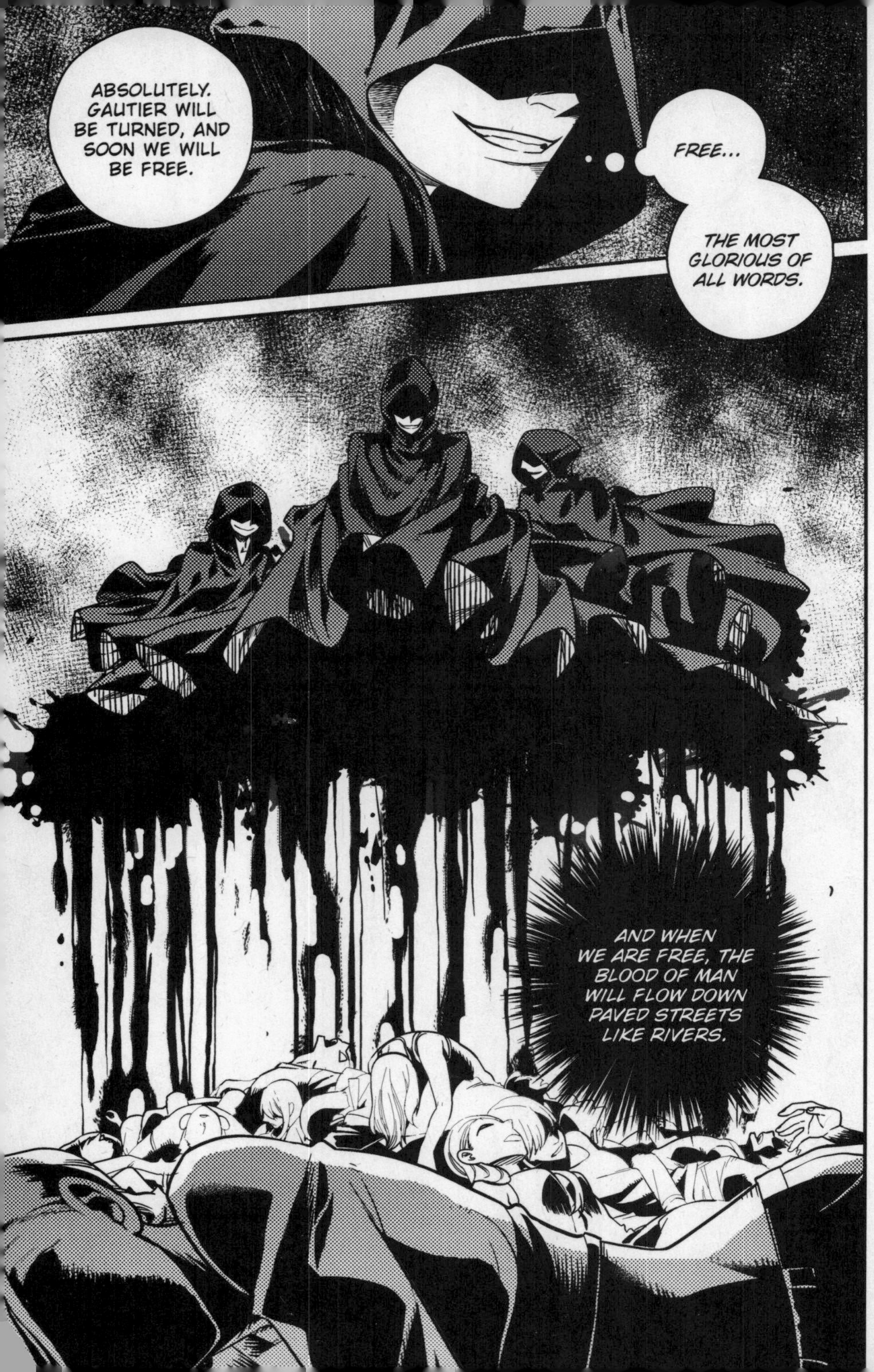
ABSOLUTELY. GAUTIER WILL BE TURNED, AND SOON WE WILL BE FREE.
FREE...
THE MOST GLORIOUS OF ALL WORDS.
AND WHEN WE ARE FREE, THE BLOOD OF MAN WILL FLOW DOWN PAVED STREETS LIKE RIVERS.

THE DARK-HUNTERS: INFINITY

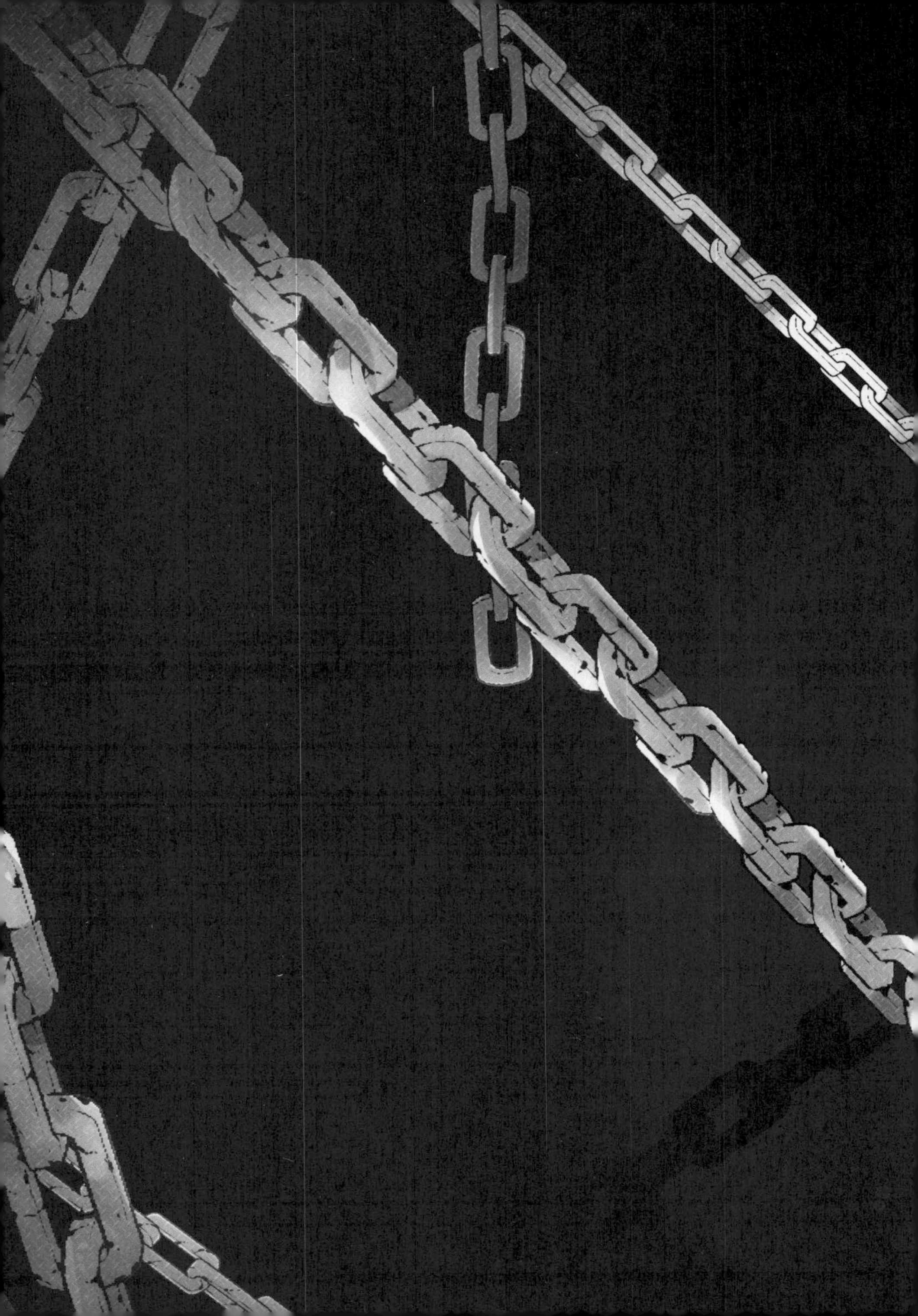

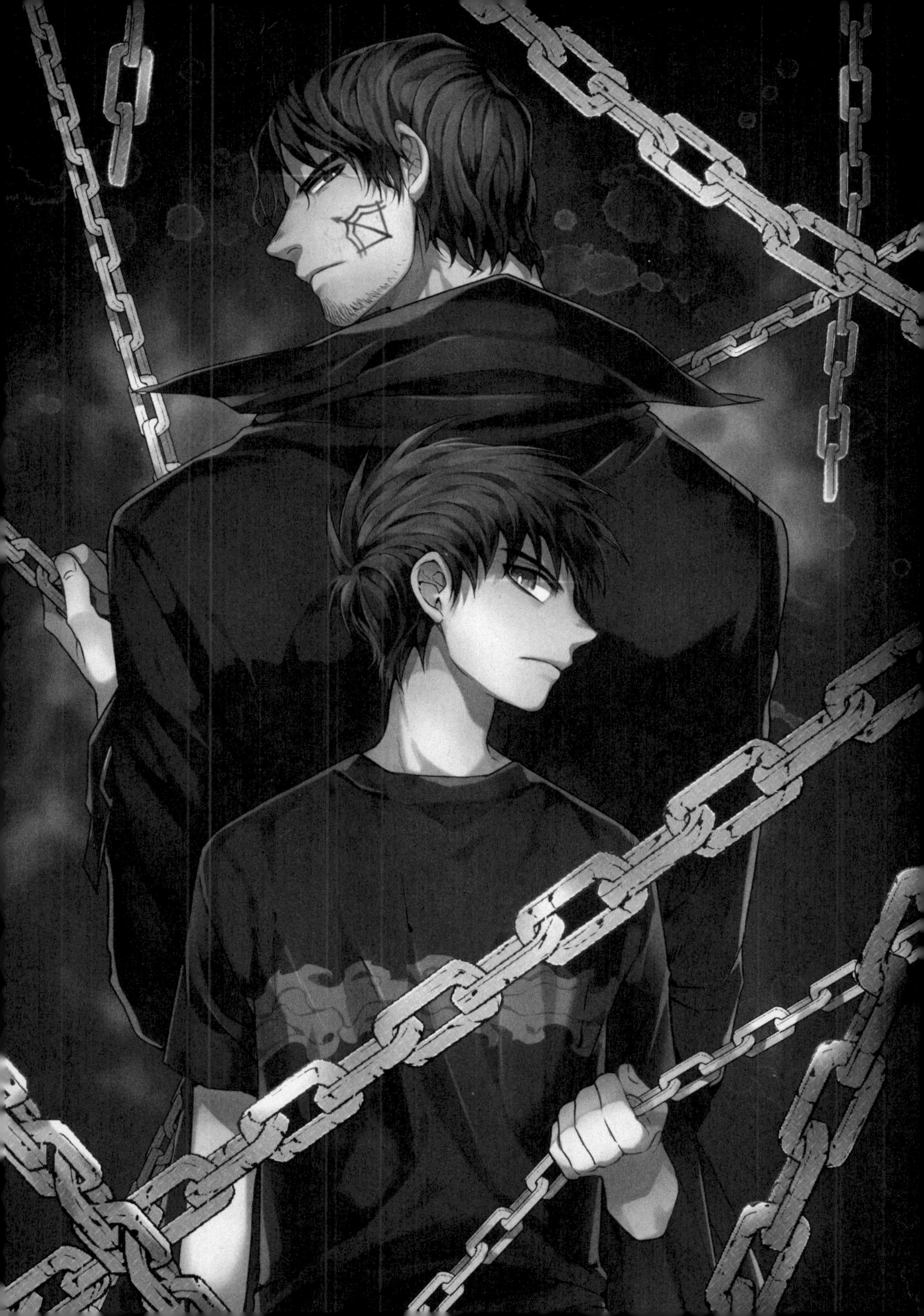

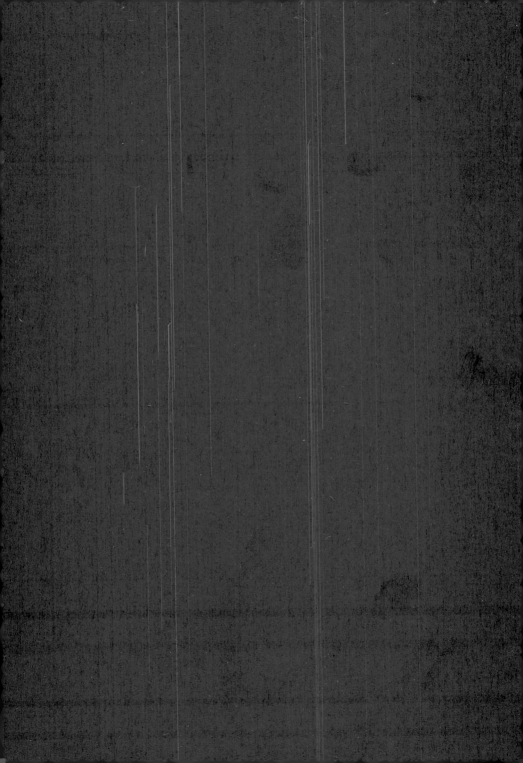